Thriving and Spirituality
Among Youth

Thriving and Spirituality Among Youth

Research Perspectives and Future Possibilities

Edited by

Amy Eva Alberts Warren
Richard M. Lerner
Erin Phelps

WILEY

John Wiley & Sons, Inc.

Library of Congress Cataloging-in-Publication Data

Thriving and spirituality among youth: research perspectives and future possibilities / edited by Amy Eva Alberts Warren, Richard M. Lerner, and Erin Phelps.
    p. cm.
  Includes index.
  ISBN 978-0-470-94830-9 (pbk.)
  ISBN 978-1-118-09982-7 (ebk)
  ISBN 978-1-118-09983-4 (ebk)
  ISBN 978-1-118-09981-0 (ebk)
  ISBN 978-1-118-09269-9 (obk)
  1. Youth–Religious life.   2. Mental health–Religious aspects.   3. Well-being–Religious aspects.
  4. Adolescent psychology.   5. Developmental psychology–Religious aspects.
  I. Warren, Amy Eva Alberts. II. Lerner, Richard M. III. Phelps, Erin.
  BL625.47.T47 2011
  204.0835–dc22

Printed in the United States of America

10 9 8 7 6 5 4 3 2 1

Contents

Foreword

I have witnessed firsthand the diverse tapestry of life in more than 130 countries. I've seen young people from many walks of life—vastly different cultures, faiths, traditions, and societies—who both succeed and fail. I have seen young people from tragic environments overcome their obstacles with amazing grace and resilience. I've talked with many young people who beat the odds of poverty, war, bad schools (or no schools at all), addiction, and family violence. And I have seen many who do not.

Over the past 35 years, I have worked as a social entrepreneur to help improve the conditions and prospects for young people where they live, learn, work, and play. These young people represent the more than 1.7 billion people today who are between the ages of 15 and 29. Eighty-five percent of them live in developing countries.

All of us who have survived adolescence know that it can be a tough time of life, a period of transition, development, and discovery. Many young people report feeling isolated and disconnected during these years, when they are undergoing major physical, social, and developmental changes. Although many people simply survive their adolescence, others fall into negative behaviors as they question who they are and their place in the world.

It is also true that the great changes and identity search during adolescence lead many young people to seek ways to contribute to something beyond themselves. Some of these young people were born into tragic circumstances, but now they serve as mentors and role models or as youth representatives on local, national, and global boards; or they work as social innovators to improve their countries and communities; or they are successful young entrepreneurs creating new enterprise.

Many girls and young women, just by the nature of being born female, have to struggle and fight for their opportunities and human rights in their countries and communities. Some of these incredible, brave young women are now furthering their education, becoming successful entrepreneurs, and challenging laws, customs, and stereotypes by serving as a whole new generation of role models in their communities and nearby towns and villages.

The reason or reasons why these young people are able to make positive differences despite their circumstances are multiple and varied. Some young people are able to connect with a positive mentor or role model who helps change the direction of their lives. Some young people are able to access programs and services that provide them with the skills and experiences they need to acquire improved opportunities. Some young people make it on their own, without any obvious outside supports from family or community. Often their own religious faith, conviction, determination, and/or sense of greater purpose propels them forward. These young people, and the millions like them around the world, inspire my work. I know they also inspire and inform the work of Richard Lerner, Amy Warren, Erin Phelps, and many of their colleagues.

I first met Richard Lerner in the early 1990s, when he was a newly arrived professor at Michigan State University, and I had recently been awarded a grant by the W. K. Kellogg Foundation (WKKF) to create and launch the International Youth Foundation (IYF). The WKKF had instituted a team of five experts who would serve as strategic consultants in advising on the evolution of IYF's work. Richard Lerner was one of those five amazing people. The team was charged with joining me and other IYF leaders as we traveled around the world to visit partner foundations (in places like Thailand, Japan, the United Kingdom, Poland, Ecuador, the Philippines, and Germany, among others) and assess IYF's effectiveness and impact. They collaborated with IYF in constantly reflecting on and improving our work.

What came through in their reports to WKKF was that the theoretical foundation upon which I had built IYF was, at the time, both innovative and effective. The theoretical foundation was based on years of my own experience, research, and conversations with young people and youth development experts in many countries. It rejected the widely accepted deficit model of youth development (*prevention*) and was built instead on the notion of *promotion* (i.e., that we should focus on the skills, attributes, behaviors, and attitudes we want to promote in young people).

In those early days, I identified the key characteristics of positive youth development as being represented by four Cs—competence, confidence, character, and connection—with detailed explanation of the meaning of each and the importance of their interrelationships. However, I had not scientifically tested these constructs, and I had no reliable evidence to prove that these constructs were well-aligned empirically with positive development. These characteristics were simply evident in so many of the young people I met in many diverse cultures, and I observed they were being promoted, both intentionally and unintentionally, in so many of the more successful youth programs I visited.

I had no idea at the time how well those four Cs—the concept of *positive youth development* and the theoretical program framework for IYF—would resonate with the research community, practitioners, and policymakers. Nor did I know how, with Richard Lerner's great leadership and genius, we would continue to build on these notions (e.g., with the addition of the constructs of caring and contribution) and eventually then be able to scientifically validate and provide evidence of the existence of the six Cs that today define *positive youth development*. Since our early days traveling the globe together with IYF, Richard Lerner has continued, at an almost inhuman pace, to provide practitioners, scholars, and policymakers with important research, thinking, and energy around the study of this emerging field.

The purpose of this book, which Amy Warren, Erin Phelps, and Richard Lerner have ably edited, is to look more closely at the sixth C (contribution) and to study the links among young people's contributions, positive development, and generosity. The editors and their colleagues posit that through contribution to self, family, and society, young people are able to transcend self and promote generosity, which, they go on to propose, is at the essence of spirituality. They go further to propose that this generosity may provide a key foundation for positive youth development.

In my own work, I have certainly met and been witness to many young people who are committed to improving not only their own lives but also the lives of others. Many of these young people have shared with me that they feel a sense of transcendence of self as a result of these contributions and that this sense of transcendence allows them to be agents both in their own healthy development and in the positive enhancement of others as well.

As this book points out, a young person's individual motivation to contribute to civil society, and the particular sense of spirituality or transcendence and positive youth development that the contribution generates, is often a result of the dynamic relationship between a young person's biological, psychological, and sociocultural characteristics. As such, the authors argue that it is important to promote such behaviors among young people (e.g., in formal, school-based, and out-of-school educational experiences). I certainly agree with this applied theoretical notion of promoting opportunities for young people to make positive contributions and that these opportunities promote positive development in youth. Imagine how the world would be different if all young people today were motivated and inspired to commit acts of generosity and make healthy, positive contributions to their world.

I am intrigued by the relationship Amy Warren, Erin Phelps, Richard Lerner, and their colleagues have found and continue to study between contribution and spirituality, and the relation of those constructs to positive youth development. Surely it is my own understanding of and beliefs about spirituality and my own definition of transcendence that informs my view and sparks my intrigue.

For me, the notion of spirituality cannot be solely explained through biology, psychology, culture, or sociological constructs. Of course, these are vitally important, and the lessons learned from this book provide us with substantive information to build on and apply. For me, it is also important to underscore the transcendent mystery of the spirit life itself. That is, equally as intriguing are the ways in which a belief in God, a belief in something (or someone) transcendent, can motivate contribution and generosity and can result in positive development. I bear personal witness from my extensive engagement in many cultures and countries to the pervasive influence of religious faith, religiosity, and some form of deeper, transcendent connection. I look to Amy Warren, Erin Phelps,

Richard Lerner, and their colleagues to continue to challenge the field and further our thinking around this complex aspect of human development.

So, with this book, we can once again thank Amy Warren, Erin Phelps, Richard Lerner, and their colleagues for inspiring the field and, more broadly, society. The editors and their colleagues have helped us think about ways to promote positive youth development and, more specifically, how to support young people in contributing to the development of a more civil society. It is a well-stated goal of the scientists collaborating in this book to build a science of adolescent spirituality and to promote future, longitudinal research about the links between spirituality and positive development during adolescence. Such work will provide practitioners and policymakers and young people themselves with the evidence they need to improve programs and policies and enhance the positive development of all young people.

RICK LITTLE
Founder and President, ImagineNations Group (www.imaginenations.org)
Chairman of the Executive Committee, Silatech (www.silatech.com)
Founder, International Youth Foundation (www.iyfnet.org)
September 25, 2010

Preface

F ollowing the theoretical framework established in *Positive Youth Development and Spirituality: From Theory to Research* (Lerner, Roeser, & Phelps, 2008), this book—*Thriving and Spirituality Among Youth: Research Perspectives and Future Possibilities*—pursues a new, empirical phase in the study of spiritual development within the social and the behavioral sciences. This book brings new data to bear on the links among spirituality, positive youth development (PYD), and young people's generosity, conceived of as their striving to matter by making valued contributions to self, family, community, and civil society.

Our prior volume (Lerner et al., 2008) provided a theoretical framework for a multimethod, cross-sectional investigation of these links, associations that were elucidated by the John Templeton Foundation (JTF)–supported study, "The Role of Spiritual Development in Growth of Purpose, Generosity, and Psychological Health in Adolescence." The present book brings together scientists who collaborated in this investigation. These researchers present data illustrating the nature and importance of the spirituality–PYD–generosity relationship. These data are useful for understanding fundamental features of adolescent development and for providing a foundation for future, longitudinal research on the role of spirituality in healthy and positive youth development.

Although the study of PYD has been a burgeoning area of scientific study for about 15 years, and has been shaped in large part by past and current members of the JTF Advisory Board, no book has empirically explored this domain of scholarship as it is linked to spirituality, especially with a set of scholars from the wide array of scientific fields represented in this book. Accordingly, we hope that this book is a watershed event in the social and behavioral sciences, one marking the emergence of a vibrant and diverse research base for generating new spiritual information about young people. Our aspiration for this book is that it will stand as a baseline against which future, developmental (longitudinal) research will be measured.

The chapters in this book provide evidence of the rich and nuanced relations that may exist between the development of thriving and of spirituality among diverse young people. Although they are well aware of the limitations of pilot, cross-sectional data, the contributors to this volume nevertheless illustrate well—through their creative exploitation of the data sets generated through the resources provided by the JTF—how the study of spiritual development enhances an understanding of the bases of positive development among diverse youth and, in turn, what additional new spiritual information might be garnered if the work presented in this volume is extended in future, longitudinal research.

The contributors to this volume present innovative and important ways of using qualitative data, physiological and brain imaging data, and a variety of quantitative information—sources of information often triangulated with additional data sets available to the authors—to elucidate the nuanced and variable links between thriving and spirituality among diverse young people. We believe that the readers of this volume will be intrigued by the findings about these links that are presented across the chapters, and that they will—as do we—see great merit in pursuing additional, developmental research about the thriving–spirituality relationship in the lives of youth.

Ultimately, then, the goal of this book, and of the scientists collaborating in the cross-sectional research discussed in it, is to build a new, developmentally rigorous (i.e., theoretically predicated, multidisciplinary, multimethod, change-sensitive, longitudinal) database for a science of "adolescent spirituality." We envision this field as integrating basic and applied scholarship and as clarifying how to foster across the adolescent years health and positive development, as well as youth contributions to families, communities, and civil society.

We would like to express our gratitude for the creativity and knowledge of the scientists who have contributed to this book. We thank all of our colleagues who have worked so hard to craft such useful and engaging chapters. Their expertise has made this book possible. The JTF-sponsored pilot project, from which contributors drew data to generate the chapters of this book, was enriched by the contributions of our colleagues from the Institute for Applied Research in Youth Development at Tufts University, who helped with the recruitment of samples and the collection of data. The study gained from the contributions of a succession of three project directors, Robert W. Roeser, Jacqueline V. Lerner, and Amy Eva Alberts Warren and, as well, from several research assistants, Mona Abo-Zena, Dan Du, Sonia Issac Koshy, Inbar Sharon, Alan Poey, Mary von Rueden, and Brian Wilson. We greatly appreciate their contributions.

We are grateful as well that Rick R. Little, Founder and Past-President of the International Youth Foundation and now President of the ImagineNations group, wrote such a powerful, provocative, and inspiring Foreword to the book. In turn, we deeply appreciate the erudite and insightful Afterword that Professor Pamela Ebstyne King, of Fuller Theological Seminary, contributed to the book. Her scholarly acumen about the nature and importance of spirituality for thriving among youth has enhanced immeasurably the quality and impact of this book.

We also appreciate the important contributions to this book that have been made by Jarrett M. Lerner, Managing Editor at the Institute for Applied Research in Youth Development. His expertise and impressive productivity in guiding the development of this work through all phases of the manuscript development and production process were invaluable to us.

We are also grateful for the support of and the commitment to quality scholarship of our publisher, John Wiley & Sons, and to our editor at Wiley, Patricia

(Tisha) Rossi. Tisha's enthusiasm for the substance of this volume and her expertise in publishing excellent scholarship have been essential in guiding us to complete this work with quality and efficiency.

We also are deeply appreciative of the support provided to us by the John Templeton Foundation. The collaborations among the scholars contributing to this volume, and the science that has been produced, could not have occurred without the vision and support of the Foundation. In addition, we are grateful to the Thrive Foundation for Youth, and to its Executive Director, Carol Gray, for her support of this volume. We deeply appreciate all that Carol has done to link our scholarship with the numerous communities within which the Thrive Foundation is working with impressive effectiveness to foster thriving among young people.

Finally, our work on *Thriving and Spirituality Among Youth: Research Perspectives and Future Possibilities* has been framed by the intellectual leadership of the late Sir John M. Templeton. Sir John stressed the importance of generating new spiritual knowledge to help direct the lives of youth along positive life paths. His life work inspired us to undertake the scholarly work represented in this volume. We dedicated the first volume derived from this project to him. Because of his vision, values, and virtues, it is fitting that we also dedicate this second book to his memory.

A. E. A. W., Medford, MA
R. M. L., Medford, MA
E. P., Medford, MA
September, 2010

REFERENCE

Lerner, R. M., Roeser, R. W., & Phelps, E. (2008). Positive development, spirituality, and generosity in youth: An introduction to the issues. In R. M. Lerner, R. W. Roeser, & E. Phelps (Eds.), *Positive youth development and spirituality: From theory to research.* West Conshohocken, PA: Templeton Foundation Press.

Contributors

Mona M. Abo-Zena
Tufts University

Aerika S. Brittian
Arizona State University

Dan Du
Tufts University

David Henry Feldman
Tufts University

Paula Taylor Greathouse
University of South Florida

Elena L. Grigorenko
Yale University

Sonia S. Issac Koshy
Tufts University

Sara W. Lazar
Harvard Medical School

Gabriel Leonard
McGill University

Jacqueline V. Lerner
Boston College

Richard M. Lerner
Tufts University

Jenni Menon Mariano
University of South Florida

Ofra Mayseless
University of Haifa

Tomáš Paus
University of Toronto

Zdenka Pausova
University of Nottingham

Michel Perron
University of Montreal

Erin Phelps
Tufts University

G. Bruce Pike
McGill University

Alan P. Poey
Tufts University

Louis Richer
University of Quebec in Chicoutimi

Robert W. Roeser
Portland State University

Pninit Russo-Netzer
University of Haifa

Hala Shehadeh
New York University

Lonnie R. Sherrod
Society for Research in Child
Development

Sukhmani Singh
New York University

Selcuk R. Sirin
New York University

Margaret Beale Spencer
University of Chicago

Gabriel S. Spiewak
Fordham University

Carola Suárez-Orozco
New York University

Roberto Toro
University of Nottingham

Heather L. Urry
Tufts University

Suzanne Veillette
University of Montreal

Amy Eva Alberts Warren
Tufts University

Wei Zhang
South China Normal University

Shuangju Zhen
South China Normal University

CHAPTER

1

⟾⟶◆⟵⟸

Research Perspectives and Future Possibilities in the Study of Thriving and Spirituality

A View of the Issues

AMY EVA ALBERTS WARREN, RICHARD M. LERNER, AND ERIN PHELPS

During adolescence, individuals undergo marked changes in body, mind, and social relations. Faced with such change, many youth seek earnestly to find their place in the world by defining who they are and how they matter (Lerner, Roeser, & Phelps, 2007). Youth search for a self definition—an identity (e.g., Erikson, 1959, 1968; Harter, 2006)—that enables them to matter to self, family, and society, both in the teenage years and in their future adult life. This search often impels the young person to transcend a cognitive and emotional focus on the self (Elkind, 1967) and to seek to contribute in important, valued, and even noble ways to his or her world. We believe that generosity derives from such transcendence, and that such noble purposes are the essence of spirituality (see too Damon, 2004), and may provide a key foundation for positive youth development (PYD) (Lerner, 2009).

Following the theoretical framework established in *Positive Youth Development and Spirituality: From Theory to Research* (Lerner et al., 2007), the purpose of this book is to bring new data to bear on the links among spirituality, PYD, and young people's generosity, that is, their striving to matter by making valued contributions to self, family, community, and civil society. The present book

1

builds on this theoretical framework with a multimethod, cross-sectional investigation of these links, the John Templeton Foundation (JTF)–supported study, "The Role of Spiritual Development in Growth of Purpose, Generosity, and Psychological Health in Adolescence" (e.g., Lerner et al., 2007; Roeser et al., 2007). Accordingly, this book brings together scientists who collaborated in this investigation and now have data illustrating the nature and importance of the spirituality–PYD–generosity relationship, both for understanding fundamental features of adolescent development and for providing a foundation for future, longitudinal research. Only such research can elucidate the interconnections among these three constructs across this life period and, therefore, provide a rich empirical basis for optimizing these relations.

Ultimately, then, the goal of the scientists collaborating in the cross-sectional research discussed in this book is to build a new, developmentally rigorous (i.e., theoretically predicated, multidisciplinary, multimethod, change-sensitive, longitudinal) database for a science of "adolescent spirituality," a field that will clarify how to foster across the adolescent years health and positive development, as well as youth contributions to families, communities, and civil society.

Such goals are ambitious and require that scientists attend to the processes of individual development, the features of the complex and changing context of youth development, and—critically, in our view—the mutually influential links between individual and context (represented as individual ↔ context relations) that propel development across the life span. Accordingly, across the chapters of this book, contributors point in different ways to the use of a broad theoretical framework—developmental systems theories—for their work, one that is useful precisely because of its focus on the system of complex individual ↔ context relations that occur within the ecology of human development (Damon & Lerner, 2008; Lerner, 2002). Table 1.1 provides a summary of the key features of developmental systems theories of human development.

As explained in Table 1.1, in developmental systems theories, the possibility of adaptive developmental relations (i.e., mutually beneficial individual ↔ context relations) between individuals and their contexts, and the potential plasticity of development across the life span (i.e., the potential for systematic change in the structure or function of behavior) are defining features of human development. Furthermore, given that the array of individual and contextual variables involved in the relations between people and their worlds constitutes a virtually open set (e.g., there are more than 70 trillion potential human genotypes, and each of them may be coupled across life with an even larger number of life course trajectories of social experiences, thus creating in effect an infinite number of human phenotypes; Hirsch, 2004), the diversity of development becomes a prime, substantive focus for developmental science (Lerner, 2004; Spencer, 2006). The diverse person, conceptualized from a strength-based perspective (in that the potential plasticity of developmental change constitutes a fundamental strength of all humans; Spencer, 2006), and approached with the expectation that positive

Table 1.1 Defining Features of Developmental Systems Theories

A relational metamodel

Predicated on a postmodern philosophical perspective that transcends Cartesian dualism, developmental systems theories are framed by a relational metamodel for human development. There is, then, a rejection of all splits between components of the ecology of human development (e.g., between nature- and nurture-based variables, between continuity and discontinuity, or between stability and instability). Systemic syntheses or integrations replace dichotomizations or other reductionist partitions of the developmental system.

The integration of levels of organization

Relational thinking and the rejection of Cartesian splits is associated with the idea that all levels of organization within the ecology of human development are integrated or fused. These levels range from the biological and physiological through the cultural and historical.

Developmental regulation across ontogeny involves mutually influential individual ↔ context relations

As a consequence of the integration of levels, the regulation of development occurs through mutually influential connections among all levels of the developmental system, ranging from genes and cell physiology through individual mental and behavioral functioning to society, culture, the designed and natural ecology, and, ultimately, history. These mutually influential relations may be represented generically as Level 1 ↔ Level 2 (e.g., Family ↔ Community) and, in the case of ontogeny, may be represented as individual ↔ context.

Integrated actions, individual ↔ context relations, are the basic unit of analysis within human development

The character of developmental regulation means that the integration of actions—of the individual on the context and of the multiple levels of the context on the individual (individual ↔ context)—constitute the fundamental unit of analysis in the study of the basic process of human development.

Temporality and plasticity in human development

As a consequence of the fusion of the historical level of analysis—and therefore, temporality—within the levels of organization constituting the ecology of human development, the developmental system is characterized by the potential for systematic change, by plasticity. Observed trajectories of intraindividual change may vary across time and place as a consequence of such plasticity.

Plasticity is relative

Developmental regulation may both facilitate and constrain opportunities for change. Thus, change in individual ↔ context relations is not limitless, and the magnitude of plasticity (the probability of change in a developmental trajectory occurring in relation to variation in contextual conditions) may vary across the life span and history. Nevertheless, the potential for plasticity at both individual and contextual levels constitutes a fundamental strength of all human development.

(Continued)

Table 1.1 (*Continued*)

Intraindividual change, interindividual differences in intraindividual change, and the fundamental substantive significance of diversity
The combinations of variables across the integrated levels of organization within the developmental system that provide the basis of the developmental process will vary at least in part across individuals and groups. This diversity is systematic and lawfully produced by idiographic, group differential, and generic (nomothetic) phenomena. The range of interindividual differences in intraindividual change observed at any point in time is evidence of the plasticity of the developmental system and makes the study of diversity of fundamental substantive significance for the description, explanation, and optimization of human development.

Optimism, the application of developmental science, and the promotion of positive human development
The potential for and instantiations of plasticity legitimate an optimistic and proactive search for characteristics of individuals and of their ecologies that, together, can be arrayed to promote positive human development across the life span. Through the application of developmental science in planned attempts (i.e., interventions) to enhance (e.g., through social policies or community-based programs) the character of humans' developmental trajectories, the promotion of positive human development may be achieved by aligning the strengths (operationalized as the potential for positive change) of individuals and contexts.

Multidisciplinarity and the need for change-sensitive methodologies
The integrated levels of organization constituting the developmental system require collaborative analyses by scholars from multiple disciplines. Multidisciplinary knowledge and, ideally, interdisciplinary knowledge is sought. The temporal embeddedness and resulting plasticity of the developmental system requires that research designs, methods of observation and measurement, and procedures for data analysis be change-sensitive and able to integrate trajectories of change at multiple levels of analysis.[1]

---

[1]Representative instances of change-sensitive methodologies may involve (a) innovations in sampling (e.g., theoretically predicated selection of participants and of x-axis divisions, or inverting the x- and the y-axis; that is, making time the dependent variable); (b) using measures designed to be sensitive to change; to possess equivalence across temporal levels (age, generation, history), different groups (sex, race, religion), and different contexts (family, community, urban-rural, culture); to provide relational indices (e.g., of person-environment fit); and to provide triangulation across different observational systems (convergent and divergent validation); (c) employing designs that are change-sensitive designs, such as longitudinal and sequential strategies, person-centered, as compared to variable-centered, analyses ("P" versus "R" approaches); and (d) data analyses that afford multivariate analyses of change (e.g., procedures such as structural equation modeling [SEM], hierarchical linear modeling [HLM], trajectory analysis, or time-series analysis).

Source: Adapted from Lerner, R. M. (2006). Developmental sciences, developmental systems, and contemporary theories of human development. In W. Damon & R. M. Lerner (Eds.), *Handbook of Child Psychology* (6th ed., Vol. 1, pp. 1–17). Hoboken, NJ: Wiley.

changes can be promoted across all instances of this diversity as a consequence of health-supportive alignments between people and settings (Benson, Scales, Hamilton, & Sesma, 2006), becomes the necessary subject of developmental science inquiry.

It is in the linkage between the ideas of plasticity and diversity that developmental systems thinking can be extended to the field of adolescence and for the field of adolescence to serve as a "testing ground" for ideas associated with developmental systems theories. This synergy has had several outcomes relevant to the focus in this book on the links among spirituality, PYD, and generosity. The synergy among the ideas of plasticity and diversity and the study of adolescent development has forged a new, strength-based vision of and vocabulary for the nature of adolescent development (Lerner, 2009). Table 1.2 summarizes the key ideas involved in the PYD perspective.

As indicated in the table, a defining feature of PYD may be acts of generosity by young people (i.e., contributions of mutual benefit to self and context). Lerner (2004) has suggested that spirituality may provide the emotional and cognitive impetus for promoting in adolescents actions that transcend a focus on the self and are of benefit to others and to society. In other words, a sense of spirituality—an orientation to invest in or devote oneself to ideas and actions that transcend self-interest—is the motivation for a positively developing youth to enact generous behaviors and to therefore make contributions that matter to the world beyond the self. In short, the plasticity–diversity linkage within developmental systems theory and method has provided the basis for the formulation of the PYD perspective and its links to generosity and spirituality.

Although the cross-sectional data discussed in this book obviously do not include the fundamental, change component that is required for understanding

Table 1.2 Key Principles of the PYD Perspective

Because of the potential to change, all youth have strengths.

All contexts have strengths as well. These strengths are resources that may be used to promote positive youth development.

These resources are termed *developmental assets*: They are the social nutrients needed for healthy development.

These assets are found in families, schools, faith institutions, youth-serving organizations, and the community more generally.

If the strengths of youth are combined with ecological developmental assets, then positive, healthy development may occur.

PYD is constituted by Five Cs (Competence, Confidence, Connection, Character, and Caring).

PYD is linked to youth contributions to the self, family, community, and civil society.

We should be optimistic that it is in our power to promote positive development among all youth.

development in general or, more specifically, for exploring changes in the associations among spirituality, PYD, and generosity, developmental systems theory is nevertheless useful in at least two ways in regard to the work presented in this book. First, because this theoretical approach was used to design the cross-sectional study on which the present volume is based (Lerner et al., 2007), the research discussed across the chapters in this book is attentive to the multiple levels of organization within the ecology of human development; these levels are always involved in the mutually influential links between individuals and contexts and, therefore, the work presented in this book provides point-in-time depictions of the nature and scope of these links and offers hypotheses regarding how, across time, individual ↔ context relations may be involved in providing positive associations among spirituality, PYD, and generosity.

The hypotheses about these relations that are drawn from the cross-sectional research discussed in this book lead to the second use of developmental systems theories for the scholarship we present. These theoretical models provide the conceptual framework for moving the burgeoning science of adolescent spirituality beyond its current status to a position within the broader field of developmental science that is based on the dynamic, across-time links between an active individual and his or her changing social, cultural, and physical ecology. By providing a framework for future, longitudinal research about not only mutually influential but also, from an optimization perspective, mutually beneficial individual ↔ context relations, the authors' use of ideas associated with developmental systems theories offers an exciting foundation for what may become a vibrant, integrated arena for a basic and applied developmental science.

We hope that the combined impact of the chapters in this book will provide a foundation for the burgeoning of this field. Indeed, as readers engage the ideas and findings presented across this book, they will realize that the scholars contributing to it stand with Sir John Templeton (1995) in believing that "No one can foresee exactly which research projects for spiritual progress should be undertaken or even the specific form that empirical inquiry may take in this realm. Nor can anyone foresee which experiments will prove fruitful" (1995, p. 70).

This book provides innovative, exciting, and important ideas for creating new spiritual knowledge about the theory-predicated empirical paths that developmental scientists may pursue in exploring the nature and importance for healthy human development of the links among PYD, spirituality, and generosity. It is useful to summarize the ways in which this book makes this contribution.

THE JOHN TEMPLETON FOUNDATION–SUPPORTED PROJECT ON THE ROLE OF SPIRITUAL DEVELOPMENT IN GROWTH OF PURPOSE, GENEROSITY, AND PSYCHOLOGICAL HEALTH IN ADOLESCENCE

Within a developmental systems approach to adolescence, the links among spirituality, PYD, and generosity involve mutually influential relations across the range of levels of organization involved in the ecology of human development. Accordingly, research framed by a developmental systems perspective must include the roles of biological-level variables (e.g., genetic and neural sources of variance) through sociocultural variables in fostering these links.

Although chapters across the book take this integrative perspective about human development as the general frame for their work, different colleagues foreground different levels of organization within the developmental system. As such, the book is organized into sections that focus on biological-level variables, on individual- and psychological-level variables, and on social- and cultural-level variables.

In order to jumpstart this effort, we embarked on research funded by the John Templeton Foundation. This project was originally conceived as a cross-sectional survey study with two intensive substudies. The first substudy was to be an interview study of youth who could be defined as spiritual exemplars, and the second substudy was to provide descriptions of brain activity that could begin to define neural contributions to the relations between spirituality and thriving. The project eventually comprised these two projects plus three additional substudies: One consisted of youth who were involved in some way in religious organizations; the second focused on physiological and brain activity measures taken while college students completed some attention and emotion regulation tasks. Because most of the research reported herein used these data, a brief description of the substudies is provided here so that we can describe the overall research context for the chapters to follow.

DESCRIPTION OF THE SUBSTUDIES

The *Religious Populations Questionnaire and Focus Group Sub-Study* was designed to obtain youth-centered perspectives on PYD ↔ spirituality relations for young people who were involved with religious organizations (i.e., schools or youth groups). Data were collected with questionnaires, followed by focus groups. Primary research questions were: How do these youth define "positive development," and do these definitions vary by age, sex, and religious tradition? How do they define "being a spiritual person," and can someone "become more spiritual over time"? Do they see themselves as "spiritual"? Who are the people who have been most influential in their spiritual development? What is the relation between PYD and spirituality among these youth?

The questionnaires were administered to 269 youth from 21 different research sites who were attending a religious school or a religious youth program in the Boston, Massachusetts area. Youth were mostly Christian, Muslim, Jewish, or Unitarian Universalist (45%, 29%, 11%, and 8%, respectively). Individuals ranged in age from 10 to 23 years, from 7th grade to 4th year of college (37% middle school, 50% high school, 14% college students); 46% were male and 54% were female.

Open-ended items were included about youth perspectives on positive development, being a spiritual person, and spiritual development. We also established closed-ended items assessing PYD, contribution, spiritual practices, and transcendence. After the questionnaire was administered, 44 focus groups comprising five to seven individuals each were conducted, to collect more qualitative data from youth concerning their conceptions of PYD and spirituality.

The *Exemplary Youth Profiles in Contribution Sub-Study* was designed to assess contribution (generosity) ↔ spirituality relations among youth who were very involved in service activities in their communities in the Boston area. This substudy was designed to assess how these young people spontaneously talk about the role of spirituality in their lives, in general, and in their service activities, in particular.

The majority of participants were recruited from three youth-serving organizations committed to the engagement of youth in community service. Additional participants were recruited for either their notable commitment to community service or their notable engagement in spiritual and religious practices. Participants were 60 ethnically and religiously diverse high school- and college-age youth (31 in high school and 29 in college), who ranged in age from 17 to 24 years. There were 24 males and 36 females.

Youth were asked to produce a spontaneous life narrative (the Life Narrative Task, LNT; Habermas, 2007), followed by participation in a semistructured interview and completion of paper-and-pencil survey measures. In the interviews, youth were asked about their life goals and values, character, spirituality and religion, community and contribution, and imagined future. Self-report assessments of open-mindedness, ego development, spirituality, contribution, well-being, attachment style, and other constructs were also collected.

The *Positive Youth Development and Spirituality Questionnaire Sub-Study* was designed to assess youth perspectives on PYD ↔ spirituality relations using questionnaires with samples of youth drawn from public schools, youth development programs, and colleges and universities. Research questions included: What are the relations among various indicators of PYD and spirituality? Are these relations differentiated by age, sex, and religious tradition?

Participants were recruited from the greater Boston area. Four hundred and eleven participants aged 10 to 22 years were recruited from middle schools, high schools, and after-school programs. An additional sample of 252 college participants aged 18 to 23 years were recruited by word of mouth and advertisements on Facebook. The overall sample, therefore, included 663 individuals ranging in age from 10 to 23 years. This included 31% middle school students, 31% high school students, and 38% college-aged students. Participants were 49% female and 51% male; were ethnically diverse; and were mostly Jewish, Catholic, Protestant, Muslim, or having no religious affiliation.

Two versions of a questionnaire were constructed and consisted of closed-ended items drawn from established measures of PYD and spirituality. The first version was delivered on a voice-enhanced personal digital assistant (PDA) for middle and high school students. The second version was a Web-based questionnaire for college-aged participants using the same items.

The *Psychophysiology Sub-Study of Emotion and Attention Regulation* was designed to investigate the behavioral and physiological consequences of emotion and attention regulation, and their relation to spiritual beliefs and practices, and PYD. It has been proposed that spiritual and religious beliefs and practices contribute to one's ability to regulate attention and emotion, which has been implicated in the maintenance of health and well-being and in PYD.

Fifty-two college participants aged 18 to 23 years were recruited. Participants were 48% female and 52% male; predominantly Caucasian (67%); and mostly identified as Christian, having multiple religions, or having no religious affiliation.

A Web-based questionnaire consisting of closed-ended items drawn from established measures of PYD and spirituality was completed. Following the questionnaire, behavioral (e.g., subjective ratings, task performance) and physiological measures (e.g., heart rate, respiration, facial muscle activity, and sweat gland activity) were collected while participants worked on three tasks. The first, an attention task, was designed to assess the ability to exhibit cognitive control by testing participants' reaction time and accuracy in the face of irrelevant distracters. In the other two, emotion and emotion regulation tasks, participants were shown pictures with emotionally negative, positive, or neutral content and asked to rate their emotional reactions to the pictures.

In the *Brain Imaging Sub-Study of Emotion Reactivity and Regulation and its Relation to Spirituality and PYD*, functional magnetic resonance imaging (fMRI) was used to investigate brain bases of emotion and emotion regulation and their relation to spiritual beliefs and practices as well as PYD. From structural scans taken of each participant's brain, features of cortical regions, like ventromedial prefrontal cortex, were measured.

A sample of 27 college participants aged 18 to 23 years was recruited. Participants were 48% female and 52% male; predominantly Caucasian (56%); and mostly identified as Christian, having multiple religions, or having no religious affiliation.

A Web-based questionnaire consisting of closed-ended items drawn from established measures of PYD and spirituality was completed (the same questionnaire used in the prior substudy). In addition, structural scans were acquired, followed by fMRIs in which participants completed two tasks in the scanner that assessed emotion reactivity and regulation (see prior description) in order to estimate the functional activity of these regions. Estimates of cortical thickness and functional brain activation were obtained.

In the chapters that follow, most of the authors used data from one or more of these substudies. In some cases, the data did not suit their purposes, which is often the case when researchers attempt to use data collected by others. In such situations, contributors to this project used other data sets and sought to triangulate findings across data sets. Whatever the specifics of the data sets they used, the work of each of the contributors to this volume supports and complements the other chapters and the overall goal of this work: to start and to advance what is, still at this writing, a largely neglected area of research on the development of youth—spirituality and PYD. A brief description of the parts of this book will illustrate the contributions made by the authors in this volume.

BIOLOGICAL CONTEXTS OF POSITIVE YOUTH DEVELOPMENT AND SPIRITUALITY

In the research reported in this book, several colleagues drew on data that were collected about how relations between biological-level variables and psychological- or social-level constructs were related to behavioral indicators of spirituality, PYD, and/or generosity. Moreover, showing one of the powerful uses of the cross-sectional data involved in the JTF study, colleagues who drew on the biological-level data were in many cases able to triangulate these data with information present in other, independently collected data sets. Such triangulation, which leverages the JTF study data in the service of cross validation, was a methodological strategy used by several colleagues involved in the research.

In the first chapter of the biological bases section, Chapter 2, Urry and her colleagues use the JTF brain imaging data on college students to consider how a psychological function can link religious/spiritual practices with well-being. In this volume, they focus on one religion/spirituality practice—meditation practice—and one psychological function—emotion regulation. They use the neuroimaging literature to propose that the prefrontal cortex region (PFC) activation might provide an individual-difference metric that captures emotion regulation ability, specifically the ability to use cognitive reappraisal to change pleasant and unpleasant feeling states. Results indicate that higher meditation practice is associated with higher PFC activation during cognitive reappraisal, and higher PFC activation is associated with positive emotion in daily life.

In turn, Grigorenko focuses in Chapter 3 on one defining feature of PYD, the social connections—the affiliations—that youth develop with other individuals and with groups. She argues that these connections form the foundation for spirituality and religiosity. She advances the hypothesis, and surveys human and animal literature in support of it, that biological agents, specifically the neuropeptides oxytocin (OXT) and arginine vasopressin (AVP), might be important for experiencing such specifically human feelings as spirituality and religiosity. This argument is based on research that shows that (a) OXT and AVP are important in the formation of the neurochemical foundation for demonstrating affiliative behavior and forming affiliation in animals and humans; (b) OXT and AVP also contribute to the development of the higher-order personality trait of affiliation; and (c) affiliative behaviors with a transcendent other are central to religiosity and spirituality.

As a precursor to the study of spirituality and brain development, Paus and his colleagues explore in Chapter 4 the connections between indicators of PYD, as indexed by the Five Cs (see Table 1.2), and variation in the thickness of the cortex of the frontal, parietal, temporal, and occipital lobes, to determine whether cortical thickness differs by PYD. These relations were assessed separately for males and females; the findings for males in the lower PYD group were the most salient. These boys with low thriving lacked the expected thinning of the temporal cortex and had lower IQs, more depression and risk-taking behaviors, and fewer adaptive personality characteristics. This finding may indicate a relatively impoverished social context that may drive the maturation on the temporal context during adolescence. The findings also indicate that sex-specific mechanisms may be mediating the relationship between PYD and cortical maturation.

After describing prior studies of changes in brain structure following meditation and prayer found in earlier research, Lazar focuses in Chapter 5 on how certain indicators of brain structure are correlated with indicators of PYD. This work is based on data collected for the JTF project, using fMRI measurements and questionnaire measures of PYD and related characteristics. She predicts that (a) the amount of time the students reported being engaged in prayer or meditation would correlate with the thickness of the right anterior insula; (b) a specific subregion of the PFC would positively correlate with measures of self-regulation; and (c) the thickness of the temporal parietal junction (TPJ) would correlate with the "connection" and "caring" components of the PYD scale. The findings lend support, although not statistical significance, to the first two predictions. While still preliminary and based on a small sample size (n = 30), these data indicate the potential of identifying the neural signatures of PYD and spirituality.

INDIVIDUAL AND PSYCHOLOGICAL CONTEXTS OF POSITIVE YOUTH DEVELOPMENT AND SPIRITUALITY

Although biological-level processes are integral to an understanding of youth development, many contributors explored psychological processes involved in the development of spirituality, positive development, and generosity during adolescence. Based on ideas of elaborative development (Ford & Lerner, 1992), Warren begins to elucidate the dynamic developmental processes involved in commitment to the *whole* of humanity in Chapter 6, as instantiated by Great Love-Compassion (GLC)—that is, the wish for *all* to have freedom and joy and for *all* to be relieved of their pain and suffering. Accordingly, she forwards a nonrecursive structural model of hypothesized relationships among adaptive developmental regulations, elaborative development, and GLC. By introducing and testing GLC as one key outcome of elaborative development, Warren seeks to explain how some developmental scenarios eventuate in the emergence of an ideational and personal style marked by commitment to the whole of humanity. Quantitative findings based on the *Exemplary Youth Profiles in Contribution Sub-Study* provide evidence of the expected, positive covariation between an index of elaborative functioning and GLC.

Feldman and colleagues examine in Chapter 7 the complex phenomenon of religious conversion, defined as movement from one (or no) religious affiliation to another religious affiliation. This chapter reports the results of an analysis of three cases, all of whom moved from a nonpracticing but Christian or Judeo-Christian affiliation to a Muslim religious identification. The primary aims of the study were to explore (a) possible relationships between religious conversion and aspects of PYD (e.g., community service) and (b) possible relationships between religious conversion and spiritual transformation (i.e., the extent to which religious conversion as a social phenomenon was associated with tangible psychological and behavioral changes in spiritual identities, commitments, and practices). Quantitative and qualitative analyses were carried out on the cases, providing a set of findings that yield three distinct interpretations, one for each adolescent. Each experience appeared to be motivated by different forces and reasons, unfolded in distinctive ways, and produced different social, psychological, and behavioral manifestations.

Spiewak and Sherrod explore in Chapter 8 whether there are shared developmental pathways between religious/spiritual engagement and PYD. They propose the 3H Model to capture the overlapping nature of development, with three domains of functioning common to both PYD and religion/spirituality: Head, Heart, and Hands. These domains capture the cognitive, affective, and behavioral dimensions of human experience. They argue that religious/spiritual development proceeds as part of the development of PYD, rather than as a separate strand. Specifically, the authors hypothesize that constructs of both religiosity/spirituality and PYD will fit into a single measurement model that involves Head, Heart, and Hands as their underlying factors. Data from the *Positive Youth Development and Spirituality Questionnaire Sub-Study* were used to construct a structural equation model to test this model, with promising results.

Using qualitative coding procedures and quantitative analyses, Mariano and her colleagues assess religious adolescents' views of success and spirituality in Chapter 9, using data from the *Religious Populations Questionnaire and Focus Group Sub-Study*. Specifically, they focus on youth responses to the following two questions: (1) "What are two or three qualities or characteristics of someone that you would say is a successful young person?" and (2) "What does it mean to be a spiritual person?" Responses were coded using an Open Coding strategy, to be responsive to what the adolescents wrote about success and spirituality. These religious youth identified success most frequently with knowledge and wisdom, moral virtues, a sense of purpose, and motivation, and with social virtues such as participation in community activities and the ability to contribute to positive relationships. Spirituality was most frequently associated with the process and outcomes of spiritual practices such as prayer and meditation, having a sense of faith, and feeling connected to something greater than the self.

Racial and ethnic variation may provide distinct opportunities for or constraints on processes of spiritual development, PYD, or the development of generosity. In Chapter 10, Brittian and Spencer study the impact of religious and racial identities on PYD, from the perspective of the Phenomenological Variant of Ecological Systems Theory (PVEST) framework (Spencer, 2006, 2008).

Accordingly, they examine the relations between and moderating effects of religious identity and ethnic identity on well-being and risk behaviors among a diverse group of American adolescents. In overview, age and sex were the strongest predictors of well-being and risk behaviors. However, for risk-taking behaviors, they found a significant ethnic identity by religious identity interaction, such that youth with higher levels of ethnic identity and lower levels of religious identity engaged in more risk behaviors. When analyses were conducted within ethnic groups (African American, European American, and Multiracial), this significant mediating effect (interaction) only occurred in the Multiracial group.

SOCIAL AND CULTURAL CONTEXTS OF POSITIVE YOUTH DEVELOPMENT AND SPIRITUALITY

Social and cultural levels of organization within the developmental system are also likely to affect spiritual development, PYD, and the development of generosity, and some of the contributors explored this possibility. In the first chapter in this section, Chapter 11, Sirin and colleagues assess Muslim youth development in two U.S. cities by triangulating JTF study data with independently collected data. Using a sample of Muslim high school and college-aged youth in the Greater New York City area and a sample of Muslim middle school, high school, and college-aged youth in the Greater Boston area, these authors explore the PYD of Muslim American youth in a post-9/11 context. Using qualitative and quantitative data from both studies, the investigators consider the roles of context and demographics in mediating religious discrimination, identity, and practice, which were used to predict Muslim youths' social conscience, well-being, social competence, general self-worth, contribution, and other helping behaviors.

In another instance of the triangulation of JTF study data with independently collected information, Suárez-Orozco and colleagues study the association between religion and social support among immigrant-origin youth in Chapter 12. Using quantitative descriptions of the parents' reports of their religious participation to provide the context, qualitative data in the youths' own words were used to explore the significance of religion in their lives using data from the *Longitudinal Immigration Student Adaptation (LISA) study* (C. Suárez-Orozco, M. M. Suárez-Orozco, & Todorova, 2008), a study of recently arrived immigrant youth from Central America, China, the Dominican Republic, Haiti, and Mexico. At the same time, they explore the mediating roles of religious identity, positive peer affiliations, and social support in predicting such positive outcomes as well-being, sense of purpose, and reduction in risk behavior from religious involvement, in immigrant youth from the JTF study.

Bringing an international focus to this work, two research groups study the national context as a framework for understanding the ecological embeddedness of the development of spirituality, PYD, and generosity.

In Chapter 13, Mayseless and Russo-Netzer explore the relationship between spirituality and emotional maturity among Israeli college youth. The questionnaire they employ overlaps considerably with the one developed for the JTF study and thus can provide some comparable results. Using several psychosocial constructs as outcomes, these authors examine the independent and intertwined relationships between spirituality and emotional maturity. They found spirituality and emotional maturity to be related, but not for every construct and not always in parallel ways. They argue that the profile of results may reflect the importance of the community, perhaps a religious community, in supporting and promoting spiritual development. Furthermore, in line with this interpretation, spiritual development was moderately to highly associated with frequency of religious practice. This finding suggests the possible importance of the religious community in promoting spiritual development in youth even in a country, such as Israel, which is highly secular.

Zhang and colleagues expand the cross-national comparative perspective in Chapter 14. They compare youth spiritual beliefs and their associations with youth development in China and America. For the study of Chinese youth, qualitative data were obtained about Chinese youths' beliefs about religion, which are quite different from American youths' beliefs. Furthermore, measures from the JTF study were adapted and translated, and combined with the information gathered from the Chinese qualitative data to develop a questionnaire that was administered to more than 900 youth in China. They found that religiosity and spirituality are core components in the spiritual belief systems of American youth and are associated with positive development and with lower levels of depression and many risk behaviors. In turn, "inner power" beliefs are the core and dominant component in the belief systems of Chinese youth, and these beliefs are associated most significantly with PYD.

CONCLUSIONS

Across the chapters in this book, readers will encounter a rich and varied array of theoretical ideas, methodological approaches to the study of youth and spiritual development, and recommendations for subsequent research. Across this variation several common perspectives exist, which together organize an agenda for innovative and programmatic scholarship aimed at producing new information about adolescent spirituality and for enhancing adaptive relations between young people and their world.

First, in the midst of theoretical variation there is also theoretical commonality. All contributors to this book embed their ideas within developmental systems notions of human development. Second, all contributors emphasize that research must be attentive to diversity—to the variation in gender, race, ethnicity, religion, family structure, and culture that makes each person an individual. All people possess generic characteristics, and all people possess group-specific attributes. However, each person also possesses specific characteristics of individuality (ranging from their genotypes to their personal history of individual ↔ context relations across the life span). The contributors share the view that, unless research is sensitive to the distinctive characteristics of people, essential features of human functioning will be missed.

Third, the contributors note that no one method can appraise adequately the general, group, and individual characteristics of people. As such, multiple methods of data collection must be used and, ideally, each method must be triangulated with other methods in order to identify what is unique and what is common about the links in adolescence among positive development, spirituality, and generosity.

Finally, the fundamental point of scientific agreement among the contributors to this book is that all of the variables involved in the relations among PYD, spirituality, and generosity are not static. They develop dynamically over the course of the second decade of life. Accordingly, all of the contributors to this book believe that the full advancement of this quest for new spiritual information rests on the design and implementation of a major and far-reaching longitudinal research project.

As will be evident across the chapters of this book, there are substantial theoretical and empirical reasons to believe that such longitudinal work can create a new era in the study of spiritual development. The chapters in this book make clear that science and scientists are poised to engage the difficult conceptual and methodological issues involved in a search for new spiritual realities about positive development in adolescence. As such, this book will mark a watershed event in the crystallization of a new domain of scientific activity.

REFERENCES

Benson, P. L., Scales, P. C., Hamilton, S. F., & Sesma, A., Jr. (2006). Positive youth development: Theory, research, and applications. In R. M. Lerner (Ed.), *Theoretical models of human development: Vol. 1, Handbook of child psychology* (6th ed., pp. 894–941). Editors-in-chief: W. Damon & R. M. Lerner. Hoboken, NJ: Wiley.

Damon, W. (2004). What is positive youth development? *Annals of the American Academy of Political and Social Science, 591*, 13–24.

Damon, W., & Lerner, R. M. (Eds.). (2008). *Child and adolescent development: An advanced course.* Hoboken, NJ: Wiley.

Elkind, D. (1967). Egocentrism in adolescents. *Child Development, 38*, 1025–1034.

Erikson, E. H. (1959). Identity and the life cycle. *Psychological Issues, 1*, 50–100.

Erikson, E. H. (1968). *Identity: Youth and crisis.* Oxford, England: Norton & Co.

Ford, D. H., & Lerner, R. M. (1992). *Developmental systems theory: An integrative approach.* Newbury Park, CA: Sage.

Habermas, T. (2007). How to tell a life: The development of the cultural concept of biography. *Journal of Cognition and Development, 8*(1), 1–31.

Harter, S. (2006). The self. In N. Eisenberg, W. Damon, & R. M. Lerner (Eds.), *Handbook of child psychology: Vol. 3, Social, emotional, and personality development.* (6th ed., pp. 505–570). Hoboken, NJ: Wiley.

Hirsch, J. (2004). Uniqueness, diversity, similarity, repeatability, and heritability. In C. Garcia Coll, E. Bearer, & R. M. Lerner (Eds.), *Nature and nurture: The complex interplay of genetic and environmental influences on human behavior and development* (pp. 127–138). Mahwah, NJ: Erlbaum.

Lerner, R. M. (2002). *Concepts and theories of human development* (3rd ed.). Mahwah, NJ: Erlbaum.

Lerner, R. M. (2004). *Liberty: Thriving and civic engagement among American youth.* Thousand Oaks, CA: Sage.

Lerner, R. M. (2009). The positive youth development perspective: Theoretical and empirical bases of a strength-based approach to adolescent development. In C. R. Snyder and S. J. Lopez (Eds.), *Handbook of positive psychology* (2nd ed.). Oxford, England: Oxford University Press.

Lerner, R. M., Roeser, R. W., & Phelps, E. (Eds.). (2007). *Positive youth development & spirituality: From theory to research.* West Conshohocken, PA: Templeton Foundation Press.

Roeser, R. W., Lerner, R. M., Phelps, E., Urry, H. L., Lazar, S., Issac, S. S., Abo-Zena, M., Alberts, A. E., & Du, D. (2007, March). The role of spiritual development in growth of purpose, generosity, and psychological health in adolescence. Invited presentation to the Fourth Biennial SRCD Pre-conference on Religious and Spiritual Development, Society for Research in Child Development (SRCD) Biennial Meeting, Boston, MA.

Spencer, M. B. (2006). Phenomenology and ecological systems theory: Development of diverse groups. In R. M. Lerner & W. Damon (Eds.), *Handbook of child psychology: Vol. 1, Theoretical models of human development* (6th ed., pp. 829–893). Hoboken, NJ: Wiley.

Spencer, M. B. (2008). Phenomenology and ecological systems theory: Development of diverse groups. In W. Damon & R. Lerner (Eds.), *Child and adolescent development: An advanced course* (pp. 696–740). Hoboken, NJ: Wiley.

Suárez-Orozco, C., Suárez-Orozco, M. M., & Todorova, I. (2008). *Learning a new land.* Cambridge, MA: Harvard University Press.

Templeton, J. M. (1995). *The humble approach: Scientists discover God.* Philadelphia, PA: Templeton Foundation Press.

Biological Contexts of Positive Youth Development and Spirituality

CHAPTER

2

Prefrontal Cortical Activation During Emotion Regulation

Linking Religious/Spiritual Practices With Well-Being[1]

HEATHER L. URRY, ROBERT W. ROESER, SARA W. LAZAR, AND ALAN P. POEY

As described by Urry and Poey (2008), it is well documented that religious/spiritual (R/S) beliefs and practices are associated with higher levels of psychological well-being. For example, use of colloquial and meditative prayer is associated with higher levels of life satisfaction and happiness (Poloma & Pendleton, 1991), and engaging in meditative practices like mindfulness meditation is associated with positive psychological outcomes (Wallace & Shapiro, 2006). In addition, religiosity has been linked to lower levels of

[1] We wish to offer our sincere thanks to the following people and organizations: Richard M. Lerner and Erin Phelps for their collegiality; the John Templeton Foundation for funding this work (PI: Richard M. Lerner); Sheeba Arnold, John D. E. Gabrieli, Steve Shannon, and Christina Triantafyllou for facilitating access to and help with operating the scanner at the Athinoula A. Martinos Imaging Center, located in the McGovern Institute for Brain Research, Massachusetts Institute of Technology; and Amy Alberts Warren and Sonia Issac Koshy for assistance with early piloting.

violent behavior in youth (Pearce, Little, & Perez, 2003), and R/S practices have been associated with decreased participation in high-risk behaviors such as substance abuse (Cotton, Zebracki, Rosenthal, Tsevat, & Drotar, 2006). With such significant outcomes at stake, an important question is raised: What factors govern the positive association between R/S beliefs and practices and well-being? We argue that emotion regulation is one important psychological function linking the two.

Emotion regulation refers to "the extrinsic and intrinsic processes responsible for monitoring, evaluating, and modifying emotional reactions, especially their intensive and temporal features, to accomplish one's goals" (Thompson, 1994, pp. 27–28). As described by Gross and Thompson (2007), there are five families of emotion-regulatory processes, each of which targets a separate stage of the emotion-generative cycle. In the present cross-sectional pilot work, we focused on cognitive reappraisal, which refers to reinterpreting emotion-triggering events in ways that modulate their emotional impact. For example, you can reduce the anger you feel when someone cuts you off on the highway by thinking that the person didn't mean to do it and probably regrets the behavior. We focused on cognitive reappraisal for two reasons. First, evidence suggests that cognitive reappraisal is effective in modifying subjective emotional experience as measured by self-report and prefrontal cortical activation as measured by functional magnetic resonance imaging (see reviews by Kalisch, 2009, and Ochsner & Gross, 2008). Second, use of cognitive reappraisal has been linked with higher psychological well-being (Gross & John, 2003).

Why do we believe that R/S practices, like meditation, might have an impact on emotion regulation abilities such as cognitive reappraisal? As reviewed by Cahn and Polich (2006), neuroimaging evidence suggests that prefrontal cortical regions, such as anterior cingulate cortex and dorsolateral prefrontal cortical (PFC), are impacted by meditation. For example, Lazar and colleagues (2000) studied experienced meditators and demonstrated greater activation in dorsolateral PFC when participants were meditating (i.e., focusing on their breath and covertly repeating mantras at inhalation and exhalation) compared to during a control condition in which they generated a random list of animals. In a later study, Lazar and colleagues (2005) demonstrated that the cortical mantle is thicker in regions of dorsolateral PFC in experienced meditators compared to control subjects. Importantly, such prefrontal regions are also involved in cognitive reappraisal, thus providing a basis for believing that meditation might have an impact on emotion regulation abilities, like reappraisal.

In sum, the studies noted previously collectively suggest that R/S practices such as meditation are positively associated with well-being and that meditation impacts prefrontal cortical regions. In addition, PFC regions implicated in meditation are known to be involved in at least one form of emotion regulation, specifically cognitive reappraisal. Finally, cognitive reappraisal is positively associated with well-being. Integrating these strands of evidence, Urry and Poey (2008) proposed a simple framework, as shown in Figure 2.1. At a psychological

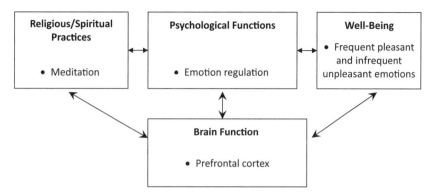

Figure 2.1   The simple framework to be tested in this chapter suggests that R/S practices, such as meditation, have a positive impact on well-being because they train
psychological functions like emotion regulation. Here we focus on the neural level
of analysis, investigating the extent to which reported meditation practice is associated with prefrontal cortical activation during volitional attempts to regulate emotional states, and whether this prefrontal cortical activation is also associated with
well-being.

Source: Adapted from Urry, H. L. & Poey, A. P. (2008). How religious/spiritual practices contribute to
well-being: the role of emotion regulation. In R. M. Lerner, R. Roeser, & E. Phelps. (Eds.), *Positive youth
development and spirituality: From theory to research.* West Conshohocken, PA: Templeton Foundation
Press.

level of analysis, they suggested that (a) R/S practices (e.g., meditation) train
psychological functions (e.g., emotion regulation), and (b) these psychological
functions then produce increases in well-being (e.g., experiencing infrequent negative and frequent positive emotions in daily life). At a neural level of analysis,
they suggested that activation in PFC regions known to be important to emotion regulation would provide one neural basis for this psychological/behavioral
cascade.

The goal of this chapter, then, is to present preliminary empirical evidence
for this framework from a pilot neuroimaging study of meditation practice and
well-being in late adolescents with a focus on emotion regulation. To this end, we
recruited a sample of late adolescents for a functional magnetic resonance imaging
(fMRI) session. We measured neural activation as participants used cognitive
reappraisal to regulate the pleasant and unpleasant emotions they experienced
in response to standardized picture stimuli. Participants also completed a web-
based survey that assessed R/S practices and well-being. Here we address two
questions as follows: (1) Does reported meditation practice correlate positively
with modulation of prefrontal cortical activation when older adolescents use
cognitive reappraisal to increase or decrease pleasant and unpleasant feelings?
(2) Is prefrontal cortical activation during cognitive reappraisal correlated with
psychological well-being, as indicated by adolescent reports of the experience of
positive and negative affect?

METHOD

In this section, we describe our participants and the materials and procedures used to answer the questions noted previously.

Participants

Twenty-seven undergraduates (13 female, ages ranged from 18 to 21 years) participated in this study. Participants endorsed the following ethnic/racial identities: $n = 4$ Asian, Asian American, or Pacific Islander (14.8%), $n = 2$ Black or African American (7.4%), $n = 2$ Hispanic or Latino/a, including Mexican American or Central American (7.4%), $n = 15$ White, Caucasian, Anglo, or European American; not Hispanic (55%), $n = 1$ Asian Indian or (Asian) Indian-American (3.7%), and $n = 3$ Multiethnic or multiracial (more than one race or ethnicity) (11.1%). All procedures were approved by the Committee on the Use of Humans as Experimental Subjects at the Massachusetts Institute of Technology. Participants provided written informed consent before their participation. They received $20 per hour in exchange for their participation.

Materials and Procedures

In this section we describe the stimuli used to elicit emotion in participants. We then describe the cognitive reappraisal task in which those stimuli were used and the manner of presentation. We also detail the specifics of the survey instrument and our analytic procedures.

Stimuli

During their laboratory session, participants viewed a set of 48 digital color photographs selected from the International Affective Picture System (IAPS; see Lang, Bradley, & Cuthbert, 2008). These pictures were designed to elicit either pleasant (24 pictures) or unpleasant (24 pictures) emotional states. Unpleasant pictures were selected on the basis of IAPS normative data across men and women to be highly arousing and unpleasant. Pleasant pictures were selected to be highly arousing and pleasant. These pictures were shown twice in counterbalanced order across participants, once under passive viewing conditions (data not shown) and once in the context of a cognitive reappraisal task.

Cognitive Reappraisal Task

Participants were trained to follow one auditory instruction during each picture trial. In this chapter, we focus on three instructions: *increase*, *decrease*, and *view*.[2] The instruction to *increase* (participants heard the word "enhance"),

---

[2]Participants also followed a fourth instruction to breathe, but this condition will not be the focus of this report.

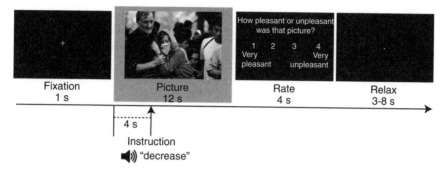

Figure 2.2   Trial structure of the cognitive reappraisal task. In this example, participants were instructed to use reappraisal to decrease unpleasant emotion.

Source: The photograph of a mourning family by Mikhail Evstafiev was reproduced with permission.

presented via headphones, served as a cue for participants to actively try to feel more emotion. For example, in response to a picture of a ferocious dog, a participant might imagine that the dog's leash broke, and therefore the dog is about to bite them. Conversely, the instruction to *decrease* (participants heard the word "suppress") signified the cue for participants to actively try to feel less emotion. For example, participants might imagine that victims of a car accident survived and healed well. Alternatively, on *view* trials, participants were instructed to view the picture carefully without trying to change how they felt. The *view* condition served as the control condition to which the others were compared. Training was provided by way of a standardized set of instructions in which example reappraisals were provided for the increase and decrease instructions in response to sample pictures.

The reappraisal trials were presented in three blocks of 16 trials pseudo-randomized such that all conditions followed one another with equal frequency, and pictures were randomly assigned to trials. As shown in Figure 2.2, each trial began with a white fixation cross presented in the center of a black screen for 1 second. The fixation cross was followed by the presentation of a picture for 12 seconds. The reappraisal instruction was delivered 4 seconds after picture onset and then participants provided a rating (data not shown; four-point scale did not provide sufficient room for variation). The rating screen was then replaced by a black screen with a central white fixation dot that lasted from 3 to 8 seconds. Trials ranged in duration from 20 to 25 seconds.

Stimulus Presentation

Stimuli were presented using E-Prime software (version 1.1.4.1, Psychology Software Tools, Inc., Pittsburgh, PA) and were delivered via a rear-projection system in which mirror images of the stimuli were projected with an LCD projector onto a 17.5-inch (horizontal measurement) screen placed at the back of the scanner bore. Participants viewed these images using a set of mirrors mounted on the head coil. The visual angle at the distance of 120 cm between the projection screen and the mirror at isocenter of the scanner bore was approximately 21 degrees.

Survey

Participants completed a web-based survey (www.SurveyMonkey.com), which, among other domains, assessed demographic information, meditation practice, and well-being. To minimize respondent burden, the entire survey was administered in two parts, one before (mean time to complete = 20.2 minutes) and one after (mean time to complete = 17.5 minutes) the experimental tasks in the scanner.

For meditation practice, participants were informed,

> For this study, we define *meditation* as the practice of sitting silently, closing the eyes, and focusing one's attention on a single thing like the breath or a holy phrase; or the practice of quieting one's mind and becoming aware of what is happening from moment to moment in an open and accepting way.

Then they responded to two items. The first was, "Given this definition, how often do you meditate by yourself?" Answers ranged from 1 (*never*) to 11 (*several times a day*). The second was, "How often, on an average weekday, do you meditate?" Answers ranged from 1 (*never*) to 8 (*11 or more hours*). Each item was standardized across subjects and averaged to form a meditation practice score.

For hedonic well-being, we used the 20-item Positive and Negative Affect Schedule (PANAS; Watson, Clark, & Tellegen, 1988), in which participants are asked to describe to what extent they generally experience 20 different feelings and emotions. The 10 positive affect (PA) items include adjectives such as *interested*, *excited*, *enthusiastic*, and *strong*. The 10 negative affect (NA) items include adjectives such as *irritable*, *upset*, *hostile*, and *scared*. Responses are provided on a five-point scale. Answers ranged from 1 (*very slightly to not at all*) to 5 (*extremely*). Items were averaged to create PA and NA scores for use in correlational analyses.

Functional Magnetic Resonance Imaging (fMRI) Data Acquisition

FMRI data were collected using a Siemens MAGNETOM Trio 3T MRI scanner (Siemens Healthcare, Erlangen, Germany) at the Athinoula A. Martinos Imaging Center, located in the McGovern Institute for Brain Research, at the Massachusetts Institute of Technology. This scanner has 32 RF receiver channels and is equipped with a 12-channel head coil. Participants lay supine on the scanner bed, and pillows were used to prevent head movements.

Blood oxygenation level–dependent (BOLD) signals were collected in three scan runs. In each run, 192 whole-brain T2*-weighted echoplanar images (EPIs) [5 mm slice thickness; 33 interleaved axial slices; TR, 2 s; TE, 30 ms; flip angle, 90°; matrix size, 64 × 64; field of view (FOV), 200; in-plane resolution, 3.125 mm] were acquired. Prior to each run, five images were recorded and discarded to allow longitudinal magnetization to reach equilibrium. For registration purposes, a short T1-weighted EPI scan was collected with the same slice prescription as the functional EPIs (TR, 10 s; TE, 34 ms). Two high-resolution, three-dimensional (3D), T1-weighted magnetization-prepared rapid gradient echo (MPRAGE) anatomical scans (TR, 2.53 s; TE, 3.39 ms; FOV, 256 mm; matrix, 256 × 256; sagittal plane; slice thickness, 1.33 mm; 128 slices) were also collected; the average of the two was used in subsequent analyses. For susceptibility artifact correction, field maps were acquired with a gradient-echo sequence using the same slice prescription as the functional EPIs (TR, 500 ms; TE 1, 2.84 ms; TE 2, 5.3 ms; flip angle, 55°).

FMRI Preprocessing and Registration

FMRI preprocessing and registration were carried out using FSL (FMRIB's Software Library, www.fmrib.ox.ac.uk/fsl; version 4.1.0). Standard preprocessing steps were applied, including realignment to compensate for small head motions, fieldmap-based B0 unwarping, and removal of residual motion artifacts and physiological noise using independent component analysis. The data were then spatially smoothed using a full-width, half-maximum Gaussian kernel of 5 mm and grand-mean intensity normalized across the entire time series by a single multiplicative factor. Finally, the data were highpass-filtered in the time domain using Gaussian-weighted least-squares straight-line fitting (sigma = 36.0 s). Prior to across-subjects analyses, the functional data were registered to MNI standard space in three steps (EPI → T1-weighted EPI → MPRAGE → MNI152), with voxels resampled to 2mm^3.

FMRI Analyses

FMRI analyses were carried out in three levels using FSL's fMRI Expert Analysis Tool (FEAT) version 5.92. At the first level, forward modeling of temporal changes in BOLD signal was achieved by convolving the original explanatory variables (EVs) with a constrained set of three optimal hemodynamic response functions and then submitting the resulting time-series to General Linear Modeling. Estimates of response amplitude (and their variances) were passed to the second-level analysis, in which we averaged across runs (fixed effects) and then tested a contrast that identifies brain regions in which the two active reappraisal conditions, increase (+1) and decrease (+1), exhibited greater activation when compared to the view (−2) condition across pleasant and unpleasant trials. Estimates of this contrast (and their variances) were passed to the third-level analysis, in which we averaged this contrast across subjects (random effects). Clusters of activation were identified by thresholding the Z statistic images with a voxelwise $Z > 3.1$ (one-tailed) and a (corrected) cluster significance threshold of $p = .05$.

Sequence of Events

After providing written informed consent, participants completed the first part of the web-based survey. They then received standardized training on the picture viewing and reappraisal tasks. After confirming eligibility for MRI scanning, participants were then positioned in the scanner, where they completed the picture viewing and reappraisal tasks. Once these tasks were complete, participants were escorted back to a computer, where they completed the second part of the web-based survey. Finally, participants completed an attention task (data not shown), were debriefed, and were compensated for their time.

RESULTS

In this section we detail the results of our analyses of the fMRI data and their relation to reported meditation practice and well-being. We focus here on reappraisal-related activation in PFC.

Prefrontal Activation

Across pleasant and unpleasant conditions, two large clusters of reappraisal-related activation (increase and decrease > view) emerged in PFC, one in dorsal medial prefrontal cortex (DMPFC) (local maximum Z at MNI $x = -6$, $y = 24$, $z = 46$; see Figure 2.3a), including paracingulate gyrus, anterior cingulate gyrus, and supplemental motor cortex, and one in left lateral PFC (local maximum Z at MNI $x = -50$, $y = 20$, $z = 22$; see Figure 2.3b), including left inferior frontal gyrus, left orbitofrontal cortex, and left insula. These two clusters served as regions of interest (ROI) for hypothesis testing as follows.

Does Meditation Practice Correlate Positively With PFC Activation During Reappraisal?

We extracted mean BOLD signal (in units of % signal change) from each of the two PFC ROI separately for the positive and negative conditions. Higher numbers signify greater activation during reappraisal (increase and decrease) relative to the view control condition. We then computed zero-order correlations between these values and meditation practice across subjects. Consistent with our simple framework, higher reported levels of meditation practice were associated with higher levels of activation in the left lateral PFC, $r = .40$, $p = .042$, and DMPFC, $r = .41$, $p = .036$, while participants regulated their positive emotions. The correlations between levels of meditation practice and activation in these

Panel a.

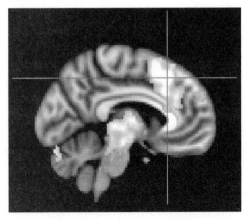

Panel b.

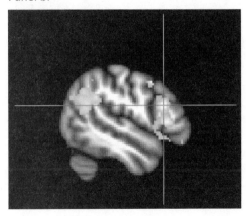

Figure 2.3   Reappraisal-related activation was found in two large regions of prefrontal cortex (PFC), including (a) dorsal medial PFC and (b) left lateral PFC.

two regions of PFC while participants regulated their negative emotions were near zero.

Does PFC Activation During Reappraisal Correlate Positively With Well-Being?

We next computed zero-order correlations between PFC activation while regulating positive emotions and well-being, as measured using PA and NA scores across subjects. Again, consistent with our simple framework, higher PFC activation in the left lateral PFC while participants regulated their positive emotions was associated with marginally higher levels of reported PA ($r = .35, p = .070$). This was also true for DMPFC ($r = .38, p = .052$). The correlations between activation in these two regions of PFC while participants regulated their negative emotions and levels of PA were near zero.

DISCUSSION

We tested a simple framework suggesting that R/S practices, with meditation practice as our primary focus, are positively associated with well-being by virtue of their association with emotion regulation. In this case, we focused on a neural level of analysis, asking whether PFC activation during volitional attempts to modulate pleasant and unpleasant emotions as they are being experienced serves as a link between meditation practice and well-being. Our preliminary results provide support for this idea. Higher reported levels of meditation practice were associated with higher levels of PFC activation when regulating pleasant emotions. Higher levels of PFC activation, in turn, were also associated with higher levels of positive affect in daily life.

Brain Regions Involved in Emotion Regulation

Several studies have focused on identifying the brain regions involved in emotion regulation using laboratory tasks like the one used here. As recently summarized by Kalisch (2009) in a meta-analysis of 13 neuroimaging studies, cognitive reappraisal to decrease unpleasant emotion relies on activation of dorsolateral, ventrolateral, and dorsomedial regions of PFC relative to a control condition. Activation of these PFC regions has also been implicated in studies assessing cognitive reappraisal to increase unpleasant emotion compared to a control condition (Ochsner et al., 2004; Urry et al., 2006; Urry, van Reekum, Johnstone, & Davidson, 2009; van Reekum et al., 2007). Such findings have been interpreted to indicate that various regions of PFC underlie the cognitive control processes necessary to deliberately regulate emotion (e.g., maintaining representations of the goal emotional state, monitoring the success of regulatory efforts, and minimizing conflicts between the prepotent and desired emotional states). Thus, our results suggest that greater cognitive control exerted during emotion regulation, as evidenced by greater PFC activation, may be both a "consequence" of R/S practices like meditation and a "cause" of higher well-being.

Directions for Future Research

The aforementioned terms *consequence* and *cause* are in quotes because clearly we cannot make claims about causal direction on the basis of these correlational findings. For that, we will need to conduct longitudinal research in which we measure all of these constructs at multiple times within individuals to test theoretically specified causal models of temporal precedence. We need to determine if brain changes underlie the emergence of emotion regulation and whether there are important windows of opportunity during which R/S practices have their biggest impact on brain structure and function, and thus psychological functions (like emotion regulation) and well-being.

Adolescence is a time of incredible change in behavior, cognition, and social functioning, and thus also a time when the brain matures to a substantial degree (Paus, 2009). Adolescence is, thus, a perfect time during which to pursue longitudinal work. We believe that such longitudinal work will be most fruitful if it incorporates both laboratory-based *and* survey-based methods, which allow us to arrive at conceptual insights based on individual differences, as demonstrated here. A need for combining laboratory and survey methods is also echoed in the work of Paus and colleagues (2011), who found expected age-related decreases in cortical thickness, but only in individuals with high scores on measures of positive youth development, and only in male adolescents. We need this work to include sufficient numbers of participants so that even small (but important) effects are detectable in statistical analyses.

CONCLUSIONS

In this chapter, we have briefly reviewed our ideas about factors that explain why R/S practices are associated with higher levels of well-being. We tested a simple framework, originally proposed by Urry and Poey (2008), suggesting that R/S practices likely have an impact on well-being via entrainment of psychological functions that are important for achieving high well-being. In this chapter, we focused on one R/S practice—meditation practice—and one psychological function—emotion regulation. We turned to a neural level of analysis, drawing on neuroimaging literature to propose that PFC activation might provide an individual difference metric that captures emotion regulation ability, specifically the ability to use cognitive reappraisal to change pleasant and unpleasant feeling states. Results indicated to us that, indeed, higher meditation practice is associated with higher PFC activation during cognitive reappraisal, and higher PFC activation is associated with positive emotion in daily life. Although some of these results were only marginally significant from a statistical perspective, they highlight great promise and a need for future research with larger samples. Studies that are designed to promote causal inference using even better measures will help us take the next, necessary steps toward understanding the mechanisms that link R/S practices to higher well-being.

REFERENCES

Cahn, B. R., & Polich, J. (2006). Meditation states and traits: EEG, ERP, and neuroimaging studies. *Psychological Bulletin, 132*, 180–211.

Cotton, S., Zebracki, K., Rosenthal, S. L., Tsevat, J., & Drotar, D. (2006). Religion/spirituality and adolescent health outcomes: A review. *Journal of Adolescent Health, 38*, 472–480.

Gross, J. J., & John, O. P. (2003). Individual differences in two emotion regulation processes: Implications for affect, relationships, and well-being. *Journal of Personality and Social Psychology, 85,* 348–362.

Gross, J. J., & Thompson, R. A. (2007). Emotion regulation: Conceptual foundations. In J. J. Gross (Ed.), *Handbook of emotion regulation* (pp. 3–24). New York, NY: Guilford Press.

Kalisch, R. (2009). The functional neuroanatomy of reappraisal: Time matters. *Neuroscience and Biobehavioral Reviews, 33,* 1215–1226.

Lang, P. J., Bradley, M. M., & Cuthbert, B. N. (2008). *International affective picture system (IAPS): Affective ratings of pictures and instruction manual* (Rep. No. A-8). Gainesville: University of Florida.

Lazar, S. W., Bush, G., Gollub, R. L., Fricchione, G. L., Khalsa, G., & Benson, H. (2000). Functional brain mapping of the relaxation response and meditation. *Neuroreport, 11,* 1581–1585.

Lazar, S. W., Kerr, C. E., Wasserman, R. H., Gray, J. R., Greve, D. N., Treadway, M. T., . . . & Fischl, B. (2005). Meditation experience is associated with increased cortical thickness. *Neuroreport, 16,* 1893–1897.

Ochsner, K. N, & Gross, J. J. (2008). Cognitive emotion regulation: Insights from social cognitive and affective neuroscience. *Current Directions in Psychological Science, 17,* 153–158.

Ochsner, K. N., Ray, R. D., Cooper, J. C., Robertson, E. R., Chopra, S., Gabrieli, J. D., & Gross, J. J. (2004). For better or for worse: Neural systems supporting the cognitive down- and up-regulation of negative emotion. *Neuroimage, 23,* 483–499.

Paus, T. (2009). Brain development. In R. M. Lerner & L. Steinberg (Eds.), *Handbook of adolescent psychology* (3rd ed., pp. 95–115). Hoboken, NJ: Wiley.

Paus, T., Leonard, G., Lerner, J. V., Lerner, R. M., Perron, M., Pike, G. B., . . . & Pausova, Z. (2011). Positive youth development and age-related changes in cortical thickness during adolescence. In A. E. Alberts Warren, R. M. Lerner, & E. Phelps (Eds.), *Thriving and spirituality among youth: Research perspectives and future possibilities* (pp. 61–76). Hoboken, NJ: Wiley.

Pearce, M. J., Little, T. D., & Perez, J. E. (2003). Religiousness and depressive symptoms among adolescents. *Journal of Clinical Child and Adolescent Psychology, 32,* 267–276.

Poloma, M. M., & Pendleton, B. F. (1991). The effects of prayer and prayer experiences on measures of general well-being. *Journal of Psychology and Theology, 19,* 71–83.

Thompson, R. A. (1994). Emotion regulation: A theme in search of definition. *Monographs of the Society for Research in Child Development, 59,* 25–52.

Urry, H. L., & Poey, A. P. (2008). How religious/spiritual practices contribute to well-being: The role of emotion regulation. In R. M. Lerner, R. Roeser, & E. Phelps (Eds.), *Positive youth development and spirituality: From theory to research* (pp. 145–163). West Conshohocken, PA: Templeton Foundation Press.

Urry, H. L., van Reekum, C. M., Johnstone, T., & Davidson, R. J. (2009). Individual differences in some (but not all) medial prefrontal regions reflect cognitive demand while regulating unpleasant emotion. *Neuroimage, 47*, 852–863.

Urry, H. L., van Reekum, C. M., Johnstone, T., Kalin, N. H., Thurow, M. E., Schaefer, H. S., . . . & Davidson, R. J. (2006). Amygdala and ventromedial prefrontal cortex are inversely coupled during regulation of negative affect and predict the diurnal pattern of cortisol secretion among older adults. *Journal of Neuroscience, 26*, 4415–4425.

van Reekum, C. M., Johnstone, T., Urry, H. L., Thurow, M. E., Schaefer, H. S., Alexander, A. L., & Davidson, R. J. (2007). Gaze fixations predict brain activation during the voluntary regulation of picture-induced negative affect. *Neuroimage, 36*, 1041–1055.

Wallace, B. A., & Shapiro, S. L. (2006). Mental balance and well-being: Building bridges between Buddhism and western psychology. *American Psychologist, 61*, 690–701.

Watson, D., Clark, L. A., & Tellegen, A. (1988). Development and validation of brief measures of positive and negative affect: The PANAS scales. *Journal of Personality and Social Psychology, 54*, 1063–1070.

3

---❯◆❮---

Closeness of All Kinds

The Role of Oxytocin and Vasopressin in the Physiology of Spiritual and Religious Behavior[1]

Elena L. Grigorenko

The spell-checker of my word-processing program (quite a well-known one, and possibly the most widely used, at least in the United States) does not know quite a few words that I think it should know. The software underlines the word in question with a red line and makes me wonder, initially, whether I misspelled the word. After I have examined the spelling, it makes me wonder whether I have made up a new word. But usually, I know that I have not made up the word; I have heard and seen it before, and I can clearly explain its meaning.

One such word is *affiliative*. I typed this word, and my word-processing program underlined it with a wavy red line. Nevertheless, I'm positive that when readers see that word, the proper semantic network is triggered, and the meaning of the word is apparent. With this network activated, an inquiry into Webster's dictionary does not bring any surprises. Specifically, Webster's presents the following words and word combinations, all of which are relevant to the triggered semantic network:

> *affiliate* (1) to bring into close association or connection . . . (6) to associate oneself, be intimately united in action or interest; *affiliated*, being

[1] The work on this essay was supported by funds from the American Psychological Foundation and Autism Speaks. I am thankful to Ms. Mei Tan for her editorial support.

in close formal or informal association; *affiliation*, the fact of affiliating, state of being affiliated or associated; *affiliative drive*, the urge to form friendships and attachments, typically prompting a person to attend social gatherings and join organizations as a way of preventing loneliness and gaining emotional security. (*Webster's new universal unabridged dictionary*, 1996, p. 33)

In the context of this semantic network, the definition of *affiliative behavior* (although not found in the pages of Webster's but existing in the research literature) as "seeking contact and social interaction with another individual when the animals have the option to freely avoid, stay close but not in contact, or interact with conspecifics"[2] (Olazábal & Young, 2005, p. 174), brings up three observations: (1) This is a completely reasonable definition that maps perfectly onto all of the related terms known to Webster's; (2) it talks about animals, and thus is likely to be used in the animal literature; and (3) the definition preserves its meaning when rewritten for humans: "seeking contact and social interaction with another individual when a person has the option to freely avoid, stay close but not in contact, or interact with other humans." Immediately, associative thinking calls forth a network of concepts such as bonding, attachment, and social interactions—relationships that involve things such as love, faithfulness, or familial devotion. But what about religiousness?

I would like to argue here that the conceptual network prompted by the words *affiliation* and *affiliative behavior* should also include concepts of spirituality and religiosity. Here this argument is supported in steps. First, I will focus on the tradition of investigating affiliation and affiliative behavior primarily in the animal literature, although several human studies will be referenced and discussed as well. Then, I will extend the discussion to humans, in particular focusing on the concepts of personality and psychopathology. Finally, I will complete the discussion of affiliation and affiliative behavior by arguing that the usage of this concept and the knowledge of its neurochemical foundation might be helpful in understanding how such human traits may be related to religiosity and spirituality.

AFFILIATIVE BEHAVIOR AND ITS NEUROCHEMICAL FOUNDATION

In animal literature, affiliative behavior is typically viewed as a type of prosocial behavior—that is, behavior that is characterized by positive social interactions (e.g., the formation of long-term bonds, demonstration of parental care). In

---

[2]Belonging to the same species.

humans, in addition to the physical connotation of affiliative behavior[3] that is similar to its typical usage in animal studies (e.g., parent-offspring bonding, partner mating), there is also a social-emotional connotation (e.g., religious, political affiliations). Thus, affiliative behaviors (and affiliation) can be viewed as one of the fundamental dimensions of social interaction throughout evolution, covering a range of such interactions from mere signaling in primitive organisms to complex human behaviors.

In this context, the reference to humans as a "highly affiliative species" (Insel, 2002, p. 3) suggests that (1) the degree of affiliativeness and the complexity of affiliative behaviors grow with the evolution of Homo sapiens; and that (2) as any trait whose transformation is notable throughout evolution, affiliation is likely to (a) form an important foundation for many other social human behaviors (e.g., commitment, social responsibility, firmness of values and beliefs); (b) exhibit marked variation in terms of its manifestation in different individuals within the species; and (c) involve biological (genetic) mechanisms that both control and ensure the individual variability in affiliation among humans. These lines of reasoning make even more sense as anthropologists redirect our understanding of grouping and sociability among human and nonhuman primates from a focus on competition and aggression to cooperative and affiliative behaviors, stressing the robustness of the observation that the latter behaviors have been shown to be substantially more common than the former in all primate species (Sussman, Garber, & Cheverud, 2005).

Throughout both evolutionary and animal-model studies of affiliation, among several agents that appear to form its biological foundation [e.g., estrogen (Cushing & Wynne-Edwards, 2006), prolactin (Odendaal & Meintjes, 2003), or opioid peptides (Panksepp & Moskal, 2005; L. J. Young, Lim, Gingrich, & Insel, 2001)], two neuropeptides, oxytocin (OXT) and arginine vasopressin (AVP), have been identified as core elements of this foundation (for reviews, see Bartz & Hollander, 2006; Heinrichs & Domes, 2008; Siever, 2008). Of particular interest for the following discussion is the observation in the literature that points to sexual dimorphism in the effects of OXT and AVP; for example, OXT has been reported to be critical in female vole partners, whereas AVP is critical in their male counterparts' partner preference formation (Bales et al., 2007).

OXT and AVP are hormones that also act as brain neurotransmitters (Carlson, 2010). OXT and AVP are synthesized in the hypothalamus and released into systemic circulation via the posterior pituitary (Caldwell & Young, 2006). Most of the time, OXT and AVP are released directly into the bloodstream; however, some doses of each hormone are released directly into the brain. OXT is a peptide

---

[3]Hereafter, the words *affiliative behavior*, *forming affiliation*, or *affiliation* are used synonymously, depending on the context.

that includes nine amino acids;[4] the action of OXT is mediated by specific, high-affinity receptors. Two genes[5] are particularly important to the OXT signaling: the oxytocin-neurophysin I preproprotein gene (*OXT*) on chromosome 20p.3 that synthesizes oxytocin, and the receptor for the oxytocin (*OXTR*) gene on 3p25.3 that produces the OXT receptor. Central OXT receptors are found in a variety of limbic brain regions; peripheral OXT receptors are present in numerous peripheral sites, including the pituitary and adrenal glands (Gimpl & Fahrenholz, 2001).

AVP is also a nanopeptide, whose sequence differs from OXT by two amino acids.[6] AVP is coded by the arginine vasopressin-neurophysin II gene (*AVP*), located on chromosome 20p.13. Its action is controlled by three receptors: the arginine vasopressin receptor 1A (coded by *AVPR1A* at 12q14.2), the arginine vasopressin receptor 1B (synthesized by *AVPR1B* at 1q32.1), and the arginine vasopressin receptor 2 (coded by *AVPR2* at Xq32.1). OXT and AVP exhibit receptor cross-reactivity, which might allow for interactions between the two hormones (Barberis & Tribollet, 1996). There are other genes whose products are relevant to the function of OXT and AVP, but their roles are not fully understood (Caldwell & Young, 2006).

Here I summarize the main findings from the animal literature that support the central role of OXT and AVP in affiliative behavior. I also discuss several collateral lines of evidence from the human literature supporting the importance of these neuropeptides in the biological basis of affiliation.

First, the neuroanatomical distribution of OXT receptors is extremely variable in different species; this variability has been stated to be associated with inter- and intra-species variability in social behavior (Tribollet, Dubois-Dauphin, Dreifuss, Barberis, & Jard, 1992; L. J. Young, 1999). For example, offspring-caring behavior (i.e., alloparental behavior[7]) onsets spontaneously in juvenile female prairie voles (approximately 20 days of age), takes one to three days of pup exposure to develop in juvenile rats, and is nearly absent in juvenile mice and meadow voles (Olazábal & Young, 2006). Remarkably, these differences correlate with the density of OXT receptors in specific brain regions. Specifically, it has been found that the receptor density in (a) the nucleus accumbens is highest in juvenile prairie voles, intermediate in juvenile rats, and lowest in juvenile mice and meadow voles; (b) in the caudate putamen is highest in prairie voles, intermediate in rats and meadow voles, and lowest in mice; and (c) in the lateral septum is highest in mice and meadow voles, and lowest in prairie voles and rats (Olazábal & Young, 2006). Moreover, this pattern of findings has been extended to explain

---

[4]Cysteine, tyrosine, isoleucine, glutamine, asparagine, cysteine, proline, leucine, and glycine.

[5]Human notation is used, but the system appears to be highly evolutionarily conserved; both rats and mice have ortholog genes.

[6]Cysteine, tyrosine, phenylalanine, glutamine, asparagine, cysteine, proline, arginine, and glycine.

[7]Raising and caring for offspring by individuals other than the biological parents.

individual differences in alloparental behavior. Specifically, when OXT receptor density was measured throughout the period when juvenile females prairie voles adopt crouching postures—viewed as one of the indicators of alloparental behavior in juveniles—alloparenting correlated with receptor density in the nucleus accumbens and in the caudate putamen, but negatively correlated with receptor density in the lateral septum (Olazábal & Young, 2006).

Second, it appears that the distribution of receptors for both OXT and AVP in the brain corresponds to the receptors' functioning with respect to processing social stimulation (Landgraf & Neumann, 2004). Specifically, OXT shows significant binding in the limbic system, including the amygdala (Huber, Veinante, & Stoop, 2005; Landgraf & Neumann, 2004). It has been found in human research that OXT reduces amygdala activity; correspondingly, deficits in OXT might plausibly contribute to hostility, fear, and mistrust—emotional states that, in turn, may provide preconditions for the emergence of aggression (Kirsch et al., 2005). Higher densities of anterior hypothalamic AVP neurons have been shown to be related to greater selective aggression toward unfamiliar conspecifics (Gobrogge, Liu, Jia, & Wang, 2007).

Third, the amount of OXT and AVP in the central nervous system (CNS) and the cerebrospinal fluid (CSF) has been associated, in different directions, with affiliative and aggressive behaviors. The amount of OXT has been positively associated with affiliative behavior and trust (Kosfeld, Heinrichs, Zak, Fischbacher, & Fehr, 2005; Winslow & Insel, 2000; Zak, Stanton, & Ahmadi, 2007) and negatively associated with aggression and anxiety (Bale, Davis, Auger, Dorsa, & McCarthy, 2001; Champagne, Diorio, Sharma, & Meaney, 2001; Ferguson et al., 2000; Windle, Shanks, Lightman, & Ingram, 1997). Relatedly, OXT knockout mice display exaggerated aggressive behavior (Ragnauth et al., 2005). AVP, on the contrary, although studied substantially less than OXT, especially in humans, has been positively associated with aggression, fear, and anxiety (Bielsky, Hu, Szegda, Westphal, & Young, 2004; Griebel et al., 2002; Landgraf & Neumann, 2004). Similarly, AVP knockout mice show decreases in aggression (Wersinger, Caldwell, Christiansen, & Young, 2007), and the administration of SRX251, the orally active AVP V1a receptor antagonist, to Syrian golden hamsters reduces aggressive behavior (Ferris et al., 2006). These differential behavior findings were reportedly associated with neuroanatomical findings.

Specifically, it has been shown (Huber et al., 2005) that these neuropeptides excite distinct neuronal populations as part of an inhibitory network in the central amygdala (Raggenbass, 2001) and modulate the integration of excitatory information from the basolateral amygdala and cerebral cortex in opposite manners. The central amygdala, in turn, provides the major output of the amygdaloid complex to the autonomic nervous system (Huber et al., 2005). In general, it has been suggested that, in the brain, AVP seems to be associated with increased vigilance, anxiety, arousal, and activation, whereas OXT seems to be associated with reduced anxiety, relaxation, growth, and restoration (Carter, 2007). Thus, both neuropeptides appear to be important in processing social information and triggering social interaction; correspondingly, the dysregulation of their metabolism might be directly related to deficiencies in social functioning (Heinrichs & Domes, 2008).

Fourth, OXT is known to participate in stress reduction (Neumann, 2002; Parker, Buckmaster, Schatzberg, & Lyons, 2005). In animals, both physical and psychological stress and fearful situations cause the release of OXT both peripherally and within the brain (Neumann, Krömer, Toschi, & Ebner, 2000; Neumann, Wigger, Torner, Holsboer, & Landgraf, 2000), dampening the activity of the hypothalamic-pituitary-adrenal (HPA) system and the amygdala (Huber et al., 2005). Similarly, behaviors associated with control, authority, or aggression increase cortisol concentrations, whereas behaviors associated with play and affiliation decrease it (Horváth, Dóka, & Miklósi, 2008). Based on these general observations, numerous studies have investigated the results of endogenous stimulation of OXT (e.g., lactation). Suckling stimuli by newborns increase OXT release and decrease basal plasma levels of adrenocorticotropic hormone (ACTH) and cortisol (e.g., Carter, Altemus, & Chrousos, 2001; Heinrichs, Neumann, & Ehlert, 2002). Likewise, other ways to stimulate an increase in the level of OXT endogenously [e.g., positive emotions and massage (Ditzen et al., 2007; Turner, Altemus, Enos, Cooper, & McGuinness, 1999)] have been found to reduce responses to physical and psychosocial stress exposure (Heinrichs & Domes, 2008).

Based on these observations, it has been suggested, conversely, that early stress might interfere with the developing hormonal system in young organisms, modifying OXT and AVP receptor binding. In turn, such alterations might form the foundation for the development of attachment disorders (Carter, 2003). Although there are no direct findings attesting to this hypothesis, there is collateral evidence of interest. For example, it has been shown (Meinlschmidt & Heim, 2007) that a single intranasal dose of OXT reduces salivary cortisol concentrations in healthy men who have a history of early parental separation in comparison with healthy control subjects. Similarly, early neglect has been shown to alter OXT signaling (Fries, Ziegler, Kurian, Jacoris, & Pollak, 2005).

Fifth, OXT exposure in young offspring appears to be associated with variation in child-rearing practices in adults. OXT is released by warmth and touch (Uvnäs-Moberg, 1998). For example, licking and grooming rodents have been reported to produce female offspring with a higher density of OXT receptors in the central amygdala and in the bed nucleus of the stria terminalis and male offspring with a higher density of AVP receptors in the central nucleus of the amygdala (Francis, Young, Meaney, & Insel, 2002). Notably, these neural differences in receptor densities eventually manifest in behavior, with offspring of high licking and grooming mothers also demonstrating high licking and grooming behavior later in life (Francis, Diorio, Liu, & Meaney, 1999).

Breast milk contains OXT (Leake, Weitzman, & Fisher, 1981). In dairy calves, a calf's plasma levels of OXT were higher when suckling from the mother than when drinking mother's milk from a bucket (Lupoli, Johansson, Uvnäs-Moberg, & Svennersten-Sjaunja, 2001). In general, in rats, early developmental exposure to OXT was reported to be associated with lower blood pressure (Holst, Uvnäs-Moberg, & Petersson, 2002; Petersson & Uvnäs-Moberg, 2007, 2008), lower corticosterone levels (Sohlstrom, Carlsson, & Uvnäs-Moberg, 2000), and optimal body weight (Petersson & Uvnäs-Moberg, 2008; Sohlstrom et al., 2000) in later life, and even the amelioration of the effects of maternal malnutrition (Olausson, Uvnäs-Moberg, & Sohlstrom, 2003).

Of interest also is evidence concerning the sexually dimorphic effects of OXT exposure. For example, neonatal exposure to OXT has been reported to change AVP binding; moreover, the reported changes were sexually dimorphic, so that the OXT exposure increased the binding in males and decreased the binding in females (Bales et al., 2007). Similarly, it has been reported that interactions with a bonded dog increase levels of plasma OXT in females but not males (Miller et al., 2009).

Sixth, the animal literature on pair-bond formation and monogamy makes references to a neurobiological model, based on the concurrent activation of the neuropeptide and the mesolimbic dopamine systems (L. J. Young & Zuoxin, 2004). This model stipulates that OXT and AVP contribute to the processing of social cues necessary for individual recognition, whereas the esolimbic dopamine triggers reinforcement and reward learning; the concurrent activation of these systems during mating results in a conditioned partner preference. Several observations made in the human literature draw certain parallels regarding the applicability of this neurobiological model in our own species. Specifically, there are studies registering the elevation of plasma OXT levels during orgasm/ejaculation in both men and women (Carmichael et al., 1987; Murphy, Seckl, Burton, Checkley, & Lightman, 1987) and plasma AVP during sexual arousal in men (Murphy et al., 1987), with findings on plasma OXT during sexual arousal being inconsistent in men (Carmichael et al., 1987; Murphy et al., 1987). Although these changes might not reflect the changes in release of OXT and AVP in the brain, they certainly provide some basis for the hypothesis that this might be the case.

Moreover, it is of interest that—keeping in mind that nipple stimulation during lactation is one of the most potent stimuli for oxytocin release (Christensson, Nilsson, Stock, Matthiesen, & Uvnäs-Moberg, 1989)—breast and nipple stimulation are, in contrast to other mammalian species, an integral part of human sexuality and hence might play a role in enhancing pair bonding with the release of the neuropeptides (L. J. Young & Zuoxin, 2004). In addition, it has been reported that the variation in pair-bonding behaviors of the monogamous prairie vole and the polygamous meadow and mountain vole can be associated, at least putatively, with a highly polymorphic repeat-containing DNA element (referred to as a *microsatellite*) located in the so-called 5'-region of the arginine vasopressin receptor 1A (*AVPR1A*) gene in mice (Hammock & Young, 2005).

Moreover, there is growing evidence in the literature that genetic variation in the *AVPR1A* gene and its surroundings is important for human behaviors as well. Specifically, the literature contains reports on associations between different variants of the *AVPR1A* gene and pair bonding in humans (Walum et al., 2008).

In particular, in one study, the researchers asked members of 552 Swedish twin pairs, all of whom were living at the time with a partner, to answer a brief self-report questionnaire with items targeting partner bonding, marital status, and marital problems. All participating twins were genotyped for the 5′-microsatellite polymorphism of the *AVPR1A* gene. It was reported that a particular allele of this polymorphism (the allele RS3 334[8]) was associated with significantly lower scores on the partner bonding items. This association was true for males only, so that males who were homozygous for this allele were twice as likely to have experienced marital problems or threat of divorce and half as likely to be married if they were involved in a committed relationship. Moreover, the presence of this allele in the male partner was reported to be correlated with reports of the quality of the relationship as reported by the female partner (Walum et al., 2008).

Seventh, it appears that OXT and AVP are important not only for sexual (J. R. Williams, Insel, Harbaugh, & Carter, 1994) but also for nonsexual (Beery, Lacey, & Francis, 2008) social behavior. As mentioned previously, pair-bonding in animals has been studied primarily in prairie voles, a socially monogamous species that forms long-lasting attachments with an opposite-sex partner (Getz, 1972; Ophir, Phelps, Sorin, & Wolff, 2008). Meadow voles, however, demonstrate behavior that is ordinary in the vast majority of rodents: that is, polygamy, both for males and females (Berteaux, Bety, Rengifo, & Bergeron, 1999; Boonstra, Xia, & Pavone, 1993; Madison, 1980). Of particular interest, however, is that during periods of short day lengths (either during the winter months in the field or when short days are artificially simulated in the laboratory), meadow voles become nonreproductive. As an outcome of this switch, they demonstrate nonsexual social behavior.

It has been argued that nonsexual social behavior is the basis for group living in many species, especially in humans (Lacey & Sherman, 2007). Researchers (Beery, Routman, & Zucker, 2009) have studied nonsexual affiliative behaviors in meadow voles during long and short days and have found a substantial difference, especially in females, in the amount of nonsexual affiliative behaviors. They have hypothesized that a contributing factor to these differences may be the OXT receptor distributions in the brains of females who have been exposed to long and short day lengths (Parker, Phillips, Kinney, & Lee, 2001). Such nonsexual affiliative behaviors are especially important for conflict resolutions that may involve not only other conflict participants but also bystanders, where bystanders can directly benefit from the engagement by warding off further aggression from those opponents (Koski & Sterck, 2009). Indeed, many animals that demonstrate social behavior engage in post-conflict affiliation between former opponents, or reconciliation (Aureli & de Waal, 2000). Such affiliation is rather common in human and nonhuman primates but has also been reported in nonprimate mammals (Arnold & Aureli, 2007; Aureli, Cords, & van Schaik, 2002).

---

[8]This variant was quickly labeled the "monogamy gene" in the mass media.

Eighth, there is a range of human studies that, individually and collectively, attest to the importance of the neuropeptide system to the manifestation of both sexual and nonsexual affiliative behavior and the formation of affiliation. Specifically, several human studies involved the exogenous administration of OXT and AVP (for review, see Heinrichs & Gaab, 2007). Specifically, both intravenous (Hollander et al., 2003, 2007) and intranasal (Born et al., 2002; Ditzen et al., 2009) infusions of OXT demonstrated interesting behavioral effects. In one study (Kosfeld et al., 2005), male volunteers were divided into two groups, one that received intranasal OXT while the other did not. Then all participants were asked to engage in the "trust game" (a variant of the well-known prisoner's dilemma), in which a sum of money is given to each of the participants, but investments should be made with an anonymous player, and the gain is dependent on the degree of cooperation among players. It was found that intranasal OXT significantly increased trust among participants as compared to a placebo; moreover, it was reported that the injected participants were willing to accept social risk, not just any risk.

It was reported in a different study (Guastella, Mitchell, & Dadds, 2008) that intranasal OXT administration, as compared to a placebo, increased the number and duration of gazes toward the eye region of emotionally neutral human faces. An intranasal infusion of OXT was reported to significantly, although not substantially ($F = 4.18$, $p = .047$), increase positive communication behavior in relation to negative behavior during a standard instructed couple conflict discussion in the laboratory and significantly, although not substantially ($F = 7.14$, $p = .011$), reduced salivary cortisol levels after the conflict compared with placebo (Ditzen et al., 2009).

Yet another study (Wolff et al., 2006) reported that users of the drug 3,4 methylenedioxymethamphetamine (MDMA, ecstasy[9]), when tested in a real club setting, had elevated levels of AVP and OXT (elevated higher than AVP) in their blood. Similarly, human brain imaging studies have generated evidence supporting the role of OXT and AVP in social processing. When intranasal OXT versus a placebo administration was followed by viewing fear-inducing social (angry and fearful faces) and nonsocial (threatening scenes) stimuli, it was observed that participants who had received OXT demonstrated reduced amygdala activation to both kinds of stimuli, and that OXT had a more pronounced effect on responses to the social stimuli (Kirsch et al., 2005). Studies have also indicated that the patterns of activation that are registered in response to the presentation to participants' photographs of their romantic partners (Bartels & Zeki, 2000) and to mothers' photographs of their children (Bartels & Zeki, 2004) engage the brain regions that are rich in OXT, AVP, or their respective receptors (Jenkins, Ang, Hawthorn, Rossor, & Iversen, 1984; Loup, Tribollet, Dubois-Dauphin, & Dreifuss, 1991). A list of behaviors that have been reported to respond to the infusion

---

[9]This drug has a widely documented ability to increase feelings of love and closeness toward others.

of OXT include empathy (Singer et al., 2008) and trust (Baumgartner, Heinrichs, Vonlanthen, Fischbacher, & Fehr, 2008), face processing (Domes et al., 2008), and memory for faces (Rimmele, Hediger, Heinrichs, & Klaver, 2009). OXT-AVP-rich areas have also been registered as active during ejaculation in men (Georgiadis, Reinders, Van der Graaf, Paans, & Kortekaas, 2007), and the infusion of OXT was related to an altered perception of sexual arousal (Burri, Heinrichs, Schedlowski, & Kruger, 2008).

Ninth, it is important to note that, although in this section of the essay the accent has been primarily on OXT and AVP as important players in the biological bases of affiliative behavior, they are not the only players. Relevant pathways have been reported to engage the serotonergic (Thompson, Callaghan, Hunt, Cornish, & McGregor, 2007; S. N. Young & Moskowitz, 2005; Zizzo, 2005) and dopaminergic (Insel, 2003; Insel & Young, 2001) systems.

To summarize, the literature indicates that between- and within-species variation in affiliative behaviors is associated, at least partially, with the function of the neuropeptides OXT and AVP. Both peptides are involved in the regulation of the behavioral and endocrine stress response and, among other stimuli, are released in response to social stimuli. It is currently thought that OXT and AVP are released primarily in response to positive and negative social stimuli, respectively. Given the distribution of OXT and AVP receptors in the brain, it is assumed that the OXT-AVP signaling is especially pronounced in the limbic areas, especially in the amygdala, so that it results in the modification of brainstem activity and autonomic arousal. Moreover, it is believed that both OXT and AVP act dimorphically, generating differential effects in different sexes of a species.

Finally, although AVP is studied substantially less than OXT, both neuropeptides have been associated with such social phenomena as overcoming natural avoidance of proximity and facilitating approach behavior (e.g., Kosfeld et al., 2005), a variety of sexual and nonsexual bonding behavior (e.g., Preston & de Waal, 2002), attachment (e.g., Insel & Young, 2001), social memory (Heinrichs, Meinlschmidt, Wippich, Ehlert, & Hellhammer, 2004), empathy, trust, and generosity (Domes, Heinrichs, Michel, Berger, & Herpertz, 2007; Kosfeld et al., 2005; Zak et al., 2007).

AFFILIATIVE BEHAVIORS, PERSONALITY, AND PSYCHOPATHOLOGY

Through all forms of their existence, at all stages of their life span, and at all levels of their society, humans exhibit a strong drive for affiliation (Mallott, Maner, DeWall, & Schmidt, 2009; Van Duuren & Di Giacomo, 1997). This drive has been characterized as one of the fundamental characteristics of humans (Baumeister & Leary, 1995). There is a tremendous amount of literature going back to the first human scripts indicating that the disruption of social connection and the inability to affiliate with other humans, whether as a result of life circumstances or social rejection, have negative and even destructive outcomes ranging from physical pain (Eisenberger, Lieberman, & Williams, 2003) to negative psychological consequences (Baumeister & Tice, 1990; Leary, 1990).

For some reason, however, the concept of affiliative behavior is not used often in the field of either personality or psychopathology, even though substantial collateral evidence shows that the functioning of the OXT-AVP system has direct links to both fields. Here I briefly discuss relevant observations.

For example, it has been found that (Uvnäs-Moberg, 1996; Uvnäs-Moberg, Widstrom, Nissen, & Bjorvell, 1990), when compared to age-matched control women, breast-feeding women score lower on scales of personality measuring muscular tension and monotony avoidance and higher on a scale measuring social desirability. In addition, positive correlations have been reported between levels of plasma OXT during breast-feeding and self-reported calmness and pleasantness (Uvnäs-Moberg, 1996; Uvnäs-Moberg et al., 1990). In a more recent study (Jonas, Nissen, Ransjö-Arvidson, Matthiesen, & Uvnäs-Moberg, 2008), breast-feeding women were recruited into groups separated according to the medical interventions that these women received during childbirth. The groups were (a) mothers having received OXT infusion during labor (OT iv group); (b) mothers having received epidural analgesia with/without OXT infusion (EDA group, OT iv+/−); (c) mothers having received OXT intramuscularly after birth (OT im); and (d) mothers having received none of these treatments. The researchers reported that women receiving no medical interventions or OXT iv or OXT im scored lower right after delivery on several of the subscales related to anxiety and aggression-hostility and scored higher on socialization when compared to the normative group. Yet, the women who received EDA did not demonstrate that profile right away, but exhibited it only two months after delivery. The profile obtained at two months was reported to be more pronounced in those mothers who were in the EDA group, OT iv+ group.

Jonas and colleagues paralleled these findings with findings from research on sheep (Levy, Kendrick, Keverne, Piketty, & Poindron, 1992) and heifers (G. L. Williams, Gazal, Leshin, Stanko, & Anderson, 2001). Specifically, it has been demonstrated that peridural anesthesia blocks the release of OXT during labor both peripherally (i.e., into plasma) and centrally (i.e., into the brain). In addition, anesthesia was reported to inhibit and delay maternal behavior and bonding to the young, although it is reportedly restored after OXT administration. Moreover, there appears to be a complex relationship between exogenous and endogenous levels of OXT (K. Jonas et al., 2009). Thus, the usage of OXT and analgesia during delivery should be considered carefully.

Similarly, in human mothers only, it has been reported that plasma OXT levels at early pregnancy and during the postpartum period are related to maternal bonding behaviors such as gaze, vocalizations, positive affect, affectionate touch, as well as attachment-related thoughts and frequent checking of the infant (Feldman, Weller, Zagoory-Sharon, & Levine, 2007). Levels of AVP have been found to be correlated with personality traits such as altruism (Israel et al., 2008; Prichard, Mackinnon, Jorm, & Easteal, 2007) and aggression (Caldwell,

Wersinger, & Young, 2008). Yet, the correlations between personality traits and states and levels of plasma OXT/AVP are sometimes contradictory. For example, there is evidence that plasma OXT was correlated with indicators of relationship distress in young women (Turner et al., 1999) and chronic feelings of attachment anxiety (e.g., desire for closeness but concerns about abandonment) in a sample of healthy men and women (Marazziti, as cited in Bartz & Hollander, 2006). Interpretations of these findings have suggested that levels of plasma OXT might act as indicators of social distress and as a motivating drive to initiate affiliative behaviors that should result in positive social contact (Taylor et al., 2006).

Researchers have also attempted to correlate levels of plasma OXT with different personality traits, sampling from different personality theories. For example, Cloninger's Psychobiological Model of Personality (Cloninger, Svrakic, & Przybeck, 1993) postulated the existence of four temperaments (novelty seeking, harm avoidance, reward dependence, and persistence) and three character dimensions (self-directedness, cooperativeness, and self-transcendence). It has been hypothesized that the temperament dimension of reward dependence is exemplified through sentimentality, social attachment, and dependence on the approval of others; a positive correlation ($p < .001$) between OXT and reward dependence was obtained in a sample of 60 individuals diagnosed with major depression disorder (Bell, Nicholson, Mulder, Luty, & Joyce, 2006). Notably, borderline or suggestive correlations were also obtained for the dimensions of novelty seeking (positive, at $p < .05$), self-directedness (negative, at $p < .10$), and persistence (negative, at $p < .10$).

Of interest also is a growing body of literature that attempts to establish associations between various indicators of personality and attachment and genes that have been discussed earlier as related to affiliative behaviors (e.g., OXT, AVP, dopaminergic, and serotonergic genes). Although often marked by small sample size (e.g., Gillath, Shaver, Baek, & Chun, 2008), these studies collectively contribute to the observation that the OXT and AVP and related systems are closely involved in the development and manifestation of affiliative behaviors in humans. More generally, these studies are thought to contribute to the field's attempt to reveal genetic bases of personality and social behavior (for reviews, see Canli, 2008; Krueger & Johnson, 2008).

The literature contains a systematic attempt to embed the concept of affiliation in the field of personality research (Depue & Morrone-Strupinsky, 2005). In this review, it is proposed that affiliation can be mapped within the interpersonal dimension of personality, which, regardless of terminological variation, is present in any (or virtually any) personality typology. Earlier models of personality have referred to this dimension as extraversion, but later conceptualizations have split this dimension into two factors (Tellegen & Waller, 2008). The first split factor has been referred to as communion, social closeness, agreeableness, and affiliation, whereas the second split factor has been referred to as agency, social dominance, the enjoyment of leadership, and assertiveness (Depue & Morrone-Strupinsky, 2005). It is notable that, before the subdivision of these factors, they were considered different aspects of extroversion and, between them, captured the richness of interpersonal behavior [e.g., Warmth-Gregariousness vs. Assertiveness (Costa & McCrae, 1997), Social Closeness vs. Social Potency (Tellegen & Waller, 2008), Warmth vs. Assertion (Goldberg, Sweeney, Merenda, & Hughes, 1996), Sociability vs. Ascendance-Dominance (Guilford & Zimmerman, 2009), Sociability vs. Ambition (Hogan, 1983), Warmhearted-Socially Enmeshed vs. Dominant-Ascendant (Cattell, Eber, & Tatsuoka, 1980), Warm-Agreeable vs. Assured-Dominant (Wiggins, Trapnell, & Phillips, 1988), and other pairs, as discussed in Depue & Morrone-Strupinsky, 2005].

A detailed analysis of the items that are used by a variety of personality inventories that capture these various pairs of factors has indicated that trait affiliation reflects preferences for experiencing particular positive emotional states educed by others that, in turn, motivate affiliative (i.e., close interpersonal) behaviors (Depue & Morrone-Strupinsky, 2005). Depue and Morrone-Strupinsky's (2005) model of affiliation views affiliation as a higher-order trait overarching the lower-order traits of warmth, affection, agreeableness, sociability, amiability, sympathy, and positive emotion; these lower-order traits, in turn, are manifested in behaviors such as friendly verbal (e.g., admiring, supportive, and encouraging comments) and nonverbal communication (e.g., facial expressions and gestures) and physical (e.g., nonsexual and sexual touch) and emotional (e.g., disclosure, comfort) proximity. Affiliation is triggered by so-called affiliative stimuli: auditory (e.g., comforting vocalization), visual (e.g., facial and bodily expressions), tactile (e.g., sexual and nonsexual touch), olfactory (e.g., pleasing odor), and multimodal (e.g., emotional need). These stimuli, in turn, initiate a set of behavior-motivation processes that are supported neurochemically: a surge for affiliative reward comprised of appetitive (associated with subjective feelings of desire, wanting, excitement, elation, enthusiasm, energy, potency, and self-efficacy) and consummatory (associated with subjective feelings of pleasure, gratification, liking, sedation, anabolism, comfort) phases, and the formation of affiliative memories.

Grounding their model in the animal literature, Depue and Morrone-Strupinsky (2005) hypothesize that the appetitive phase engages primarily the dopaminergic system and OXT and AVP; the consummatory phase engages primarily the opiates and OXT and AVP; and the formation of memories engages GABA and glutamate. Thus, Depue and Morrone-Strupinsky (2005) offer a complex multilevel model of affiliation, viewing it as a higher-order personality trait and attempting to bring together multiple layers of literature. Although not exclusive, the role of OXT and AVP is central to the formation of affiliation in this model. It has been argued that the trait of affiliation is disrupted and, thus, can be viewed as an endophenotype (i.e., intermediate correlated phenotype) in many psychiatric disorders, such as autism spectrum disorders (ASD), schizoid personality, primary psychopathy, dismissing attachment, depression, and anxiety disorders (Troisi & D'amato, 2005).

The connection between affiliation, psychopathology, and OXT and AVP has been explored, although to a limited degree. Thus, there is a growing body of literature connecting ASD and OXT and AVP. This connection is based on three related observations. First, there is evidence of lower plasma OXT levels in individuals with ASD (Modahl et al., 1998), which might be indicative of deficient synthesis of OXT from its precursor (Green et al., 2001). Second, there are genetic studies showing associations between OXT and its receptor genes (Wu et al., 2005; Ylisaukko-oja et al., 2006; Yrigollen et al., 2008). Similarly, genetic association has been reported between the AVP-related genes and ASD (Kim et al., 2002; Wassink et al., 2004; Yirmiya et al., 2006). Finally, the intravenous administration of OXT to individuals with ASD has been reported to decrease repetitive and stereotypic behaviors (Hollander et al., 2003) and enhance social information processing (Hollander et al., 2007) in ASD.

There is also suggestive evidence connecting obsessive compulsive disorder (OCD) and OXT. Specifically, women suffering from OCD appear to experience worsening of their symptoms during pregnancy or immediately after delivery (for review, see McDougle, Barr, Goodman, & Price, 1999). Moreover, increased levels of CSF OXT has been reported in some subgroups of individuals with OCD (Leckman et al., 1994). Yet studies that involved the administration of intranasal OXT to individuals with OCD or OCD-spectrum disorders have not revealed any symptom improvement (den Boer & Westenberg, 1992; Epperson, McDougle, & Price, 1996a, 1996b).

In addition, there is evidence connecting OXT to depression (Cyranowski et al., 2008) and AVP to aggression in disorders of personality (Coccaro, Kavoussi, Hauger, Cooper, & Ferris, 1998). Yet, although these findings are of interest, they are sporadic and not all replicated; correspondingly, further investigation of these associations is needed.

To summarize, the literature explores the concepts of affiliation and affiliative behaviors in the context of both studies of personality and psychopathology. Although the research on these concepts in humans is rather limited—compared to the vast research on these concepts in animals—the emerging picture is rather coherent. Affiliation is one of the most important human traits, and it is no surprise that it is captured, although in different terms, in most, if not all, theories of personality. When the neurochemical foundation of affiliation-related personality traits is investigated, the revealed associations are consistent in implicating the neuropeptides OXT and AVP. Moreover, affiliation is supposed to be disrupted in many psychiatric conditions. There is now limited but growing evidence that, at least in some of these conditions, there might be a disruption of the OXT-AVP signaling pathway.

AFFILIATIVE BEHAVIOR AND SPIRITUALITY

The last portion of this essay is aimed at understanding the connection between affiliative behavior (affiliation), personality, and religiosity and spirituality. Here I propose, along the lines of the argument on the material nature of the human soul (Farah & Murphy, 2009), that spirituality, being connected to affiliation, is at least partially grounded in the functional properties of OXT and AVP. The following observations from the literature support this argument.

Religiosity [and spirituality, when defined as "beliefs about the existence of gods or *spirits* and their involvement in human life" ([italics added] McCullough & Willoughby, 2009, p. 71)] has been positively associated with a wide variety of indicators of health, well-being, achievement, and social prosperity (for a review, see McCullough & Willoughby, 2009). Yet, the mechanisms of these connections are not well understood. A recent review (McCullough & Willoughby, 2009) has provided a systematic account of empirical evidence supporting the assertions that religious people tend to live longer; be more mentally healthy; demonstrate less disorderly, amoral, or criminal conduct; do better in school; and have stronger, longer-lasting, and more satisfying marriages. It then concluded that religious belief, cognition, and behavior (at least some of their types) promote self-regulation and self-control, which, in turn, result in better health and social and emotional outcomes. In line with their argument, McCullough and Willoughby (2009) focus primarily on the correlations between personality traits that capture or correlate with self-regulation and self-control. However, what is notable even from their analysis is that the traits that capture affiliation (see the previous discussion) in different personality taxonomies also correlate with religiosity.

For example, from the Big Five taxonomy, religiosity positively and consistently correlates with agreeableness (Ashton, Kibeom, & Goldberg, 2004; McCullough, Tsang, & Brion, 2003; Saroglou & Fiasse, 2003; Wink, Ciciolla, Dillon, & Tracy, 2007). Of note is that this association appears to hold across different ages (Ciarrocchi, Dy-Liacco, & Deneke, 2008; Cramer, Griffin, & Powers, 2008), cultures (Mendonca, Oakes, Ciarrocchi, Sneck, & Gillespie, 2007), and religions (Dy-Liacco, Piedmont, Murray-Swank, Rodgerson, & Sherman, 2009). Moreover, it has been reported that, at least for women, agreeableness and religiosity have reciprocal relationships, so that religiosity enhances agreeableness and agreeableness strengthens religiosity throughout the life span (Wink et al., 2007).

It has also been noted that lifelong (rather than sudden, caused by life turmoil) religiosity is related to indicators of early secure attachment, once again stressing the role of affiliation and affiliative behavior (Granqvist, Ivarsson, Broberg, & Hagekull, 2007). In the case of the development of religiosity, the affiliation is formed with God, but reportedly love of God is similar in many ways to love for a human (Gallup & Jones, 1989; Stevens, 2006). According to believers, religious affiliative behaviors include "seeking closeness to God in prayer and rituals, using God as a safe haven during distress, and using God as a secure base for exploring the environment" (Granqvist et al., 2007, p. 591). Moreover, the God of individuals whose religiosity, reportedly, is associated with secure attachment, is itself loving and caring (Kirkpatrick, 1998), further stimulating affiliative behaviors.

Yet, this connection between religiosity and affiliation is not straightforward and might be nonlinear, depending on the extent of religiosity and the types of prosocial behavior exhibited (Rokeach, 1968). For example, it has been reported that the frequency of church visits was negatively related to expressed social compassion (Rokeach, 1970). Of great interest and importance also is the association between religious fundamentalism and feelings of affiliation with one group, along with a high degree of prejudice against another (Rokeach, 1970). Thus, it might be that the connection between religiosity and affiliative behaviors is heterogeneous, depending on type and degree of religiosity and type and extent of affiliation.

The concept of spirituality is not crystal clear, but the meaning of it is such that it enhances religiosity and secular spirituality (defined in a variety of ways) as well (e.g., Koenig, 2008). Although not clearly defined and not precisely measured, the concept demonstrates similar patterns of associations with personality traits (Ozer & Benet-Martínez, 2006; Saucier & Skrzypinska, 2006; Saroglou & Muños-García, 2008), stressing, again, its natural link to affiliative behaviors (Kiesling, Sorell, Montgomery, & Colwell, 2006) and better mental and physical health (Carmody, Reed, Kristeller, & Merriam, 2008; Leak, DeNeve, & Greteman, 2007). Definitions of spirituality stress its relational, affiliative component (Kiesling et al., 2006; Saucier & Skrzypinska, 2006; Sinnott, 2002; Wink & Dillon, 2002). For example, spirituality has been referred to as "one's personal relation to the sacred or transcendent, a relation that then informs other relationships and the meaning of one's own life" (Sinnott, 2002, p. 199). Of note also is the finding that personality traits related to religiosity and spirituality (e.g., Self-Transcendence and its subscale Spiritual Acceptance in the Cloninger Temperament and Character Inventory) have been reported to be associated with variation in the genes involved in serotonergic turnover (Nilsson et al., 2007).

In summary, features of spirituality and religiosity, such as their anxiolytic relaxing effects, reduced emotional arousal, and feelings of trust and calm, parallel the OXT-related experiences of bonding and affiliation (Heinrichs & Domes, 2008). The theoretical work of personality taxonomies has suggested that affiliation might be a higher-order personality trait that subsumes other traits, capturing the stable features of a person's social interaction. Moreover, the overlap between the widespread distribution of OXT and AVP receptors in the brain (Landgraf & Neumann, 2004) and the distribution of the neural network underlying social cognition and emotion (Adolphs, 2003) and religious experiences (Lutz, Brefczynski-Lewis, Johnstone, & Davidson, 2008) make the hypotheses of the involvement of the OXT-AVP system in the experiences of religiosity and spirituality plausible.

CONCLUSION

Although still sporadic in the literature, the findings presented here appear to converge, at least preliminarily, on the fact/possibility that the neuropeptides OXT and AVP might be important for experiencing such specifically human feelings as spirituality and religiosity. This argument is based on the observations that (a) OXT and AVP have been shown to be important players in the formation of the neurochemical foundation for demonstrating affiliative behavior and forming affiliation in animals and humans; (b) they also contribute to the development of the foundation for the manifestation of the higher-order personality trait of affiliation; and (c) affiliative behaviors (although with a transcendent, not a real other) are central to religiosity and spirituality. Yet, at this point, ideas regarding the role of OXT and AVP in spirituality and religiosity are only hypotheses. Empirical work—ideally longitudinal in design—is needed to verify them.

REFERENCES

Adolphs, R. (2003). Cognitive neuroscience of human social behavior. *Nature Review Neuroscience, 4*, 165–178.

Arnold, K., & Aureli, F. (2007). Postconflict reconciliation. In C. J. Campbell, A. Fuentes, K. C. MacKinnon, M. Panger, & S. K. Bearder (Eds.), *Primates in perspective* (pp. 592–608). New York, NY: Oxford University Press.

Ashton, M. C., Kibeom, L., & Goldberg, L. R. (2004). A hierarchical analysis of 1,710 English personality descriptive adjectives. *Journal of Personality and Social Psychology, 87*, 707–721.

Aureli, F., Cords, M., & van Schaik, C. P. (2002). Conflict resolution following aggression in gregarious animals: A predictive framework. *Animal Behavior, 64*, 325–343.

Aureli, F., & de Waal, F. B. M. (2000). *Natural conflict resolution*. Berkeley: University of California Press.

Bale, T. L., Davis, A. M., Auger, A. P., Dorsa, D. M., & McCarthy, M. M. (2001). CNS region-specific oxytocin receptor expression: Importance in regulation of anxiety and sex behavior. *Journal of Neuroscience, 21*, 2546–2552.

Bales, K. L., Plotsky, P. M., Young, L. J., Lim, M. M., Grotte, N., Ferrer, E., & Carter, C. S. (2007). Neonatal oxytocin manipulations have long-lasting, sexually dimorphic effects on vasopressin receptors. *Neuroscience, 144*, 38–45.

Barberis, C., & Tribollet, E. (1996). Vasopressin and oxytocin receptors in the central nervous system. *Critical Reviews in Neurobiology, 10*, 119–154.

Bartels, A., & Zeki, S. (2000). The neural basis of romantic love. *Neuroreport, 11*, 3829–3834.

Bartels, A., & Zeki, S. (2004). The neural correlates of maternal and romantic love. *Neuroimage, 21*, 1155–1166.

Bartz, A. J., & Hollander, E. (2006). The neuroscience of affiliation: Forging links between basic and clinical research on neuropeptides and social behavior. *Hormones and Behavior, 50*, 518–528.

Baumeister, R. F., & Leary, M. R. (1995). The need to belong: Desire for interpersonal attachments as a fundamental human motivation. *Psychological Bulletin, 117*, 497–529.

Baumeister, R. F., & Tice, D. M. (1990). Anxiety and social exclusion. *Journal of Social & Clinical Psychology, 9*, 165–195.

Baumgartner, T., Heinrichs, M., Vonlanthen, A., Fischbacher, U., & Fehr, E. (2008). Oxytocin shapes the neural circuitry of trust and trust adaptation in humans. *Neuron*, 58, 639–650.

Beery, A. K., Lacey, E. A., & Francis, D. D. (2008). Oxytocin and vasopressin receptor distributions in a solitary and a social species of tuco-tuco (*Ctenomys haigi* and *Ctenomys sociabilis*). *Journal of Comparative Neurology*, 507, 1847–1859.

Beery, A. K., Routman, D. M., & Zucker, I. (2009). Same-sex social behavior in meadow voles: Multiple and rapid formation of attachments. *Physiology & Behavior*, 97, 52–57.

Bell, C. J., Nicholson, H., Mulder, R. T., Luty, S. E., & Joyce, P. R. (2006). Plasma oxytocin levels in depression and their correlation with the temperament dimension of reward dependence. *Journal of Psychopharmacology*, 20, 656–660.

Berteaux, D., Bety, J., Rengifo, E., & Bergeron, J. M. (1999). Multiple paternity in meadow voles (Microtus pennsylvanicus): Investigating the role of the female. *Behavioral Ecology and Sociobiology*, 45, 283–291.

Bielsky, I. F., Hu, S. B., Szegda, K. L., Westphal, H., & Young, L. J. (2004). Profound impairment in social recognition and reduction in anxiety-like behavior in vasopressin V1a receptor knockout mice. *Neuropsychopharmacology*, 29, 483–493.

Boonstra, R., Xia, X., & Pavone, L. (1993). Mating system of the meadow vole, *Microtus pennsylvanicus*. *Behavioral Ecology*, 4, 83–89.

Born, J., Lange, T., Kern, W., McGregor, G. P., Bickel, U., & Fehm, H. L. (2002). Sniffing neuropeptides: A transnasal approach to the human brain. *Nature Neuroscience*, 5, 514–516.

Burri, A., Heinrichs, M., Schedlowski, M., & Kruger, T. H. (2008). The acute effects of intranasal oxytocin administration on endocrine and sexual function in males. *Psychoneuroendocrinology*, 33, 591–600.

Caldwell, H. K., Wersinger, S. R., & Young, W. S. (2008). The role of the vasopressin 1b receptor in aggression and other social behaviours. *Progress in Brain Research*, 170, 65–72.

Caldwell, H. K., & Young, W. S. (2006). Oxytocin and vasopressin: Genetics and behavioral implications. In A. Lajtha & R. Lim (Eds.), *Handbook of neurochemistry and molecular neurobiology: Neuroactive proteins and peptides* (3rd ed., pp. 573–607). Berlin, Germany: Springer.

Canli, T. (2008). Toward a "molecular psychology" of personality. In O. P. John, J. R. Robbins, & L. A. Pervin (Eds.), *Handbook of personality* (pp. 311–327). New York, NY: Guilford Press.

Carlson, N. R. (2010). *Physiology of behavior*. Boston, MA: Allyn & Bacon.

Carmichael, M. S., Humbert, R., Dixen, J., Palmisano, G., Greenleaf, W., & Davidson, J. M. (1987). Plasma oxytocin increases in the human sexual response. *Journal of Clinical Endocrinology & Metabolism*, 64, 27–31.

Carmody, J., Reed, G., Kristeller, J., & Merriam, P. (2008). Mindfulness, spirituality, and health-related symptoms. *Journal of Psychosomatic Research*, 64, 393–403.

Carter, C. S. (2003). Developmental consequences of oxytocin. *Physiology & Behavior, 79,* 383–397.

Carter, C. S. (2007). Sex differences in oxytocin and vasopressin: Implications for autism spectrum disorders? *Behavioural Brain Research, 176,* 170–186.

Carter, C. S., Altemus, M., & Chrousos, G. P. (2001). Neuroendocrine and emotional changes in the post-partum period. *Progress in Brain Research, 133,* 241–249.

Cattell, R., Eber, H., & Tatsuoka, M. (1980). *Handbook for the sixteen personality questionnaire (16PF).* Champaign, IL: Institute for Personality and Ability.

Champagne, F. A., Diorio, J., Sharma, S., & Meaney, M. J. (2001). Naturally occurring variations in maternal behavior in the rat are associated with differences in estrogen-inducible central oxytocin receptors. *Proceedings of the National Academy of Sciences of the United States of America, 98,* 12736–12741.

Christensson, K., Nilsson, B. A., Stock, S., Matthiesen, A. S., & Uvnäs-Moberg, K. (1989). Effect of nipple stimulation on uterine activity and on plasma levels of oxytocin in full-term, healthy, pregnant women. *Acta Obstetricia et Gynecologica Scandinavica, 68,* 205–210.

Ciarrocchi, J. W., Dy-Liacco, G. S., & Deneke, E. (2008). Gods or rituals? Relational faith, spiritual discontent, and religious practices as predictors of hope and optimism. *The Journal of Positive Psychology, 3,* 120–136.

Cloninger, C. R., Svrakic, D. M., & Przybeck, T. R. (1993). A psychobiological model of temperament and character. *Archives of General Psychiatry, 50,* 975–990.

Coccaro, E. F., Kavoussi, R. J., Hauger, R. L., Cooper, T. B., & Ferris, C. F. (1998). Cerebrospinal fluid vasopressin levels: Correlates with aggression and serotonin function in personality-disordered subjects. *Archives of General Psychiatry, 55,* 708–714.

Costa, P. T., Jr., & McCrae, R. R. (1997). Stability and change in personality assessment: The revised NEO personality inventory in the year 2000. *Journal of Personality Assessment, 68,* 86–94.

Cramer, R. J., Griffin, M. P., & Powers, D. V. (2008). A five-factor analysis of spirituality in young adults: Preliminary evidence. *Research in the Social Scientific Study of Religion, 19,* 43–57.

Cushing, B. S., & Wynne-Edwards, K. E. (2006). Estrogen receptor-alpha distribution in male rodents is associated with social organization. *The Journal of Comparative Neurology, 494,* 595–605.

Cyranowski, J. M., Hofkens, T. L., Frank, E., Seltman, H., Cai, H. M., & Amico, J. A. (2008). Evidence of dysregulated peripheral oxytocin release among depressed women. *Psychosomatic Medicine, 70,* 967–975.

den Boer, J. A., & Westenberg, H. G. (1992). Oxytocin in obsessive compulsive disorder. *Peptides, 13,* 1083–1085.

Depue, R. A., & Morrone-Strupinsky, J. V. (2005). A neurobehavioral model of affiliative bonding: Implications for conceptualizing a human trait of affiliation. *Behavioral and Brain Sciences, 28,* 313–350.

Ditzen, B., Neumann, I. D., Bodenmann, G., von Dawans, B., Turner, R. A., Ehlert, U., & Heinrichs, M. (2007). Effects of different kinds of couple interaction on cortisol and heart rate responses to stress in women. *Psychoneuroendocrinology, 32*, 565–574.

Ditzen, B., Schaer, M., Gabriel, B., Bodenmann, G., Ehlert, U., & Heinrichs, M. (2009). Intranasal oxytocin increases positive communication and reduces cortisol levels during couple conflict. *Biological Psychiatry, 65*, 728–731.

Domes, G., Heinrichs, M., Glascher, J., Buchel, C., Braus, D. F., & Herpertz, S. C. (2008). Oxytocin attenuates amygdala responses to emotional faces regardless of valence. *Biological Psychiatry, 62*, 1187–1190.

Domes, G., Heinrichs, M., Michel, A., Berger, C., & Herpertz, S. C. (2007). Oxytocin improves "mind-reading" in humans. *Biological Psychiatry, 61*, 731–733.

Dy-Liacco, G. S., Piedmont, R. L., Murray-Swank, N. A., Rodgerson, T. E., & Sherman, M. F. (2009). Spirituality and religiosity as cross-cultural aspects of human experience. *Psychology of Religion and Spirituality, 1*, 35–52.

Eisenberger, N. I., Lieberman, M. D., & Williams, K. D. (2003). Does rejection hurt? An FMRI study of social exclusion. *Science, 302*, 290–292.

Epperson, C. N., McDougle, C. J., & Price, L. H. (1996a). Intranasal oxytocin in obsessive-compulsive disorder. *Biological Psychiatry, 40*, 547–549.

Epperson, C. N., McDougle, C. J., & Price, L. H. (1996b). Intranasal oxytocin in trichotillomania. *Biological Psychiatry, 40*, 559–560.

Farah, M. J., & Murphy, N. (2009). Neuroscience and the soul. *Science, 323*, 1168.

Feldman, R., Weller, A., Zagoory-Sharon, O., & Levine, A. (2007). Evidence for a neuroendocrinological foundation of human affiliation: Plasma oxytocin levels across pregnancy and the postpartum period predict mother-infant bonding. *Psycholological Science, 18*, 965–970.

Ferguson, J. N., Young, L. J., Hearn, E. F., Matzuk, M. M., Insel, T. R., & Winslow, J. T. (2000). Social amnesia in mice lacking the oxytocin gene. *Nature Genetics, 25*, 284–288.

Ferris, C. F., Lu, S. F., Messenger, T., Guillon, C. D., Heindel, N., Miller, M., . . . & Simon, N. G. (2006). Orally active vasopressin V1a receptor antagonist, SRX251, selectively blocks aggressive behavior. *Pharmacology, Biochemistry & Behavior, 83*, 169–174.

Francis, D. D., Diorio, J., Liu, D., & Meaney, M. J. (1999). Nongenomic transmission across generations of maternal behavior and stress responses in the rat. *Science, 286*, 1155–1158.

Francis, D. D., Young, L. J., Meaney, M. J., & Insel, T. R. (2002). Naturally occurring differences in maternal care are associated with the expression of oxytocin and vasopressin (V1a) receptors: Gender differences. *Journal of Neuroendocrinology, 14*, 349–353.

Fries, A. B., Ziegler, T. E., Kurian, J. R., Jacoris, S., & Pollak, S. D. (2005). Early experience in humans is associated with changes in neuropeptides critical for regulating social behavior. *Proceedings of the National Academy of Sciences of the United States of America, 102*, 17237–17240.

Gallup, G., Jr., & Jones, S. (1989). *One hundred questions and answers: Religion in America.* Princeton, NJ: Princeton Religious Research Center.

Georgiadis, J. R., Reinders, A. A., Van der Graaf, F. H., Paans, A. M., & Kortekaas, R. (2007). Brain activation during human male ejaculation revisited. *Neuroreport, 18,* 553–557.

Getz, L. L. (1972). Social structure and aggressive behavior in a population of *Microtus pennsylvanicus. Journal of Mammalogy, 53,* 310–317.

Gillath, O., Shaver, P. R., Baek, J.-M., & Chun, D. S. (2008). Genetic correlates of adult attachment style. *Personality and Social Psychology Bulletin, 34,* 1396–1405.

Gimpl, G., & Fahrenholz, F. (2001). The oxytocin receptor system: Structure, function, and regulation. *Physiological Reviews, 81,* 629–683.

Gobrogge, K. L., Liu, Y., Jia, X., & Wang, Z. (2007). Anterior hypothalamic neural activation and neurochemical associations with aggression in pair-bonded male prairie voles. *Journal of Comparative Neurology, 502,* 1109–1122.

Goldberg, L. R., Sweeney, D., Merenda, P. F., & Hughes, J. E. J. (1996). The Big-Five factor structure as an integrative framework: An analysis of Clarke's AVA model. *Journal of Personality Assessment, 66,* 441–471.

Granqvist, P., Ivarsson, T., Broberg, A. G., & Hagekull, B. (2007). Examining relations among attachment, religiosity, and new age spirituality using the Adult Attachment Interview. *Developmental Psychology, 43,* 590–601.

Green, L., Fein, D., Modahl, C., Feinstein, C., Waterhouse, L., & Morris, M. (2001). Oxytocin and autistic disorder: Alterations in peptide forms. *Biological Psychiatry, 50,* 609–613.

Griebel, G., Simiand, J., Serradeil-Le Gal, C., Wagnon, J., Pascal, M., Scatton, B., ... & Soubrie, P. (2002). Anxiolytic- and antidepressant-like effects of the non-peptide vasopressin V1b receptor antagonist, SSR149415, suggest an innovative approach for the treatment of stress-related disorders. *Proceedings of the National Academy of Sciences of the United States of America, 99,* 6370–6375.

Guastella, A. J., Mitchell, P. B., & Dadds, M. R. (2008). Oxytocin increases gaze to the eye region of human faces. *Biological Psychiatry, 63,* 3–5.

Guilford, J. P., & Zimmerman, W. (2009). *The Guilford-Zimmerman temperament survey.* New York, NY: Pearson.

Hammock, E. A. D., & Young, L. J. (2005). Microsatellite instability generates diversity in brain and sociobehavioral traits. *Science, 308,* 1630–1634.

Heinrichs, M., & Domes, G. (2008). Neuropeptides and social behaviour: Effects of oxytocin and vasopressin in humans. *Progress in Brain Research* (Vol. 170, pp. 337–350). New York, NY: Elsevier.

Heinrichs, M., & Gaab, J. (2007). Neuroendocrine mechanisms of stress and social interaction: Implications for mental disorders. *Current Opinion in Psychiatry, 20,* 158–162.

Heinrichs, M., Meinlschmidt, G., Wippich, W., Ehlert, U., & Hellhammer, D. H. (2004). Selective amnesic effects of oxytocin on human memory. *Physiology and Behavior, 83,* 31–38.

Heinrichs, M., Neumann, I. D., & Ehlert, U. (2002). Lactation and stress: Protective effects of breast-feeding in humans. *Stress, 5*, 195–203.

Hogan, R. (1983). A socioanalytic theory of personality. In M. Page (Ed.), *1982 Nebraska Symposium on Motivation* (pp. 55–89). Lincoln: University of Nebraska Press.

Hollander, E., Bartz, A. J., Chaplin, W., Phillips, A., Sumner, J., Soorya, L., & Wasserman, S. (2007). Oxytocin increases retention of social cognition in autism. *Biological Psychiatry, 61*, 498–503.

Hollander, E., Novotny, S., Hanratty, M., Yaffe, R., DeCaria, C. M., Aronowitz, B. R., & Mosovich, S. (2003). Oxytocin infusion reduces repetitive behaviors in adults with autistic and Asperger's disorders. *Neuropsychopharmacology, 28*, 193–198.

Holst, S., Uvnäs-Moberg, K., & Petersson, M. (2002). Postnatal oxytocin treatment and postnatal stroking of rats reduce blood pressure in adulthood. *Autonomic Neuroscience-Basic & Clinical, 99*, 85–90.

Horváth, Z., Dóka, A., & Miklósi, Á. (2008). Affiliative and disciplinary behavior of human handlers during play with their dog affects cortisol concentrations in opposite directions. *Hormones and Behavior, 54*, 107–114.

Huber, D., Veinante, P., & Stoop, R. (2005). Vasopressin and oxytocin excite distinct neuronal populations in the central amygdala. *Science, 308*, 245–248.

Insel, T. R. (2002). Social anxiety: From laboratory studies to clinical practice. *Biological Psychiatry, 51*, 1–3.

Insel, T. R. (2003). Is social attachment an addictive disorder? *Physiology & Behavior, 79*, 351–357.

Insel, T. R., & Young, L. J. (2001). The neurobiology of attachment. *Nature Reviews Neuroscience, 2*, 129–136.

Israel, S., Lerer, E., Shalev, I., Uzefovsky, F., Reibold, M., Bachner-Melman, R., . . . & Ebstein, R. P. (2008). Molecular genetic studies of the arginine vasopressin 1a receptor (AVPR1a) and the oxytocin receptor (OXTR) in human behaviour: From autism to altruism with some notes in between. *Progress in Brain Research, 170*, 435–449.

Jenkins, J. S., Ang, V. T., Hawthorn, J., Rossor, M. N., & Iversen, L. L. (1984). Vasopressin, oxytocin and neurophysins in the human brain and spinal cord. *Brain Research, 291*, 111–117.

Jonas, K., Johansson, L. M., Nissen, E., Ejdeback, M., Ransjo-Arvidson, A. B., & Uvnas-Moberg, K. (2009). Effects of intrapartum oxytocin administration and epidural analgesia on the concentration of plasma oxytocin and prolactin, in response to suckling during the second day postpartum. *Breastfeeding Medicine: The Official Journal of the Academy of Breastfeeding Medicine, 4*, 71–82.

Jonas, W., Nissen, E., Ransjö-Arvidson, A., Matthiesen, A. S., & Uvnäs-Moberg, K. (2008). Influence of oxytocin or epidural analgesia on personality profile in breastfeeding women: A comparative study. *Archives of Women's Mental Health, 11*, 335–345.

Kiesling, C., Sorell, G. T., Montgomery, M. J., & Colwell, R. K. (2006). Identity and spirituality: A psychosocial exploration of the sense of spiritual self. *Developmental Psychology, 42*, 1269–1277.

Kim, S. J., Young, L. J., Gonen, D., Veenstra-VanderWeele, J., Courchesne, R., Courchesne, E.,...& Insel, T. R. (2002). Transmission disequilibrium testing of arginine vasopressin receptor 1A (AVPR1A) polymorphisms in autism. *Molecular Psychiatry, 7,* 503–507.

Kirkpatrick, L. A. (1998). God as a substitute attachment figure: A longitudinal study of adult attachment style and religious change in college students. *Personality and Social Psychology Bulletin, 24,* 961–973.

Kirsch, P., Esslinger, C., Chen, Q., Mier, D., Lis, S., Siddhanti, S.,...& Meyer-Lindenberg, A. (2005). Oxytocin modulates neural circuitry for social cognition and fear in humans. *Journal of Neuroscience, 25,* 11489–11493.

Koenig, H. G. (2008). Concerns about measuring "spirituality" in research. *Journal of Nervous & Mental Disease, 196,* 349–355.

Kosfeld, M., Heinrichs, M., Zak, P. J., Fischbacher, U., & Fehr, E. (2005). Oxytocin increases trust in humans. *Nature, 435,* 673–676.

Koski, S. E., & Sterck, E. H. M. (2009). Post-conflict third-party affiliation in chimpanzees: What's in it for the third party? *American Journal of Primatology, 71,* 409–418.

Krueger, R. F., & Johnson, W. (2008). Behavior genetics and personality: A new look at the integration of nature and nurture. In O. P. John, J. R. Robbins, & L. A. Pervin (Eds.), *Handbook of personality* (pp. 287–310). New York, NY: Guilford Press.

Lacey, E. A., & Sherman, P. W. (2007). The ecology of sociality in rodents. In J. O. Wolff & P. W. Sherman (Eds.), *Rodent societies: An ecological and evolutionary perspective* (pp. 243–254). Chicago, IL: University of Chicago Press.

Landgraf, R., & Neumann, I. D. (2004). Vasopressin and oxytocin release within the brain: A dynamic concept of multiple and variable modes of neuropeptide communication. *Frontiers in Neuroendocrinology, 25,* 150–176.

Leak, G. K., DeNeve, K. M., & Greteman, A. J. (2007). The relationship between spirituality, assessed through self-transcendent goal strivings, and positive psychological attributes. *Research in the Social Scientific Study of Religion, 18,* 263–279.

Leake, R. D., Weitzman, R. E., & Fisher, D. A. (1981). Oxytocin concentrations during the neonatal period. *Biology of the Neonate, 39,* 127–131.

Leary, M. R. (1990). Responses to social exclusion: Social anxiety, jealousy, loneliness, depression, and low self-esteem. *Journal of Social & Clinical Psychology, 9,* 221–229.

Leckman, J. F., Goodman, W. K., North, W. G., Chappell, P. B., Price, L. H., Pauls, D. L.,...& McDougle, C. J. (1994). Elevated cerebrospinal fluid levels of oxytocin in obsessive-compulsive disorder: Comparison with Tourette's syndrome and healthy controls. *Archives of General Psychiatry, 51,* 782–792.

Levy, F., Kendrick, K. M., Keverne, E. B., Piketty, V., & Poindron, P. (1992). Intracerebral oxytocin is important for the onset of maternal behavior in inexperienced ewes delivered under peridural anesthesia. *Behavioral Neuroscience, 106,* 427–432.

Loup, F., Tribollet, E., Dubois-Dauphin, M., & Dreifuss, J. J. (1991). Localization of high-affinity binding sites for oxytocin and vasopressin in the human brain: An autoradiographic study. *Brain Research, 555,* 220–232.

Lupoli, B., Johansson, B., Uvnäs-Moberg, K., & Svennersten-Sjaunja, K. (2001). Effect of suckling on the release of oxytocin, prolactin, cortisol, gastrin, cholecystokinin, somatostatin and insulin in dairy cows and their calves. *Journal of Dairy Research, 68,* 175–187.

Lutz, A., Brefczynski-Lewis, J. A., Johnstone, T., & Davidson, R. J. (2008). Regulation of the neural circuitry of emotion by compassion meditation: effects of meditative expertise. *PLoS ONE, 3,* e1897.

Madison, D. M. (1980). Space use and social structure in meadow voles, *Microtus pennsylvanicus. Behavioral Ecology and Sociobiology, 7,* 65–71.

Mallott, M. A., Maner, J. K., DeWall, N., & Schmidt, N. B. (2009). Compensatory deficits following rejection: The role of social anxiety in disrupting affiliative behavior. *Depression and Anxiety, 26,* 438–446.

McCullough, M. E., Tsang, J., & Brion, S. L. (2003). Personality traits in adolescence as predictors of religiousness in early adulthood: Findings from the Terman Longitudinal Study. *Personality and Social Psychology Bulletin, 29,* 980–991.

McCullough, M. E., & Willoughby, B. L. (2009). Religion, self-regulation, and self-control: Associations, explanations, and implications. *Psychological Bulletin, 135,* 69–93.

McDougle, C. J., Barr, L. C., Goodman, W. K., & Price, L. H. (1999). Possible role of neuropeptides in obsessive compulsive disorder. *Psychoneuroendocrinology, 24,* 1–24.

Meinlschmidt, G., & Heim, C. (2007). Sensitivity to intranasal oxytocin in adult men with early parental separation. *Biological Psychiatry, 61,* 1109–1111.

Mendonca, D., Oakes, K. E., Ciarrocchi, J. W., Sneck, W. J., & Gillespie, K. (2007). Spirituality and God-attachment as predictors of subjective well-being for seminarians and nuns in India. *Research in the Social Scientific Study of Religion, 18,* 121–140.

Miller, S. C., Kennedy, C., DeVoe, D., Hickey, M., Nelson, T., & Kogan, L. (2009). An examination of changes in oxytocin levels in men and women before and after interaction with a bonded dog. *Anthrozoos, 22,* 31–42.

Modahl, C., Green, L., Fein, D., Morris, M., Waterhouse, L., Feinstein, C., & Levin, H. (1998). Plasma oxytocin levels in autistic children. *Biological Psychiatry, 43,* 270–277.

Murphy, M. R., Seckl, J. R., Burton, S., Checkley, S. A., & Lightman, S. L. (1987). Changes in oxytocin and vasopressin secretion during sexual activity in men. *Journal of Clinical Endocrinology & Metabolism, 65,* 738–741.

Neumann, I. D. (2002). Involvement of the brain oxytocin system in stress coping: Interactions with the hypothalamo-pituitary-adrenal axis. *Progress in Brain Research, 139,* 147–162.

Neumann, I. D., Krömer, S. A., Toschi, N., & Ebner, K. (2000). Brain oxytocin inhibits the (re)activity of the hypothalamo-pituitary-adrenal axis in male rats: Involvement of hypothalamic and limbic brain regions. *Regulatory Peptides, 96,* 31–38.

Neumann, I. D., Wigger, A., Torner, L., Holsboer, F., & Landgraf, R. (2000). Brain oxytocin inhibits basal and stress-induced activity of the hypothalamo-pituitary-adrenal axis in male and female rats: Partial action within the paraventricular nucleus. *Journal of Neuroendocrinology, 12,* 235–243.

Nilsson, K. W., Damberg, M., Ohrvik, J., Leppert, J., Lindstrom, L., Anckarsater, H., & Oreland, L. (2007). Genes encoding for AP-2beta and the serotonin transporter are associated with the personality character spiritual acceptance. *Neuroscience Letters, 411,* 233–237.

Odendaal, J. S., & Meintjes, R. A. (2003). Neurophysiological correlates of affiliative behaviour between humans and dogs. *Veterinary Journal, 165,* 296–301.

Olausson, H., Uvnäs-Moberg, K., & Sohlstrom, A. (2003). Postnatal oxytocin alleviates adverse effects in adult rat offspring caused by maternal malnutrition. *American Journal of Physiology—Endocrinology & Metabolism, 284,* E475–E480.

Olazábal, D. E., & Young, L. J. (2005). Variability in "spontaneous" maternal behavior is associated with anxiety-like behavior and affiliation in naive juvenile and adult female prairie voles (*Microtus ochrogaster*). *Developmental Psychobiology, 47,* 166–178.

Olazábal, D. E., & Young, L. J. (2006). Species and individual differences in juvenile female alloparental care are associated with oxytocin receptor density in the striatum and the lateral septum. *Hormones and Behavior, 49,* 681–687.

Ophir, A. G., Phelps, S. M., Sorin, A. B., & Wolff, J. O. (2008). Social but not genetic monogamy is associated with greater breeding success in prairie voles. *Animal Behaviour, 75,* 1143–1154.

Ozer, D. J., & Benet-Martínez, V. (2006). Personality and the prediction of consequential outcomes. *Annual Review of Psychology, 57,* 401–421.

Panksepp, J., & Moskal, J. R. (2005). Loving opioids in the brain. *Behavioral and Brain Sciences, 28,* 361–362.

Parker, K. J., Buckmaster, C. L., Schatzberg, A. F., & Lyons, D. M. (2005). Intranasal oxytocin administration attenuates the ACTH stress response in monkeys. *Psychoneuroendocrinology, 30,* 924–929.

Parker, K. J., Phillips, K. M., Kinney, L. F., & Lee, T. M. (2001). Day length and sociosexual cohabitation alter central oxytocin receptor binding in female meadow voles (*Microtus pennsylvanicus*). *Behavioral Neuroscience, 115,* 1349–1356.

Petersson, M., & Uvnäs-Moberg, K. (2007). Effects of an acute stressor on blood pressure and heart rate in rats pretreated with intracerebroventricular oxytocin injections. *Psychoneuroendocrinology, 32,* 959–965.

Petersson, M., & Uvnäs-Moberg, K. (2008). Postnatal oxytocin treatment of spontaneously hypertensive male rats decreases blood pressure and body weight in adulthood. *Neuroscience Letters, 440,* 166–169.

Preston, S. D., & de Waal, F. B. M. (2002). Empathy: Its ultimate and proximate bases. *Behavioral and Brain Sciences, 25,* 1–20.

Prichard, Z. M., Mackinnon, A. J., Jorm, A. F., & Easteal, S. (2007). AVPR1A and OXTR polymorphisms are associated with sexual and reproductive behavioral phenotypes in humans. Mutation in brief no. 981. Online. *Human Mutation, 28,* 1150.

Raggenbass, M. (2001). Vasopressin- and oxytocin-induced activity in the central nervous system: Electrophysiological studies using in-vitro systems. *Progress in Neurobiology, 64,* 307–326.

Ragnauth, A. K., Devidze, N., Moy, V., Finley, K., Goodwillie, A., Kow, L. M., . . . & Pfaff, D. W. (2005). Female oxytocin gene-knockout mice, in semi-natural environment, display exaggerated aggressive behavior. *Genes, Brain and Behavior, 4,* 229–239.

Rimmele, U., Hediger, K., Heinrichs, M., & Klaver, P. (2009). Oxytocin makes a face in memory familiar. *Journal of Neuroscience, 29,* 38–42.

Rokeach, M. (1968). The paradox of religious belief. *Proceedings of the Christian Association for Psychological Studies* (April), 51–58.

Rokeach, M. (1970). Faith, hope and bigotry. *Psychology Today, 3,* 33–37, 58.

Saroglou, V., & Fiasse, L. (2003). Birth order, personality, and religion: A study among young adults from a three-sibling family. *Personality and Individual Differences, 35,* 19–29.

Saroglou, V., & Muños-García, A. (2008). Individual differences in religion and spirituality: An issue of personality traits and/or values. *Journal for the Scientific Study of Religion, 47,* 83–101.

Saucier, G., & Skrzypinska, K. (2006). Spiritual but not religious? Evidence for two independent dispositions. *Journal of Personality, 74,* 1257–1292.

Siever, L. J. (2008). Neurobiology of aggression and violence. *American Journal of Psychiatry, 165,* 429–442.

Singer, T., Snozzi, R., Bird, G., Petrovic, P., Silani, G., Heinrichs, M., & Dolan, R. J. (2008). Effects of oxytocin and prosocial behavior on brain responses to direct and vicariously experienced pain. *Emotion, 8,* 781–791.

Sinnott, J. D. (2002). Introduction. *Journal of Adult Development, 9,* 199–200.

Sohlstrom, A., Carlsson, C., & Uvnäs-Moberg, K. (2000). Effects of oxytocin treatment in early life on body weight and corticosterone in adult offspring from ad libitum-fed and food-restricted rats. *Biology of the Neonate, 78,* 33–40.

Stevens, B. A. (2006). "Love Supreme": On spiritual experience and change in personality structure. *Journal of Psychology & Theology, 34,* 318–326.

Sussman, R. W., Garber, P. A., & Cheverud, J. M. (2005). Importance of cooperation and affiliation in the evolution of primate sociality. *American Journal of Physical Anthropology, 128,* 84–97.

Taylor, S. E., Gonzaga, G. C., Klein, L. C., Hu, P., Greendale, G. A., & Seeman, T. E. (2006). Relation of oxytocin to psychological stress responses and hypothalamic-pituitary-adrenocortical axis activity in older women. *Psychosomatic Medicine, 68,* 238–245.

Tellegen, A., & Waller, N. G. (2008). Exploring personality through test construction: Development of the Multidimensional Personality Questionnaire. In G. J. Boyle, G. Matthews, & D. H. Saklofske (Eds.), *The SAGE handbook of personality theory and assessment* (Vol. 2: Personality measurement and testing, pp. 261–292). Thousand Oaks, CA: Sage.

Thompson, M. R., Callaghan, P. D., Hunt, G. E., Cornish, J. L., & McGregor, I. S. (2007). A role for oxytocin and 5-HT1A receptors in the prosocial effects of 3,4 methylenedioxymethamphetamine ("ecstasy"). *Neuroscience, 146,* 509–514.

Tribollet, E., Dubois-Dauphin, M., Dreifuss, J. J., Barberis, C., & Jard, S. (1992). Oxytocin receptors in the central nervous system: Distribution, development, and species differences. *Annals of the New York Academy of Sciences, 652*, 29–38.

Troisi, A., & D'amato, F. R. (2005). Deficits in affiliative reward: An endophenotype for psychiatric disorders? *Behavioral and Brain Sciences, 28*, 365–366.

Turner, R. A., Altemus, M., Enos, T., Cooper, B., & McGuinness, T. (1999). Preliminary research on plasma oxytocin in normal cycling women: Investigating emotion and interpersonal distress. *Psychiatry, 62*, 97–113.

Uvnäs-Moberg, K. (1996). Neuroendocrinology of the mother-child interaction. *Trends in Endocrinology and Metabolism, 7*, 126–131.

Uvnäs-Moberg, K. (1998). Oxytocin may mediate the benefits of positive social interaction and emotions. *Psychoneuroendocrinology, 23*, 819–835.

Uvnäs-Moberg, K., Widstrom, A.-M., Nissen, E., & Bjorvell, H. (1990). Personality traits in women 4 days postpartum and their correlation with plasma levels of oxytocin and prolactin. *Journal of Psychosomatic Obstetrics and Gynecology, 11*, 261–273.

Van Duuren, F., & Di Giacomo, J. P. (1997). Degrading situations, affiliation and social dependency. *European Journal of Social Psychology, 27*, 495–510.

Walum, H., Westberg, L., Henningsson, S., Neiderhiser, J. M., Reiss, D., Igl, W.,... & Lichtenstein, P. (2008). Genetic variation in the vasopressin receptor 1a gene (AVPR1A) associates with pair-bonding behavior in humans. *Proceedings of the National Academy of Sciences of the United States of America, 1105*, 14153–14156.

Wassink, T. H., Piven, J., Vieland, V. J., Pietila, J., Goedken, R. J., Folstein, S. E., & Sheffield, V. C. (2004). Examination of AVPR1a as an autism susceptibility gene. *Molecular Psychiatry, 9*, 968–972.

Webster's new universal unabridged dictionary. (1996). New York, NY: Barnes & Noble.

Wersinger, S. R., Caldwell, H. K., Christiansen, M., & Young, W. S. (2007). Disruption of the vasopressin 1b receptor gene impairs the attack component of aggressive behavior in mice. *Genes, Brain, & Behavior, 6*, 653–660.

Wiggins, J., Trapnell, P., & Phillips, N. (1988). Psychometric and geometric characteristics of the revised Interpersonal Adjective Scales (IAS-R). *Multivariate Behavioral Research, 23*, 517–530.

Williams, G. L., Gazal, O. S., Leshin, L. S., Stanko, R. L., & Anderson, L. L. (2001). Physiological regulation of maternal behavior in heifers: Roles of genital stimulation, intracerebral oxytocin release, and ovarian steroids. *Biology of Reproduction, 65*, 295–300.

Williams, J. R., Insel, T. R., Harbaugh, C. R., & Carter, C. S. (1994). Oxytocin administered centrally facilitates formation of a partner preference in female prairie voles (*Microtus ochrogaster*). *Journal of Neuroendocrinology, 6*, 247–250.

Windle, R. J., Shanks, N., Lightman, S. L., & Ingram, C. D. (1997). Central oxytocin administration reduces stress-induced corticosterone release and anxiety behavior in rats. *Endocrinology, 138*, 2829–2834.

Wink, P., Ciciolla, L., Dillon, M., & Tracy, A. (2007). Religiousness, spiritual seeking, and personality: Findings from a longitudinal study. *Journal of Personality, 75,* 1051–1070.

Wink, P., & Dillon, M. (2002). Spiritual development across the adult life course: Findings from a longitudinal study. *Journal of Adult Development, 9,* 79–94.

Winslow, J. T., & Insel, T. R. (2000). The social deficits of the oxytocin knockout mouse. *Neuropeptides, 36,* 221–229.

Wolff, K., Tsapakis, E. M., Winstock, A. R., Hartley, D., Holt, D., Forsling, M. L., & Aitchison, K. J. (2006). Vasopressin and oxytocin secretion in response to the consumption of ecstasy in a clubbing population. *Journal of Pharmacology, 20,* 400–410.

Wu, S., Jia, M., Ruan, Y., Liu, J., Guo, Y., Shuang, M., . . . & Zhang, D. (2005). Positive association of the oxytocin receptor gene (OXTR) with autism in the Chinese Han population. *Biological Psychiatry, 58,* 74–77.

Yirmiya, N., Rosenberg, C., Levi, S., Salomon, S., Shulman, C., Nemanov, L., . . . & Ebstein, R. P. (2006). Association between the arginine vasopressin 1a receptor (AVPR1a) gene and autism in a family-based study: Mediation by socialization skills. *Molecular Psychiatry, 11,* 488–494.

Ylisaukko-oja, T., Alarcón, M., Cantor, R. M., Auranen, M., Vanhala, R., Kempas, E., . . . & Peltonen, L. (2006). Search for autism loci by combined analysis of Autism Genetic Resource Exchange and Finnish families. *Annals of Neurology, 59,* 145–155.

Young, L. J. (1999). Frank A. Beach Award. Oxytocin and vasopressin receptors and species-typical social behaviors. *Hormones & Behavior, 36,* 212–221.

Young, L. J., Lim, M. M., Gingrich, B., & Insel, T. R. (2001). Cellular mechanisms of social attachment. *Hormones & Behavior, 40,* 133–138.

Young, L. J., & Zuoxin, W. (2004). The neurobiology of pair bonding. *Nature Neuroscience, 7,* 1048–1054.

Young, S. N., & Moskowitz, D. S. (2005). Serotonin and affiliative behavior. *Behavioral and Brain Sciences, 28,* 367–368.

Yrigollen, C. M., Han, S. S., Kochetkova, A., Babitz, T., Chang, J. T., Volkmar, F. R., . . . & Grigorenko, E. L. (2008). Genes controlling affiliative behavior as candidate genes for autism. *Biological Psychiatry, 63,* 911–916.

Zak, P. J., Stanton, A. A., & Ahmadi, S. (2007). Oxytocin increases generosity in humans. *PLoS ONE, 2,* 1–5.

Zizzo, D. J. (2005). Serotonin, dopamine, and cooperation. *Behavioral and Brain Sciences, 28,* 370–370.

4

Positive Youth Development and Age-Related Changes in Cortical Thickness During Adolescence[1]

Tomáš Paus, Gabriel Leonard, Jacqueline V. Lerner,
Richard M. Lerner, Michel Perron, G. Bruce Pike, Louis Richer,
Roberto Toro, Suzanne Veillette, and Zdenka Pausova

The human brain continues to develop throughout childhood and adolescence. Using magnetic resonance imaging (MRI), a growing number of studies have described age-related changes in the volume of gray matter (GM) and cortical thickness, as well as the volume of white matter (WM) and its structural properties (reviewed in Durston et al., 2001; Giedd et al., 2009; Lenroot et al.,

---

[1]The Saguenay Youth Study project is funded by the Canadian Institutes of Health Research (TP, ZP), Heart and Stroke Foundation of Quebec (ZP), and the Canadian Foundation for Innovation (ZP). We thank the following individuals for their contributions in designing the protocol and acquiring and analyzing the data: psychometricians (Chantale Belleau, Mélanie Drolet, Catherine Harvey, Stéphane Jean, Hélène Simard, Mélanie Tremblay, Patrick Vachon), ÉCOBES team (Nadine Arbour, Julie Auclair, Marie-Ève Blackburn, Marie-Ève Bouchard, Annie Houde, Dr. Luc Laberge, Catherine Lavoie), laboratory technicians (Denise Morin and Nadia Mior), Julie Bérubé, Celine Bourdon, Dr. Rosanne Aleong, Dr. Jennifer Barrett, Candice Cartier, Dale Einarson, Helena Jelicic, and Valerie Legge. We thank Dr. Jean Mathieu for the medical follow-up of participants in whom we detected any medically relevant abnormalities. We thank Manon Bernard for designing and managing our online database.

2007; Paus et al., 2001; Paus, 2005, 2010). The main features of brain maturation during adolescence include age-related *decreases* in the volume of cortical GM (e.g., Giedd et al., 1999; Paus et al., 2009) and cortical thickness (O'Donnell, Noseworthy, Levine, & Dennis, 2005; Shaw et al., 2006; Sowell et al., 2007) and *increases* in the volume of WM (e.g., de Bellis et al., 2001; Giedd et al., 1999; Perrin et al., 2008), as well as age-related changes in WM microstructure assessed with diffusion tensor imaging and magnetization-transfer imaging (e.g., Lebel, Walker, Leemans, Phillips, & Beaulieu, 2008; Perrin et al., 2008; Schmithorst, Holland, & Dardzinski, 2008).

What is the relationship between behavior and these structural changes in the adolescent brain? First, it is assumed that even subtle deviations from normal trajectories of brain maturation, whether related to genes or environment, could lead to psychopathology (Paus, Keshavan, & Giedd, 2008). For example, we have speculated that testosterone-driven changes in axonal caliber and, consequently, volume and properties of white matter during male adolescence may contribute to the emergence of symptoms of schizophrenia in late adolescence—a proposal that needs to be tested in future studies (Paus & Toro, 2009). Putting pathology aside, do healthy individuals with different life experiences differ in their brain structure? Several imaging studies carried out in adults suggest that this is the case, although we do not know the directionality of the function-structure relationships in all of the following examples: musical training (reviewed in Schlaug, 2001; Stewart, 2008), profession (Maguire, Woollett, & Spiers, 2006; Sluming et al., 2002), or the long-term practice of meditation (Luders, Toga, Lepore, & Gaser, 2009), and even those of a short-term engagement in specific behaviors, such as juggling (Draganski et al., 2004; Driemeyer, Boyke, Gaser, Büchel, & May, 2008), mirror reading (Ilg et al., 2008), or studying for medical examinations (Draganski et al., 2006). These findings indicate a great deal of brain plasticity but, for the most part, it is not known how such (normal) environmental influences interact with the developmental trajectories described previously.

One way to address this issue is to compare trajectories in brain development of children and adolescents with different cognitive abilities, personality, or, more broadly, of individuals with different experiences with their peers, family, and neighborhood. Shaw et al. (2006) examined age-related changes in cortical thickness in a large sample ($N = 307$, mixed cross-sectional and longitudinal design) of children and adolescents, and compared trajectories in three groups with different intelligence quotients (IQ): superior intelligence (IQ range 121–149), high intelligence (IQ range 109–120), and average intelligence (IQ range 83–108). The three groups differ in cortical-thickness trajectories both during childhood (about 6 to 11 years) and adolescence (about 12 to 19 years); during adolescence, age-related decreases in the thickness of several frontal and temporal regions appear steeper in the superior- and high-intelligence groups, as compared with the average-intelligence group. Overall, the rate of cortical thinning during adolescence was higher in the superior-intelligence group as compared with the other two groups.

Forces driving the observed dynamics of cortical maturation are unknown, however. Theoretically, cortical thinning during adolescence may be driven by a predetermined (genetic) plan of cortical development, or it might reflect environmental influences/experiences that are likely to differ across the three groups. In fact, the results of twin-based studies of intelligence and other cognitive abilities (Bouchard, 1998) and cortical thickness (Lenroot et al., 2009) suggest that both genetic and environmental factors contribute to these phenotypes to a degree that varies across specific brain regions, age of participants, and type of cognitive abilities.

POSITIVE YOUTH DEVELOPMENT

In this chapter, we will employ an approach similar to that of Shaw et al. (2006) and test whether adolescents with low and high scores of positive youth development, rather than intelligence, differ in the cortical-thickness trajectories. Current theories of youth development emphasize that positive, or healthy, psychological and social functioning includes characteristics of successful and adaptive behavior. The presence of psychosocially and physically healthy change is indexed by increases in attributes indicative of thriving, such as the Five Cs of Positive Youth Development (PYD): Competence, Confidence, Connection, Character, and Caring (Eccles & Gootman, 2002; Lerner, Fisher, & Weinberg, 2000; Lerner et al., 2005; Roth & Brooks-Gunn, 2003). These Cs have been found to be the outcomes of *functionally and developmentally appropriate (adaptive) interactions between the young person and his or her social ecology*; these attributes appear to be inversely related to indicators of both internalizing and externalizing risk/problem behaviors (Jelicic, Bobek, Phelps, Lerner, & Lerner, 2007; Lewin-Bizan et al., 2010; Phelps et al., 2007; Zimmerman, Phelps, & Lerner, 2008). Overall, we predict that adolescents with high PYD scores will show the normative age-related decrease in cortical thickness; this relation will not be the case of adolescents with low PYD.

PARTICIPANTS AND METHODS

All participants were white Caucasians recruited from a French Canadian population living in the Saguenay Lac Saint-Jean (SLSJ) region of Quebec, Canada. Details of the recruitment and testing procedures are provided in Pausova et al., 2007.

Briefly (adolescents 12 to 18 years of age) were recruited in high schools in the SLSJ region. The recruitment began with the team visiting all classrooms in a given school and presenting the study to the students. At the same time, letters containing an information brochure, a letter from the principal, and a consent form for a telephone interview were sent to the parents. Subsequently, a research nurse conducted a structured telephone interview with interested families (most commonly with the child's mother) to verify their eligibility. Additional information was acquired using a medical questionnaire filled out by the child's biological parent.

The main exclusion criteria were (1) positive history of alcohol abuse during pregnancy; (2) positive medical history for meningitis, malignancy, and heart disease requiring heart surgery; (3) severe mental illness (e.g., autism, schizophrenia) or mental retardation (IQ < 70); and (4) MRI contraindications. The Research Ethics Committee of the Chicoutimi Hospital approved the study protocol.

Assessment of Positive Youth Development

Positive youth development (PYD) was assessed with a questionnaire based on the Five Cs model: Competence, Confidence, Character, social Connection, and Caring or compassion (Lerner et al., 2005). The questionnaire contains more than 300 questions that are answered by the adolescent. To calculate the score for each of the five scales (i.e., the Five Cs), all individual items were first rescaled on a 0-to-12-point scale. Overall, the scoring is such that a high score indicates more positive behavior on each of the 5 Cs scales. The average of the five scales represents the PYD score.

Magnetic Resonance Imaging

MRI data were collected on a Phillips 1.0-T superconducting magnet. High-resolution anatomical T1-weighted (T1W) images were acquired using the following parameters: three-dimensional (3D) RF-spoiled gradient echo scan with 140–160 sagittal slices, 1-mm isotropic resolution, TR = 25 ms, TE = 5 ms, flip angle = 30°. We measured cortical thickness using FreeSurfer, a set of automated tools for reconstruction of the brain cortical surface (Fischl & Dale, 2000). For every participant, FreeSurfer segments the cerebral cortex, the white matter, and other subcortical structures, and then computes triangular meshes that recover the geometry and the topology of the pial surface and the gray/white interface of the left and right hemispheres. The local cortical thickness is measured based on the difference between the position of equivalent vertices in the pial and gray/white surfaces. A correspondence between the cortical surfaces across the participants is established using a nonlinear alignment of the principal sulci in each participant's brain with an average brain (Fischl, Sereno, Tootell, & Dale, 1999).

Statistical Analysis

The main hypothesis tested here is that the relationship between cortical thickness and age will differ between adolescents with low (below median) and high (above median) PYD. This hypothesis was evaluated separately in male and female adolescents by testing significance of age (in months) by PYD (low vs. high) interaction using analysis of variance.

Table 4.1 Demographics

	Males		Females	
	Low PYD	High PYD	Low PYD	High PYD
Number of adolescents	75	74	83	82
Age (months)	182 ± 22	184 ± 23	181 ± 23	184 ± 25
PYD	6.6 ± 0.9	9.2 ± 0.9	7.7 ± 0.8	9.7 ± 0.7
Confidence	7.9 ± 1.9	9.9 ± 1.5	6.8 ± 1.9	9.7 ± 1.6
Competence	7.4 ± 1.3	9.1 ± 1.1	7.8 ± 1.2	9.5 ± 1.3
Character	5.9 ± 1.4	8.5 ± 1.5	7.8 ± 1.4	9.5 ± 1.2
Connection	6.7 ± 1.5	8.7 ± 1.1	7.5 ± 1.2	9.1 ± 0.9
Caring	5.4 ± 2.7	9.7 ± 2.2	8.5 ± 2.4	10.5 ± 1.7
Puberty (Tanner) stage	3.5 ± 0.8	3.6 ± 0.9	4.1 ± 0.8	4.2 ± 0.7
Household income (CAD)	52266 ± 26333	61369 ± 20228	50375 ± 25579	57037 ± 25221
Full scale IQ	101.3 ± 13.2	107.9 ± 12.1	102.9 ± 13	105.9 ± 11

PYD, Positive Youth Development; CAD, Canadian Dollars; IQ, intelligence quotient.
Low and High PYD adolescents are those with PYD values below and above sex-specific median, respectively (Males: 7.74; Females: 8.65).
Reported values are Means ± Standard Deviations.

Cortical thickness was assessed for each of the four lobes: frontal, parietal, temporal, and occipital. Using FreeSurfer-based parcellation, these regions were determined automatically in each participant based on the nonlinear transformation of the participant's surface reconstructions into an average cortical surface.

RESULTS

Table 4.1 describes the sample of 314 adolescents included in this report. Median values of PYD in male and female adolescents were, respectively, 7.74 and 8.65. Note that the low (below sex-specific median) and high (above sex-specific median) PYD subgroups do not differ in their age and puberty stage in either the male or female groups. But, male adolescents with low and high PYD differ in their Full-scale IQ ($F_{1,147} = 9.9$, $p = .002$) and Household Income ($F_{1,147} = 5.5$, $p = .02$). This difference is not found for female adolescents (IQ: $F_{1,162} = 2.6$, $p = .1$; Household Income: $F_{1,160} = 2.8$, $p = .1$).

As expected, cortical thickness decreases with age in both male and female adolescents in all lobes (Table 4.2). A significant interaction between Age (in months) and Sex was observed only in the case of the frontal cortex, with

Table 4.2 **Main Effects of Age (in months), Sex and Age × Sex Interaction on Cortical Thickness in the Frontal, Parietal, Temporal and Occipital Lobes**

	Age	Sex	Age × Sex
Frontal cortex	$-7.9(< .0001)$[1]	$3.3(.001)$[2]	$2.0(.05)$
Parietal cortex	$-8.7(< .0001)$	$1.7(.09)$	$1.0(.3)$
Temporal cortex	$-4.2(< .0001)$	$1.4(.2)$	$1.2(.25)$
Occipital cortex	$-5.1(< .0001)$	$-2.6(.009)$[3]	$0.5(.6)$

[1] t ratio (p value).
[2] Females > Male.
[3] Males > Females.

male adolescents showing a steeper decrease in cortical thickness than female adolescents.

Trajectories in cortical thickness do not differ between the low and high PYD subgroups of female adolescents (Figure 4.1), whereas male adolescents with low PYD do not show the expected decrease in cortical thickness in the case of the temporal cortex (Figure 4.2); this finding contrasts with age-related cortical thinning shown by male adolescents with high PYD (Age × PYD interaction: t ratio $= -2.1, p = .03$).

Given the significant interactive effect of Age and PYD on the thickness of the temporal cortex in male adolescents, we decided to examine the contribution of the individual PYD components, namely Confidence, Competence, Character, Connection, and Caring. As seen in Figure 4.3, the low and high PYD subgroups of male adolescents show a similar pattern of differences in cortical-thickness trajectories across all five Cs, but only Confidence interacts significantly ($p = .0001$) with Age, reflecting an absence of age-related changes in cortical thickness in the low Confidence subgroup and a steep decrease in thickness in the high Confidence subgroup.

To test possible confounding effects of IQ on these findings obtained in male adolescents, we reanalyzed these data while including full-scale IQ (FIQ) in the respective statistical models. In the case of PYD, including IQ in the model reduced the significance of the Age × PYD interaction from $p = .03$ to $p = .055$. In the case of Confidence, including IQ in the model did not change the high significance ($p = .0001$) of the Age × Confidence interaction.

DISCUSSION

Positive youth development has been conceptualized as an outcome of *functionally and developmentally appropriate (adaptive) interactions between the young person and his or her social ecology* (Lerner et al., 2005). In this study we found that cortical maturation during adolescence differs in individuals with high and low

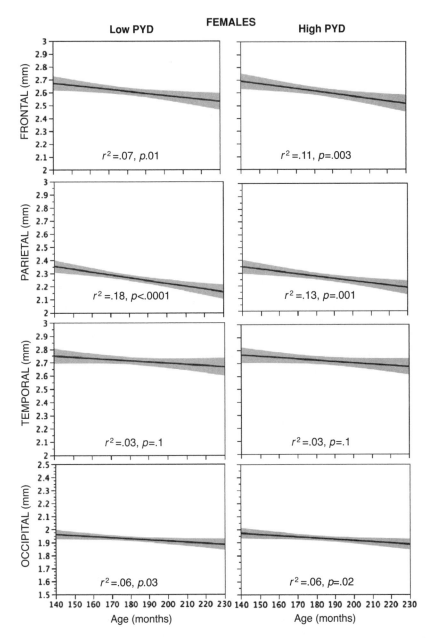

Figure 4.1   Age-related changes in cortical thickness of the frontal, parietal, temporal, and occipital lobes in female adolescents with low (*left*) and high (*right*) PYD. PYD, Positive Youth Development; Low and High PYD adolescents are those with PYD values below and above 8.65, respectively. Age × PYD interaction was not significant in any of the four lobes; Frontal: *t* ratio = 0.4, *p* = .7; Parietal: *t* ratio = .5, *p* = .6; Temporal: *t* ratio = −.1, *p* = .9; and Occipital: *t* ratio = −.2, *p* = .9. Note different Y scale for Occipital lobe.

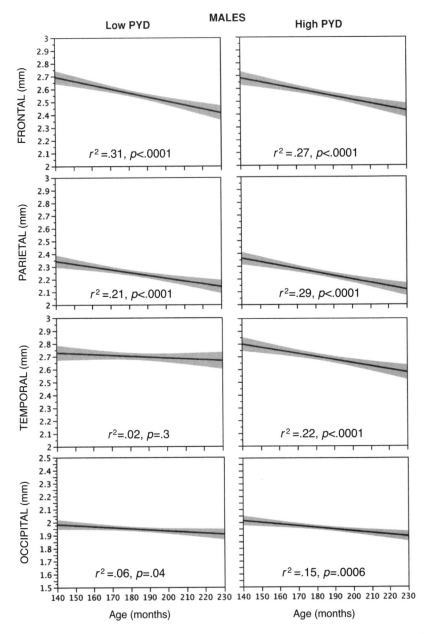

Figure 4.2   Age-related changes in cortical thickness of the frontal, parietal, temporal, and occipital lobes in male adolescents with low (*left*) and high (*right*) PYD. PYD, Positive Youth Development; Low and High PYD adolescents are those with PYD values below and above 7.74, respectively. Age × PYD interaction was significant in the temporal lobe; Frontal: t ratio $= 0.4$, $p = .7$; Parietal: t ratio $= -.7$, $p = .5$; Temporal: t ratio $= -2.1$, $p = .03$; and Occipital: t ratio $= -.9$, $p = .3$. Note different Y scale for Occipital lobe.

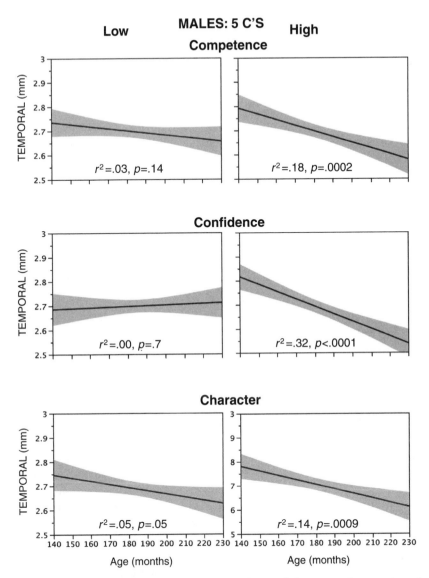

Figure 4.3   Age-related changes in cortical thickness of the temporal cortex in male adolescents with low (*left*) and high (*right*) Competence, Confidence, Character, Connection, and Caring. Low and High adolescents are those with values below and above median in a given "C" (Competence: 8.3; Confidence: 9.08; Character: 7.43; Connection: 7.86; and Caring: 7.2). Age x "C" interaction was significant for Confidence only; Competence: t ratio $= -1.8$, $p = .08$; Confidence: t ratio $= -13.97$, $p = .0001$; Character: t ratio $= -.7$, $p = .5$; Connection: t ratio $= -1.37$, $p = .2$; and Caring: t ratio $= -1.6$, $p = .1$.

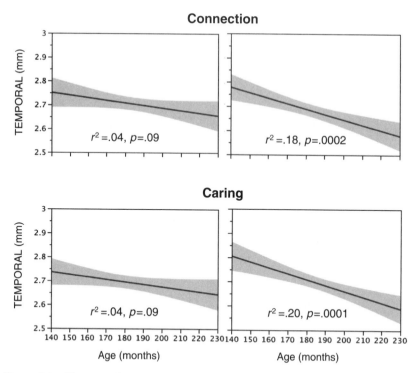

Figure 4.3   (*Continued*)

PYD, respectively. In male adolescents, the expected pattern of cortical maturation, namely age-related decreases in cortical thickness, is observed only in individuals with high—but not low—PYD and, especially, with high—but not low—Confidence. In both cases, this finding is true only for the temporal cortex. In female adolescents, we saw no such differences between individuals with low and high PYD (or any of the Five Cs) in any of the lobes. In the following discussion, we will focus on possible neurobiological and psychological interpretations of these findings.

Let us begin by briefly discussing current views on neurobiological processes that might underlie age-related changes in cortical thickness, as measured with MRI, during childhood and adolescence. The most common concept invoked in explaining changes in the volume of cortical GM or cortical thickness is that of synaptic pruning (e.g., Giedd et al., 1999; Sowell, Thompson, Tessner, & Toga, 2001). There is no evidence to support this view, however.

As reviewed in detail elsewhere (Paus et al., 2008, 2010), several cellular compartments other than synapses are possible candidates for mediating age-related changes in cortical thickness. For example, given the large amount of neuropil consisting of dendritic and axonal processes (60% of the mouse cortex; Braitenberg & Schüz, 1998), it is possible that age-related variations in dendritic arborization affect cortical thickness. In turn, it may be that myelination of intracortical axons and/or white matter at the gray-white boundary of the cerebral cortex influence MR signal in a manner resulting in an *apparent* cortical thinning. Furthermore, a recent *postmortem* study (albeit with small sample size) of 12- to 24-year-old individuals suggests that there are age-related differences in the size of nerve-cell bodies in different cortical layers, with no differences in cortical thickness (Rabinowicz, Petetot, Khoury, & de Courten-Myers, 2009).

Overall, neurobiological underpinnings of age-related decreases in cortical GM volume and (apparent) cortical thickness during adolescence are unknown. Nonetheless, it is clear that whatever cellular processes underlie these maturational changes observed in many previous studies and in this report, these processes do not occur to the same extent in the temporal cortex of male adolescents with low PYD. We will come back to the issue of (possible) regional specificity after considering some psychological differences between individuals with low and high PYD.

As pointed out in the introductory section of this chapter, PYD attempts to index the degree of adaptive, or healthy, interactions of young people with their social environment. In the five domains (i.e., Five Cs), adolescents indicate their self-perception of academic, social, and physical competence (Competence), relationships with parents and friends (Connection), their own behavior and conduct as well as their sense of positive values (Character), their self-worth and confidence in physical posture and appearance and control over their lives (Confidence), and the degree to which they feel sorry for the distress of others (Caring). In addition to measuring the Five Cs, the assessment of youth used in this study includes indices of the social environment of the adolescent. This context is assessed at several levels, including family (e.g., parental warmth, involvement), school (e.g., level of care and encouragement provided by the school), and community (e.g., quality of neighborhood and presence of adult role models).

Overall, the broad spectrum of the PYD measures provides a holistic view of adolescents and their social environment without attempting to distinguish between causes and consequences of the interindividual differences in the level of thriving. Our findings suggest that male adolescents with a relatively low level of thriving lack the expected maturational pattern of age-related thinning of the temporal cortex. Who are those individuals? First, it has been previously established that PYD scores are inversely related to scores for depression indexed by the Center for Epidemiological Studies Depression (CES-D) measure (Radloff, 1977), both within a given grade level (e.g., 5th grade; Lerner et al., 2005) and across grades (from 5th grade to 6th grade; Jelicic et al., 2007; Lewin-Bizan et al., 2010; Phelps et al., 2007; Zimmerman, Phelps, & Lerner, 2008). Similarly, in these same reports, scores for PYD are inversely related to indices of smoking, bullying, and drug use (Jelicic et al., 2007; Lerner et al., 2005; Lewin-Bizan et al., 2010; Phelps et al., 2007; Zimmerman, Phelps, & Lerner, 2008). In our sample, we have also found higher levels of psychopathology, as assessed with DISC

Predictive Scales (Lucas et al., 2001), in low versus high PYD adolescents. Furthermore, we have examined the possible relationship between PYD and personality, as assessed with the NEO-PI-R scale (Costa & McCrae, 1992), and observed that low versus high PYD adolescents scored higher on Neuroticism and lower on Extroversion, Openness, Agreeableness, and Conscientiousness. Thus, it appears that (male and female) adolescents with low PYD display less adaptive personality characteristics and present with more psychopathology, as compared with adolescents with high PYD.

Taken together, *male* adolescents with low versus high PYD have a slightly lower IQ (by six IQ points), more psychopathology, less adaptive personality characteristics, and, most importantly, they lack the normative age-related decrease in cortical thickness in the temporal lobe. It might be that, in male adolescents, such a six-point IQ advantage translates to better social skills and social intelligence needed to enhance PYD. This cross-sectional study does not allow us to determine, however, the directionality of the observed structure-function relationship: is the maladaptive behavior a consequence of an abnormal trajectory in brain development or *vice versa*?

We will be exploring this question in an ongoing longitudinal study in which the same measures are being collected. In this study, we may also be able to address possible reasons of the relative regional specificity of our findings, namely the involvement of the temporal cortex. Given the importance of the temporal cortex in processing of visual information, including information about human faces and bodies (Aleong & Puce, 2009; Allison, Puce, & McCarthy, 2000), we will be examining brain activity measured with functional MRI during observation of faces and bodies (Grosbras & Paus, 2006; Grosbras et al., 2007). At this point, we can only speculate that the structural findings reported here may indicate a relatively impoverished social environment, which is mostly visual in nature, that may drive normal maturation of the temporal cortex during adolescence.

Finally, the clear difference in the findings obtained here in male and female adolescents suggests sex-specific mechanisms mediating the relationship between PYD and cortical maturation. First, age-related changes in cortical thickness in female adolescents seem to be less pronounced than those in male adolescents across the brain; note, however, that Age × Sex interaction is significant only in frontal cortex. Second, in neither high nor low PYD female adolescents did the thickness of the temporal cortex differ with age. Third, unlike males, female adolescents with low and high PYD do not differ in their IQ. In both male and female adolescents, however, low and high PYD subgroups differ in the rate of psychopathology and personality, despite showing different patterns of cortical maturation (in the temporal lobe). Thus, the relationship between PYD, psychopathology and personality, and cortical maturation is likely to be distinct in the two sexes.

Future studies should carefully consider possible sex differences in the role of various environmental factors in shaping brain and behavior during adolescence.

Ideally, longitudinal research should be conducted to study the potentially differential links between brain and behavior for adolescent boys versus adolescent girls.

REFERENCES

Aleong, R., & Paus, T. (2010). Neural correlates of human body perception. *Journal of Cognitive Neuroscience, 22*(3), 482–495.

Allison, T., Puce, A., & McCarthy, G. (2000). Social perception from visual cues: Role of the STS region. *Trends in Cognitive Sciences, 4,* 267–278.

Bouchard, T. J., Jr. (1998). Genetic and environmental influences on adult intelligence and special mental abilities. *Human Biology, 70,* 257–279.

Braitenberg, V., & Schüz, A. (1998). *Cortex: Statistics and geometry of neuronal connectivity.* Berlin, Germany: Springer Verlag.

Costa, P. T., Jr., & McCrae, R. R. (1992). *Revised NEO Personality Inventory (NEO-PI-R) and NEO Five-Factor Inventory (NEO-FFI) professional manual.* Odessa, FL: Psychological Assessment Resources.

De Bellis, M. D., Kreshavan, M. S., Beers, S. R., Hall, J., Frustaci, K., Masalehdan, A., . . . & Boring, A. M. (2001). Sex differences in brain maturation during childhood and adolescence. *Cerebral Cortex, 11,* 552–557.

Draganski, B., Gaser, C., Busch, V., Schuierer, G., Bogdahn, U., & May, A. (2004). Neuroplasticity: Changes in grey matter induced by training. *Nature, 427,* 311–312.

Draganski, B., Gaser, C., Kempermann, G., Kuhn, H. G., Winkler, J., Büchel, C., & May, A. (2006). Temporal and spatial dynamics of brain structure changes during extensive learning. *Journal of Neuroscience, 26,* 6314–6317.

Driemeyer, J., Boyke, J., Gaser, C., Büchel, C., & May, A. (2008). Changes in gray matter induced by learning—revisited. *PLoS One, 3,* e2669.

Durston, S., Hulshoff Pol, H. E., Casey, B. J., Giedd, J. N., Buitelaar, J. K., & van Engeland, H. (2001). Anatomical MRI of the developing human brain: What have we learned? *Journal of the American Academy of Child and Adolescent Psychiatry, 40,* 1012–1020.

Eccles, J., & Gootman, J. A. (Eds). (2002). *Community programs to promote youth development.* Washington, DC: National Academy Press.

Fischl, B., & Dale, A. M. (2000). Measuring the thickness of the human cerebral cortex from magnetic resonance images. *Proceedings of the National Academy of Sciences of the United States of America, 97,* 11050–11055.

Fischl, B., Sereno, M. I., Tootell, R. B., & Dale, A. M. (1999). High-resolution intersubject averaging and a coordinate system for the cortical surface. *Human Brain Mapping, 8,* 272–284.

Giedd, J. N., Blumenthal, J., Jeffries, N. O., Castellanos, F. X., Liu, H., Zijdenbos, A., . . . & Rapoport, J. L. (1999). Brain development during childhood and adolescence: A longitudinal MRI study. *Nature Neuroscience, 2,* 861–863.

Giedd, J. N., Lalonde, F. M., Celano, M. J., White, S. L., Wallace, G. L., Lee, N. R., & Lenroot, R. K. (2009). Anatomical brain magnetic resonance imaging of typically developing children and adolescents. *Journal of the American Academy of Child and Adolescent Psychiatry, 48*, 465–470.

Grosbras, M. H., & Paus, T. (2006). Brain networks involved in viewing angry hands or faces. *Cerebral Cortex, 16*, 1087–1096.

Grosbras, M. H., Osswald, K., Jansen, M., Toro, R., McIntosh, A. R., Steinberg, L., . . . & Paus, T. (2007). Neural mechanisms of resistance to peer influence in early adolescence. *Journal of Neuroscience, 27*, 8040–8045.

Ilg, R., Wohlschläger, A. M., Gaser, C., Liebau, Y., Dauner, R., Wöller, A., . . . & Mühlau, M. (2008). Gray matter increase induced by practice correlates with task-specific activation: A combined functional and morphometric magnetic resonance imaging study. *Journal of Neuroscience, 28*, 4210–4215.

Jelicic, H., Bobek, D., Phelps, E., Lerner, J. V., & Lerner, R. M. (2007). Using positive youth development to predict contribution and risk behaviors in early adolescence: Findings from the first two waves of the 4-H Study of Positive Youth Development. *International Journal of Behavioral Development, 31*(3), 263–273.

Lebel, C., Walker, L., Leemans, A., Phillips, L., & Beaulieu, C. (2008). Microstructural maturation of the human brain from childhood to adulthood. *Neuroimage, 40*, 1044–1055.

Lenroot, R. K., Gogtay, N., Greenstein, D. K., Wells, E. M., Wallace, G. L., Clasen, L. S., . . . & Giedd, J. N. (2007). Sexual dimorphism of brain developmental trajectories during childhood and adolescence. *Neuroimage, 36*, 1065–1073.

Lenroot, R. K., Schmitt, J. E., Ordaz, S. J., Wallace, G. L., Neale, M. C., Lerch, J. P., . . . & Giedd, J. N. (2009). Differences in genetic and environmental influences on the human cerebral cortex associated with development during childhood and adolescence. *Human Brain Mapping, 30*, 163–174.

Lerner, R. M., Fisher, C. B., & Weinberg, R. A. (2000). Toward a science for and of the people: Promoting civil society through the application of developmental science. *Child Development, 71*, 11–20.

Lerner, R. M., Lerner, J. V., Almerigi, J., Theokas, C., Phelps, E., Gestsdottir, S., . . . & von Eye, A. (2005). Positive youth development, participation in community youth development programs, and community contributions of fifth-grade adolescents: Findings from the first wave of the 4-H Study of Positive Youth Development. *Journal of Early Adolescence, 25*, 17–71.

Lewin-Bizan, S., Lynch, A. D., Fay, K., Schmid, K., McPherran, C., Lerner, J. V., & Lerner, R. M. (2010). Trajectories of positive and negative behaviors from early- to middle-adolescence. *Journal of Youth and Adolescence, 39*(7), 751–763.

Lucas, C. P., Zhang, H., Fisher, P. W., Shaffer, D., Regier, D. A., Narrow, W. E., . . . & Friman, P. (2001). The DISC Predictive Scales (DPS): Efficiently screening for diagnoses. *Journal of the American Academy of Child and Adolescent Psychiatry, 40*, 443–449.

Luders, E., Toga, A. W., Lepore, N., & Gaser, C. (2009). The underlying anatomical correlates of long-term meditation: Larger hippocampal and frontal volumes of gray matter. *Neuroimage*, *45*, 672–678.

Maguire, E. A., Woollett, K., & Spiers, H. J. (2006). London taxi drivers and bus drivers: A structural MRI and neuropsychological analysis. *Hippocampus*, *16*, 1091–1101.

O'Donnell, S., Noseworthy, M. D., Levine, B., & Dennis, M. (2005). Cortical thickness of the frontopolar area in typically developing children and adolescents. *Neuroimage*, *24*, 948–954.

Paus T. (2005). Mapping brain maturation and cognitive development during adolescence. *Trends in Cognitive Science*, *9*, 60–68.

Paus, T. (2009). Brain development. In R. M. Lerner & L. Steinberg (Eds.), *Handbook of adolescent psychology* (3rd ed., pp. 95–115). Hoboken, NJ: Wiley.

Paus, T. (2010). Growth of white matter in the adolescent brain: Myelin or axon? *Brain Cognition*, *72*, 26–35.

Paus, T., Collins, D. L., Evans, A. C., Leonard, G., Pike, B., & Zijdenbos, A. (2001). Maturation of white matter in the human brain: A review of magnetic-resonance studies. *Brain Research Bulletin*, *54*, 255–266.

Paus, T., Keshavan, M., & Giedd, J. N. (2008). Why do many psychiatric disorders emerge during adolescence? *Nature Reviews Neuroscience*, *9*, 947–957.

Paus, T., Nawaz-Khan, I., Leonard, G., Perron, M., Pike, G. B., Pitiot, A., ... & Pausova, Z. (2010). Sexual dimorphism in the adolescent brain: Role of testosterone and androgen receptor in global and local volumes of grey and white matter. *Hormones and Behavior*, *57*(1), 63–75.

Paus, T. & Toro, R. (2009). Could sex differences in white matter be explained by g ratio? *Frontiers in Neuroanatomy*, doi:10.3389/neuro.05.014.2009.

Pausova, Z., Paus, T., Abrahamowicz, M., Almerigi, J., Arbour, N., Bernard, M., ... & Watkins, K. (2007). Genes, maternal smoking, and the offspring brain and body during adolescence: Design of the Saguenay Youth Study. *Human Brain Mapping*, *28*, 502–518.

Perrin, J. S., Herve, P. Y., Leonard, G., Perron, M., Pike, G. B., Pitiot, A., ... & Paus, T. (2008). Growth of white matter in the adolescent brain: Role of testosterone and androgen receptor. *Journal of Neuroscience*, *28*, 9519–9524.

Phelps, E., Balsano, A., Fay, K., Peltz, J., Zimmerman, S., Lerner, R. M., & Lerner, J. V. (2007). Nuances in early adolescent development trajectories of positive and problematic/risk behaviors: Findings from the 4-H Study of Positive Youth Development. *Child and Adolescent Psychiatric Clinics of North America*, *16*(2), 473–496.

Rabinowicz, T., Petetot, J. M., Khoury, J. C., & de Courten-Myers, G. M. (2009) Neocortical maturation during adolescence: Change in neuronal soma dimension. *Brain Cognition*, *69*, 328–336.

Radloff, L. S. (1977). The CES-D scale: A self-report depression scale for research in general population. *Applied Psychological Measurement*, *1*, 385–401.

Roth, J. L., & Brooks-Gunn, J. (2003). What exactly is a youth development program? Answers from research and practice. *Applied Developmental Science, 7*, 94–111.

Schlaug, G. (2001). The brain of musicians. A model for functional and structural adaptation. *Annals of the New York Academy of Science, 930*, 281–299.

Schmithorst, V. J., Holland, S. K., & Dardzinski, B. J. (2008). Developmental differences in white matter architecture between boys and girls. *Human Brain Mapping, 29*, 696–710.

Shaw, P., Greenstein, D. K., Lerch, J. P., Clasen, L. S., Lenroot, R. K., Gogtay, N., . . . & Giedd, J. (2006). Intellectual ability and cortical development in children and adolescents. *Nature, 440*, 676–679.

Sluming, V., Barrick, T., Howard, M., Cezayirli, E., Mayes, A., & Roberts, N. (2002). Voxel-based morphometry reveals increased gray matter density in Broca's area in male symphony orchestra musicians. *Neuroimage, 17*, 1613–1622.

Sowell, E. R., Thompson, P. M., Tessner, K. D., & Toga, A. W. (2001). Mapping continued brain growth and gray matter density reduction in dorsal frontal cortex: Inverse relationships during postadolescent brain maturation. *Journal of Neuroscience, 21*, 8819–8829.

Sowell, E. R., Peterson, B. S., Kan, E., Woods, R. P., Yoshii, J., Bansal, R., . . . & Toga, A. W. (2007). Sex differences in cortical thickness mapped in 176 healthy individuals between 7 and 87 years of age. *Cerebral Cortex, 17*, 1550–1560.

Stewart, L. (2008). Do musicians have different brains? *Clinical Medicine, 8*, 304–308.

Zimmerman, S., Phelps, E., & Lerner, R. M. (2008). Positive and negative developmental trajectories in U.S. adolescents: Where the PYD perspective meets the deficit model. *Research in Human Development, 5*(3), 153–165.

5

Neural Correlates of Positive Youth Development

Sara W. Lazar

The volume of human brain research has exploded in the past 10 years, thanks in large part to the advent of magnetic resonance imaging (MRI) as an experimental tool. Investigators have used this tool to study a myriad of questions, from basic neurobiological questions such as how vision works to more abstract neural constructs such as how the brain differentially responds to beautiful versus visually awkward images (Di Dio, Macaluso, & Rizzolatti, 2007). In the last few years, social scientists have also started to embrace this technology to address more esoteric human qualities such as empathy (Cacioppo, Norris, Decety, Monteleone, & Nusbaum, 2009), moral reasoning (Greene & Paxton, 2009), and unconditional love (Beauregard, Courtemanche, Paquette, & St-Pierre, 2009).

Our laboratory and others now use this powerful tool to explore the neural correlates of various spiritual practices, including Buddhist meditation (Brefczynski-Lewis, Lutz, Schaefer, Levinson, & Davidson, 2007; Hölzel et al., 2007, 2008, 2010, 2011; Lazar et al., 2000, 2005; Luders, Toga, Lepore, & Gaser, 2009; Pagnoni, Cekic, & Guo, 2008; Vestergaard-Poulsen et al., 2009) and Christian prayer (Schjoedt, Stodkilde-Jorgensen, Geertz, & Roepstorff, 2008, 2009). We have recently begun to use this tool to study the neural correlates of positive youth development (PYD). Our long-term goal is to understand how brain structure and function is related to PYD. Such information will help us understand how different aspects of PYD are related to one another, and also how environmental and behavioral factors influence the development of PYD. We are particularly interested in understanding how behavior modification programs may influence PYD at the neurological level. Specifically, we are interested in determining whether undertaking a new spiritual practice, or becoming more engaged in an existing practice, can lead to changes in brain structure and function associated with PYD. Before presenting the results from our pilot study of the neural correlates of PYD, we will first discuss what is currently known about the development of the adolescent brain.

PLASTICITY AND THE ADOLESCENT BRAIN

Although we are born with most of the neurons (i.e., gray matter) we will ever have, the brain continues to develop in numerous ways throughout our lives. Development of the brain is complex, with multiple factors influencing the shape and composition of neural tissue. Most of the growth occurs during the period from birth through our mid-twenties (Giedd et al., 1999; Lenroot et al., 2009; O'Donnell, Noseworthy, Levine, & Dennis, 2005; Shaw et al., 2006). Perhaps the most dramatic change in brain structure is the growth of white matter, which comprises various types of helper cells that surround the neurons and influence their activity (Dong & Greenough, 2004). Development of white matter proceeds in stages through different brain regions, and as the brain matures, so does our behavior. For instance, late adolescence is typically when the frontal cortex—the part of the brain responsible for reasoning, decision making, and abstract conceptualization—undergoes the most development and reshaping (Lenroot et al., 2009).

Not coincidentally, this is also a time of great spiritual growth, self-realization, and development of personal assets such as the Five Cs that define positive youth development: Competence, Confidence, Connection, Character, and Caring (Lerner, Fisher, & Weinberg, 2000). Although we now know that the frontal cortex plays an important role in the instantiation of these higher-order faculties, it is largely unknown where within this vast territory these functions lay, what other brain regions might be involved, or how the brain regions interact. We and others are engaged in ongoing research to address these questions.

The rate and timing of these large-scale normal developmental changes in brain structure can be influenced by nonspecific factors such as gender and genetics (Lenroot et al., 2009; Paus, 2009; Wilke, Krageloh-Mann, & Holland, 2007). Neuroimaging techniques such as MRI have enhanced our knowledge of how these factors influence neural development and also how the development of the brain influences cognition and behavior. For instance, several studies that followed large cohorts of subjects demonstrated that the average thickness of the entire cortical mantle is related to various cognitive measures such as IQ (Shaw et al., 2006), and recently Paus and colleagues (2011) have demonstrated positive correlations between large-scale changes in cortical structure and measures of positive youth development.

In addition to these developmental changes in neural structure that are pre-programmed to occur over large areas of the brain in all individuals, numerous changes are also occurring throughout the brain within small, discrete loci. These smaller-scale changes can be caused by specific individual differences related to personal experiences, genetics, or learning new information or skills (Draganski et al., 2004; Drevets, Price, & Furey, 2008; Hulshoff Pol et al., 2006). In MRI images these changes appear as increased gray matter volume or density (Draganski et al., 2004; Ilg et al., 2008) and may be caused by the formation of new synapses (the connections between neurons), although other cellular mechanisms are also possible (Black, Zelazny, & Greenough, 1991; Dong & Greenough, 2004). A growing body of literature suggests that these small differences in brain structure may underlie individual differences in personality traits (Omura, Todd Constable, & Canli, 2005), as well as differences in behavioral characteristics including empathy (Rankin et al., 2006; Sterzer, Stadler, Poustka, & Kleinschmidt, 2007), impulsivity (Matsuo et al., 2009), emotional susceptibility (Iaria et al., 2008), experience seeking (Martin et al., 2007), conduct disorder (De Brito et al., 2009; Huebner et al., 2008), and violence (Tiihonen et al., 2008). These data provide important clues about the neural bases of behavior and suggest that much of our behavior can be explained by the hard-wiring of our brains.

This is not to say, however, that our behavior is completely predetermined or immalleable. The human nervous system has the capacity for plasticity, and the structure of the brain can change in response to training (Draganski et al., 2004; Gage, 2002). For instance, several studies have demonstrated growth of brain gray matter after learning abstract information (Draganski et al., 2006), motor skills (Draganski et al., 2004), and specific cognitive skills (Ilg et al., 2008). Recently we have demonstrated changes in the amygdala related to changes in perceived stress (Hölzel et al., 2009), suggesting that brain regions related to affect are also malleable. These studies also indicate that training-induced plasticity of the brain is possible within a relatively short period, generally a few weeks to a few months. Finally, the data suggest that regular practice of any behavior can lead to changes in brain structure that will help transform these behaviors into habits or character traits. This suggestion has led to our exploration of the impact of spiritual practices on brain structure. We wish to understand how regularly engaging in spiritual practices alters the wiring and shape of our brains, and in turn, how this altered wiring influences daily behavior. In the next section we describe our findings on how practice of meditation alters the brain, and then we conclude with our studies of brain structure differences associated with PYD.

SPIRITUAL PRACTICES AND BRAIN STRUCTURE

Our laboratory has used MRI to assess how Buddhist meditation practice can influence both the function and structure of the brain (Hölzel et al., 2010, 2011; Lazar et al., 2000, 2005). Our initial cross-sectional study, which compared highly experienced meditation practitioners to demographically matched controls, identified specific brain regions that were larger in the meditators relative to the controls (Lazar et al., 2005). The most prominent difference was significantly more gray matter in the right anterior insula of the meditators compared to the controls. The insula is well-known to be involved in visceral awareness (Critchley, Wiens, Rotshtein, Ohman, & Dolan, 2004) as well as in empathic responses (Singer et al., 2004). More generally, a recent review points to the fundamental role of the insula in human awareness and consciousness (Craig, 2009). Three other laboratories have since performed similar analyses, replicating and extending our findings (Hölzel et al., 2008; Luders et al., 2009; Vestergaard-Poulsen et al., 2009). Our other significant finding was a region of the lateral prefrontal cortex (PFC). The PFC is well known to downregulate the amygdala, which is important for responding to emotionally salient stimuli, particularly those that induce fear and anger (Banks, Eddy, Angstadt, Nathan, & Phan, 2007; Coccaro, McCloskey, Fitzgerald, & Phan, 2007; Monk et al., 2008).

Recently, we finished a longitudinal study with meditation-naïve individuals that documented changes in specific regions of gray matter just eight weeks after these participants began to practice meditation (Hölzel et al., 2010, 2011). Although gray matter density increased within the right anterior insula (Figure 5.1a), it was not statistically significant compared to the wait-list control group. However, significant between-group changes did occur in several other brain regions including the temporal parietal junction. (TPJ; Figure 5.1b), which is important for perspective taking and empathy (Akitsuki & Decety, 2009; Cacioppo et al., 2009; Jackson, Brunet, Meltzoff, & Decety, 2006; Saxe, Moran, Scholz, & Gabrieli, 2006; Saxe, Whitfield-Gabrieli, Scholz, & Pelphrey, 2009), and the posterior cingulate, which is important for assessing the relevance of a stimulus for oneself (Gusnard, Akbudak, Shulman, & Raichle, 2001; Schmitz & Johnson, 2007) and for the integration of self-referential stimuli in the emotional and autobiographical context of one's own person (Northoff & Bermpohl, 2004).

We also identified a region of the brainstem that produces several neurotransmitters, including those involved in mood and homeostatic regulation (Lowry, Lightman, & Nutt, 2009). The change in the gray matter of the brainstem was positively correlated with measures of personal growth, self-acceptance, and purpose in life. Finally, the amygdala—best known for its central role in mediating fear responses—appeared to become smaller in many participants, and the change in size was correlated with a reduction in perceived stress. Together, our data indicate that regularly engaging in spiritual activities such as meditation can lead to detectable changes in gray matter in brain regions that subserve functions known to be impacted by spiritual practices. Demonstrating gray matter increases in regions associated with empathy, self-awareness, and mood, the data presented here suggest a plausible neural mechanism underlying these changes—namely, that such increases represent enduring changes in brain structure that could support improved mental functioning, even when individuals are not actively practicing meditation techniques.

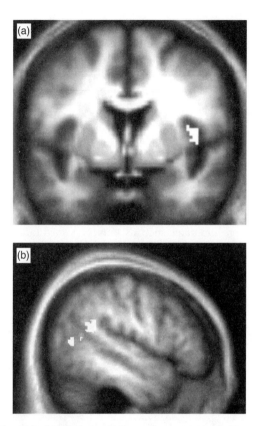

Figure 5.1   Bright white highlighting indicates brain regions of increased gray matter density following an eight-week meditation-based stress reduction intervention. (a) Right anterior insula. (b) Temporal-parietal junction.

NEURAL CORRELATES OF PYD

Our data with meditation raises many questions: Do the changes in brain structure actually lead to changes in behavior? Do other contemplative practices yield similar results? Do individuals with a natural predisposition to contribute to society have brain structure similar to those who have become this way after practicing meditation? Does undertaking a new spiritual practice, or becoming more engaged in an existing practice, lead to changes in brain structure associated with PYD? As a first step to address these questions, we performed a small pilot study in collaboration with Heather Urry of Tufts University. This research was part of the John Templeton Foundation (JTF)–supported study, "The Role of Spiritual Development in Growth of Purpose, Generosity, and Psychological Health in Adolescence" (Richard M. Lerner, Principal Investigator). We recruited 30 college-aged students, who then underwent a MRI scanning session and completed the PYD survey that was common to all arms of the project. The questionnaires included measures of social contribution and religious participation, as well as metrics of various psychological constructs that are related to PYD, such as self-regulation. Our goal was two-fold: First, Urry had the students perform a series of emotion regulation tasks to test how PYD was related to emotion regulation. She details the findings of this part of the study elsewhere in this book. Second, we wished to test whether factors related to PYD were correlated with cortical thickness of very specific brain regions, based on our findings with meditation as well as other published reports of empathy, moral behavior, and emotion regulation. We had three specific hypotheses:

1. Based on our study of meditation practitioners described previously, we predicted the amount of time the students reported being engaged in contemplative practices such as prayer or meditation would correlate with the thickness of the right anterior insula.

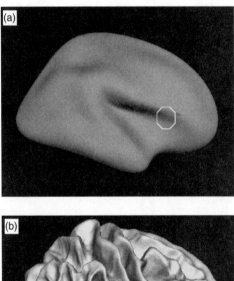

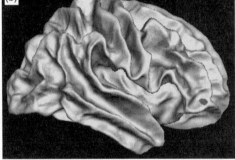

Figure 5.2   White regions indicate brain loci whose gray matter thickness correlated with questionnaires related to PYD. (a) Thickness of right anterior insula correlates with amount of spiritual practice (note: $p = .1$, not significant). (b) Thickness of frontal cortex correlates with self-regulation.

2. Based on the work of the neural basis of empathy and perspective taking (Akitsuki & Decety, 2009; Cacioppo et al., 2009; Jackson et al., 2006; Saxe et al., 2006, 2009), we predicted the thickness of the temporal parietal junction (TPJ) would correlate with the Connection and Caring components of the PYD scale.

3. Based on the work of Greene and colleagues (Greene & Paxton, 2009) on the neural basis of moral behavior as well as the extensive body of work demonstrating the role of lateral PFC in regulating the amygdala (Banks et al., 2007; Monk et al., 2008), we predicted a specific subregion of the PFC would positively correlate with measures of self-regulation.

The results of these analyses are depicted in Figure 5.2. Because of the small sample size, the findings did not meet statistical significance, but they did approach significance for two of our three hypotheses. First, the exact same region of anterior insula that we identified in our studies of meditation correlated with amount of prayer or meditation practiced by the students ($p = .1$; Figure 5.2a). Second, the predicted region of PFC was correlated with self-regulation ($p = .053$; Figure 5.2b). Although the spatial localization of the findings were precisely as predicted, the statistical significance of the findings failed to meet appropriate thresholds, and therefore must be considered with extreme caution.

CONCLUSIONS

These data, although preliminary, indicate the potential for this line of research and are highly suggestive of the possibility of identifying the neural signatures of PYD. Our recent work, demonstrating that practicing meditation for as little as two months leads to changes in brain structure, gives credence to the hypothesis that PYD may be malleable and that the use of contemplative-based interventions may be an effective way to help individuals with low PYD move in a more positive direction. In conjunction with the Kripalu Center for Yoga and Health, we will soon be embarking on a study to test this hypothesis, using the preliminary data generated here to calculate sample sizes. We will evaluate changes in resilience, empathy, and spirituality in high school students starting a yoga practice, and we will test whether any such changes are correlated with changes in brain regions identified in this pilot study. Additional longitudinal studies will be required to determine whether other contemplative practices impact the brain in similar or different fashions.

REFERENCES

Akitsuki, Y., & Decety, J. (2009). Social context and perceived agency affects empathy for pain: An event-related fMRI investigation. *Neuroimage, 47*(2), 722–734.

Banks, S. J., Eddy, K. T., Angstadt, M., Nathan, P. J., & Phan, K. L. (2007). Amygdala-frontal connectivity during emotion-regulation. *Social Cognitive and Affective Neuroscience, 2*(4), 303–312.

Beauregard, M., Courtemanche, J., Paquette, V., & St-Pierre, E. L. (2009). The neural basis of unconditional love. *Psychiatry Research, 172*(2), 93–98.

Black, J. E., Zelazny, A. M., & Greenough, W. T. (1991). Capillary and mitochondrial support of neural plasticity in adult rat visual cortex. *Experimental Neurology, 111*(2), 204–209.

Brefczynski-Lewis, J. A., Lutz, A., Schaefer, H. S., Levinson, D. B., & Davidson, R. J. (2007). Neural correlates of attentional expertise in long-term meditation practitioners. *Proceedings of the National Academy of Sciences of the United States of America, 104*(27), 11483–11488.

Cacioppo, J. T., Norris, C. J., Decety, J., Monteleone, G., & Nusbaum, H. (2009). In the eye of the beholder: Individual differences in perceived social isolation predict regional brain activation to social stimuli. *Journal of Cognitive Neuroscience, 21*(1), 83–92.

Coccaro, E. F., McCloskey, M. S., Fitzgerald, D. A., & Phan, K. L. (2007). Amygdala and orbitofrontal reactivity to social threat in individuals with impulsive aggression. *Biological Psychiatry, 62*(2), 168–178.

Craig, A. D. (2009). How do you feel—now? The anterior insula and human awareness. *Nature Reviews Neuroscience, 10*(1), 59–70.

Critchley, H. D., Wiens, S., Rotshtein, P., Ohman, A., & Dolan, R. J. (2004). Neural systems supporting interoceptive awareness. *Nature Neuroscience, 7*(2), 189–195.

De Brito, S. A., Mechelli, A., Wilke, M., Laurens, K. R., Jones, A. P., Barker, G. J., . . . & Viding, E. (2009). Size matters: Increased grey matter in boys with conduct problems and callous-unemotional traits. *Brain, 132*(Pt. 4), 843–852.

Di Dio, C., Macaluso, E., & Rizzolatti, G. (2007). The golden beauty: Brain response to classical and renaissance sculptures. *PLoS ONE, 2*(11), e1201.

Dong, W. K., & Greenough, W. T. (2004). Plasticity of nonneuronal brain tissue: Roles in developmental disorders. *Mental Retardation and Developmental Disabilities Research Reviews, 10*(2), 85–90.

Draganski, B., Gaser, C., Busch, V., Schuierer, G., Bogdahn, U., & May, A. (2004). Changes in grey matter induced by training. *Nature, 427*, 311–312.

Draganski, B., Gaser, C., Kempermann, G., Kuhn, H. G., Winkler, J., Buchel, C., & May, A. (2006). Temporal and spatial dynamics of brain structure changes during extensive learning. *Journal of Neuroscience, 26*(23), 6314–6317.

Drevets, W. C., Price, J. L., & Furey, M. L. (2008). Brain structural and functional abnormalities in mood disorders: Implications for neurocircuitry models of depression. *Brain Structure and Function, 213*(1–2), 93–118.

Gage, F. H. (2002). Neurogenesis in the adult brain. *Journal of Neuroscience, 22*(3), 612–613.

Giedd, J. N., Blumenthal, J., Jeffries, N. O., Castellanos, F. X., Liu, H., Zijdenbos, A., . . . & Rapoport, J. L. (1999). Brain development during childhood and adolescence: A longitudinal MRI study. *Nature Neuroscience, 2*(10), 861–863.

Greene, J. D., & Paxton, J. M. (2009). Patterns of neural activity associated with honest and dishonest moral decisions. *Proceedings of the National Academy of Sciences of the United States of America, 106*(30), 12506–12511.

Gusnard, D. A., Akbudak, E., Shulman, G. L., & Raichle, M. (2001). Medial prefrontal cortex and self-referential mental activity: Relation to a default mode of brain function. *Proceedings of the National Academy of Sciences of the United States of America, 98*(7), 4259–4264.

Hölzel, B. K., Carmody, J., Evans, K. C., Hoge, E. A., Dusek, J. A., Morgan, L., . . . & Lazar, S. W. (2010). Stress reduction correlates with structural changes in the amygdala. *Social Cognitive and Affective Neuroscience, 5*(1), 11–17.

Hölzel, B. K., Carmody, J., Vangel, M., Congleton, C., Yerramsetti, S. M., & Lazar, S. W. (2011). Mindfulness practice leads to increases in regional brain gray matter density. *Psychiatry Research: Neuroimaging, 19*(1), 36–43.

Hölzel, B. K., Ott, U., Gard, T., Hempel, H., Weygandt, M., Morgen, K., . . . & Vaitl, D. (2008). Investigation of mindfulness meditation practitioners with voxel-based morphometry. *Social Cognitive and Affective Neuroscience, 3*(1), 55–61.

Hölzel, B. K., Ott, U., Hempel, H., Hackl, A., Wolf, K., Stark, R., & Vaitl, D. (2007). Differential engagement of anterior cingulate and adjacent medial frontal cortex in adept meditators and non-meditators. *Neuroscience Letters, 421*(1), 16–21.

Huebner, T., Vloet, T. D., Marx, I., Konrad, K., Fink, G. R., Herpertz, S. C., & Herpertz-Dahlmann, B. (2008). Morphometric brain abnormalities in boys with conduct disorder. *Journal of the American Academy of Child and Adolescent Psychiatry, 47*(5), 540–547.

Hulshoff Pol, H. E., Schnack, H. G., Posthuma, D., Mandl, R. C., Baare, W. F., van Oel, C., . . . & Kahn, R. S. (2006). Genetic contributions to human brain morphology and intelligence. *Journal of Neuroscience, 26*(40), 10235–10242.

Iaria, G., Committeri, G., Pastorelli, C., Pizzamiglio, L., Watkins, K. E., & Carota, A. (2008). Neural activity of the anterior insula in emotional processing depends on the individuals' emotional susceptibility. *Human Brain Mapping, 29*(3), 363–373.

Ilg, R., Wohlschlager, A. M., Gaser, C., Liebau, Y., Dauner, R., Wöller, A., . . . & Mühlau, M. (2008). Gray matter increase induced by practice correlates with task-specific activation: A combined functional and morphometric magnetic resonance imaging study. *Journal of Neuroscience, 28*(16), 4210–4215.

Jackson, P. L., Brunet, E., Meltzoff, A. N., & Decety, J. (2006). Empathy examined through the neural mechanisms involved in imagining how I feel versus how you feel pain. *Neuropsychologia, 44*(5), 752–761.

Lazar, S. W., Bush, G., Gollub, R. L., Fricchione, G. L., Khalsa, G., & Benson, H. (2000). Functional brain mapping of the relaxation response and meditation. *Neuroreport, 11*(7), 1581–1585.

Lazar, S. W., Kerr, C. E., Wasserman, R. H., Gray, J. R., Greve, D. N., Treadway, M. T., . . . & Fischl, B. (2005). Meditation experience is associated with increased cortical thickness. *Neuroreport, 16*(17), 1893–1897.

Lenroot, R. K., Schmitt, J. E., Ordaz, S. J., Wallace, G. L., Neale, M. C., Lerch, J. P., . . . & Giedd, J. N. (2009). Differences in genetic and environmental influences on the human cerebral cortex associated with development during childhood and adolescence. *Hum Brain Mapp, 30*(1), 163–174.

Lerner, R. M., Fisher, C. B., & Weinberg, R. A. (2000). Toward a science for and of the people: Promoting civil society through the application of developmental science. *Child Development, 71*(1), 11–20.

Lowry, C. A., Lightman, S. L., & Nutt, D. J. (2009). That warm fuzzy feeling: Brain serotonergic neurons and the regulation of emotion. *Journal of Psychopharmacology, 23*(4), 392–400.

Luders, E., Toga, A. W., Lepore, N., & Gaser, C. (2009). The underlying anatomical correlates of long-term meditation: Larger hippocampal and frontal volumes of gray matter. *Neuroimage, 45*(3), 672–678.

Martin, S. B., Covell, D. J., Joseph, J. E., Chebrolu, H., Smith, C. D., Kelly, T. H., . . . & Gold, B. T. (2007). Human experience seeking correlates with hippocampus volume: Convergent evidence from manual tracing and voxel-based morphometry. *Neuropsychologia, 45*(12), 2874–2881.

Matsuo, K., Nicoletti, M., Nemoto, K., Hatch, J. P., Peluso, M. A., Nery, F. G., & Soares, J. C. (2009). A voxel-based morphometry study of frontal gray matter correlates of impulsivity. *Human Brain Mapping, 30*(4), 1188–1195.

Monk, C. S., Telzer, E. H., Mogg, K., Bradley, B. P., Mai, X., Louro, H. M., . . . & Pine, D. S. (2008). Amygdala and ventrolateral prefrontal cortex activation to masked angry faces in children and adolescents with generalized anxiety disorder. *Archives of General Psychiatry, 65*(5), 568–576.

Northoff, G., & Bermpohl, F. (2004). Cortical midline structures and the self. *Trends in Cognitive Science, 8*(3), 102–107.

O'Donnell, S., Noseworthy, M. D., Levine, B., & Dennis, M. (2005). Cortical thickness of the frontopolar area in typically developing children and adolescents. *Neuroimage, 24*(4), 948–954.

Omura, K., Todd Constable, R., & Canli, T. (2005). Amygdala gray matter concentration is associated with extraversion and neuroticism. *Neuroreport, 16*(17), 1905–1908.

Pagnoni, G., Cekic, M., & Guo, Y. (2008). "Thinking about not-thinking": Neural correlates of conceptual processing during Zen meditation. *PLoS ONE, 3*(9), e3083.

Paus, T. (Ed.). (2009). *Brain development.* (3rd ed.). Hoboken, NJ: Wiley.

Paus, T., Leonard, G., Lerner, J. V., Lerner, R. M., Perron, M., Pike, G. B., . . . & Pausova, Z. (2011). Positive youth development and age-related changes in cortical thickness during adolescence. In A. E. Alberts Warren, R. M. Lerner, & E. Phelps (Eds.), *Thriving and spirituality among youth: Research perspectives and future possibilities* (pp. 61–76). Hoboken, NJ: Wiley.

Rankin, K. P., Gorno-Tempini, M. L., Allison, S. C., Stanley, C. M., Glenn, S., Weiner, M. W., & Miller, B. L. (2006). Structural anatomy of empathy in neurodegenerative disease. *Brain*, *129*(Pt. 11), 2945–2956.

Saxe, R., Moran, J. M., Scholz, J., & Gabrieli, J. (2006). Overlapping and non-overlapping brain regions for theory of mind and self reflection in individual subjects. *Social and Cognitive Affective Neuroscience*, *1*(3), 229–234.

Saxe, R., Whitfield-Gabrieli, S., Scholz, J., & Pelphrey, K. A. (2009). Brain regions for perceiving and reasoning about other people in school-aged children. *Child Development*, *80*(4), 1197–1209.

Schjoedt, U., Stodkilde-Jorgensen, H., Geertz, A. W., & Roepstorff, A. (2008). Rewarding prayers. *Neuroscience Letters*, *443*(3), 165–168.

Schjoedt, U., Stodkilde-Jorgensen, H., Geertz, A. W., & Roepstorff, A. (2009). Highly religious participants recruit areas of social cognition in personal prayer. *Social and Cognitive Affective Neuroscience*, *4*(2), 199–207.

Schmitz, T. W., & Johnson, S. C. (2007). Relevance to self: A brief review and framework of neural systems underlying appraisal. *Neuroscience Biobehavioral Review*, *31*(4), 585–596.

Shaw, P., Greenstein, D. K., Lerch, J. P., Clasen, L. S., Lenroot, R., Gogtay, N., . . . & Giedd, J. (2006). Intellectual ability and cortical development in children and adolescents. *Nature*, *440*(7084), 676–679.

Singer, T., Seymour, B., O'Doherty, J., Kaube, H., Dolan, R. J., & Frith, C. D. (2004). Empathy for pain involves the affective but not sensory components of pain. *Science*, *303*(5661), 1157–1162.

Sterzer, P., Stadler, C., Poustka, F., & Kleinschmidt, A. (2007). A structural neural deficit in adolescents with conduct disorder and its association with lack of empathy. *Neuroimage*, *37*(1), 335–342.

Tiihonen, J., Rossi, R., Laakso, M. P., Hodgins, S., Testa, C., Perez, J., . . . & Frisoni, G. B. (2008). Brain anatomy of persistent violent offenders: more rather than less. *Psychiatry Research*, *163*(3), 201–212.

Vestergaard-Poulsen, P., van Beek, M., Skewes, J., Bjarkam, C. R., Stubberup, M., Bertelsen, J., & Roepstorff, A. (2009). Long-term meditation is associated with increased gray matter density in the brain stem. *Neuroreport*, *20*(2), 170–174.

Wilke, M., Krageloh-Mann, I., & Holland, S. K. (2007). Global and local development of gray and white matter volume in normal children and adolescents. *Experimental Brain Research*, *178*(3), 296–307.

PART

II

Individual and Psychological
Contexts of Positive Youth
Development and Spirituality

6

Strengthening Human Potential for Great Love-Compassion Through Elaborative Development[1]

AMY EVA ALBERTS WARREN

The perception of living entities as self-contained, closed systems is one expression of the *individualist paradigm* regarding human nature and interaction (Lee, 2002). Impervious to external influence, closed systems provide no theoretical basis for commitment to the collective's health and well-being; the health of one closed system is inconsequential to the health of another (Thelen & Smith, 1998, 2006). Such a split conception of self and other (Overton, 1998, 2006) rationalizes commitment to only a *part* of the *whole*, to at best only the few, proximal individuals with whom relationship and influence are tangible and obvious. "The rest"—to whom we are imperceptibly fused—receive neither our commitment nor our care.

The individualist belief in the possibility of *no-influence* by others is false, as it fails to appreciate the systemic interconnection/fusion of living systems and, thus,

[1]This research was supported by a grant to Dr. Richard M. Lerner from the John Templeton Foundation. I thank Drs. Richard M. Lerner (Principal Investigator), Erin Phelps (Co-Investigator), and Robert Roeser (Project Director); Sonia S. Issac Koshy, Mona M. Abo-Zena, and Dan Du (graduate research assistants); and Inbar Sharon, Mary von Rueden, and Brian Wilson (project assistants) for their assistance with this project.

the *inevitability* of influence (Morgan, 1968; Overton, 2006; Tobach & Schneirla, 1968). The systemic organization and embeddedness of all living entities makes them open systems (Ford & Lerner, 1992) and, thus, "integrally fused together" (Thelen & Smith, 1998, p. 572). "To be," then, "is to be related" to the *whole* (Krishnamurti, 1992, p. 20; see also Adler, 1927/1998; Buber, 1923/1970; Jung, 1977; Tobach, 1981; Tobach & Schneirla, 1968). There is no absolute break, or split (Overton, 1998, 2006, 2010), between self and other. There is no isolated *part* pocketed off from the rest. There is only the *whole*, to which we are integrally fused and by which we are inevitably influenced. Our entanglement with the whole, then, provides a theoretical basis for commitment to the whole; the health of one facet of the overall open system *is consequential* to the health of all other facets (see Warren, 2009, for a review of the interdisciplinary bases for this position).

This integrative conception has not been a prominent part of the extant literature of social and behavioral science. In fact, scholarship about split conceptions of humanity has dominated the literature (Overton, 2010). Although labeled differently (e.g., White-positive/Black-negative racial stereotypes, negative prejudice, extrinsic religious orientation, implicit antidemocratic trends, traditional family ideology, contrient interdependence and the competitive process, moral exclusion, and character-conditioned hate) and associated with different bodies of work, the phenomena examined in these research programs converge as instantiations of the tendency to split humanity into desirable and undesirable groupings (e.g., Adorno, Frenkel-Brunswik, Levinson, & Sanford, 1950; Allport, 1954, 1963; Clark & Clark, 1939a, 1939b, 1940; Deutsch, 1949a, 1949b; Fromm, 1973/1992; Levinson & Huffman, 1955; Opotow, 1990, 2005; Staub, 1990; see Warren, 2009, for a review). These research programs have the shared goal of understanding humans' tendency to commit to only a *part* of the whole (Overton, 1998, 2006, 2010).

The documentation of humans' tendency to split humanity into desirable and undesirable groupings is a worthwhile endeavor. However, to mend such split conceptions, a complementary endeavor must take place, one with the goal of understanding human connection. Although arguably less developed than scholarship about split conceptions of humanity (Allport, 1950), scholarship about *mending* split conceptions has been underway just as long. Several scholars over the years have had the shared goal of understanding humans' potential to perceive their systemic interconnection, to commit to the *whole* of humanity (e.g., Adler, 1938/1964; Allport, 1954; Colby & Damon, 1992; Deutsch & Coleman, 2000; Fehr, Sprecher, & Underwood, 2009; Loevinger, 1966; Post, 2003; see Warren, 2009, for a review). As with split conceptions, the phenomena under study pertain to different substantive areas (e.g., the tolerant personality, conflict resolution, social interest, ego development, extraordinary moral commitment, wisdom, unlimited love, and compassionate love). Yet, these research programs converge in their emphasis on human connection, on mending or preventing perceived and actual splits within humanity.

The present research follows in this tradition but, as elaborated as follows, advances beyond past mending scholarship in several ways. Based on ideas of elaborative development (Ford & Lerner, 1992), this chapter begins to elucidate the dynamic developmental processes involved in commitment to the *whole* of humanity, as instantiated by Great Love-Compassion (GLC), which is the wish for *all* to have freedom and joy and for *all* to be relieved of their pain and suffering. By introducing and testing GLC as one key outcome of elaborative development, this work will seek to explain how some developmental scenarios eventuate in the emergence of an ideational and personal style marked by commitment to the whole of humanity.

The methodology used in the present investigation also builds on past research concerned with the introduction of new constructs not yet operationalized in the literature. Quantitative data from the John Templeton Foundation (JTF)–sponsored study of "The Role of Spiritual Development in Growth of Purpose, Generosity, and Psychological Health in Adolescence" were employed to document both the purported developmental antecedent, elaborative status, and the theoretically believed outcome, GLC, by using a construct validation methodology developed in particular by Block (1971) and employed in subsequent research (e.g., Bobek, 2008; Perkins, 1996). The details and bases of this methodology, and of the methodological tradition from which it was derived (Block, 1971; see also Bobek, 2008; Lerner, Dowling, & Chaudhuri, 2005; Perkins, 1996; Teti, 2005), may be found in Warren (2009). Here, however, I turn to the theoretical architecture of this work—a nonrecursive structural model of hypothesized relationships among adaptive developmental regulations, elaborative development, and GLC—derived from several social and behavioral science fields (e.g., developmental science, social psychology, personality psychology, evolutionary psychology, cognitive psychology, transpersonal psychology, and humanistic psychology).

GREAT LOVE-COMPASSION: AN EXEMPLARY INSTANTIATION OF COMMITMENT TO THE WHOLE AND ITS DIVERSITY[2]

> *A human being is a part of a whole, called by us "universe," a part limited in time and space. He experiences himself, his thoughts and feelings as something separated from the rest . . . a kind of optical delusion of his consciousness.*

---

[2] Although broad and multidimensional constructs such as GLC are admittedly uncommon in social science research, there is reason to believe that the zeitgeist is changing in this direction. Sternberg's (1997, 2003, 2005, 2006; see also Sternberg & Barnes, 1988; Sternberg, Hojjat, Barnes, 2001) work on love and hate, Baltes' (see Baltes, Glück, & Kunzmann, 2002; Baltes & Kunzmann, 2003; Baltes & Smith, 2008) work on wisdom, and Damon's (2003) work on noble purpose are notable examples of research programs concerned with such challenging foci.

This delusion is a kind of prison for us, restricting us to our personal desires
and to affection for a few persons nearest to us. Our task must be to free
ourselves from this prison by widening our circle of compassion to embrace
all living creatures *and the whole of nature in its beauty [emphasis added].*
————Albert Einstein[3]

I propose that *great love-compassion* (GLC)—the wish for *all* to have freedom
and joy, and the complementary wish born of clear perception, for *all* to be relieved of their pain and suffering (Glaser, 2005; see also Dalai Lama & Cutler,
1998; Fromm, 1956)—is an exemplary instantiation of commitment to the whole
of humanity, to all facets of the integrated overall open human system (Ford &
Lerner, 1992; Thelen & Smith, 1998, 2006). GLC is a cognitive and emotional
attribute of the person that contributes to his or her commitment and contributions to this system, and thus to a win-win orientation to life, in that the system
supports the individual in any life path that as well maintains or enhances the
system (Lerner, 2004a). "It is the *finest* expression of our relationship to self and
others" and "is the foundation, process, and goal of psychological health and
wholeness" (Glaser, 2005, pp. 11–12).

Given that the absence of deficit does not ensure the presence of well-being
(Lerner, 2004a), the wish to relieve pain and suffering alone is an incomplete
wish; it does not ensure the presence of freedom and joy. Love and compassion,
then, are necessarily spoken of together, even as a single word: *love-compassion*
(Glaser, 2005). Love-compassion is arguably abundant, *but often limited in scope*,
concerned with the welfare of only the few, proximal individuals with whom
relationship and influence are tangible and obvious. Based on the individualist
paradigm, we may wish for a *selection* of others to experience freedom from suffering
and happiness; this is assuredly love-compassion, but it is *ordinary*—as opposed
to *great*—in its scope. *Ordinary* love-compassion (OLC) is limited to only a *few*
privileged individuals, to only a *part* of the whole (Glaser, 2005). Regardless of
how sincere and deeply felt it is, OLC is incomplete; it is a split conception and
approach to others (Overton, 1998, 2006, 2010), a commitment to only a *part*
of the *whole*. In short, while OLC is focused on one separate and self-contained
part of life—selecting, rejecting, and privileging one *section* of humanity—GLC
dissolves the synthetic borders that partition humanity and holds the whole of
human life in awareness.

The eventual apex of GLC, what makes it great and not merely ordinary,
is both its universal scope *and* its commitment to action (Glaser, 2005). GLC
begins with a wish, born of broadening empathic awareness, but (theoretically)
ultimately evolves into a commitment to help all human beings triumph over
suffering and attain freedom and joy. It is, thus, a way of being *and* of doing, a
noun and a verb. In other words, indicators of the presence of GLC will necessarily
involve both an ideological and an action component.

---

[3]From Letter of 1950, as quoted in Sullivan, W. (1972, March 29). The Einstein Papers:
A Man of Many Parts. *The New York Times*, p. 20.

GLC and Concepts From Past Mending Scholarship

GLC differs from the related concepts of unlimited love (Post, 2003, 2005, 2008) and compassionate love (Fehr & Sprecher, 2004; Fehr, Sprecher, & Underwood, 2009; Underwood, 2002, 2004, 2005). For example, in contrast to unlimited love, GLC offers a nonsectarian—and, thus, a more broadly applicable—conception of love. According to the Institute for Research on Unlimited Love (IRUL), unlimited love is defined, in part, as "a *Creative Presence* underlying and integral to all of reality" [italics added] (http://www.unlimitedloveinstitute.org/mission/index.html). Moreover, IRUL's President, Stephen Post, has noted that, in its purest form, unlimited love is "identified with the very essence of *divine* nature across the great religious cultures of the world" [italics added] (Post, Johnson, McCullough, & Schloss, 2003, p. 1). To be sure, drawing upon common, social constructions and traditions (religious or otherwise) is an important method for *exemplifying* a new construct. However, to include theological criteria within the definition of a construct, to make a construct theo-centric, may considerably limit its applicability and usefulness. GLC is conceived in nonsectarian language, which means it genuinely regards the whole of humanity by honoring humanity's (ideological) diversity.

Another limitation of the unlimited love construct is that it does not emphasize the importance of clear perception (Dalai Lama & Cutler, 1998; Glaser, 2005), or of an accurate cognitive and emotional understanding of the other (Underwood, 2002, 2005, 2009). Arguably, genuine love and compassion is born of such knowledge, which requires "pure and fearless openness" (Trungpa, 1973, p. 213). This notion of being *unconditionally* awake to the *diversity* of humanity is integral to the present conceptualization of GLC and, as well, to earlier conceptions of cognitive and emotional functioning that were proposed to counter the in-group–out-group attitudes that frame negative prejudice (Allport, 1954).

In addition, unlimited love is, in some respects, adevelopmental. Post (2008) concluded that "one of the healthiest things a person can do is to step back from self-preoccupation and self-worry . . . [by] focusing attention on helping others" (p. 1). While this is a seemingly logical conclusion as it relates to adulthood, Post (2008) went on to underscore the importance of "getting started" at a young age. However, self-preoccupation and self-worry are common, if not essential, features of early development. Several developmental theories point to the negative effects of prematurely possessing an other-centered orientation (Elkind, 1967, 1981; Erikson, 1959; Maslow, 1958).

The construct of compassionate love has similar limitations. A central criterion of compassionate love is commitment to others "at a cost to self" (Underwood, 2009, p. 4). Salient across multiple definitions of compassionate love is the prominent theme of selflessness and sacrifice, as instantiated by placing others' needs *above* one's own (Shacham-Dupont, 2003). Arguably, such behavior early in development would be counterproductive to the goal of development. Moreover, considerable evidence suggests that caring for the self is neither mutually exclusive nor incompatible with caring for the whole of humanity (Baltes, Lindenberger,

& Staudinger, 2006; Cialdini, Brown, Lewis, Luce, & Neuberg, 1997; Colby & Damon, 1995; Lerner, 2004a; Lerner, Alberts, & Bobek, 2007; Sternberg, 1999; Templeton, 2004). For example, unity (integration) of self and moral goals is the central, defining feature of extraordinary moral commitment (Colby & Damon, 1992, 1995). Colby and Damon (1995) noted, however, that "the prevailing culture in contemporary Western society emphasizes a *split* between personal self-interest and morality such that they are often assumed to be fundamentally in opposition to each other" [italics added] (p. 367). They continued, "We believe that the intellectual climate of our culture would do better to emphasize the potential for unity in personal and moral goals rather than a seemingly inevitable conflict between them" (Colby & Damon, 1995, p. 368). The construct of GLC, what has been called "the *finest* expression of our relationship to self and others" (Glaser, 2005, pp. 11–12), answers this call.

In addition, compassionate love, as conceptualized by Underwood and colleagues (Fehr, Sprecher, & Underwood, 2009; Underwood, 2009), does not specifically speak to the range of humanity. Although these scholars may intend for this construct to apply to the whole of humanity, such complete inclusion has not been presented as a necessary criterion. As such, there is no distinction between compassionate love for one's in-group (OLC) and compassionate love for the whole group (GLC). In contrast, Great Love-Compassion is explicitly directed to the breadth of humanity.

Finally, GLC differs from compassionate love in the equal emphasis given to love and compassion. Compassionate (i.e., adjective) love (i.e., noun) makes "love" the centerpiece and "compassion" a mere qualification. Compassionate love, then, is a type of love, not an equal marriage of love (freedom, joy, and every form of happiness) and compassion (desire to alleviate or reduce pain and suffering). In contrast, Love-Compassion (noun-noun) places equal emphasis on commitment to love and commitment to compassion. If the reduction of suffering and the promotion of flourishing are two sides of a single coin (Lerner, 2004a), then compassionate love is an imbalanced conception.

In these respects, GLC differs from, and arguably advances beyond, the related conceptions of unlimited love and compassionate love. The construct of GLC, then, will be used in the current investigation.

Whether or not we realize our potential for GLC, for commitment to the whole of humanity and its diversity, depends on how we traverse birth to maturity, on the *nature of our developmental (structural) change*. Murphy (1958) noted that

> one of the greatest problems of the release of human potentials [is whether] . . . the fires of infancy can be gently transferred to the new furnaces of high creativeness, preserving the primitive intensities of the first vital responses but channeling them into the infinitely diverse realms in which discovery and creativeness may flourish. (p. 166)

What we have reborn with every child is the release of our potential for GLC.

THE POTENTIAL FOR PLASTICITY (ENHANCEMENT) WITHIN AN INDIVIDUAL ↔ CONTEXT (RELATIONAL) SYSTEM: DIVERSITY OF AND AMONG PARTICIPATING VARIABLES

Current, cutting-edge conceptions of human development indicate that the basic processes of systematic ontogenetic change involve mutually regulative relations between individuals and their contexts, represented as individual ↔ context relations (Lerner, 2002, 2006). Developmental contextualism, an instance of developmental systems theory, assumes a nonreductionistic, interlevel, and synthetic relation among variables from the multiple levels of organization comprising the ecology of human development (Lerner, 2006). This model portrays the essential process of development as involving dynamic interactions (i.e., changing, reciprocal relations) between individuals and the multilevel contexts in which they are embedded (Lerner, 2002; Lerner & Kauffman, 1985). No single variable is the cause of human functioning and development. Rather, the relational structure of the system—the constellation of relations—is the cause of current functioning; and changes in the configuration of these relations are the cause of development. Such dynamic interactions among variables mean that human life is characterized by relative plasticity, or the potential for systematic change, in *all* manifestations and contexts of human life (Brim & Kagan, 1980; Lerner, 2004b).

The individual's diversity represents a central basis of the plasticity of the overall system, and of its potential to change toward an enhanced status. Diverse individuals, who have been given the time and space to realize their own multiple dimensions of individuality, to have diverse experiences, to be exposed to diverse perspectives, and to derive a diverse mental and behavioral repertoire, will be more "plastic"—*better able to form diverse constellations of relations*, to identify with and potentially commit to diverse others. Thus, the promotion of intrapersonal *diversity* is fundamental to the *optimization* of the individual and, because of the effects of individuals on their contexts (Lerner, 2004b), of societal health.

PRESERVATION OF OUR PROLONGED YOUTH: INCREASING INTRAPERSONAL DIVERSITY AND THE POTENTIAL OF PLASTICITY

Developmental change across ontogeny may be evaluated as either elaborative or decremental (Baltes, 1987; Ford & Lerner, 1992). According to Ford and Lerner (1992), an elaborative change *increases* (whereas a decremental change *reduces*) "the size, diversity, or complexity of organization of a person or of his or her characteristics, capabilities, and relationships with their environments" (p. 35). Elaborative changes in structure and function provide the foundation for and are demonstrative of, respectively, development toward greater, positive capitalization on plasticity (Lerner & Busch-Rossnagel, 1981).

From a species perspective, humans have a specific level of plasticity; thus, the issue becomes one of actualizing or capitalizing on it in a positive way. If optimal development may be regarded as the capacity to enhance the self and other selves (Lerner, Dowling, & Anderson, 2003), then elaborative change—intrapersonal diversification—should be an indication of optimal development, of the potential for enhancement through plastic relations.

Humans' exhibit greater potential for elaborative change compared with other species (Lerner, 1984). This potential is made possible by a protracted period of childhood dependency—paedomorphy produced by neoteny—during which humans *may eventually* acquire high-level capacities (Gottlieb, 1997; Lerner, Freund, De Stefanis, & Habermas, 2001). The size, diversity, and complexity of these capacities have implications for the regulation of organism–context relations and, thus, for capitalizing on plasticity and actualizing the potential for enhancement. It would be foolish, then, to "prune" during such a generative "growing season," as is afforded by neoteny (Elkind, 1987, p. 10; Gould, 1977).

Behavioral and physical neoteny, a slowing down or retardation of development such that juvenile characteristics are retained across life, is largely responsible for the complex and flexible behavior that undergirds human plasticity (Bjorklund, 1997; Gould, 1977; Lerner, 2002). Neoteny is an instance of the process of heterochrony—changes across phylogeny in developmental (ontogenetic) timing of ancestral characteristics. To delay the time of appearance of developmental characteristics, decrease the rate of change, and, ultimately, postpone the attainment of maturity, is to increase time for "construction." Humans' life history patterns are sequentially delayed compared to other living primates (Gould, 1977; McKinney, 2000). The average life span, including the periods of infancy and puberty, is prolonged in humans. Fossil dentition has provided evidence that human evolution has involved an increasing delay in major developmental events (Gould, 1977). This extension of growth has advanced humans' somatic and brain morphology compared with other living relatives (McKinney & McNamara, 1991). The prolongation of brain myelinization, which fosters effective nerve transmission, has increased human potential for language, memory, and intelligence (Case, 1992). Increases in evolutionary brain size is a result of disproportionately more growth in sections of the brain (e.g., neocortex) produced relatively *late* in development (Finlay & Darlington, 1995). Neocortical size positively correlates with the capacity to process diverse kinds of information requisite for behavioral and cognitive complexity. This prolongation of brain maturation has resulted in humans' prolonged learning. Humans have an initially large endowment of neurons, dendrites, and synapses, which enables the retention and manipulation of information; the delay of their maturation means that peak rates and pruning occur later in life (Gibson, 1991).

For example, myelination progresses well into adulthood (Baltes et al., 2006; Keating, 2004; Nelson, Thomas, & De Haan, 2006). On a coarse though sufficient level, contemporary humans' extraordinary capacity for behavioral and cognitive flexibility is linked in large part to the prolongation of childhood and the life span in general (McKinney, 2000). From an evolutionary standpoint, prolongation or *extension* (McKinney, 1998) was the easiest way to alter the potential for complexity. Early developmental interactions have become increasingly resistant to evolutionary alteration, as a result of the canalizing effect of stabilizing selection. Developmental evolution, then, has favored modifications that alter later development, thereby leading to a prolongation of the "constructive" years (McKinney, 1998).

It may be, then, that our neoteny, our prolonged physiological immaturity (e.g., prolonged brain growth and the development of diverse associations), has an important contemporary impact on our potential for behavioral diversification and adaptation (Bjorklund, 1997). The complexity and variability of our perceptions, of the meanings we associate with a particular sensation, is an indication of the diversity of our behavioral repertoire. The ability to mentally simulate actions and their effects makes us aware of the diversity of behavioral options and may inform our thoughtful selection of behaviors. The acquisition of a diverse behavioral repertoire, as the one potentially obtained by humans, requires substantial ontogenetic time. This process of diversification may not be rushed, given that experience required for the development of associations is limited by maturational status (Elkind, 1998; Lerner, 2002). That is, the same experience will have different meanings and generate different associations depending on the organism's level of growth and differentiation. As such, the development of diverse associations and, ultimately, a diverse behavioral repertoire requires substantial time for construction.

Childhood, then, is not merely an anteroom to genuine advancement, but rather involves a variety of adaptive limitations that serve the needs of the developing organism (Bjorklund & Green, 1992). The adaptive role of neoteny in human development cautions us not to hurry children to overcome developmental limitations mistakenly viewed as liabilities (Elkind, 1981). Development involves dramatic changes in function and form, and the elaboration of these new, increasingly complex capacities is a slow process. To recognize children's limitations—or, better, age/stage-specific adaptive capacities—and to treat them differently from adults is not discriminatory; on the contrary, such developmentally sensitive actions honor the tremendous potential of childhood development and help to actualize plasticity's potential (Elkind, 1981).

Preservation of our prolonged youth, of its various processes of diversification, may be related to children's eventual flexibility and, thus, capacity for plastic partnerships with their contexts. As proposed in the previous section, the *potential* for enhancement of an individual ↔ context (relational) system is dependent on system-changing relations and, thus, on the *diversity* (flexibility) of those people doing the relating. Individuals, as interacting levels of the system, contribute considerably to the plasticity of their partnerships (Lerner & Busch-Rossnagel, 1981). Diverse individuals, who have been given the time and space to realize their own multiple dimensions of individuality, to have diverse experiences, to be exposed to diverse perspectives, and to derive a diverse mental and behavioral repertoire, will arguably be more plastic—*better able to form diverse constellations of relations*, to identify with and potentially commit to diverse others. Theoretically, then, elaboratively developed individuals are in an opportune position to enhance the system, to realize their potential for commitment to the whole of humanity and its *diversity*, for GLC. In other words, GLC may be one key *content* of an elaborative developmental *structure*.

STRENGTHENING OUR POTENTIAL FOR GREAT LOVE-COMPASSION THROUGH ELABORATIVE DEVELOPMENT: TRANSFORMING "IT" INTO "YOU" VIA THE DIVERSIFICATION OF "I"

> *So many things fail to interest us, simply because they don't find in us enough surface on which to live. And what we have to do then is to increase the number of planes in our mind, so that a much larger number of themes can find a place in it at the same time.*

—José Ortega y Gasset[4]

If elaborative development increases the potential for plasticity—for forming *diverse configurations of relations* within the developmental system—then elaborative status (i.e., a defining functional attribute of an adaptive individual ↔ context structure) should be linked to GLC status (arguably, one key content of an elaborative developmental structure). The basis of commitment (e.g., love-compassion), at its most fundamental level, is the sense of "at-homeness" with another, the extent to which the self and other are perceived to overlap/correlate (Zohar, 1990; see also Aron & Aron, 1986; Aron et al., 2005; Hornstein, 1982).

Based on the premise that crucial features of the self are located outside the body of the individual, inside known others (Geertz, 1973; Gilligan, 1982; Markus & Kitayama, 1991), Cialdini et al. (1997) reinterpreted data proposed to support the empathy-altruism model of helping (i.e., that empathic concern eventuates in selflessness and true altruism). These authors argue that the circumstances leading to empathic concern simultaneously lead to greater perceived self-other overlap, which raises the possibility that seemingly selfless and altruistic acts are, in fact, directed toward the self. In three studies, the influence of empathic concern on willingness to help was rendered nonsignificant when oneness (i.e., perceived self-other overlap) was considered (Cialdini et al., 1997). Moreover, in all three studies, the proportion of variance accounted for by oneness was several times greater than that for empathic concern (Study 1: 30% vs. 0.36%; Study 2: 10.4% vs. 1.4%; Study 3: 13.5% vs. 0.9%). These findings suggest the central relevance of self-other overlap in commitment to another (e.g., as instantiated here by willingness to help). Thus, it may be that those seen as an extension of the self

---

[4]As quoted in Warshall, P. (1999, Fall). The Great Arsenic Lobster. *Whole Earth*, 13.

are imbued with the self's human identity; in essence, they are transformed from *It* into *You* (Buber, 1923/1970; Lévinas, 1989).

Buber (1923/1970) and, more recently, Lévinas (1989) distinguished between *I-It* and *I-You* (or *I-Thou*) relationships. In *I-It* relationships, others are regarded in the third person, as an *It*, as split from and antithetical to the self, the Real (Lévinas, 1989; Overton, 2006; Putnam, 1987; see also Descartes, 1969). Such others, sharing no perceivable co-relation with the self, are divested of human characteristics as we have come to know them within the self. *Its* are talked to rather than attuned to, explained, avoided, and used, mastered, and controlled; whether they are revered or disposed of depends on their utility to the self (Morgan, 1968).

To contrast, in *I-You* relationships, others are seen as an extension of/fused to/synthetic with the self. In the absence of self-other splits, these humanized others are just as Real as the self, and just as deserving of another's commitment. Indeed, a defining feature of *I-You* relationships is "feeling with"/"feeling felt" (Buber, 1923/1970). At the neural level, *I-You* engagement involves resonance with another's emotional patterns and mental maps (Goleman, 2006). The more our patterns and maps overlap, the more at-home we feel with one another, the greater our potential for commitment, for love-compassion.

If the basis of commitment (e.g., love-compassion) is self-other overlap, how might we strengthen our potential for GLC? As previously stated, the *potential* for enhancement of an individual ↔ context (relational) system is dependent on system-changing relations and, thus, on the *diversity* (flexibility) of those people doing the relating. It follows that diverse individuals will be more plastic—better able to form *diverse constellations of relations* within the developmental system. When we increase "the size, diversity, or complexity of organization of [our] . . . characteristics, capabilities, and relationships with the environment" (Ford & Lerner, 1992, p. 35), we effectively increase our potential for overlapping with others—for perceiving diverse others as an extension of the self, and, thus, for GLC. Others are perceived as *Its* "simply because they don't find in us enough surface on which to live" (Gasset, n.d., i.e., quotation cited at the beginning of this section). If *Its* become *Yous* via overlap with *I*, then the diversified *I*—the *I* with a notable number of "planes" or "plurality of selves" (Ogbonnaya, 1994; Seligman, 1951)—should have a greater potential for *I-You* relationships, for GLC (Figure 6.1).

Substantial empirical evidence shows that the diversification of self (via elaborative development) is related to the potential for (various instantiations of) self-other overlap, for perceiving others as *Yous* rather than *Its* (Allport, 1954; Brewer & Pierce, 2005; Cassell, 2002; Csíkszentmihályi, 1996; Deutsch, 1973; Kang & Shaver, 2004; Pettigrew, 1997, 1998; Roccas & Brewer, 2002; Staub, 1989, 2005a; Suedfeld, Leighton, & Conway, 2006; Tibon, 2000; Winter, 2007; see McFarland & Mathews, 2005; Pettigrew & Tropp, 2000, for a meta-analysis; see Warren, 2009, for a review). For example, social psychologists have long postulated that amount and variety of experience—an elaboratively developed

**In the case of
elaborative development...**

**In the case of
decremental development...**

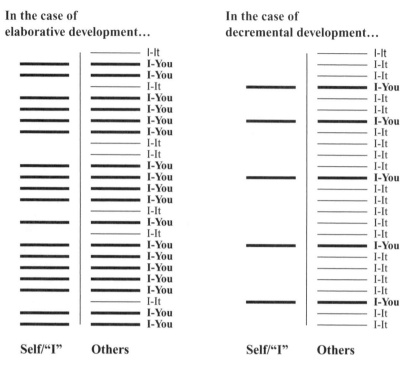

Figure 6.1   Increasing the self's dimensions ("planes"; Gasset, n.d.) effectively increases the self's capacity for *I-You* relations, for GLC.

experiential repertoire—are associated with inclusive caring (Staub, 2002a, 2002b, 2005a), moral development (Kohlberg, 1972), and the humanization of different (even despised) others (Staub & Pearlman, 2003; Staub, Pearlman, & Miller, 2003), as well as decreases in prejudice and hostility (e.g., Allport, 1954; Deutsch, 1973; Pettigrew, 1997, 1998, see Pettigrew & Tropp, 2000, for a meta-analysis). In two studies, Kang and Shaver (2004) found significant associations between emotional complexity (i.e., the possession of a wide-ranging and well-differentiated set of emotional experiences) and empathic tendencies, as well as interpersonal adaptability. Similarly, the elaborative development of one's general knowledge base via formal education and, specifically, of one's world knowledge is positively associated with concern for human rights (Barrows, 1981; Grace & Van Velzer, 1951; McFarland & Mathews, 2005). In turn, authoritarianism and ethnocentrism, plausibly indicative of limited intrapersonal range/latitude, of decremental development, predicts less concern for human rights (McFarland & Mathews, 2005; Moghaddam & Vuksanovic, 1990).

Taken together, these findings support the proposed relationship between the diversification of self (via elaborative development) and the self's potential for overlap with others, for perceiving others as *Yous* rather than *Its*. In the diversified, elaborated, self, "a much larger number of themes can find a place" to live (Gasset, n.d., i.e., quotation cited at the beginning of this section; see also Dabrowski, 1972). Diverse individuals simply have more opportunities to overlap with others, to perceive others as an extension of the self. Indeed, "the deeper we go into ourselves as particular and unique [the more differentiated we become] . . . the more we find the whole human species" (Rogers, 1961, p. 42). If the basis of commitment (e.g., love-compassion) is self-other overlap, then elaborative development (intrapersonal diversity) is arguably fundamental to the actualization of commitment to the whole of humanity, of GLC.

Intrapersonal diversification or the *elaborative development* of the individual (Ford & Lerner, 1992) is most optimally fostered in the context of mutually beneficial regulations between the individual and context (Warren, 2009). Development, elaborative or otherwise, is the result of changing individual ↔ context relations and, thus, the regulation of these relations determines the nature of developmental change. Developmental regulations that mutually benefit both the individual and context represent a structural fit between the individual's attributes and the demands or needs of his or her context. Given the nonstationary quality of both an individual's attributes and the context's demands, fit must be fluid to remain structurally intact and functionally relevant over time. Such adaptive developmental regulations, through their provision of adequate *space* (fit) and *time* (fluidity of fit), theoretically foster change in an elaborative (vs. a decremental) direction and, thus, help actualize our human potential for a diverse, flexible self, and—therefore—for GLC (Warren, 2009).

CONCLUSIONS

The systemic organization and multilevel ecological embeddedness of all living entities makes them open systems (Ford & Lerner, 1992) and, thus, "integrally fused together" (Thelen & Smith, 1998, p. 572). Such entanglement with the whole provides a theoretical basis for commitment to the whole; the health of one facet of the overall open system is consequential to the health of all other facets (Warren, 2009). Although commitment of this kind may take numerous forms, GLC (vs. OLC; Glaser, 2005) is arguably an exemplary instantiation of commitment to the whole of humanity, to all facets of the integrated overall open human system (Ford & Lerner, 1992; Thelen & Smith, 1998, 2006).

In this regard, the present investigation has the goal of understanding humans' potential to commit to the *whole* of humanity, of *preventing* split conceptions of humanity (via elaborative development). How do we strengthen our potential for GLC? How do we "gently transfer" the "fires of infancy" (Murphy, 1958, p. 166)—traverse birth to maturity—in order to realize this human potential?

Diverse individuals, who have been given the time and space to realize their own multiple dimensions of individuality, to have diverse experiences, to be exposed to diverse perspectives, and to derive a diverse mental and behavioral repertoire, will be more plastic—better able to identify with and potentially commit to diverse others. Arguably, the basis of commitment (e.g., love-compassion), at its most fundamental level, is perceived self-other overlap (Zohar, 1990). It follows simply that the diversified, elaborated self—the self with a notable number of "planes" or "plurality of selves" (Ogbonnaya, 1994; Seligman, 1951)—should be more likely to commit to the whole, to have GLC. The preceding literature review has provided empirical evidence that the diversification of self (a defining functional attribute of an adaptive individual ↔ context structure) is related to the potential for (various instantiations of) self-other overlap (Allport, 1954; Brewer & Pierce, 2005; Cassell, 2002; Csíkszentmihályi, 1996; Deutsch, 1973; Kang & Shaver, 2004; Pettigrew, 1997, 1998; Roccas & Brewer, 2002; Staub, 1989, 2005a; Suedfeld, Leighton, & Conway, 2006; Tibon, 2000; Winter, 2007; see McFarland & Mathews, 2005; Pettigrew & Tropp, 2000, for a meta-analysis).

Thanks to our paedomorphic-neotenous characteristics (Gould, 1977), we are afforded an extended period of elaborative developmental change (Ford & Lerner, 1992). The optimization of elaborative development, and of GLC, then, is dependent on the preservation of our prolonged youth, of the time and space needed to diversify our psychosocial repertoire. It is proposed that adaptive developmental regulations—mutually beneficial regulations between the individual and context—provide the developmentally protective time and space requisite for optimal, elaborative development. Adaptive developmental regulations, in turn, benefit the collective, with which these diverse individuals may have high levels of resourceful partnerships (e.g., as instantiated by GLC). Such partnerships theoretically represent *continued* adaptive developmental regulations—the mutually beneficial individual ↔ context relations that foster *continued* elaborative development that fosters *continued* GLC, and so on, nonrecursively. Figure 6.2, the culmination of this literature review, presents a nonrecursive structural model of the hypothesized relationships among adaptive developmental regulations (i.e., the *structure* of elaborative development), elaborative development (i.e., a defining *functional* attribute of an adaptive individual ↔ context structure), and GLC (arguably, one key *content* of an elaborative developmental structure).

HYPOTHESIS AND RESEARCH QUESTIONS

Given the vast and abstract nature of the theoretical architecture presented in this chapter, the present empirical study was admittedly only a preliminary step toward its elucidation. The purpose of the present study was to move toward an empirical understanding of the core hypothesized relation between elaborative development (a defining functional attribute of an adaptive individual ↔ context structure) and GLC (one key content of an elaborative developmental structure). The present study utilized cross-sectional quantitative data. As such, this research did not examine elaborative *development* per se or the hypothesized relationship between GLC and *continued* adaptive developmental regulations (Figure 6.2);

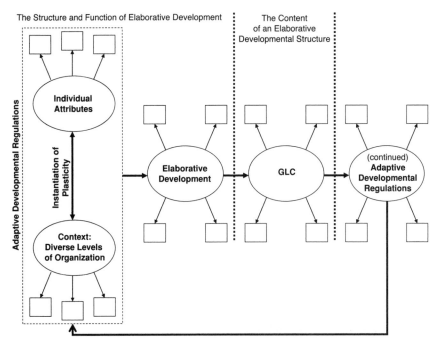

Figure 6.2   A nonrecursive structural model of the hypothesized relationships among adaptive developmental regulations, elaborative development, and GLC.

rather, it explored the hypothesized relation between elaborative *status* (intra-personal diversity at a single point in time) and GLC (Figure 6.3).

Theoretically, the labels of elaborative and decremental *status* would equate to elaborative and decremental *development* in the context of longitudinal data. These preliminary analyses, then, may provide bases for future (ideally longitudinal) research on this topic.

Accordingly, per the structural model (Figure 6.2), the hypothesized link between elaborative status and GLC was assessed (Figure 6.3). Specifically, to what extent does individuals' elaborative status predict their GLC scores? Moreover, does this relationship differ for the members of certain subgroups (as defined by age, sex, religion, and ethnicity)? The method employed to answer these research questions is discussed in the following section.

METHOD

The current investigation used quantitative data available from the John Templeton Foundation (JTF)–sponsored study, "The Role of Spiritual Development in Growth of Purpose, Generosity, and Psychological Health in Adolescence," a cross-sectional and multimethod study conducted in the greater Boston area (Richard M. Lerner, Principal Investigator). Full details of the methodology of

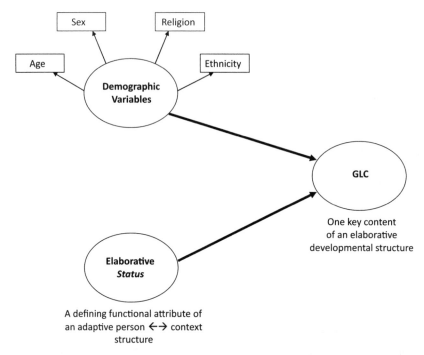

Figure 6.3   Measurement model of the hypothesized link between elaborative status and GLC.

the JTF study have been presented in prior reports (e.g., Lerner, Roeser, & Phelps, 2008; Roeser et al., 2007). Accordingly, I present only those features of methodology pertinent to the focus of this investigation.

Design

The data employed in the present investigation come from the Exemplary Youth Profiles in Contribution substudy, which was conducted during the spring semester of the 2006–2007 academic year. This substudy was designed with the primary goal of assessing contribution (generosity) ↔ spirituality relations among youth in the Boston, Massachusetts area. The overarching hypothesis guiding the substudy was that for some unknown percentage of young people highly involved in service activities, spirituality is an important underlying system of meaning and motivation.

A two-hour, multimethod protocol was designed for this substudy that included a brief introduction to the study foci/objectives and an overview of the data collection tasks; the acquisition of consent and review of confidentiality procedures; a sentence completion task (i.e., the Sentence Completion Test for Children and Youths, SCT-Y; Westenberg, Treffers, & Drewes, 1998); the production of a spontaneous life narrative (the Life Narrative Task, LNT;

Habermas, 2007); a semistructured interview covering multiple content areas (i.e., life goals and values, character, spirituality and religion, community and contribution, and imagined future); paper-and-pencil survey measures; and, finally, a wrap-up/debriefing session. For the present research report, I used information from the paper-and-pencil survey measures. As such, while complete details of the Exemplary Youth Profiles in Contribution substudy protocol can be found in Roeser et al. (2007), I describe as follows only those portions that were used in the present study.

Sample

The sample for this study consisted of 58 ethnically and religiously diverse high-school-age youth ($n = 30$; 10 males, 20 females) and college-age youth ($n = 28$; 14 males, 14 females) living in the Boston, Massachusetts area. Given the general purpose of the substudy reported in this chapter—i.e., to assess contribution (generosity) ↔ spirituality relations—the majority of participants ($n = 30$) were recruited from three youth-serving organizations committed to the engagement of youth in community service. Additional participants were recruited for either their notable commitment to community service or their notable engagement in spiritual and religious practices. These additional participants came from local public and private educational institutions ($n = 12$), and from the personal networks of the project staff ($n = 16$). Participants varied in regard to race/ethnicity and religious affiliation. Table 6.1 summarizes the demographic characteristics of the sample.

Procedure

Data collections lasted approximately two hours and were conducted by study staff. Each data collection took place between one participant and one research assistant in a quiet, private space (i.e., in participants' homes, schools, local libraries, youth-serving organizations and, as well, at locations at Tufts University). Following a brief description of the study foci and objectives, consent was acquired and confidentiality procedures reviewed. Participants were told that their personal information would be kept confidential and would not be released without their written permission, except as required by law. Finally, it was made clear that participation was entirely voluntary, that participants were free to withdraw from the study at any time, and that such a decision would not affect them. Once consent was acquired the data collection commenced, following the sequence noted previously (i.e., sentence completion task, life narrative task, semistructured interview, and paper-and-pencil survey measures).

Relevant to the present investigation, the last substantive task to be completed by participants was a 206-item paper-and-pencil survey, which took approximately 30 minutes to complete. The survey was designed to tap multiple content areas including positive youth development, spirituality and religiousness, personality characteristics, time use, nature and the outdoors, as well as

Table 6.1 Demographic Characteristics of the Study Participants

Category	Percentage (%)
Sex	
Male	41.4
Female	58.6
Age (range in years)	16–24
Race/Ethnicity	
African American	16.4
Asian American	5.5
European American	41.8
Latino/a American	12.7
Arab-American	3.6
Multiracial	10.9
Other	5.5
Does not identify with any ethnic group(s)	3.6
Religious Affiliation	
Christian	45.6
Jewish	15.8
Muslim	15.8
Other religious affiliation	5.3
Nonreligious	17.5

demographic characteristics. More details about the procedure may be found in Warren (2009).

Measures

The measures employed in this study come from the 206-item paper-and-pencil survey administered in the Exemplary Youth Profiles in Contribution substudy. As detailed in Warren (2009), an expert rater validation process was undertaken in order to extract from the survey a set of items pertinent to the formation of measures of elaborative status and GLC. In addition to these substantive items, information regarding age, sex, religion, and ethnicity was also used in the present investigation.

Elaborative Status and Great Love-Compassion

Given the absence of existing measures of elaborative status and GLC, Warren (2009) undertook an expert rater validation process in order to identify closed-ended items within the survey that could be used to operationalize these constructs. The methodology for this construct validation work has its roots in the theory and method of Jack Block (1971; see also Lerner, Dowling, & Chaudhuri, 2005; J. V. Lerner & Galambos, 1985; J. V. Lerner, Hertzog, Hooker, Hassibi, & Thomas, 1988; Teti, 2005). In his book *Lives through Time*, a study of personality development and change across the adolescent period, Block (1971) exploited archival data from two initially separate but, for his purposes, conjoined longitudinal studies. Block (1971) had the formidable task of regularizing and transforming the diverse materials (e.g., from interview protocols to X-rays to news clippings regarding the participants), comprising the two data sets into usable data. Both studies were conceived in an earlier era, so Block (1971) also had the task of organizing archival information using contemporary concepts, which differed considerably from those that guided the data collection. However, "given archival resources of sufficient intrinsic richness, the opportunity is developed of letting information collected in another time, for another purpose, speak to the conceptual questions of today" (Block, 1971, p. 34).

As described in Warren (2009), the present methodology follows in this tradition of employing expert raters to systematically codify existing information (belonging to disparate measures) in order to (1) place such diverse information within "the same conceptual and metrical framework" and (2) introduce "contemporaneous variables not specifically of interest at earlier times" (Block, 1971, p. 39). This process involved several steps *per construct* (i.e., for both elaborative status and GLC) for establishing convergent and divergent validation and, as well, measurement reliability. In addition, there was an interrelation of the processes for each construct in order to appraise convergent and divergent validity. These analyses of convergent and divergent validation and of internal consistency yielded a psychometrically useful set of 33 items indicative of elaborative status ($\alpha = .65$) and 17 items indicative of GLC ($\alpha = .86$). The specifics of this procedure may be found in Warren (2009).

Demographic Variables

In addition to the substantive items noted earlier, information regarding age, sex, religion, and ethnicity from the Exemplary Youth Profiles in Contribution substudy survey was also used in the present investigation. Inclusion of these standard demographic items enabled an examination of group differences in the link between elaborative status and GLC. However, the primary reason for including these items was so that they could be held constant while examining this link.

Age was determined by subtracting participants' date of birth from the date of testing. In addition to being treated as a continuous variable, age was recoded as a dichotomous variable in order to compare high-school-age and college-age participants along ES-DS and GLC.

Sex was measured with a single item in which participants were asked to check one of the following options: female or male.

Religion was measured with a single open-ended question: "What religion do you consider yourself currently, if any?" The following categories were created based on the responses obtained: Christian (i.e., Roman Catholic, Protestant, Unitarian Universalist), Jewish, Muslim, other religious affiliations (i.e., other religion, multiple religions), and nonreligious (i.e., atheist/agnostic).

Ethnicity was measured with a single open-ended question from Phinney's (1992) Ethnic Identity Scale: "In terms of my racial or ethnic group(s), I consider myself to be . . ." The following categories were created based on the responses obtained: African American (i.e., Black or African American, Somalian), Asian American, European American (i.e., White or European American, Caucasian), Latino/a American (i.e., Hispanic or Latino/a, Mexican American), Arab-American, Multiracial (i.e., more than one race or ethnicity), other, and does not identify with any ethnic group(s).

RESULTS

Before an examination of the hypothesized link between elaborative status and GLC, descriptive statistics (i.e., means, standard deviations, and sample sizes) were calculated for these two variables. These findings are presented in Table 6.2.

In addition, a series of one-way analyses of variance were conducted to identify any subgroup differences in elaborative status and GLC (Table 6.2). Although sex was not a significant factor for elaborative status and GLC, age was a significant factor for GLC, $F(1, 56) = 11.033$, $p < .01$. That is, college-age participants had significantly higher GLC scores than their high-school-age counterparts. Religion was also found to be a significant factor for GLC, $F(4, 52) = 3.493$, $p < .05$. Post hoc tests revealed that Jewish participants had significantly higher GLC scores than did nonreligious participants ($M = .3610$ and $M = -.4528$, respectively, $p < .05$). All other religious group differences were nonsignificant. Ethnic group differences could not be determined because of small subgroup sizes. These preliminary analyses underscored the potential relevance of age and religion to any exploration of the relationship between elaborative status and GLC. As such, both demographic variables were included in the regression analyses reported as follows.

Next, to examine the relationships among the variables of interest, elaborative status, GLC, age, sex, and religion were correlated. These correlations are summarized in Table 6.3. Again, ethnicity was excluded from this examination because of small subgroup sizes. Of course, these analyses were in accord with the previous findings: age and GLC were significantly correlated, $r(58) = .357$, $p < .01$. In addition, affiliation with the Jewish religion was significantly related to GLC in the positive direction, $r(58) = .270$, $p < .05$, whereas the absence of a religious affiliation was inversely related to GLC, $r(58) = -.342$, $p < .01$. These preliminary analyses underscored the potential relevance of age and religion to any exploration of the relationship between elaborative status and GLC. As such,

Table 6.2 Descriptive Statistics (Means, Standard Deviations, and Sample Sizes) for ES-DS and GLC

	ES-DS(z)	GLC (z)
Sex		
Male ($n = 24$)	−.0035 (.25)	.0786 (.57)
Female ($n = 34$)	.0046 (.30)	−.0747 (.61)
Age		
High-school-age ($n = 30$)	−.0637 (.33)	−.2424 (.56)*
College-age ($n = 28$)	.0708 (.20)	.2364 (.54)*
Race/Ethnicity		
African American ($n = 9$)	.0801 (.23)	.0327 (.56)
Asian American ($n = 3$)	−.0276 (.29)	.1595 (.39)
European American ($n = 23$)	−.0930 (.28)	−.1745 (.62)
Latino/a American ($n = 7$)	.0482 (.27)	.0932 (.36)
Arab-American ($n = 2$)	−.1103 (.49)	−.5783 (.50)
Multiracial ($n = 6$)	.1287 (.23)	−.1887 (.71)
Other ($n = 3$)	.1987 (.17)	.3445 (.58)
Does not identify with any ethnic group(s) ($n = 2$)	.4012 (.13)	.9051 (.28)
Religious Affiliation		
Christian ($n = 26$)	−.0309 (.32)	.0074 (.53)
Jewish ($n = 9$)	.1600 (.21)	.3610 (.53)**
Muslim ($n = 9$)	−.0034 (.24)	.2559 (.60)
Other religious affiliation ($n = 3$)	.0164 (.20)	−.2865 (.45)
Nonreligious ($n = 10$)	−.0447 (.30)	−.4528 (.54)**
Total sample ($n = 58$)	.0012 (.28)	−.0113 (.59)
Range	−.72 to .65	−1.12 to 1.10

Note: ES-DS = Elaborative Status-Decremental Status and GLC = Great Love-Compassion.
*High-school-age and College-age participants significantly differed in their GLC scores, $p < .01$.
**Jewish and Nonreligious participants significantly differed in their GLC scores, $p < .05$.

both demographic variables were included in the regression analyses reported as follows.

As noted in Table 6.3, age was also found to be positively related to affiliation with the Muslim religion, $r(58) = .486, p < .01$, and inversely related to affiliation with the Christian religion, $r(58) = −.445, p < .01$. These findings reflect the distribution of Christian and Muslim participants across the age range of this sample. That is, Muslim participants were skewed in favor of older ages and

Table 6.3 Correlations Among ES-DS, GLC, Age, Sex, and Religious Categories for the Quantitative Sample ($n = 58$)

	1.	2.	3.	4.	5.	6.	7.	8.	9.
1. ES-DS	–	.362**	.169	.014	−.104	.245	−.007	.013	−.075
2. GLC	.362**	–	.357**	−.128	.029	.270*	.194	−.109	−.342**
3. Age	.169	.357**	–	−.152	−.445**	.019	.486**	.037	.120
4. Sex***	.014	−.128	−.152	–	.124	−.123	−.123	.038	.013
5. R_1	−.104	.029	−.445**	.124	–	–	–	–	–
6. R_2	.245	.270*	.019	−.123	–	–	–	–	–
7. R_3	−.007	.194	.486**	−.123	–	–	–	–	–
8. R_4	.013	−.109	.037	.038	–	–	–	–	–
9. R_5	−.075	−.342**	.120	.013	–	–	–	–	–

Note: ES-DS = Elaborative Status-Decremental Status; GLC = Great Love-Compassion; R_1 = Christian; R_2 = Jewish; R_3 = Muslim; R_4 = Other religious affiliation; and R_5 = Non-religious. Key: *$p < .05$; **$p < .01$; ***0 = Male and 1 = Female.

Christian participants were skewed in favor of younger ages. Regression analyses reported as follows assess whether this multicollinearity between age and religion is reflected as redundancy between the individual coefficients of the two groups.

The first step in examining the hypothesized link between elaborative status and GLC was to correlate participants' quantitative scores on these measures. As presented in Table 6.3, elaborative status and GLC share a significant, positive correlation, $r(58) = .362$, $p < .01$. To explore whether this relationship differed for the members of specific subgroups (as defined by age, sex, religion, and ethnicity), additional correlations were conducted. Elaborative status and GLC were significantly correlated for high-school-age participants, $r(30) = .416$, $p = .022$; for girls, $r(34) = .444$, $p = .009$; and for European Americans, $r(23) = .460$, $p = .027$. However, these variables were nonsignificantly related across other ethnic and all religious subgroups, for college-age participants, and for boys. The small sample size for various subgroups limited the power of this exploration.

Hierarchical multiple regression analyses were conducted to determine the extent to which elaborative status predicts GLC, after controlling for the relevant demographic variables identified in the preliminary analyses. Three regression models were fitted to the data. Parameter estimates, approximate p values, and goodness-of-fit statistics are presented in Table 6.4.

The introduction of elaborative status in Model 3 significantly increased the overall model fit ($\Delta R^2 = .051$, $p < .05$). This model accounted for 42.8% of the variance in GLC. In regard to the individual predictor variables, and of great interest to this investigation, elaborative status had a positive, significant coefficient ($p < .05$), when controlling for sex, age, and religion. The other

Table 6.4 Hierarchical Multiple Regression of GLC on Sex, Age, Religion, and ES-DS: Parameter Estimates, Approximate p Values, and Goodness of Fit Tests ($n = 58$)

	Models		
	M1	M2	M3
Intercept	−1.828*	−3.030**	−2.664**
Sex****	−.090	−.035	−.055
Age	.105**	.136**	.120**
Jewish		.888***	.773**
Muslim		.496*	.497*
Christian		.684**	.653**
Other religious affiliation		.218	.184
ES-DS			.506*
R^2	.133*	.377***	.428***
dfE	55	51	50
ΔR^2		.245**	.051*
$Df(\Delta R^2)$	2	4	1

Note: ES-DS = Elaborative Status-Decremental Status and GLC = Great Love-Compassion.
Key: *$p < .05$; **$p < .01$; ***$p < .001$; ****1 = Male and 2 = Female.

predictor variables retained the significance they had in Model 2 (and in Model 1 in the case of age), with the exception of the Jewish dummy variable that lost significance (from $p < .001$ in M2 to $p < .01$ in M3) with the introduction of elaborative status. Such a loss in significance might suggest that these two variables are somewhat correlated. Although not presented in Table 6.4, an additional model was fitted to the data to test possible interaction effects. None of the interactions was significant.

Taken together, these quantitative findings provide evidence for the hypothesized link between elaborative status and GLC. That is, as predicted, elaborative status accounted for a significant proportion of the variance in GLC, after controlling for sex, age, and religion. Interpretation of these findings, methodological limitations, and suggestions for future directions are presented in the next section.

DISCUSSION

The problem that guided this work is the high prevalence of split conceptions of humanity (Overton, 1998, 2006); conceptions that undergird commitment to a *part* of humanity (*without* reference to the whole). Such incomplete commitment—as instantiated by war and genocide; dehumanization and moral exclusion; racialism and nationalism; and even *ordinary* love and compassion (Glaser, 2005)—is a major roadblock to the healthy functioning of humanity. The systemic organization and embeddedness of all living entities makes them open systems (Ford & Lerner, 1992) and, thus, "integrally fused together" (Thelen & Smith, 1998, p. 572). If to be is to be related to the *whole* of humanity, then commitment to a *part*—to the exclusion of the rest—will arguably compromise the healthy functioning of the whole (see Warren, 2009).

Overton (2006) wrote that the splitting of the whole into mutually exclusive parts is *coexistent* with the assertion that one of the parts constitutes the ultimate Real, the truth, and is, *alone*, worthy of our commitment. Mending the splits, then, eliminates the basis for such assertions. In the absence of splits, there are no logical grounds for incomplete commitment.

Accordingly, the purpose of this chapter was to outline, and begin to explore, the dynamic developmental processes involved in strengthening the human potential for Great Love-Compassion, for commitment to the *whole* of humanity. Following in the social-behavioral science tradition of scholarship about mending split conceptions of humanity (e.g., Adler, 1938/1964; Allport, 1954; Colby & Damon, 1992; Deutsch & Coleman, 2000; Fehr, Sprecher, & Underwood, 2009; Loevinger, 1966; Post, 2003; Staub, 2005a), I forwarded a nonrecursive structural model of hypothesized relationships among adaptive developmental regulations (i.e., the *structure* of elaborative development), elaborative development (i.e., a defining *functional* attribute of an adaptive person ↔ context structure), and GLC (one key *content* of an elaborative developmental structure; Figure 6.2). In short, GLC was proposed to be one key *content* of an elaborative developmental structure; a content that, in turn, theoretically perpetuates the *structure* and *function* of elaborative development, and so on, nonrecursively.

In the context of this structural model, the present study empirically examined the hypothesized relation between elaborative development and GLC, as it might exist at a single point in time. These preliminary analyses, then, may provide bases for future (ideally longitudinal) research on this topic.

ASSESSMENT OF THE HYPOTHESIZED LINK BETWEEN ELABORATIVE STATUS AND GLC

Before assessing the hypothesized link between elaborative status and GLC, preliminary analyses were conducted to obtain descriptive information about the variables under study. This information illuminated certain features of the present sample and helped determine the potential relevance of certain demographic variables to assessment of the hypothesized link. Both age and religion were found to be significant factors for GLC. First, college-age participants had significantly higher GLC scores than their high-school-age counterparts. When age was treated as a continuous variable in subsequent hierarchical multiple regression analyses, it predicted a significant proportion of the variance in GLC across models. Theoretically, we would expect to see GLC—awareness and actions on behalf of the whole—increase as a function of chronological age and of the various cognitive, emotional, social, and behavioral capacities that tend to co-vary with age. Affirmative responses on nearly all of the items comprising GLC reflect an other-centered orientation, which is considered by many scholars to be a developmental achievement (Elkind, 1967, 1981; Erikson, 1959; Loevinger, 1966; Maslow, 1958). Similarly, the frequency of certain helping behaviors depends on particular life circumstances (e.g., independence, mobility, gainful employment) that tend to co-vary with age. For example, helping "someone you don't know" requires contact with strangers, which is likely to increase with one's independence and mobility (see Warren, 2009, for a list of all items used in the present report). In turn, giving "money to charity" implies the financial means to do so (e.g., that one is gainfully employed). We would expect, then, affirmative responses to these helping behavior items to increase with participants' age. Longitudinal research is needed to move beyond this finding of covariation to examine whether and how GLC develops across ontogeny.

Second, religion was found to be a significant factor for GLC. Although the small sample size for certain religious subgroups limited the power of this exploration, post hoc tests indicated that the difference was between Jewish and nonreligious participants. That is, Jewish participants had significantly higher GLC scores than nonreligious participants. Regression analyses further indicated that Jewish, Muslim, and Christian participants had significantly higher GLC scores than nonreligious participants. Generally speaking, we might expect religion to be an important factor for GLC. Indeed, love and compassion are central to most religious doctrines, and religious institutions often encourage and even provide opportunities for many of the community service activities that are a part of the GLC index. Interestingly, however, participants affiliated with only certain religions were found to have significantly higher scores than nonreligious participants. Future research will need to increase the power of these analyses to determine whether this relationship exists as well within other religious subgroups. The use of qualitative data regarding the role of religion in participants' lives might further illuminate why this relationship exists for some religious individuals and not for others (Warren, in preparation).

Preliminary analyses also revealed that age was positively related to affiliation with the Muslim religion and inversely related to affiliation with the Christian religion. These findings speak to the skewed distribution of Christian and Muslim participants across the age range of this sample. Although age and religion were not completely redundant in their prediction of GLC, multicollinearity hampers the accuracy of findings. As such, future research should involve a larger, more representative sample so that the predictive utility of various demographic variables may be accurately determined.

These preliminary analyses underscored the potential relevance of age and religion to any exploration of the relationship between ES-DS and GLC. As such, both demographic variables were included in the regression analyses discussed as follows. The relevance of ethnicity could not be determined because of small ethnic subgroup sizes. Future research will need to employ a larger sample so that ethnic group differences may be tested and, if found to be significant, added to explanatory models of the variation in GLC.

In the context of the structural model (Figure 6.2), I assessed the hypothesized link between elaborative status and GLC (Figure 6.3). Evidence of the expected co-relation was first provided by correlation analyses. A significant, positive correlation was found within the overall sample. Additional subgroup analyses revealed that elaborative status and GLC were significantly correlated among high-school-age participants, girls, and European Americans, but not across other ethnic and all religious subgroups, among college-age participants, and among boys. As noted earlier, the small sample size for various subgroups limited the power of this exploration. Additional research is needed to examine whether and why this relationship holds for certain subgroups and not for others.

Finally, the hypothesized link was assessed through a series of hierarchical multiple regression analyses. As predicted, elaborative status accounted for a significant proportion of the variance in GLC, after controlling for sex, age, and religion.

This empirical validation of the hypothesized link between elaborative status and GLC has implications for theory, research, and practice concerned with the promotion of GLC, of commitment to the *whole* of humanity. If GLC is one key content of an elaborative developmental structure, then the promotion of GLC will require an understanding of how mutually beneficial individual ↔ context regulations emerge and are maintained across the life span and across diverse people and places. As noted earlier, such adaptive developmental regulations involve congruence between a person's individual attributes and the demands of his or her context (Lerner, 1982). Given the nonstationary quality of both an individual's attributes and the context's demands, fit must be fluid to remain structurally intact and functionally relevant over time. What, then, is the role of families, schools, and youth-serving organizations in supporting such fluid fit? Staub's (2005a) research on the frustration and fulfillment of basic human needs (i.e., the need for security, positive identity, feelings of effectiveness and control, positive connection to other human beings, autonomy, among others) is movement toward answering this question. However, more work is needed to identify the idiosyncratic variables that comprise elaborative developmental structures across diverse peoples and places.

Although this investigation provided empirical evidence of the hypothesized link between elaborative status and GLC, a majority of the variance in GLC was not explained by elaborative status. What do we think is happening when GLC emerges in the absence of elaborative developmental structures? What other variables help explain the presence of GLC? One potentially important factor may be the presence of opportunities (and, in turn, barriers to opportunities) to act on behalf of the whole. Such opportunities and their barriers may be indicated, for example, by participants' socioeconomic status, geographic location, and school and community resources. Future research concerned with expanding our explanatory model of GLC should examine the predictive utility of these contextual variables.

Additional predictor variables may be identified through qualitative assessments of "off-diagonal" (i.e., low elaborative status/high GLC) cases (see Warren, in prep). Salient features of the lives of these individuals may help explain the variance in GLC unaccounted for by elaborative status. In her qualitative analysis of four exemplary cases representing four possible relationships between elaborative status and GLC (i.e., high-high, low-low, high-low, and low-high), Warren (in prep) identified certain familial and religious social structures (external supports) that might facilitate the presence of GLC in the absence of high elaborative status. Future (longitudinal) research should expand the present explanatory model of GLC to include these and other variables, as well as determine whether the presence of these social structures is adequate for the emergence of (sustainable) GLC.

LIMITATIONS OF THE RESEARCH AND FUTURE DIRECTIONS

There are several limitations of this research. The first issue concerns the clear discrepancy between the structural model (Figure 6.2) and the measurement model (Figure 6.3), which poses a challenge to external validity (generalizability). Given the existence of several methodological limitations (e.g., the employment of cross-sectional data, a convenience sample, and the use of initially nonvalidated measures), the measurement model can only begin to illustrate the potential validity of the overall theoretical architecture. For instance, this research cannot speak to elaborative *development* per se or to the hypothesized relationship between GLC and *continued* adaptive developmental regulations (Figure 6.2). Instead, the research can only involve an examination of elaborative *status* (intrapersonal diversity) and its hypothesized relation to GLC (Figure 6.3).

Of course, there will always be an imperfect match between a structural model and its measurement model. This fact is especially true when one's conception is guided by a developmental systems view of organism-context relations, arguably the most complex model of human life currently involved in defining the theoretical architecture of developmental science (Lerner, 2006). Moreover, my use of an existing data set makes it difficult to establish such goodness-of-fit, in that existing measures may not be likely to map perfectly onto a new set of theoretical objectives. Nevertheless, the expert rater validation process yielded measures of elaborative status and GLC that provided patterns of covariation reflective of reliability and of convergent and divergent validity (Warren, 2009). Despite the challenges of poor structural and measurement model alignment, these preliminary analyses may provide bases for future (optimally longitudinal) research on this topic.

An additional limitation of measurement regards the sole use of self-report data. While self-report survey data may be one legitimate means for indexing elaborative status and GLC, the triangulated measurement of these constructs is recommended for future research. For example, behavioral observations as well as contextual data regarding possible "barriers to elaborative development" (i.e., constraints on adaptive developmental regulations) might better align the structural and measurement models. Moreover, the validity of self-report data may be compromised by the need to respond in socially desirable ways. This concern is especially relevant to the GLC measure. Favorable responses to items regarding equality, democracy, and universal caring are more socially acceptable than responses of disagreement. If possible, future research might include an "objective" report of self-other interactions or even a test of implicit attitudes (Carney, Nosek, Greenwald, & Banaji, 2007; Nosek & Banaji, 2009) to better assess this construct.

Future research might also consider triangulating these quantitative findings with qualitative data (see Warren, in preparation). Because this work represents a new area of empirical inquiry, it would be useful to build on quantitative depictions of elaborative status and GLC with qualitative depictions of how these constructs manifest within specific lives. As noted previously, such illustrative information may inform future measurement development, as well as offer insight into the circumstances surrounding the failure of elaborative developmental structures to eventuate in GLC. Considering the substance underlying the numbers would also bring into focus the discrepancy between the measurement and conceptual models, as well as the challenge that faces us of decreasing it.

Another limitation of measurement concerns the treatment of elaborative-decremental status as a single dimension. In light of theory and research that reveals development as a gradual process, wherein stage transitions result from modal (and not absolute) functioning (e.g., see Turiel, 1969, regarding *stage mixture*, and Piaget, 1972, regarding *décalage*), it is likely that elaborative and decremental status do not share a simple inverse relation. As such, future research should take steps to dimensionalize the measure of elaborative and decremental status, in order to reflect the possibility that individuals might be at once "high" *and* "low" on both constructs across domains. For example, the development of a coding scheme that treats elaborative and decremental status as separate dimensions would yield a more nuanced measure of these constructs.

Another set of limitations pertains to the participant sample used in the present investigation. Given the general purpose of the substudy reported in this chapter—i.e., to assess contribution (generosity) ↔ spirituality relations—the majority of participants were purposively sampled because of their exceptionality with regard to community service or spiritual and religious practices. This purposive sampling approach produced a very specialized sample, which poses a challenge to the generalizability of the present findings. Without knowing the underlying "true" distribution of elaborative status and GLC, these findings cannot be unequivocally interpreted. In addition, the relatively small sample size

($N = 58$) offers limited statistical power for assessing group differences. Future research would do well to involve a larger sample with more diverse participants in order to better understand the true range constituting the elaborative-decremental developmental continuum.

Nevertheless, despite the limitations of this project and partially independent of the specific findings, this chapter serves as an illustration of the possibility of launching an empirical line of research about concepts central to adaptive development and positive relations among the diversity of humanity. If only as an impetus, then, to further methodologically more sophisticated research, this chapter will have served a valuable purpose.

REFERENCES

Adler, A. (1927/1998). *Understanding human nature* (C. Brett, Trans.). Center City, MN: Hazelden.

Adler, A. (1938/1964). *Social interest: A challenge to mankind.* New York, NY: Capricorn.

Adorno, T. W., Frenkel-Brunswik, E., Levinson, D. J., & Sanford, R. N. (1950). *The authoritarian personality.* Oxford, England: Harpers.

Allport, G. W. (1950). A psychological approach to the study of love and hate. In P. A. Sorokin (Ed.), *Explorations in altruistic love and behavior* (pp. 145–164). Oxford, England: Beacon Press.

Allport, G. W. (1954). *The nature of prejudice.* Reading, MA: Addison-Wesley.

Allport, G. W. (1963). Behavioral science, religion, and mental health. *Journal of Religion and Health, 2,* 187–197.

Aron, A., & Aron, E. N. (1986). *Love and the expansion of self: Understanding attraction and satisfaction.* Washington, DC: Hemisphere.

Aron, A., McLaughlin-Volpe, T., Mashek, D., Lewandowski, G., Wright, S. C., & Aron, E. N. (2005). Including others in the self. In W. Stoebe & M. Hewstone (Eds.), *European review of social psychology, Vol. 14* (pp. 101–132). Hove, England: Psychology Press.

Baltes, P. B. (1987). Theoretical propositions of life-span developmental psychology: On the dynamics between growth and decline. *Developmental Psychology, 23,* 611–626.

Baltes, P. B., Glück, J., & Kunzmann, U. (2002). Wisdom: Its structure and function in regulating successful lifespan development. In C. R. Snyder & S. J. Lopez (Eds.), *Handbook of positive psychology* (pp. 327–347). New York, NY: Oxford University Press.

Baltes, P. B., & Kunzmann, U. (2003). Wisdom. *The Psychologist, 16,* 131–132.

Baltes, P. B., Lindenberger, U., & Staudinger, U. M. (2006). Life span theory in developmental psychology. In R. M. Lerner & W. Damon (Eds.), *Handbook of child psychology: Vol. 1, Theoretical models of human development* (6th ed., pp. 569–664). Hoboken, NJ: Wiley.

Baltes, P. B., & Smith, J. (2008). The fascination of wisdom: Its nature, ontogeny, and function. *Perspectives on Psychological Science, 3,* 56–64.

Barrows, T. S. (1981). *College students' knowledge and beliefs: A survey of global understanding.* New Rochelle, NY: Change Magazine Press.

Bjorklund, D. F. (1997). The role of immaturity in human development. *Psychological Bulletin, 122*(2), 153–169.

Bjorklund, D. F., & Green, B. L. (1992). The adaptive nature of cognitive immaturity. *American Psychologist, 47*(1), 46–54.

Block, J. (1971). *Lives through time.* Berkeley, CA: Bancroft.

Bobek, D. (2008). Maintaining civil society and democracy: Examining the role of youth development organizations in promoting civic identity development. *Dissertation Abstracts International: Section B, The Sciences and Engineering, 68*(7-B), pp. 4862.

Brewer, M. B., & Pierce, K. P. (2005). Social identity complexity and outgroup tolerance. *Personality and Social Psychology Bulletin, 31*(3), 428–437.

Brim, O. G., Jr., & Kagan, J. (Eds.). (1980). *Constancy and change in human development.* Cambridge, MA: Harvard University Press.

Buber, M. (1923/1970). *I and thou* (W. Kaufmann, Trans.). New York, NY: Charles Scribner's Sons.

Carney, D. R., Nosek, B. A., Greenwald, A. G., & Banaji, M. R. (2007). Implicit Association Test (IAT). In R. Baumeister & K. Vohs (Eds.), *Encyclopedia of social psychology* (pp. 463–464). Thousand Oaks, CA: Sage.

Case, R. (1992). The role of the frontal lobes in the regulation of cognitive development. *Brain and Cognition, 20*, 51–73.

Cassell, E. J. (2002). Compassion. In C. R. Snyder & S. J. Lopez (Eds.), *Handbook of positive psychology* (pp. 434–445). New York, NY: Oxford University Press.

Cialdini, R. B., Brown, S. L., Lewis, B. P., Luce, C., & Neuberg, S. L. (1997). Reinterpreting the empathy-altruism relationship: When one into one equals oneness. *Journal of Personality and Social Psychology, 73*(3), 481–494.

Clark, K. B., & Clark, M. K. (1939a). The development of consciousness of self and the emergence of racial identification in Negro preschool children. *Journal of Social Psychology, 10*, 591–599.

Clark, K. B., & Clark, M. K. (1939b). Segregation as a factor in the racial identification of Negro pre-school children. *Journal of Experimental Education, 8*, 161–163.

Clark, K. B., & Clark, M. K. (1940). Skin color as a factor in racial identification of Negro preschool children. *Journal of Social Psychology, 11*, 159–169.

Colby, A., & Damon, W. (1992). *Some do care: Contemporary lives of moral commitment.* New York, NY: The Free Press.

Colby, A., & Damon, W. (1995). The development of extraordinary moral commitment. In M. Killen & D. Hart (Eds.), *Morality in everyday life: Developmental perspectives* (pp. 342–370). New York, NY: Cambridge University Press.

Csíkszentmihályi, M. (1996). *Creativity: Flow and the psychology of discovery and invention.* New York, NY: HarperCollins.

Dabrowski, K. (1972). *Psychoneurosis is not an illness.* London, England: Gryf.

Dalai Lama, H. H., & Cutler, H. (1998). *The art of happiness*. New York, NY: Riverhead Books.

Damon, W. (2003). *Noble purpose: The joy of living a meaningful life*. Philadelphia, PA: Templeton Foundation Press.

Descartes, R. (1969). *The philosophical works of Descartes* (E. S. Haldane & G. R. T. Ross, Trans.). Cambridge, England: Cambridge University Press.

Deutsch, M. (1949a). A theory of cooperation and competition. *Human Relations, 2*, 129–151.

Deutsch, M. (1949b). An experimental study of the effects of cooperation and competition upon group process. *Human Relations, 2*, 199–231.

Deutsch, M. (1973). *The resolution of conflict: Constructive and destructive processes*. New Haven, CT: Yale University Press.

Deutsch, M., & Coleman, P. T. (Eds.). (2000). *The handbook of conflict resolution: Theory and practice*. San Francisco, CA: Jossey-Bass.

Elkind, D. (1967). Egocentrism in adolescence. *Child Development, 38*, 1025–1034.

Elkind, D. (1981). *The hurried child: Growing up too fast too soon*. Reading, MA: Addison-Wesley.

Elkind, D. (1987). The child yesterday, today, and tomorrow. *Young Children, 42*(4), 6–11.

Elkind, D. (1998). Behavioral disorders: A postmodern perspective. *Behavioral Disorders, 23*(3), 153–159.

Erikson, E. H. (1959). *Identity and the life cycle: Selected papers*. Oxford, England: International Universities Press.

Fehr, B., & Sprecher, S. (2004, July). *Compassionate love: Conceptual, relational, and behavioral issues*. Paper presented at the Conference for the International Association for Relationship Research, Madison, WI.

Fehr, B., Sprecher, S., & Underwood, L. G. (Eds.). (2009). *The science of compassionate love: Theory, research, and applications*. Oxford, England: Wiley-Blackwell.

Finlay, B. L., & Darlington, R. B. (1995). Linked regularities in the development and evolution of mammalian brains. *Science, 268*, 1578–1584.

Ford, D. H., & Lerner, R. M. (1992). *Developmental systems theory: An integrative approach*. Newbury Park, CA: Sage.

Fromm, E. (1956). *The art of loving*. New York, NY: Harper Perennial.

Fromm, E. (1973/1992). *Anatomy of human destructiveness*. New York, NY: Holt.

Geertz, C. (1973). *The interpretation of cultures*. New York, NY: Basic Books.

Gibson, K. R. (1991). Myelination and behavioral development: A comparative perspective on questions of neoteny, altriciality, and intelligence. In K. Gibson & A. Petersen (Eds.), *Brain maturation and cognitive development* (pp. 29–64). New York, NY: deGruyter.

Gilligan, C. (1982). *In a different voice: Psychological theory and women's development*. Cambridge, MA: Harvard University Press.

Glaser, A. (2005). *A call to compassion: Bringing Buddhist practices of the heart into the soul of psychology.* Berwick, ME: Nicolas-Hays.

Goleman, D. (2006). *Social intelligence: The new science of human relationships.* New York, NY: Bantam Books.

Gottlieb, G. (1997). *Synthesizing nature-nurture: Prenatal roots of instinctive behavior.* Mahwah, NJ: Erlbaum.

Gould, S. J. (1977). *Ontogeny and phylogeny.* Cambridge, MA: Harvard University Press.

Grace, H. A., & Van Velzer, V. (1951). Attitudes toward the Universal Declaration of Human Rights. *International Journal of Opinion and Attitude Research, 5,* 541–552.

Habermas, T. (2007). How to tell a life: The development of the cultural concept of biography. *Journal of Cognition and Development, 8*(1), 1–31.

Hornstein, H. A. (1982). Promotive tension: Theory and research. In V. Derlega & J. Grzelak (Eds.), *Cooperation and helping behavior: Theories and research* (pp. 229–248). New York, NY: Academic Press.

Jung, C. G. (1977). *Two essays on analytical psychology.* Princeton, NJ: Princeton University Press.

Kang, S., & Shaver, P. R. (2004). Individual differences in emotional complexity: Their psychological implications. *Journal of Personality, 72*(4), 687–726.

Keating, D. P. (2004). Cognitive and brain development. In R. M. Lerner & L. Steinberg (Eds.), *Handbook of adolescent psychology* (2nd ed., pp. 45–84). Hoboken, NJ: Wiley.

Kohlberg, L. (1972). A cognitive-developmental approach to moral education. *Humanist, 32*(6), 13–16.

Krishnamurti, J. (1992). *On relationship.* New York, NY: HarperCollins.

Lee, R. G. (2002). Ethics: A gestalt of values/the values of gestalt: A next step. *Gestalt Review, 6*(1), 27–51.

Lerner, J. V., & Galambos, N. L. (1985). Maternal role satisfaction, mother-child interaction, and child temperament. *Developmental Psychology, 21,* 1157–1164.

Lerner, J. V., Hertzog, C., Hooker, K. A., Hassibi, M., & Thomas, A. (1988). A longitudinal study of negative emotional/behavioral states and adjustment from early childhood through adolescence. *Child Development, 59,* 356–366.

Lerner, R. M. (1982). Children and adolescents as producers of their own development. *Developmental Review, 2,* 342–370.

Lerner, R. M. (1984). *On the nature of human plasticity.* New York: Cambridge University Press.

Lerner, R. M. (2002). *Concepts and theories of human development* (3rd ed.). Mahwah, NJ: Erlbaum.

Lerner, R. M. (2004a). *Liberty: Thriving and civic engagement among America's youth.* Thousand Oaks, CA: Sage.

Lerner, R. M. (2004b). Diversity in individual ↔ context relations as the basis for positive development across the life span: A developmental systems perspective for theory, research, and application. *Research in Human Development, 1*(4), 327–346.

Lerner, R. M. (2006). Developmental science, developmental systems, and contemporary theories of human development. In R. M. Lerner & W. Damon (Eds.), *Handbook of child psychology: Vol. 1, Theoretical models of human development* (6th ed., pp. 1–17). Hoboken, NJ: Wiley.

Lerner, R. M., Alberts, A. E., & Bobek, D. (2007). *Thriving youth, flourishing civil society: How positively developing young people may contribute to democracy and social justice: A Bertelsmann Foundation White Paper.* Gutersloh, Germany: The Bertelsmann Foundation.

Lerner, R. M., & Busch-Rossnagel, N. A. (Eds.). (1981). *Individuals as producers of their development: A life-span perspective.* New York, NY: Academic Press.

Lerner, R. M., Dowling, E. M., & Anderson, P. M. (2003). Positive youth development: Thriving as the basis of personhood and civil society. *Applied Developmental Science, 7*(3), 172–180.

Lerner, R. M., Dowling, E. M., & Chaudhuri, J. (2005). Methods of contextual assessment and assessing contextual methods: A developmental contextual perspective. In D. M. Teti (Ed.), *Handbook of research methods in developmental science* (pp. 183–209). Cambridge, MA: Blackwell.

Lerner, R. M., Freund, A. M., De Stefanis, I., & Habermas, T. (2001). Understanding developmental regulation in adolescence: The use of the selection, optimization, and compensation model. *Human Development, 44,* 29–50.

Lerner, R. M., & Kauffman, M. B. (1985). The concept of development in contextualism. *Developmental Review, 5,* 309–333.

Lerner, R. M., Roeser, R. W., & Phelps, E. (2008). Positive youth development and spirituality: From theory to research. West Conshohocken, PA: Templeton Foundation Press.

Lévinas, E. (1989). Martin Buber and the theory of knowledge. In S. Hand (Ed.), *The Lévinas reader.* Oxford, England: Blackwell.

Levinson, D. J., & Huffman, P. E. (1955). Traditional family ideology and its relation to personality. *Journal of Personality, 23,* 251–273.

Loevinger, J. (1966). The meaning and measurement of ego development. *American Psychologist, 21*(3), 195–206.

Markus, H. R., & Kitayama, S. (1991). Culture and the self: Implications for cognition, emotion, and motivation. *Psychological Review, 98*(2), 224–253.

Maslow, A. H. (1958). Higher and lower needs. In C. L. Stacey & M. DeMartino (Eds.), *Understanding human motivation* (pp. 48–51). Cleveland, OH: Howard Allen.

McFarland, S., & Mathews, M. (2005). Who cares about human rights? *Political Psychology, 26*(3), 365–385.

McKinney, M. L. (1998). Cognitive evolution by extending brain development: On recapitulation, progress, and other heresies. In J. Langer & M. Killen (Eds.), *Piaget, evolution, and development* (pp. 9–31). Mahwah, NJ: Erlbaum.

McKinney, M. L. (2000). Evolving behavioral complexity by extending development. In S. T. Parker, J. Langer, & M. L. McKinney (Eds.), *Biology, brains, and behavior:*

The evolution of human development (pp. 25–40). Santa Fe, NM: School of American Research Press.

McKinney, M. L., & McNamara, K. J. (1991). *Heterochrony: The evolution of ontogeny*. New York, NY: Plenum.

Moghaddam, F. M., & Vuksanovic, V. (1990). Attitudes and behavior toward human rights across different contexts: The role of right-wing authoritarianism, political ideology, and religiosity. *International Journal of Psychology, 25*(4), 455–474.

Morgan, G. W. (1968). *The human predicament: Dissolution and wholeness*. Providence, RI: Brown University Press.

Murphy, G. (1958). *Human potentialities*. New York, NY: Basic Books.

Nelson, C. A., Thomas, K. M., & De Haan, M. (2006). Neural bases of cognitive development. In R. M. Lerner & W. Damon (Eds.), *Handbook of child psychology: Vol. 2, Theoretical models of human development* (6th ed., pp. 3–57). Hoboken, NJ: Wiley.

Nosek, B. A., & Banaji, M. R. (2009). Attitude, implicit. In T. Bayne, A. Cleeremans, & P. Wilken, (Eds.), *Oxford companion to consciousness* (pp. 84–86). Oxford, England: Oxford University Press.

Ogbonnaya, A. O. (1994). Person as community: An African understanding of the person as an intrapsychic community. *Journal of Black Psychology, 20*(1), 75–87.

Opotow, S. (1990). Moral exclusion and injustice: An introduction. *Journal of Social Issues, 46*, 1–20.

Opotow, S. (2005). Hate, conflict, and moral exclusion. In R. J. Sternberg (Ed.), *The psychology of hate* (pp. 121–153). Washington, DC: American Psychological Association.

Overton, W. F. (1998). Developmental psychology: Philosophy, concepts, and methodology. In W. Damon & R. M. Lerner (Eds.), *Handbook of child psychology: Vol. 1, Theoretical models of human development* (5th ed., pp. 107–188). Hoboken, NJ: Wiley.

Overton, W. F. (2006). Developmental psychology: Philosophy, concepts, methodology. In R. M. Lerner & W. Damon (Eds.), *Handbook of child psychology: Vol. 1, Theoretical models of human development* (6th ed., pp. 18–88). Hoboken, NJ: Wiley.

Overton, W. F. (2010). Life-span development: Concepts and issues. In W. R. Overton (Ed.), *Cognition, biology, and methods across the life span: Vol. 1, Handbook of life-span development*. Editor-in-chief: R. M. Lerner. Hoboken, NJ: Wiley.

Perkins, D. F. (1996). An examination of the organismic, behavioral, and contextual covariates of risk behaviors among diverse groups of adolescents. *Dissertation Abstracts International Section A: Humanities and Social Sciences, 57* (2-A), pp. 0878.

Pettigrew, T. F. (1997). Generalized intergroup contact effects on prejudice. *Personality and Social Psychology Bulletin, 23*, 173–185.

Pettigrew, T. F. (1998). Intergroup contact theory. *Annual Review of Psychology, 49*, 65–85.

Pettigrew, T. F., & Tropp, L. R. (2000). Does intergroup contact reduce prejudice? Recent meta analytic findings. In S. Oskamp (Ed.), *Reducing prejudice and discrimination* (pp. 93–114). London, England: Erlbaum.

Phinney, J. S. (1992). The multigroup ethnic identity measure: A new scale for use with diverse groups. *Journal of Adolescent Research, 7*(2), 156–176.

Piaget, J. (1972). Intellectual evolution from adolescence to adulthood. *Human Development, 15*(1), 1–12.

Post, S. G. (2003). *Unlimited love: Altruism, compassion, and service.* West Conshohocken, PA: Templeton Foundation Press.

Post, S. G. (2005). Altruism, happiness, and health: It's good to be good. *International Journal of Behavioral Medicine, 12*(2), 66–77.

Post, S. G. (2008). It's good to be good: Health and the generous heart. http://www.unlimitedloveinstitute.com/publications/goodtobegood.html.

Post, S. G., Johnson, B., McCullough, M. E., & Schloss, J. P. (Eds.). (2003). *Research on altruism and love: An annotated bibliography of major studies in psychology, sociology, evolutionary biology, and theology.* West Conshohocken, PA: Templeton Foundation Press.

Putnam, H. (1987). *The many faces of realism.* Cambridge, England: Cambridge University Press.

Roccas, S., & Brewer, M. B. (2002). Social identity complexity. *Personality and Social Psychology Review, 6*(2), 88–106.

Roeser, R. W., Lerner, R. M., Phelps, E., Urry, H. L., Lazar, S., Issac, S. S., . . . & Du, D. (2007, March). *The role of spiritual development in growth of purpose, generosity, and psychological health in adolescence.* Invited presentation to the Fourth Biennial SRCD Pre-conference on Religious and Spiritual Development, Society for Research in Child Development (SRCD), Boston, MA.

Rogers, C. R. (1961). *On becoming a person.* Boston, MA: Houghton Mifflin.

Seligman, C. G. (1951). Multiple souls in Negro Africa. *Ancient Egypt, 3,* 103–106.

Shacham-Dupont, S. (2003). Compassion and love in relationships—Can they coexist? *Relationship Research News, 2,* 13–15.

Staub, E. (1989). *The roots of evil: The origins of genocide and other group violence.* New York, NY: Cambridge University Press.

Staub, E. (1990). Moral exclusion, personal goal theory, and extreme destructiveness. *Journal of Social Issues, 46*(1), 47–64.

Staub, E. (2002a). From healing past wounds to the development of inclusive caring: Contents and processes of peace education. In G. Salomon & B. Nevo (Eds.), *Peace education: The concepts, principles, and practices around the world* (pp. 73–89). Mahwah, NJ: Erlbaum.

Staub, E. (2002b). Preventing terrorism: Raising "inclusively" caring children in the complex world of the 21st century. In C. E. Stout (Ed.), *The psychology of terrorism* (pp. 119–131). New York, NY: Praeger.

Staub, E. (2005a). The roots of goodness: The fulfillment of basic human needs and the development of caring, helping and nonaggression, inclusive caring, moral courage, active bystandership, and altruism born of suffering. In G. Carlo & C. P. Edwards

(Eds.), *Moral motivation through the life span* (pp. 33–72). Lincoln: University of Nebraska Press.

Staub, E. (2005b). The origins and evolution of hate, with notes on prevention. In R. J. Sternberg (Ed.), *The psychology of hate* (pp. 51–66). Washington, DC: American Psychological Association.

Staub, E., & Pearlman, L. A. (2003). *Advancing healing and reconciliation in Rwanda and elsewhere.* Unpublished manuscript, University of Massachusetts at Amherst.

Staub, E., Pearlman, L. A., & Miller, V. (2003). Healing the roots of genocide in Rwanda. *Peace Review, 15*(3), 287–294.

Sternberg, R. J. (1997). Construct validation of a triangular love scale. *European Journal of Social Psychology, 27*(3), 313–335.

Sternberg, R. J. (1999). A balance theory of wisdom. *Review of General Psychology, 3,* 347–365.

Sternberg, R. J. (2003). A duplex theory of hate: Development and application to terrorism, massacres, and genocide. *Review of General Psychology, 7*(3), 299–328.

Sternberg, R. J. (Ed.). (2005). *The psychology of hate. Washington,* DC, US: American Psychological Association.

Sternberg, R. J. (2006). A duplex theory of love. In R. J. Sternberg & K. Weis (Eds.), *The new psychology of love* (pp. 184–199). New Haven, CT: Yale University Press.

Sternberg, R. J., & Barnes, M. L. (Eds.). (1988). *The psychology of love.* New Haven, CT: Yale University Press.

Sternberg, R. J., Hojjat, M., & Barnes, M. L. (2001). Empirical tests of aspects of a theory of love as a story. *European Journal of Personality, 15*(3), 199–218.

Suedfeld, P., Leighton, D. C., & Conway, L. G., III. (2006). Integrative complexity and cognitive management in international confrontations: Research and potential applications. In M. Fitzduff & C. Stout (Eds.), *The psychology of resolving global conflicts: From war to peace: Vol. 1, Nature vs. nurture* (pp. 211–237). Westport, CT: Praeger Security International.

Sullivan, W. (1972, March 29). The Einstein Papers: A Man of Many Parts. *The New York Times,* pp. 1, 20.

Templeton, J. M., Jr. (2004). *Thrift and generosity.* West Conshohocken, PA: Templeton Foundation Press.

Teti, D. M. (Ed.). (2005). *Handbook of research methods in developmental science.* Cambridge, MA: Blackwell.

Thelen, E., & Smith, L. B. (1998). Dynamic systems theories. In W. Damon & R. M. Lerner (Eds.), *Handbook of child psychology: Vol. 1, Theoretical models of human development* (5th ed., pp. 563–633). Hoboken, NJ: Wiley.

Thelen, E., & Smith, L. B. (2006). Dynamic systems theories. In R. M. Lerner & W. Damon (Eds.), *Handbook of child psychology: Vol. 1, Theoretical models of human development* (6th ed., pp. 258–312). Hoboken, NJ: Wiley.

Tibon, S. (2000). Personality traits and peace negotiations: Integrative complexity and attitudes toward the Middle East peace process. *Group Decision and Negotiation*, 9(1), 1–15.

Tobach, E. (1981). Evolutionary aspects of the activity of the organism and its development. In R. M. Lerner & N. A. Busch-Rossnagel (Eds.), *Individuals as producers of their development: A life-span perspective* (pp. 37–68). New York, NY: Academic Press.

Tobach, E., & Schneirla, T. C. (1968). The biopsychology of social behavior of animals. In R. E. Cooke & S. Levin (Eds.), *Biologic basis of pediatric practice* (pp. 68–82). New York, NY: McGraw-Hill.

Trungpa, C. (1973). *Cutting through spiritual materialism*. Boston, MA: Shambhala.

Turiel, E. (1969). Developmental processes in the child's moral thinking. In P. H. Mussen, J. Langer, & M. Covington (Eds.), *Trends and issues in developmental psychology*. New York, NY: Holt, Rinehart, & Winston.

Underwood, L. G. (2002). The human experience of compassionate love: Conceptual mapping and data from selected studies. In S. G. Post, L. G. Underwood, J. P. Schloss, & W. B. Hurlbut (Eds.), *Altruism and altruistic love* (pp. 72–88). New York, NY: Oxford University Press.

Underwood, L. G. (2004). Compassionate love. In S. G. Post (Ed.), *Encyclopedia of bioethics* (3rd ed., pp. 483–488). New York, NY: Macmillan Reference.

Underwood, L. G. (2005). Interviews with Trappist monks as a contribution to research methodology in the investigation of compassionate love. *Journal for the Theory of Social Behavior*, 35, 285–302.

Underwood, L. G. (2009). Compassionate love: A framework for research. In B. Fehr, S. Sprecher, & L. G. Underwood (Eds.), *The science of compassionate love: Theory, research, and applications* (pp. 3–25). Oxford, England: Wiley-Blackwell.

Warren, A. E. A. (2009). Strengthening human potential for great love-compassion through elaborative development. *Dissertation Abstracts International: Section B, The Sciences and Engineering*, 70(1-B), pp. 719.

Warren, A. E. A. (In preparation). The link between great love–compassion and elaborative development: A qualitative analysis.

Warshall, P. (1999, Fall). The Great Arsenic Lobster. *Whole Earth*. Retrieved from http://www.wholeearth.com

Westenberg, P. M., Treffers, P. D. A., & Drewes, M. J. (1998). A new version of the WUSCT: The sentence completion test for children and youths (SCT-Y). In J. Loevinger (Ed.), *Technical foundations for measuring ego development: The Washington University sentence completion test*. Mahwah, NJ, Erlbaum.

Winter, D. G. (2007). The role of motivation, responsibility, and integrative complexity in crisis escalation: Comparative studies of war and peace crises. *Journal of Personality and Social Psychology*, 92(5), 920–937.

Zohar, D. (1990). *The quantum self: Human nature and consciousness defined by the new physics*. New York, NY: William Morrow.

⟫◈⟪

When Beliefs Fit and When They Don't

Religious Conversion, Spirituality, and Positive Youth Development

DAVID HENRY FELDMAN, MONA M. ABO-ZENA, ROBERT W. ROESER, AND AMY EVA ALBERTS WARREN

For young adults, does religious conversion merely mark a religious change, or can it represent personal or religious development? The frequency and context of religious conversions warrant the attention of researchers and practitioners. According to a Pew Forum study of 35,000 people (2007), there is relatively high fluidity of faith commitments in the United States given that 28% of U.S. adults have left the faith in which they were raised during childhood in favor of another religion or no religion at all. The number of U.S. adults who identify with no religion is 16%, and it is 25% among emerging adults. Religious conversion is a complex process that provides a window onto a specific kind of religious/spiritual development. Given an integrated, holistic view of human development, religious/spiritual development is likely to affect and be affected by other aspects of development (Overton, 2006).

This chapter reports the results of an analysis of three cases of religious conversion during the adolescent/early adulthood periods. Data come from the John Templeton Foundation (JTF)–sponsored pilot study (PI: Richard M. Lerner). Religious conversion is defined as movement from one (or no) religious affiliation to another religious affiliation. All three cases in this study moved from a nonpracticing, or Christian or Jewish affiliation to a Muslim religious identification.

The primary aims of this study were to explore (a) possible relationships between religious conversion and aspects of positive youth development (e.g., community service) and (b) possible relationships between religious conversion and spiritual transformation (i.e., the extent to which religious conversion as a social phenomenon is associated with tangible psychological and behavioral changes in spiritual identities, commitments, and practices). In other words, when is religious conversion associated with spiritual growth and transformation and when is it not?

RELIGIOUS CONVERSION: PREVIOUS RESEARCH

The topic of religious conversion is one that has historically received substantial consideration by both psychology and religion scholars (Hall, 1904; Starbuck, 1899). Psychologists who studied meaning-systems tried to explain how an act performed repeatedly may begin to take on a new meaning for a person and become a moral necessity. In other words, how do new interests of religious import grow so salient that they dispel a previous mental or religious system (James, 1902/1985)?

Although conversion has continued to receive attention over the decades, the literature does not provide clear and widely referenced conceptualizations of what constitutes conversion (Snow & Machalek, 1984). For the purpose of this study, religious conversion will be marked by a shift from one religion to another or by a change from being nonreligious to being religious. Current literature on religious conversion is largely divided into two camps surrounding its antecedents. Proponents of a conceptualization of gradual conversion describe a long-term developmental process that is similar to normative religious development in which individuals develop new identity and worldview beliefs, new values and purpose, and new social networks over time (Kox, Meeus, & Hart, 1991; Paloutzian & Park, 2005; Zinnabauer & Pargament, 1998). So, the gradual unfolding of a life story with its related psychosocial changes is punctuated by a religious conversion that is publicly noticeable because it is manifest in alternative thinking, feelings, and behavior (Clendenen, 2006).

In contrast, conceptualizations of sudden conversion describe a "pseudo-solution for dealing with extreme disintegrating conflicts" (Salzman, 1953, p. 179). There are also accounts of what are perceived as positive sudden conversions (e.g., Saul on the road to Damascus) embedded in sacred religious texts (Clendenen, 2006). Finally, even when exploring what may seem a sudden instance of conversion, there are likely a series of early indications or antecedents that may help explain the shift.

A range of empirical studies have explored how variables such as personality, cognitive levels, and religious affiliation may affect conversion. It is thought that both levels of anxiety and well-being measures are related to conversion (Cooley, Ewing, & Jerry, 1965; Spellman, Baskett, & Byrne, 1971; Ullman,

1982). Post-conversion studies explore personality correlates (Stanley, 1964) and suggest a range between minimal and profound changes to different levels or aspects of personality, irrespective of whether the conversion appeared to be sudden or gradual or to a Western or Eastern faith tradition (Paloutzian, Richardson, & Rambo, 1999). Conversion requires an assessment of at least two religious systems and a comparative appraisal of the relative merits of each. Nonetheless, a study that compared 40 religious converts from four religious groups and 30 nonconverts found no evidence that cognitive factors are related to religious conversion (Ullman, 1982). Finally, it has been found that religious affiliation may both directly and indirectly inform the processes, attitudes about, and rates of exploring the merits of alternate religious systems, and thus conversion itself (Smith & Denton, 2005; Ullman, 1989).

CONVERSION AND ADOLESCENT DEVELOPMENT

The marked changes youth undergo during adolescence include ones related to body, mind, and social relations. Pubertal development and the intensification of emotion and emotionally guided behavior precede prefrontal lobe development and executive functioning by which youth can regulate emotion, reflect on behavioral functioning, and plan (Dahl, 2004). An adolescent's more sophisticated thinking includes being able to engage in hypothetical thought, deductive reasoning, and other analytic approaches conducive to comparisons between religious meaning systems (Piaget, 1972). From the perspective of social psychology, adolescents deepen their foray into peer culture and broader society. Increasingly aware of the conventional nature of social constructions, adolescents seek to integrate their concepts of self with the family and social influences (Erikson, 1950, 1968). The identity development process is widely considered to crystallize during adolescence; religious beliefs and attitudes were features of Erikson's original ideas about identity (1950, 1968), and questions about religion were incorporated into the identity formation interview Marcia developed (1966). From a developmental systems perspective (Lerner, 2002), the range of psychosocial factors both influence and are influenced by each other, culminating in assertions that there may be a sensitive period during adolescence regarding religious exploration (Good & Willoughby, 2008). As a result, even though conversion can occur at any age, adolescence by virtue of its special qualities is considered a more likely period for conversion (Spilka, Hood, Hunsberger, & Gorsuch, 2003).

Despite critical reviews of the conversion literature that point out that empirical studies are largely retrospective, cross-sectional, and lack methodological rigor (Paloutzin et al., 1993; Spilka et al., 2003), empirical evidence suggests that conversion largely occurs during adolescence. Spilka and others (2003) report a review of major studies of conversion with a total sample size exceeding 15,000 participants and find adolescence as the customary conversion time, with the age varying by study and location (see Argyle & Beit-Hallahmi, 1975; Beit-Hallahmi & Argyle, 1997; Gillespie, 1991; Roberts, 1965).

Although 40 years of empirical studies have consistently found adolescence to be the main period for conversion (Spilka et al., 2003), conversion and adolescents are notably absent from the developmental science literature, particularly the literature focusing on the religious and spiritual development of children and adolescents. *The Handbook of Spiritual Development in Childhood and Adolescence* has no entries related to conversion or converts (Roehlkepartain, Benson, King, & Wagener, 2006). The largest representative study of the religious/spiritual lives of adolescents in the United States focuses on a range of denominations within religious majority and minority groups, but it has no qualitative or quantitative data about youth converts (Smith & Denton, 2005), presumably because of low incidence in a representative sample. The Smith and Denton study (2005) does, however, explore the degree to which alternative religious traditions may be attractive given the participant's worldview, but notes that children's beliefs and practices largely track with those of their parents.

As indicated earlier, this minimal attention afforded to adolescent conversion is inconsistent with what is thought about the developmental processes related to the role of religion in development and religious development. Erikson's seminal writings about the identity development process (1950, 1968) consider religion one of the central issues of adolescence. Given widespread engagement in interactions that involve religion or religious questioning during childhood across cultures, religion has been described as a pancultural experience that is universal across cultures, but because of religious variation may take different forms (Feldman, 1994). The increase in the salience of religion during adolescence may encourage youth to seek religious/spiritual guidance, because it is thought to provide a moral meaning system as well as a social community to channel positive development (Dahl, 2004). Developmental theories invoked to explain most of the differentiated religiosity of adolescents focus on variations in adults' efforts to actively socialize or channel youth toward certain religious experiences, social learning, and spiritual modeling (Martin, White, & Perlman, 2003).

The developmental science and psychological literatures that focus on conversion consider broad issues of conversion and well-being, or provide case studies for particular individuals or groups that may illustrate a range of topics. Some studies consider the intersection between societal and political pressures and how they may manifest themselves in an individual's conversion (see Beaucage, Meintel, & Mossiere, 2007, for a study on religious transformation of migrants). Other studies use a range of methods and sample sizes to explore various outcomes of conversion, including self-discovery and well-being (Brandt, 2005), maturation and integration of concepts from a psychoanalytic perspective (Cohen, 2002), promoting resilience of at-risk youth (Coles, Elkind, Monroe, Sheldon, & Soaries, 1995), and the identity development outcomes of religious conversion (Carrothers, 2010; Speelman, 2006). Some studies attempt to reconstruct the beginning of the conversion narrative, such as an exploration of the motivation for converts that differentiates between primarily religious motivations and other primary motivations (Carrothers, 2010), mental health issues and conversion (Rosen, Greenberg, Schmeidler, & Shefler, 2008), or cognitive and emotional antecedents to conversion (Ullman, 1982).

Of the psychological conversion literature dealing with a particular social or religious group, the preponderance of the literature focused on converts to Islam (Sultán, 1999; Wohlrab-Sahr, 1999). Perhaps the most sustained focus on conversion to Islam has been forwarded by Köse and includes descriptive explorations of converts in Great Britain, their pre-conversion motifs, and their post-conversion outcomes (Köse, 1994, 1996, 1999; Köse & Lowenthal, 2000). The literature on Muslim converts is further specialized to reflect a focus on particular subgroups. For example, some literature considers conversion as rehabilitation with a focus on converts to Islam among prison or inmate populations (Ammar, Weaver, & Saxson, 2004; Dannin, 1996; Spalek & El-Hassan, 2007). Given the widely held views of Islam being a religion that oppresses women (Sensoy & DiAngelo, 2006), numerous studies explore women converts to Islam generally (Balchin, 2008; Rehman & Dziegielewski, 2003), and in particular contexts such as feminist approaches among Muslim converts in Sweden (McGinty, 2007).

RELIGIOUS CONVERSION: CHANGE OF SYSTEM OR RELIGIOUS DEVELOPMENT

Language regarding the terms currently represented in the literature regarding religious conversion (e.g., *alternation*, *transformation*) suggests a central tension within the field: Does religious conversion simply mark the change from one fixed system to another system with few new benefits, or does religious conversion mark some developmental change (Feldman, 2008)? The present study focuses on the qualities that distinguish a change, however radical, from a developmental, forward step. It also tries to identify some of the qualities that may distinguish the likely convert from his or her peers in tolerance for ambiguity, attachment style, and participation in religious activities.

Method

This investigation used quantitative and qualitative data available from the John Templeton Foundation (JTF)–sponsored study, "The Role of Spiritual Development in Growth of Purpose, Generosity, and Psychological Health in Adolescence," a cross-sectional and multimethod study conducted in the greater Boston area (Richard M. Lerner, Principal Investigator). Full details of the methodology of the JTF study are presented in the introduction to this book and in prior reports (e.g., Lerner, Roeser, & Phelps, 2008; Roeser et al., 2007). Accordingly, we present only those features of methodology pertinent to the research presented in this chapter.

Overall Study Design

The JTF study consists of multiple substudies. Modularization was employed in order to accomplish a multimethod, developmental systems theory–derived assessment of positive youth development, spirituality, and contribution among ethnically and religiously diverse adolescents and young adults (Roeser et al., 2007). Moreover, modularization allowed for the triangulated measurement of the study's key constructs. From a developmental systems theoretical perspective, outcomes such as contribution and generosity emerge as a result of dynamic interactions among the multiple levels of the developmental system (Lerner, 2002, 2006). A multimethod approach, enabled by modularization, was used to generate data about different facets of these complex relations.

The data employed in the present investigation come from the *Exemplary Youth Profiles in Contribution Sub-Study*. This substudy was conducted during the spring semester of the 2006–2007 academic year. The primary goal was to examine exemplary cases of religious conversion, spiritual transformation, and contribution to community; and to examine potential interactions among these focal areas of interest: spirituality, development, contribution. The overall hypothesis was that for some unknown percentage of young people who were highly involved in service activities, spirituality would be an important, long-term developmental influence on the motivation for activities that contribute to the community. The substudy was designed to assess how much, if at all, young people who had already demonstrated some level of community commitment would spontaneously talk about the role of spirituality in their lives, in general, and in relation to their service activities, in particular. As we began to conduct these interviews, we had occasion to learn about and meet three individuals who, rather than being notable for their service, were notable for their conversion to Islam in the post-9/11 period in the United States. Aware of the uniqueness of such individuals and the kinds of insights into spiritual development that might be gleaned from such atypical cases, we decided to include them in the data collection effort.

SAMPLE

The overall substudy sample consists of 60 ($n = 36$ females, 60%) ethnically and religiously diverse high-school-age adolescents ($n = 31$; 52%) and college students ($n = 29$) growing up or going to school in the Northeastern United States. These youth ranged in age from 17 to 24 years old (median = 19 years, 3 months). Ethnically, these youth self-identified as European American ($n = 22$, 37%), Hispanic or Latin American ($n = 7$, 12%), African American ($n = 6$, 10%), multiethnic heritage ($n = 6$, 10%), Asian American ($n = 2$, 3%), Arab American ($n = 2$, 3%), Asian Indian/Asian Indian American ($n = 1$, 2%), none

($n = 2$, 3%), other ($n = 3$, 5%), or missing/blank ($n = 9$, 15%). Religiously, participants self-identified as Christian ($n = 25$, 42%), Muslim ($n = 9$, 15%), Jewish ($n = 9$, 15%), Unitarian Universalist ($n = 1$, 2%), no religion ($n = 8$, 13%), multiple religions ($n = 1$, 2%), atheist ($n = 1$, 2%), other religions ($n = 2$, 3%), or missing/blank ($n = 4$, 7%).

As noted earlier, three of the cases included in the sample reported that they had changed their religious status (i.e., they converted religions). Specifically, each of these three individuals reported undergoing a religious conversion from self-identification as a Christian ($n = 2$) or as of mixed religious background (Christian/Jewish) to self-identification as Muslim or Sufi. These three cases are the focus of the present investigation. Case 1 is a 21-year-old Haitian-born female who was raised Christian and who came to the United States when she was 8 years old. Named Neara (pseudonym), this person identifies as "Black, West Indian" and "Muslim." Case 2 is a 22-year-old, U.S.-born male who had a Christian mother and a Jewish father. Ken (pseudonym) elected not to identify his ethnicity/race and self-identified as a Sufi. Case 3 is a 23-year-old, U.S.-born female who was raised in a Catholic Christian family. Penny (pseudonym) identifies as "Italian-American" and "Muslim."

PROCEDURES

All participants in the *Exemplary Youth Profiles in Contribution Sub-Study*, including the three individuals who converted, participated in a two-hour research protocol. The assessment protocol included a brief introduction to the study objectives and an overview of the data collection tasks, a review of confidentiality procedures and the acquisition of written consent by the individual to participate in the study, and the series of assessment tasks for the study. Consent was obtained directly from the participants, who were all 18 years of age or older.

Data collection took place between one participant and one research assistant in a quiet, private space (i.e., in participants' homes, schools, local libraries, youth-serving organizations, and at the university). Participants were told that the focus of the study was on how young people develop and construct their life stories, as well as how these stories reflect important life values, goals, and priorities. The reason for framing the study in these general terms was to keep participants unaware of the purpose of the substudy (i.e., to examine exemplary cases of religious conversion, spiritual transformation, and contribution), so as to allow these themes to emerge (or not) without specific cues during the course of the data collection.

Following a brief overview of the data collection tasks, consent was acquired and confidentiality procedures reviewed. Participants were told that their personal information would be kept confidential and would not be released without their written permission, except as required by law (e.g., in the case of reporting an instance of abuse or of hurting one's self or another person). Finally, it was made clear that participation was entirely voluntary, that participants were free to withdraw from the study at any time, and that such a decision would not affect them or their relationship with Tufts University.

The tasks included, in the following order: a paper-and-pencil sentence completion task, a life narrative task (LNT), a semistructured interview, and a paper-and-pencil survey. At the close of the data collection, participants were told a bit more about the purposes of the substudy and the larger JTF study, as well as the reasons behind their recruitment (e.g., their affiliation with an organization committed to the engagement of youth in community service).

Digital audio recordings were made of the LNT and semistructured interview. The audio files were transcribed verbatim by a professional transcription service. These transcriptions were checked by students who were trained to check the accuracy of the transcriptions by reading them while listening to the original audio files. All edits were made using the Track Changes function in Microsoft Word. These edited files, in turn, were checked by graduate school students, who either accepted or rejected the first-order edits in the course of following the same editing process (listening to original recording, reading the first corrected transcript).

MEASURES

Because identity formation and development is an important way we have conceptualized spirituality and spiritual development (see Furrow, King, & White, 2004; Roeser, Issac, Abo-Zena, Brittian, & Peck, 2008), a series of measures that assessed key aspects of adolescents' and emerging adults' identity development were administered. These included a sentence completion measure that assesses level of ego development (i.e., the *Sentence Completion Test for Children and Youths*, SCT-Y; Westenberg, Treffers, & Drewes, 1998); the production of a spontaneous life narrative concerning the seven most important events that have happened to the person in their life so far (the Life Narrative Task, LNT; Habermas, 2007); a semistructured interview covering multiple areas of identity and positive development (i.e., life goals and values, character, spirituality and religion, community and contribution, and imagined future; Roeser, Lerner, & Phelps, unpublished); and paper-and-pencil survey measures of spirituality, contribution, and other aspects of positive development. In this paper, we focus our analysis on the quantitative survey data and the qualitative data the participants gave in their life story narratives and interview responses. We describe these measures in more detail as follows.

Quantitative Survey Measures

The quantitative measures employed in this study come from a 206-item survey developed for this study. This survey took approximately 30 minutes to complete. The survey was designed to tap multiple content areas, including positive youth development, spirituality and religiousness, personality characteristics, time use, nature and the outdoors, and demographic characteristics. Before beginning the survey, participants were reminded that their answers would not be judged as right or wrong, and that they should answer with complete honesty. They were also instructed to skip any question they did not wish to answer. In a few cases, participants completed the survey at home and then returned it in a self-addressed, stamped envelope provided for them.

For the purposes of this study, we examined five main sets of factors assessed in the survey. These sets of factors pertained to participants' self-reported demographic information, attachment style, tolerance for ambiguity, personal well-being, and engagement in social and personal forms of religious practices.

Demographics

Participants' age was determined by subtracting participants' date of birth from the date of testing. Sex was measured with a single item in which participants were asked to check one of the following options: female or male. Religion was measured with a single open-ended question: "What religion do you consider yourself currently, if any?" Ethnicity was measured with a single open-ended question from Phinney's (1992) Ethnic Identity Scale: "In terms of my racial or ethnic group(s), I consider myself to be . . . "

Attachment Style

Participants' categorical, self-nominated attachment style was assessed with the *Adult Attachment Style* instrument (Bartholomew & Horowitz, 1991). This assessment tool involves one forced-choice item and four follow-up Likert scale items. First, participants respond to the following instructions: Following are four general relationship styles that people often report. Place a checkmark next to the letter corresponding to the style that best describes you or is closest to the way you are in relationships with others:

A. It is easy for me to become emotionally close to others. I am comfortable depending on them and having them depend on me. I don't worry about being alone or having others not accept me (i.e., secure attachment).

B. I am uncomfortable getting close to others. I want emotionally close relationships, but I find it difficult to trust others completely, or to depend on them. I worry that I will be hurt if I allow myself to become too close to others (i.e., fearful avoidant attachment).

C. I want to be completely emotionally intimate with others, but I often find that others are reluctant to get as close as I would like. I am uncomfortable being without close relationships, but I sometimes worry that others don't value me as much as I value them (i.e., preoccupied attachment).

D. I am comfortable without close emotional relationships. It is very important to me to feel independent and self-sufficient, and I prefer not to depend on others or have others depend on me (i.e., dismissive avoidant attachment).

Next, participants are asked to indicate the relevance of each description to their own general relationship style using a 7-point Likert scale ranging from 1 = *disagree strongly* to 7 = *agree strongly*.

Tolerance for Ambiguity

We assessed participants' tolerance for ambiguity using a subscale of the *Need for Closure Scale* (NFC; Webster & Kruglanski, 1994). Survey items are designed to measure participants' cognitive style regarding certainty/uncertainty. This subscale comprises nine items; however, in the process of scale construction, one item was omitted because of low reliability, thereby resulting in an eight-item scale. The response format ranges from 1 = *strongly disagree* to 6 = *strongly agree*. Examples of items include "I don't like situations that are uncertain" and "I like to know what people are thinking all the time." When all items are reverse-coded, higher scores indicate greater tolerance for ambiguity. In the full substudy sample, the Cronbach's alpha for this subscale was .69.

Personal Well-Being

Participants' well-being was assessed with a three-item scale (Roeser et al., 2008). Participants rated (using a scale from 1 = *not at all* to 5 = *very*) their overall happiness, stress level, and physical health at the time of testing. When the stress-level item is reverse-coded, higher scores indicate greater perceived well-being. In the present data set, Cronbach's alpha is .68.

Engagement in Religious Practices

The frequency of religious practice was assessed with a five-item scale constructed for the purposes of the present investigation. Three items regarding frequency and context of prayer (i.e., by oneself, with the family, and in a group) came from Smith & Denton's (2005) *Prayer Scale*. Two items regarding frequency and context of meditation (by oneself and with a group) came from Roeser's (2005) *Meditation Scale*. Meditation was defined for participants as "the practice of sitting silently, closing the eyes, and focusing one's attention on a single thing like the breath or a holy phrase; or the practice of quieting one's mind and becoming aware of what is happening from moment to moment in an open and accepting way." In the present data set, these items were combined to form a religious practices scale. The Cronbach's alpha for the combined prayer and meditation items was .79.

In addition to these survey data, data from two qualitative measures were examined in this study: the *Life Narrative Task* (LNT) and the semistructured interview.

Qualitative Life Narrative Task

Participants were asked to produce a spontaneous, 20-minute-long narrative of the most important events of their life so far (*Life Narrative Task*, LNT; Habermas, 2007). The LNT was administered with a script that was read verbatim. Participants were asked to think about the seven most important events that have happened to them and to write down each memory on a separate index card. Participants were then asked to temporally order the seven cards on the table in front of them, from the earliest to the most recent memory. Using these cards as a reference point, participants were asked to tell the story of their lives to date. Interviewers were instructed to remain silent during the course of the monologue, with the exception of alerting participants when they had five minutes left.

Qualitative Semistructured Interview Data

Participants also engaged in a semistructured interview covering multiple content areas (i.e., life goals and values, character, spirituality and religion, community and contribution, and imagined future).

DATA ANALYSIS

In order to describe the three conversion cases, we examined their scores on the survey measures and then compared their scores to a subsample of 22 same-aged participants drawn from the wider substudy. We compared these religious converts to a group of same-aged peers (50% female). Were the religious converts similar to this comparison group, or did their development, well-being, and current functioning suggest that their conversions were less associated with positive development than with a life of challenge and difficulty? Were these three cases of conversion also cases of positive and resilient development or of problematic changes or responses to life challenges?

In Figure 7.1, the scores of the 22 participants and the three conversion cases on the tolerance for ambiguity scale were plotted (range 1–6). Figure 7.1 shows that Ken stands out with respect to the other two conversion cases, as well as the sample of 22 individuals as a whole, as having a very strong tolerance for ambiguity as measured by this self-report subscale. In contrast, Neara has considerably less such tolerance, falling below the mean, whereas Penny rates herself as near the average on this measure.

Figure 7.2 shows the scores for the comparison sample and the three conversion cases on the personal well-being scale (range 1–5). As seen in Figure 7.2, Ken again stands out with respect to the other two conversion cases, as well as the sample of 22 individuals as a whole, in terms of having a very strong reported personal well-being. In contrast, Penny reports below-average levels of well-being, whereas Neara rates herself as near the sample average on personal well-being.

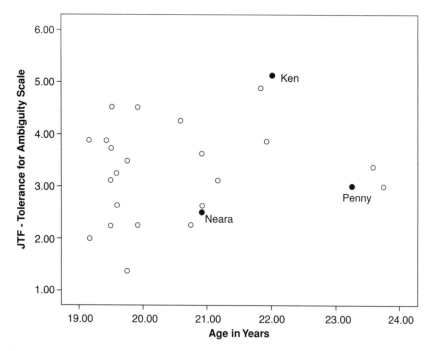

Figure 7.1   Scatterplot of tolerance for ambiguity scores for college youth ($n = 25$).

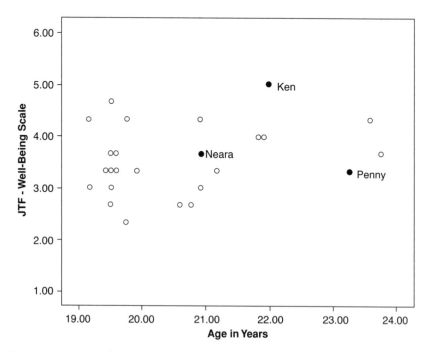

Figure 7.2   Scatterplot of well-being scores for college youth ($n = 25$).

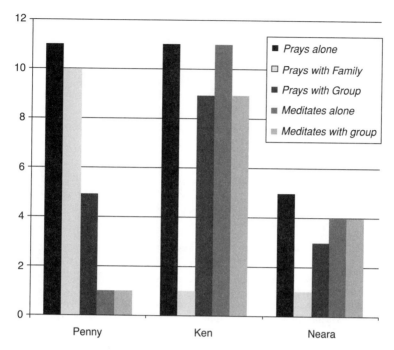

Figure 7.3   Bar graphs of frequency of religious practices for three conversion youth (1: Never, 2: Less than once a year, 3: About once or twice a year, 4: Several times a year, 5: About once a month, 6: 2-3 times a month, 7: Nearly every week, 8: Every week, 9: Several times a week, 10: Every day, 11: Several times a day)

Figure 7.3 presents the differential patterns of engagement in religious practices that characterize these three individuals. In this figure, the scores of these three cases are plotted with respect to how often they pray alone, with family, and with groups; and how often they meditate by themselves or with others, respectively. Penny indicates frequent engagement in prayer by herself and with her family; Ken reports frequent engagement in each of these five practices except praying with his family; and Neara reports relatively little engagement in prayer or meditation generally.

Finally, we examined the converts' self-reported attachment styles on both the categorical and dimensional measures of self-reported attachments described previously (Figure 7.4). On the categorical measures, Ken and Neara reported secure attachments (e.g., choice A = "It is easy for me to become emotionally close to others. I am comfortable depending on them and having them depend on me. I don't worry about being alone or having others not accept me"); whereas Penny rated herself as insecurely attached (e.g., choice C = "I want to be completely emotionally intimate with others, but I often find that others are reluctant to get as close as I would like. I am uncomfortable being without close relationships,

KEN	A. It is easy for me to become emotionally close to others. I am comfortable depending on them and having them depend on me. I don't worry about being alone or having others not accept me. (SECURE ATTACHMENT)
NEARA	B. I am uncomfortable getting close to others. I want emotionally close relationships, but I find it difficult to trust others completely, or to depend on them. I worry that I will be hurt if I allow myself to become too close to others. (FEARFUL AVOIDANT ATTACHMENT)
PENNY	C. I want to be completely emotionally intimate with others, but I often find that others are reluctant to get as close as I would like. I am uncomfortable being without close relationships, but I sometimes worry that others don't value me as much as I value them. (PRE-OCCUPIED ATTACHMENT)
	D. I am comfortable without close emotional relationships. It is very important to me to feel independent and self-sufficient, and I prefer not to depend on others or have others depend on me. (DISMISSIVE AVOIDANT ATTACHMENT)

Figure 7.4 Attachment styles of religious converts.

but I sometimes worry that others don't value me as much as I value them";
i.e., preoccupied attachment). In terms of the dimensional ratings of how much
each of the four attachment categories represented themselves, Ken rated himself
highest on the dimensional ratings for attachment style A only (e.g., a "5") and a
"1" on all three of the other styles. Neara rated herself highest on the dimensional
ratings for attachment style A ("6") and also the fearful avoidant style B ("5").
Neara rated herself lower for styles C ("3") and D ("2"). In contrast, Penny
rated herself highest on the dimensional ratings for both secure and insecure
attachment: Styles C ("6") and D ("6") for the insecure styles and lower on the
secure styles A ("5") and B ("3").

In summary, the results of the quantitative analyses suggest that these are
three very different people, although they all converted to Islam. Ken appears
as an open-minded, securely attached individual who is characterized by strong
personal well-being at this point in his life. Neara appears as someone who,
despite a general sense of security, experiences some fear in relationships and
tends to avoid ambiguity. She seems average in terms of her personal well-being
compared to her highly contributing peers, and she also does not seem to engage
very often in religious acts of devotion or contemplation. Finally, Penny seems
to be struggling a bit more to find her footing in relationships and to achieve a
sense of well-being.

To elaborate on these results and explore the validity of these conjectures
further, we next turned to an exploration of the interview and life narrative data
generated by these individuals.

THREE CASE STUDIES OF CONVERSION

We recognize that the obstacles to generalization from small numbers of cases are substantial, and these cases perhaps more than most because of their selection as part of a targeted sample. Our purposes were to begin to identify qualities, patterns, or issues that might emerge from this very limited set of cases that might help guide future research. Results should be interpreted in the context of these very limited aims.

As part of the larger study of civic engagement, community involvement, and religious and spiritual activities, we chose to study cases of conversion as perhaps the most extreme examples of religious commitment in our sample. If the adolescent years are a "sensitive period" for spiritual development, as has been recently claimed (Good & Willoughby, 2008), conversion would seem to be a particularly intense form of spiritual development. Converting and embracing a new religious affiliation is almost certainly perceived as a positive change for those who choose it, but it is not clear what kinds of changes, positive or less so, may accompany or follow the conversion decision.

Our goals in this part of the study were to attempt to understand what led each of our cases to the decision to convert; what changes in the individual's beliefs, attitudes, identity, and contributions to community may have accompanied conversion; and what contributions conversion may have made to positive youth development as defined in the literature and within this project (e.g., R. L. Lerner, 2009; R. M. Lerner et al., 2005; R. M. Lerner, Roeser, & Phelps, 2008). We also looked for changes that may not have been positive, that may raise cautions about the role of conversion in positive development.

In the current study, all three of the cases of conversion changed from relatively superficial affiliations with Jewish or Christian religions to stronger affiliations with the Muslim faith (although, to be sure, each individual embraced Islam differently as well). Within contemporary U.S. culture, the individuals in this study moved from majority to minority status by virtue of their decision to convert (at least one of the three individuals was also an ethnic minority).

We began with the assumption that the decision to convert to a minority religion, particularly to embrace the Muslim faith in this country at this time (post-9/11), was a complex process. We recognized that the information gathered about conversion in the study was largely a byproduct of its data gathering techniques; there were few parts of the questionnaires and interviews that dealt directly with conversion.

Because the larger study tended to constrain the sample to individuals who are positively involved in their communities, we did not expect to find in this study cases where conversion was a form of protest or defiance of majority culture. In a future study we would hope to compare the cases described here with other cases where there are fewer constraints on motives and reasons for deciding to convert. In general, the three cases described were positively motivated, (i.e., they saw the new religious affiliation as one that matched more closely their emerging core beliefs and that offered practices that were more satisfying than those they left behind).

Neara: Strength, Courage, and Determination in the Face of Adversity

Interviewed in 2007 when she was a 21-year-old college student, Neara was living with her mother and several siblings. The number of siblings in the family is not altogether clear; different answers were given to questions about members of her immediate family. The number is as large as 15 (7 brothers, 8 sisters), along with "11 cousins" who apparently live in the same place. In another question, Neara answered "13" to a question about how many brothers and sisters she has. She listed herself as a "middle" child, although she did not specify where in the sequence of brothers and sisters she is.

Neara was born in Haiti in 1986 and spent her first eight years in Port-au-Prince living with her mother and/or relatives in an extended family. Her father lived with the rest of the family only briefly, and when the family relocated to the United States, her father remained in Haiti. Neara's mother preceded her to the United States by about a year. With a brother and a sister, Neara arrived in 1994, which she reported to be a difficult transition.

> So it was really hard at first when I'd get up and I'd wake up in the morning and there were all these weird, different kind of people walking around my neighborhood. . . . And I'm like, "This is really strange and I don't know if I can deal with it." (p. 4)

Neara and her family were very poor, homeless at times, until 1996 when her mother, a nurse, found work in Cambridge, and the family's prospects improved. Neara, however, became increasingly upset with her mother's tendency to have too many children with too many men, a period she describes as very troubling; and she began to act out in school: ". . . every single day I'd show up and I'd be just in a terrible mood and start bullying people around" (p. 5).

Neara's life in school might well have deteriorated beyond repair, but in the seventh grade her teacher took a special interest in her, despite Neara's persistently negative behavior:

> I make fun of you. I talk back to you. I don't do your work. Why do you insist on, like, being so nice and coming to my house? . . . I never understood it at the time, but he was really dedicated into making me a better person. And he's still in my life to this day. (p. 5)

The other person who was a powerful influence in Neara's life was her grandmother, who took care of her in Haiti as a little girl. A year before the study interview, Neara's grandmother died. She described what her grandmother meant to her:

> She was handicapped. . . . And she would cook from her wheelchair. . . .
> She was my everything, you know. . . . She was the one that taught us
> about religion and how to be good people.
>   . . . So I got all the money that I had together. I was so broke. I went
> to her funeral [in Haiti] and said my piece. . . (p. 7).

And later, when asked where her ideas about good and bad, right and wrong came from, Neara immediately replied: "Not from my parents. From my grandmother. . . She was the bank. She was Oprah. She was Johnnie Cochran" (pp. 13, 15).

At about sixteen, Neara made a conscious decision to change her life, especially her relationship with her mother: "So I started getting my grades back together and not getting into as much trouble" (p. 6). But soon thereafter, Neara "discovered Islam," putting a new strain on her relationship with her mother. As she reported, the conflict between them was real but not as bad as it was earlier. By the time of the interview for this study, Neara had reached her 21st birthday, was in college, engaged, paying her own way, and hoping to move out of her mother's apartment within a year.

Religious Background

Neara was raised in Haiti as a Catholic and went to a Catholic school there. Neara, however, was not enthusiastic about her religion: "But I didn't have my first communion. By that time, I was just so sick of it, I didn't want to go there" (p. 15). When asked about converting to Islam, Neara described her reaction to the loose moral climate of her school, neighborhood, and home:

> Before I became a Muslim, there was a lot of judging. . . a very superficial
> thing. You know, you're in high school, you're a sophomore, that girl
> walked by, her skirt's like, up to her hips and you're like, "Ew, what a
> whore" type of thing. And [t]hen I started studying Islam, talking to
> people and seeing different things. (p. 19)

It was also a reaction to the church:

> . . . I remember when I was in sixth grade, and I went to church, and this
> guy walks in, and he had no shoes on, and his shirt was torn. He was
> homeless, and they were like, "No, sorry. You can't come in.". . . And
> I'm like, "But the guy is here to praise God."
>   [My Muslim brothers and sisters]. . . are not there to judge. They're
> willing to work with who you are because you're still a vital part of their

life and you're willing to change. . . . So to me, that was something like [eyebrow raising], like "Wow, that's powerful." (pp. 19–20)

When she describes her own approach to religiosity, Neara emphasizes the importance of the opportunity to grow: "I don't close my heart and my experiences with other people, because to me, that's stunting my growth and I don't want to do that" (p. 20). As we will see, this theme of growth and of seeking opportunities for growth is a central theme of Neara's presentation of herself. For Neara, religious experience is a very personal, almost visceral reality. She describes early experiences in the Catholic church as superficial and lacking authentic religious spirit:

It was when I was six years old. . . . I was going to be in the first grade and my grandmother was teaching me how to pray, because it's also part of the entrance exams . . . very prestigious. . . . And she knew that it wasn't really important that I believed it, it was important that I looked like I believed it. (p. 24)

Then, in contrast, Neara described her first genuine religious experience:

. . . it was the first time I went to the mosque and prayed. . . . I wanted to have something to pray for. . . . I prayed that my mom would accept Islam. And that was the first time that I actually experienced, had this warmth in my chest, and I couldn't even see straight because I was so concentrated on it. . . . If I was having a new drug, that's what it would feel like. Like I was high on that one prayer. (pp. 24–25)

As Neara describes it, the "tingling feeling" that she sometimes gets in prayer has become the lodestone for her life. She seeks that feeling in relationships, in her work as a teacher, and in her service activities. The primary basis for her judgments rests on what she perceives as a fundamental resonance in her body affirming the value of an experience, decision, or direction in her life.

Neara, however, is not particularly observant in her Muslim faith. She embraces its broad values and some of its specific practices and rejects others. She is, for example, engaged to a non-Muslim man. She does not cover her body in the prescribed ways. She does not heed the call to prayers five times a day. She does, however, embrace the tolerant, community-oriented ideal of service that she has found in Islam. As she said in her interview: "I consider myself a spiritual person. Religion, not so much" (p. 16).

She sees Islam as offering her the opportunity to strive to be a good person and to grow in her spirituality, yet sees other religious traditions as offering positive lessons and spiritual guidance. She is an "à la carte" Muslim, where the religion serves her as much as she serves it.

The Theme of Growth

Compared with our other two cases, there is a striking theme in Neara's materials of the importance of growth and development. In Neara's narrative and in her answers to questions, she often judges matters on the basis of their growth potential or lack of it. For example, in a sentence completion item that began with the prompt: "My biggest fear . . . " Neara completed the item with "is not progressing."

Another example was in response to a question about why school was currently the most important thing in Neara's life. She responded:

> I'd wake up, go to work, and come back. That's not age appropriate. There's no growth there. I'm not learning anything new. I'm not learning anything that's going to further my life. It's just—I'm going to get stuck there. (p. 9)

For Neara, becoming a Muslim serves her need to grow and become a better, more productive, more successful person judged by her own sense of what she should be doing. She is guided by her religious affiliation, but not to the extent that it controls her decisions. She sees herself as a strong, independent, and resilient person who will find what she needs to continue her growth and development.

When asked about her three wishes for the future, Neara replied that she wanted to "have my own place," be rich, and start an orphanage in Haiti. Being rich, she adds, would be nice, but the orphanage "I'm willing to spend time. It's not money, but I'm willing to spend time on it" (p. 30). One has the sense that this complex, self-reliant, ambitious, devoted young woman is likely to achieve her wishes.

Penny: A Devoted But Uneasy Convert

Penny is a young woman in her midtwenties who converted from being a nonobservant Catholic to a very observant Muslim when she was about 21. Her story appears on the surface to be one of a young woman who converts because she falls in love with a Muslim man, but this would be a serious misinterpretation. Penny gets angry when people (including fellow Muslims) describe her conversion as an effort to marry the Muslim man she was seeing at the time she began her conversion.

> "Oh, you just did it to marry him, blah, blah, blah." It's not true, you know? . . . Because he himself even said to me, "You know, . . . I don't want you to convert for me." I said, "I know there's a possibility that we're not going to be together, you know? . . . But I don't have any doubts." (Penny, 2007, p. 47)

A more accurate account would acknowledge that Penny was very much in love with a young Muslim man from Morocco, and would acknowledge that she was motivated to learn as much as she could about his faith and his culture. She began reading about the Muslim faith, and especially the Koran, in an effort to become closer to this young man. It became apparent very quickly, however, that her lover was not comfortable with Penny's interest in Islam; it also became apparent from her reading that their relationship was profoundly problematic within the framework of Islam. She understood that a decision to pursue her growing interest in the Muslim faith threatened her relationship.

Knowing this, Penny decided to continue her quest for knowledge about Islam. At the same time, she fought hard to continue the relationship, hoping to find a way to marry in the faith. The relationship was put in great jeopardy by an acquaintance from Diwa's (a pseudonym) country, who contacted his parents and told them that Diwa was seeing Penny. Diwa claimed that he pleaded with his parents to be able to continue the relationship with Penny, but it seems more likely that he recognized that he had been caught in a sinful (within the Muslim faith) transgression and had to stop seeing Penny, using his parents' unwillingness to accept Penny (even if she converted) as an excuse to end the affair.

Penny was (and is) profoundly devastated by the loss of her relationship with Diwa, and she clearly still has deep feelings for him:

> But I just—it still breaks my heart because, I'm sorry, I don't know. Something happened that's out of our control, and [crying] but he means a lot to me because that's why I learned about Islam. . . . (pp. 5–6)
>
> And sometimes I still, you know, at night, I have him in my dreams sometimes. (p. 6)

Penny reveals these thoughts and feelings as a newly married woman; she seems to be able to accept that her love for Diwa continues even as she has begun to build an observant Muslim life and marriage. Although she is still very much trying to transcend her loss, Penny used her new Muslim community to help her find an acceptable husband within the faith. Now married to a man a decade her senior, Penny seems to have made a commitment to have all facets of her life reflect her new faith. She seems content with her choices, although they appear to lack the intensity of her earlier relationships.

Penny's Experience Growing Up

As a child of poverty, Penny, her mother, and her father moved frequently. She was born in Massachusetts, but she lived as far away as Oregon before her family settled in Eastern Massachusetts where they lived for seven years before Penny (at age 21) left for Boston to get married for the first time. She had graduated from high school, gone to college for a year, lived in Eastern Massachusetts for another year, met a young man from the Dominican Republic working between academic years, and married him that September.

The marriage was almost immediately abusive, and Penny quickly decided that it was not viable. She left the marriage, but she was determined not to go back to her family and to make it on her own in the Boston area. She worked two jobs, found her own place, and was able to sustain herself. She met and fell in love with Diwa, the young Moroccan man, and she started to learn about the Muslim faith as part of her desire to know Diwa better. Penny continued to work, read the Koran at breaks, and before long it became clear to her that she wanted to convert and become a Muslim.

Although she is from a poor family, Penny described her experience growing up as loving and healthy. She had only positive and happy things to say about her mother and father. When asked if her relationship with her parents had always been positive, Penny replied:

> Oh, very much so, because it's always been all three of us, and we've been through so much, so many bad things.... (p. 14)
> I can't remember any time when they really forced anything upon me. And that's why I really, really love them. (p. 17)

Penny was an only child, but Penny's mother had a boy and a girl from a prior marriage, although these children did not live with Penny and her parents. The family unit was tightknit, supportive, healthy, and happy, despite occasional homelessness and almost constant poverty. By all accounts, Penny's parents have been consistently positive and supportive of her, including through the turmoil of her first marriage, the pain of her relationship with Diwa, her conversion to Islam, and her recent marriage to Nomar, a Muslim man almost a decade her senior.

Penny's parents were both Italian American Catholic, but neither was observant. Their church experience was pretty much limited to the major holidays:

> I remember that every Palm Sunday we would sneak into the church and grab a palm for my mom, because she didn't want to go to church, but she wanted, you know, the palm thing. So we would get her one. (p. 43)
> **Interviewer:** ... Well, why didn't you just grow up Catholic, then, and commit to that?
> I was like if he lets that happen to his son, I'm scared, you know?... (p. 44)
> [And earlier she said:] Well, the reasoning that Islam believes that Jesus was a prophet, it just made sense to me. Because I always kind of feared God in the way of why would he send down his son and have him killed like that? That always really, really bothered me a lot. (p. 20)
> **Interviewer:** So you didn't have any formal religious education...?
> Oh, no. I went to Sunday School, or CCD, but it was just a couple of times, really... (p. 44)

And when asked if she felt positively about God, Penny replied:

> ... I always felt like God loved me.... There was always that feeling,
> you know, they [her parents] always told me, you know, God loves you,
> and he forgives. And there were never bad, any bad connotations mixed
> up with religion.... (p. 43)

Penny remembered learning about the five pillars of wisdom of the Muslim
faith during high school and feeling that she would love to be able to follow them.
The possibility of doing so seemed unlikely then, but she was impressed with even
that small exposure to the Muslim faith, and perhaps the seeds of conversion were
sown then, emerging as she became involved with a Muslim man.

A positive relationship with God but skepticism about the religion she knew
as a child, consistent support and acceptance from her parents, some minimal
exposure to Islam among other world religions in high school, and the motivation
to become closer to the man with whom she was in love, these seem to have been
the main ingredients that combined to lead Penny to Islam. Not that they explain
her choice completely, but we can see that she moved from a base of secure and
consistent parenting, knowing that her parents would accept her decisions, and
entertained serious questions about the particular religion of her childhood.

As she began her explorations of Islam, two experiences helped galvanize the
direction she was taking. In one of these, a stranger came up to her when she
was reading the Koran during a break from her job as a cashier in an airport
restaurant:

> Yeah, because he just came—he was a younger brother, and he had
> glasses. I still remember what he—[big smile], he was just so pleased that
> I was reading Koran. And it made such an impact. I was like "What?",
> and I was like—After, I was just happy that I was, you know, because I
> guess, because you don't see a lot of Americans doing that [reading the
> Koran]. (p. 45)

The second experience was also at the airport, and this time Penny noticed
a young woman, a white American like Penny, who came to Penny's restaurant
and was covering her body in Muslim fashion. Penny asked this young woman:

> "Can I ask you a question?... What does it feel like to be an Ame-
> rican Muslim?"... And she said, "Well, you know, it's absolutely won-
> derful."... And she was just so enthusiastic about it....
>
> So she went back to her job.... And [later] she came back with a
> piece of paper. And she said to me, "Oh, I just wrote some things down."
> And I'm like, "Wow, she thought about me? She wrote stuff down? She
> came back?"

> . . . And then the next day she came to me, and she said, "You know, I just wanted to tell you that you should say, I mean you should do, your shahadah.". . . And I looked at her and I was like, she's really right. . . . "Well, do you have to go to a mosque?" And she said, "You just take a shower, and then you say the shahadah, and you're a Muslim." And I did that night. And then the next morning I put on my hijab, and I went to work. And everybody was so surprised. (p. 4)

When asked how her parents reacted to this change in her life, she responded that her parents were happy for her:

> They said, "Oh, that's good.". . . And my mom said, you know, "As long as you feel like you're closer to God, that's really good." So when I called and told them, "I did convert," they're like, "Wow, really?" It surprised them. . . . My mom, she has her beliefs, but she never tries to push them in an ignorant way. . . . My dad, he studied some world religions. . . . So I said, "Well, I wear the head scarf." And they said, "Oh, okay.". . . And my dad's like, "You look so pretty." (pp. 16, 17)

Before long, her father converted to Islam, and Penny is hoping that her mother will do so as well. One has the impression that her parents are totally devoted to Penny and trust her implicitly. She seems to be at the center of their lives; embracing Islam to sustain their closeness appears to be a natural decision for them.

As for how Penny experiences Islam so far, it seems to include intellectual, emotional, spiritual, and practical qualities, a clear guide as to how to live. Penny reports having thought about God a great deal while growing up, as in the example earlier of finding the logic of the Jesus story neither compelling nor uplifting. Later, after converting, Penny finds Islam more coherent and plausible, as in this comment:

> . . . Before I started learning about Islam, I thought, you know, if you're good you go to heaven. But what good is that? Like, do you just not lie and steal? . . . Islam is more guideline oriented, you know? Do this . . . If you do this, it'll be a good thing.
> . . . Because I feel more engaged than before. I mean, I felt less guided. Because I felt even when I talked to God, I felt like, well, is he listening? . . . And I just felt really kind of lost. And then once I learned about Islam, it all made sense, and it came into place. (pp. 20–21)

When asked what role religion now plays in her life, Penny replied:

> A big one. I think it's changed almost everything for the better. I mean, I have a better life. I have more goals, and I just feel more guided. And

I feel like if I follow the teachings of the prophet, salla sallam, that I'll be okay, that my life will be okay, you know? And, you know, hopefully I can achieve the level of Allah. (p. 24)

Becoming a Minority

Conversion for Penny meant shifting from mainstream majority to double minority: She is a minority within the larger, contemporary U.S. culture as a Muslim woman who wears a hijab, and she is a minority within Muslim culture in that she is not of Middle Eastern descent, speaks little Arabic, and is just beginning to learn the customs and practices of her new affiliations. These changes have not been easy for Penny; she reports being upset at being treated with hostility as a Muslim, as well as being treated with condescension as a new member of her Muslim community.

This theme of not being accepted is a central one in Penny's interview. An example of how she feels mistreated within the Muslim community shows how intensely she feels being shunned:

I mean, the community—I get offended if I say "Salaam" to a sister and she doesn't say it back, even if it's an obligation. My husband says don't worry about it. Let her be her. But I feel like the community should [n't] be like that, you know?
    Interviewer: Yeah, it's like an obligation and a common courtesy.[1]
    Right, yeah. And even if you don't consider me your sister because I'm white or whatever—(pp. 29–30)
    Interviewer: Do you feel like that happens for you [for] that reason?
    Yeah, very much. Mm-hmm.

A powerful example of being treated badly in the wider culture was when Penny went to the post office. As Penny recalls the incident:

And this white older man, he was at the desk . . . and I was standing in line, and the man decided to explain in extent how to fill out the change of address form. . . .
    Interviewer: Just assumed that you don't know the language?
    No, no, I wasn't—I was just in the line, right. But he looked at me. That's why he was doing it, to stall so he didn't have to wait on me. Because it was a white girl at the desk, you know, a customer. . . .

---

[1]It should be mentioned that the person interviewing Penny from the research team is herself a Muslim woman who covers herself and is part of the greater Boston Muslim community. This may well have influenced how Penny responded to questions and what words she chose to use. For example, Penny used many phrases from Islam, undoubtedly knowing that her interviewer was familiar with them.

There is no need to explain that much in detail.... But he kept looking at me, and he kept talking, and he kept looking at me.... I get up there...and I said, "I need a money order for $800." And I put the money on the counter, and I just stood there. Because I was really upset at that time, because I knew how he was treating me.... So I took the thing. And then I went over to the table, and I put my stuff in my bag. And I said, "Oh, I forgot, Nomar, the minute I put this on, I'm not a human being anymore..." I almost sometimes want to go ["D]o you realize I'm the same race as you? Number one, you shouldn't discriminate against any different race. But your own people? Are you kidding me?" (pp. 32–33)

When asked about volunteer or community-based activities, Penny described a high degree of involvement, although mostly outside of her Muslim community. She works in a homeless shelter and with a tutoring program that helps prepare inner-city girls for college. Her main contribution, though, is informally helping fellow students at her current school.

Penny appears to be academically talented, mentioning that she has the highest grades in her school. She is trained as an emergency medical technician (EMT), but she desires to attend medical school to become an emergency room physician. When asked about the volunteer work she does at her school, Penny said:

And I just, you know, I feel, like, a responsibility to help them, because these girls, the girls that go to that particular school, they're just high-school educated. They're not—they're what people would consider ghetto. I mean, they live in the poorest parts. Some of them are on welfare. They're young mothers. They're teen mothers. But I help them out a lot because maybe they weren't given the advantages that I am, that I did, that I had, you know.... Basically every day I help them out. (p. 41)

When asked for her three wishes for the future, Penny said that she wanted to become a mother, lose weight, and spend more time with her husband, all in the context of being a good Muslim woman. As she said,

And I know that I will be Muslim for the rest of my life. But I don't have any doubts. I mean, the only doubt I have is I don't know if I'm being good enough, you know? Insha'Allah, but it's hard.... I'm just trying my best, Insha'Allah. (p. 47)

Although her adjustment to her new faith and her new community has not been without its challenges, Penny seems deeply committed to the process of being an observant and devoted Muslim woman and defines her future in relation to that goal. At this stage of her life, she seems to be content with her choice and certain that she has made the right choice in converting to Islam.

Ken: A Natural Seeker of God

Ken, a child of the western suburbs of Boston, would seem an unlikely person to become a seeker of God and spiritual enlightenment through service and religious practice in the small Sufi Muslim Nimatullahi Order. His upbringing and early experience were typical and uneventful, as he describes them, and as he started college as a pre-med student. Within a year, Ken changed directions and set himself on a remarkable path of religious inquiry, culminating in a commitment to join the Sufi movement and live in the Sufi House in Boston.

Born of a relatively nonobservant Jewish mother and an equally nonpracticing Christian father, Ken describes celebrating the major Christian and Jewish holidays, but little else by way of religious training or experience. The family broke up when Ken was about three; Ken lived with his mother in the same house after his parents' divorce. Ken's mother remarried when he was in early elementary school, and he inherited a stepbrother his same age. Ken reports having a good, if not especially close, relationship with his new sibling, and he reports being on good terms with his stepbrother now that they are in their midtwenties.

An Improbable Conversion

As with the other cases in this study, Ken was not a particularly observant young man when he began the process that would lead to his involvement with the Sufi Muslim order to which he now belongs. In this respect, his conversion was not a major, wrenching process where he gave up a deeply held set of beliefs only to embrace an alternative set of beliefs. For Ken, conversion was the culmination of a search for a religion that matched his emerging needs and best understandings of what his life could become. Ken spoke of his early religious experiences as relatively casual:

> ... I was not raised religious, but I did celebrate Hanukkah and Christmas and Easter. ... We'd celebrate with friends Rosh Hashanah, Passover, Yom Kippur—but we would never go to temple or anything. So I was raised for the most part secular. (Ken, 2007, p. 1)

As for his town and its inhabitants, Ken describes them as disinterested in religious matters:

> We were just friends. It's America. You played sports together. Most of the kids didn't want to go to church on Sunday. ... There is very little connection between the youth and the church. ... No one talked about religion. It was a joke for most people. (p. 11)

Similarly, when Ken described his experience through high school, there is at first little that would indicate the intense spiritual search that would begin in his second year of college:

> ...I had a nice time in high school, played football and track and did musicals—and I had a very, very core group of friends. I was very close and I'm still close with them. (p. 2)

There is one important set of experiences, though, that Ken describes that may have helped prepare him for the major shift he would undergo as a college junior. Although the suburb where Ken and his mother lived was overwhelmingly white, Catholic, and middle class, a Hindu family of Indian descent lived next door. The family included four daughters, each of whom babysat for Ken when they became old enough to do so:

> ...I lived next door to a Hindu family, and they had four sisters, and they all basically took care of me. Because my mother was single, they all babysat for me in descending order.... I [sic] had a nice multicultural feel to just my little neighborhood.... The religion didn't really directly influence me, but the practice of the family, the wholesome values did. (p. 5)

In high school, although he did mostly typical social, sports, and school activities, Ken reported that he did have an interest in philosophy and religion. And he had one friend who shared his interests:

> Very busy, studying, sports, we didn't have time to breathe.... My friend Karl, we went on meditation retreats together. (pp. 12–13)
> Well, in high school, there was the search, too. But because there was a sort of negative feeling around religion, I had a negative feeling around religion, that people were brainwashed or very dogmatic. There was nothing attractive about that, nothing. So we searched in things like philosophy.... I was actually studying the biographies of the [philosophers].... And very often, philosophers were very sick.... Let's say, having a wholesome family versus people who are sleeping with multiple women, had many wives in a culture that didn't support having many wives. (p. 12)

More directly related to his religious search, Ken reported that he, as did some of his peers, engaged in some risky and unhealthy behaviors during his first two years of college. But Ken also described a period during which he began to reflect on what he was doing and how it was affecting and would likely affect him and his friends:

> And every party we would have...in college, our friends would get together and drink, we'd be outside philosophizing or talking about religion under the stars.... (p. 13)

Even as his search for a spiritual/religious home base was underway, Ken engaged in, from his perspective, some risky and dangerous behavior:

> Yeah. Of course I did bad things. People. I hurt people. I didn't make the safest decisions. (p. 10)
>
> ...I was involved in a sort of a circle of friends that weren't the most constructive people—there was a lot of drinking and many of the kids were doing cocaine and drugs and really a depressing atmosphere. I...studied philosophy, and I realized most philosophers were depressed. [laughs] I started studying...the saints—and they seemed to be the closest to sort of a wholeness and something that was lacking in my immediate environment. (pp. 3–4)
>
> So that was very important that—sort of that valley, and I'm very thankful for it because without it I'd just be still in the muck of things. (p. 4)

The Crystallizing Experiences

For Ken, an experience in his second year of college provided the needed catalyst to give direction to his quest. He had realized that philosophy was unlikely to provide answers to his questions about how to lead a good life, to be happy and fulfilled. He began to focus his studies on religions, especially on the most exemplary spiritual/religious individuals in each religious tradition. Switching from pre-med to film and religious studies followed after Ken enrolled in an elective course that involved meditation practice:

> And one of the best courses I took...was actually a meditation course, because it opened my mind up to my heart, up to a sort of spiritual practice. After the meditation course, I started looking at religions again.... I was very interested in Eastern thought and religion—but through the meditation I was able to read the Christian, the Jewish, and the Muslim texts from a different sort of heart-related viewpoint. And so then I started taking more courses and doing much more reading and more studies on basically all the religions. (pp. 2–3)

For Ken, it was reading the poetry of the Sufi Muslim tradition that most resonated with his heart and spirit:

> What gripped me most was actually the Sufi Muslims, the poetry. (p. 3)...

It was where my heart felt most at peace, where I felt the most peace.... I was very attracted to the Sufi poets... At first I was mostly practicing Buddhism.... But I felt it was missing this sort of passion, this yearning for the sort of divine. And the discussion of Buddhism largely focuses on emptiness.... [In] the Sufi poetry, I felt a lot of sort of the striving of this divine.... And also I found the Koran very poetic at the heart of it.... It's very beautiful with a great sense of truth coming from it. (p. 7)

... And I knew what I was looking for was in the mystic teachings. Largely the Sufis. So I stopped by the local Sufi House in Boston. And even there... I still didn't feel the connection. There was the director there... I felt a great deal of humility from him, and I was very attracted to his sort of spiritual qualities. So he invited me to go see the master of the orders..., the sheikh since 1953.

It was in the fall of his junior year of college that the director of the Sufi House took Ken and one other young man to London to meet the head of their Sufi order. This experience was life transforming for Ken:

... meeting him was the ultimate expression of someone who truly followed his spiritual path to the end and just his selflessness how he thought of himself. He just opened his house, didn't ask for money or anything, just felt he was very close to God. So that was the closest I had, where my heart felt closest to God was when I was with the Sufi master. (p. 8)

Ken does not see himself as limited by his involvement in the Nimatullahi Sufi order, but rather sees that order as the home base from which he pursues his spiritual goals:

Interviewer: So, you describe your religion now as Sufism?

Yes and no. I live in the Sufi House. As far as Sufism, again, I've never been a fan of -isms. And even the Sufis themselves said it's important not to self-identify yourself with Sufism.... I hope to stay in the Sufi order I'm in. I don't jump around too much. My devotion is there.... (p. 15)

But you have to be able to let go of the practice [of meditation]. You can be very attached to the practice of meditation, the solitude. But the real challenge and the real perfection is bringing it into society. This is the main teaching of Sufism that I've felt was lacking in Buddhism is how to integrate this experience of God in society. (pp. 29–30)

That's one of the greatest features of Islam is it's truly the middle path of religions. In Christianity, there's a great deal of focus on spirituality, at least at the core in the [early] history. . . . So Islam's kind of the middle way, which I like. (p. 30)

When asked to describe himself as more religious or more spiritual, Ken said:

Both. I still love religion. That's a caveat of mine. I do, both the outer and inner teachings.

Interviewer: And is that how you would sort of differentiate religion from spirituality?

Somewhat—it's difficult, because spirituality today can mean a lot of things. . . . So there's different senses of spiritual, and there's also people who are truly spiritual, and they don't follow, say, any religion. . . . They always think of others. . . . Just personally, I was very attracted to the teachings of religion. (pp. 16–17)

Parents' Roles and Reactions to Ken's Conversion

Ken's father seems to have had little influence on his conversion. As Ken remarked, after his parents' divorce he saw little of his father and did not look to him for support or guidance. Ken's stepfather, however, did play an important if largely negative role. Ken described his stepfather as self-indulgent and selfish, an example of everything Ken did not want to be. His mother, however, seemed to play a benign but not powerful role in the process:

My father I don't see so much, so it was never an issue with him. My mother I'm very close with, and . . . when . . . she saw I was doing the [unintelligible] prayer, she was like, "You're Jewish." [laughs] And I was, "Mom, I didn't go to Hebrew school. I wasn't raised Jewish." But she definitely saw the positive transformation. (p. 9) . . .

My stepfather was very self-centered, and especially with finances. . . . I found I have to do the opposite of whatever he's doing. . . . Because I saw he was very unhappy, and he'd get very angry—so that negative, that really showed me. (p. 6)

Interviewer: You mentioned, it was striking, how your mother recognized a difference in terms of just watching TV, helping around the house . . . (p. 25) . . . She noticed a transformation somehow? Did she see it that you just felt, you seemed more content or at peace? Or did she start seeing different types of choices?

Helping more . . . Let's say offering my help. Where I would [have been] lazy watching TV, let's say, or playing video games before, I'd be trying to help as much as I could with whatever I could. (p. 10)

Ken's Life and Practice as a Sufi Muslim

Ken is now a recent college graduate. He has been living in the Sufi House for more than two years. Here is how he describes his living situation and introduces his new girlfriend:

> ... I moved into the Sufi House and I essentially gave up all possessions and personal space because I lived in the tearoom, and every Thursday and Sunday people would gather in the tearoom before going up for the [Zek]—the remembrance. So I couldn't have anything out ever. So it was a great practice. So I still live there now, and I just graduated college as a writing and communications major. And I hope to be working as an EMT after the summer. And I just recently met my new girlfriend and she moved in with me, and she actually just became initiated as well. So that should be an interesting journey for both of us. (p. 3)

When asked to describe those things that he most values and what his main goals are, Ken emphasized service to the community as the best expression of service to God:

> The most important thing is finding—seeking help from God and finding where I can best help people and best serve in this world with these two hands that I'm given, this heart, this mind. So essentially what I care about most is helping people and finding the best way to help people to love everyone. (p. 5)
> ... Hopefully, you always grow. And every day is part of our Sufi practice. We're supposed to, it's called self-examination or calculation. You add up all your good deeds and all your bad deeds.... The emphasis on the moment, constantly aware of God, praying with every breath ... making sure that I'm always moving in a positive direction, always moving closer to God.... (p. 19) We're constantly supposed to be conscious and aware of God in every breath. So right is remembering God; wrong is forgetting about God. (p. 21)

In a statement that makes clear why Ken believes that religion is vital for success in serving the community, he contrasts spirituality without religion and spirituality in the context of a religious community:

> ... You can't walk the path alone. So ... the religious community really helps inspire you and keep you going during—let's say you've lost energy. A person walking beside is just going to help you.... That's another thing about spirituality versus religious ... Often people who define themselves as spiritual don't have a community [and] are at a lost for a lot of growth.... It's really impossible without other people helping you. (p. 21)

Ken appears to have found his path, recognizes that it is a long and challenging one, and eagerly submits himself to the goal of serving his God through serving his community. When discussing Ken, we agreed that he seemed to possess a spiritual/religious vitality and energy that, while difficult to describe, nonetheless was definitely there. It would not surprise us if Ken were one day to be called a Sufi master.

CONCLUSION

In this chapter we have examined the topic of religious conversion in three young people. Religious conversion has been a venerable topic in the study of religion, but it has not received much scholarly attention within developmental science. Within the overall framework of positive youth development (R. M. Lerner et al., 2005; J. V. Lerner, Phelps, Forman, & Bowers, 2009) that guides our work, we focused on the topic of conversion for what it might reveal about religious and/or spiritual transformation as a developmental process and as a possible marker for positive development of various kinds.

We examined three cases from the larger study sample, who chose to change their religious affiliation during adolescence or early adulthood, first on measures that were taken on variables such as tolerance of ambiguity, attachment style, and frequency of religious activities, like prayer. We then searched their interviews and life narratives for information about why and how they converted, what the conversion experience may have revealed about their involvement in community activities, and, more generally, to what extent religious conversion seemed related to positive development in these young people.

We found that the three religious converts (all to Islam in our study) differed from their peers, all of whom were chosen for the sample because of their in-volvement in their communities, on the quantitative variables as well as from each other. The three cases did not cluster into a distinct subgroup, but rather were different from each other as well as from the overall group. One of them, for example, had extremely high tolerance for ambiguity, whereas another had relatively low tolerance relative to the rest of the group. Even on the amount of religious practice activities measure, the three conversion subjects differed from each other: One stood out as having a high number of such activities, another for having a low number. From the quantitative measures, then, we found that our subjects were distinctive, as much from each other as from the overall sample.

When we looked at the quantitative data in the context of the case material, a more coherent picture of each of the three individuals began to emerge. We learned that each of the three had a unique set of experiences that gave rise to the decision to convert, that each converted in a different way, and that the form of Islam to which they converted also differed. One subject, for example, joined a Sufi order, another became a member of a largely Arabic-speaking Muslim community.

In all three cases, there was evidence to support the relationship between religious conversion and positive youth development. The decision to convert was made for different reasons by each participant, but the reasons were positive and growth seeking in each case. It is fair to say that each individual has tried to become a better person through the conversion process, better in terms of the criteria of the new faith community as well as better in terms of the wider society as they perceived it.

This is not to say that the conversion process was free of stress or that there were not problems associated with the decision and its implementation. In one case, for example, the newly converted Muslim woman found that she felt like a minority within her new community because she did not speak Arabic and because her appearance as a Western white woman made her stand out. She felt pride and satisfaction in having joined her new faith community, mixed with anger and frustration at being relegated to a secondary status. This may explain why her participation in religious practices was significantly less than the typical person in the sample and less than the other two converts.

In another case, we found that the interview and life narrative accounts gave a striking picture of a person at peace with himself, open to new experience, and devoted to serving others. His high score on the tolerance for ambiguity measure seemed consistent with the qualitative impressions based on interview and LNT data. Similar conclusions could be drawn from the attachment style measure, where this individual was rated as securely attached and open to very close emotional relationships, consistent with the way he described his life experiences.

As compelling as the pictures may be of our three cases, we recognize that the data from this study, quantitative and qualitative, were not gathered specifically for the purposes of studying conversion as a possible expression of positive youth development. Our sample was an opportunity sample, the study data were culled for relevant information but were not designed for these purposes, and our interpretations may be colored by what we knew about the purposes of the study and the individuals.

Overall, we can say that the results of this initial study were promising but limited, best used as guides for future research. We look forward to continuing our investigation into conversion as it relates to positive youth development in studies designed specifically for this purpose. Conversion from one religion to another, for example, may or may not be similar regardless of where one begins and where one ends. At this point we have only seen the process in three individuals, all of whom converted to Islam. Would the picture have been similar if they had converted to Catholicism or Judaism or Baha'i? Are there patterns that mark the conversion process that are distinct to each faith? Does it make a difference from what faith one leaves and to what faith one converts?

To begin to answer these and many other questions, studies are needed that follow larger numbers of cases from before conversion through the process and beyond. As part of a large-scale study, it would seem eminently feasible to include conversion as one of the ways that religion, spiritual development, and positive youth development may be fruitfully explored.

REFERENCES

Argyle, M., & Beit-Hallahmi, B. (1975). *The social psychology of religion*. London: Routledge & Kegan Paul.

Ammar, N. H., Weaver, R. R., & Saxson, S. (2004). Muslims in prison: A case study from Ohio State prisons. *International Journal of Offender Therapy and Comparative Criminology, 48*(4), 414–428.

Balchin, C. (2008). Women embracing Islam: Gender and conversion in the West. *Development in Practice, 18*(1), 150–152.

Bartholomew, K. & Horowitz, L. M. (1991). Attachment styles among young adults: A test of a four-category model. *Journal of Personality and Social Psychology, 61*(2), 226–244.

Beaucage, P., Meintel, D., & Mossiere, G. (2007). Introduction: Social and political dimensions of religious conversion. *Anthropologica, 49*(1), 11–16.

Beit-Hallahmi, B., & Argyle, M. (1997). *The psychology of religious behavior, belief, and experience*. London: Routledge.

Brandt, P. (2005). Religious conversion: A creative process. *Archives de Psychologie, 71,* 278–279.

Carrothers, R. M. (2010). Identity consequences of religious changing: Effects of motivation for change on identity outcomes. *Sociological Focus, 43*(2), 150–162.

Clendenen, A. (2006). In E. M. Dowling & W. G. Scarlett (Eds.), *Encyclopedia of religious and spiritual development*. Thousand Oaks, CA: Sage.

Cohen, M. (2002). Convergence: Maturation and integration in the course of a religious conversion. *Journal of the American Academy of Psychoanalysis & Dynamic Psychiatry, 30*(3), 383–400.

Coles, R., Elkind, D., Monroe, L., Shelton, C., & Soaries, B. (1995). *The ongoing journey: Awakening spiritual life in at-risk youth*. Boys Town, NE: Boys Town Press.

Cooley, C., Ewing, H., & Jerry, B. (1965). Adolescent response to religious appeal as related to IPAT anxiety. *Journal of Social Psychology, 67*(2), 325–327.

Dahl, R. E. (2004). Adolescent brain development: Vulnerabilities and opportunities, *Annals of the New York Academy of Sciences, 1021,* 1–22.

Dannin, R. (1996). Island in a sea of ignorance: Contours and dimensions of the prison mosque. In B. Metcalf (Ed.), *Making Muslim space* (pp. 131–146). Berkeley: University of California Press.

Erikson, E. (1950) *Childhood and society*. New York: Norton.

Erikson, E. (1968). *Identity, youth, and crisis*. New York: Norton.

Feldman, D. H. (1994). *Beyond universals in cognitive development* (2nd ed.). Norwood, NJ: Ablex.

Feldman, D. H. (2008). The role of developmental change in spiritual development. In R. M. Lerner, R. Roeser, & E. Phelps (Eds.), *Positive youth development and spirituality: From theory to research*. West Conshohocken, PA: Templeton Foundation Press.

Furrow, J. L., King, P. E., & White, K. (2004). Religion and positive youth development: Identity, meaning, and prosocial concerns. *Applied Developmental Science, 8*(1), 17–26.

Gillespie, V. B. (1991). *The dynamics of religious conversion: Identity and transformation*. Birmingham, AL: Religious Education Press.

Good, M., & Willoughby, T. (2008). Adolescence as a sensitive period for spiritual development. *Child Development Perspectives, 2*(1), 32–37.

Habermas, T. (2007). How to tell a life: The development of the cultural concept of biography. *Journal of Cognition and Development, 8*(1), 1–31.

Hall, G. S. (1904). *Adolescence: Its psychology and relations to physiology, anthropology, sociology, sex, crime, religion and education* (2 vols.). New York, NY: Appleton.

Ken (2007). *The life narrative of Ken/Interviewer Dr. Mona M. Abo-Zena*. The Role of Spiritual Development in Growth of Purpose, Generosity, and Psychological Health in Adolescence, Tufts University, Medford, MA.

James, W. (1902/1985). *The varieties of religious experience*. Cambridge, MA: Harvard University Press.

Köse, A. (1994). Post-conversion experiences of native British converts to Islam. *Islam and Christian-Muslim Relations, 5*(2), 195–206.

Köse, A. (1996). *Conversion to Islam: A study of native British converts*. New York, NY: Kegan Paul International.

Köse, A. (1999). The journey from the secular to the sacred: Experiences of native British converts to Islam. *Social Compass, 46*(3), 301–312.

Köse, A., & Loewenthal, K. M. (2000). Conversion motifs among British converts to Islam. *The International Journal for the Psychology of Religion, 10*, 101–110.

Kox, W., Meeus, W., & Hart, H. (1991). Religious conversion of adolescents: Testing the Lofland and Stark Model of religious conversion. *Sociology of Religion, 52*(3), 227–240.

Lerner, J. V., Phelps, E., Forman, Y., & Bowers, E. P. (2009). Positive youth development. In R. M. Lerner & L. Steinberg (Eds.), *Handbook of adolescent psychology* (3rd ed., pp. 524–558). Hoboken, NJ: Wiley.

Lerner, R. M. (2002). *Concepts and theories of human development* (3rd ed.). Mahwah, NJ: Erlbaum.

Lerner, R. M. (2006). Developmental science, developmental systems, and contemporary theories of human development. In R. M. Lerner & W. Damon (Eds.), *Handbook of child psychology: Vol. 1. Theoretical models of human development* (6th ed., pp. 1–17). Hoboken, NJ: Wiley.

Lerner, R. M. (2009). The positive youth development perspective: Theoretical and empirical bases of a strength-based approach to adolescent development. In C. R. Snyder & S. J. Lopez (Eds.), *Oxford handbook of positive psychology* (2nd ed., pp. 149–163). Oxford, England: Oxford University Press.

Lerner, R. M., Lerner, J. V., Almerigi, J., Theokas, C., Phelps, E., Gestsdottir, S., . . . & von Eye, A. (2005). Positive youth development, participation in community youth development programs, and community contributions of fifth grade adolescents: Findings from the first wave of the 4-H Study of Positive Youth Development. *Journal of Early Adolescence, 25,* 17–71.

Lerner, R. M., Roeser, R. W., & Phelps, E. (Eds.). (2008). *Positive youth development and spirituality: From theory to research.* West Conshohocken, PA: Templeton Foundation Press.

Marcia, J. E. (1966). Development and validation of ego identity status. *Journal of Personality and Social Psychology, 3,* 551–558.

Martin, T. F., White, J. M., & Perlman, D. (2003). Religious socialization: A test of the channeling hypothesis of parental influence on adolescent faith maturity. *Journal of Adolescent Research, 18,* 169–187.

McGinity, A. M. (2007). Formation of alternative femininities through Islam: Feminist approaches among Muslim converts in Sweden. *Women's Studies International Forum, 30*(6), 474–485.

Neara (2007). *The life narrative of Neara/Interviewer Dr. Amy Eva Alberts Warren.* The Role of Spiritual Development in Growth of Purpose, Generosity, and Psychological Health in Adolescence, Tufts University, Medford, MA.

Overton, W. S. (2006). Developmental psychology: Philosophy, concepts, methodology. In W. Damon & R. M. Lerner (Vol. Eds.), *Handbook of child psychology* (6th ed.), Vol. 1: *Theoretical models of human development* (pp. 18–88). Hoboken, NJ: Wiley.

Paloutzian, R. F., & Park, C. L. (Eds.). (2005). *Handbook of the psychology of religion and spirituality.* New York, NY: Guilford Press.

Paloutzian, R. F., Richardson, J. R., & Rambo, L. R. (1999). Religious conversion and personality change. *Journal of Personality, 67,* 1047–1079.

Penny (2007). *The life narrative of Penny/Interviewer Dr. Mona M. Abo-Zena.* The Role of Spiritual Development in Growth of Purpose, Generosity, and Psychological Health in Adolescence, Tufts University, Medford, MA.

Pew Forum on Religion and Public Life. (2008). *U.S. religious landscape survey.* Washington, DC: Pew Research Center.

Phinney, J. S. (1992). The multigroup ehtnic identity measure: A new scale for use with diverse groups. *Journal of Adolescent Research, 7*(2), 156–176.

Piaget, J. (1972). Intellectual evolutions from adolescence to adulthood. *Human Development, 15*(1), 1–12.

Rehman, T., & Dziegielewski, S. (2003). Women who choose Islam: Issues, changes, and challenges in providing ethnic-diverse practice. *International Journal of Mental Health, 32*(3), 31–49.

Roberts, F. J. (1965). Some psychological factors in religious converstion. *British Journal of Social and Religious Psychology, 4,* 185–187.

Roehlkepartain, E. C., Benson, P. L., King, P. E., & Wagener, L. M. (2006). Spiritual development in childhood and adolescence: Moving to the scientific mainstream. In

E. C. Roehlkepartain, P. E. King, L. Wagener, & P. L. Benson (Eds.), *The handbook of spiritual development in childhood and adolescence* (pp. 1–15). Thousand Oaks, CA: Sage.

Roeser, R. W. (2005). An introduction to Hindu India's contemplative spiritual views on human motivation, selfhood, and development. In M. L. Maehr & S. A. Karabenick (Eds), *Advances in motivation and achievement, Volume 14: Religion and Motivation* (pp. 297–345). New York: Elsevier.

Roeser, R. W., Lerner, R. M., Phelps, E., Urry, H. L., Lazar, S., Issac, S. S., Abo-Zena, M., Alberts, A. E., & Du, D. (2007, March). *The role of spiritual development in growth of purpose, generosity, and psychological health in adolescence.* Invited presentation to the Fourth Biennial SRCD Pre-conference on Religious and Spiritual Development, Society for Research in Child Development (SRCD), Boston, MA.

Roeser, R. W., Issac, S. S., Abo-Zena, M., Brittian, A., & Peck, S. C. (2008). Self and identity processes in spirituality and positive youth development. In R. Roeser, E. Phelps, & R.M. Lerner (Eds.), *Positive youth development and spirituality: From theory to research.* (pp. 74–105). West Conshohocken, PA: Templeton Foundation Press.

Rosen, D., Greenberg, D., Schmeidler, J., & Shefler, G. (2008). Stigma of mental illness, religious change, and explanatory models of mental illness among Jewish patients at a mental-health clinic in North Jerusalem. *Mental Health, Religion & Culture, 11*(2), 193–209.

Salzman, L. (1953). The psychology of religious and ideological conversion. *Psychiatry, 53,* 177–187.

Sensoy, O., & DiAngelo, R. (2006). "I wouldn't want to be a woman in the Middle East": White female student teachers and the narrative of the oppressed Muslim woman. *Radical Pedagogy, 1*(8).

Smith C., & Denton, M. L. (2005). *Soul searching: The religious and spiritual lives of American teenagers.* New York, NY: Oxford University Press.

Snow, D. A., & Machalek, R. (1984). The sociology of conversion. *Annual Review of Sociology, 10,* 167–190.

Spalek, B., & El-Hasssan, S. (2007). Muslim converts in prison. *Howard Journal of Criminal Justice, 46*(2), 99–114.

Speelman, G. (2006). Conversion as (dis)continuity of identity. *Psyche en Geloof, 17*(1), 22–31.

Spellman, C. M., Baskett, G. D., & Byrne, D. (1971). Manifest anxiety as a contributing factor in religious conversion. *Journal of Consulting and Clinical Psychology, 36,* 245–247.

Spilka, B., Hood, R. W., Hunsberger, B., & Gorsuch, R. (2003). *The psychology of religion* (3rd ed.). New York, NY: Guilford Press.

Stanley, G. (1964). Personality and attitude correlates of religious conversion. *Journal for the Scientific Study of Religion, 4*(1), 60–63.

Starbuck, E. D. (1899). *The psychology of religion: An empirical study of the growth of religious consciousness.* Ann Arbor, MI: Walter Scott.

Sultán, M. (1999). Choosing Islam: A study of Swedish converts. *Social Compass, 46*(3), 325–335.

Ullman, C. (1982). Cognitive and emotional antecedents of religious conversion. *Journal of Personality and Social Psychology, 43*(1), 183–192.

Ullman, C. (1989). *The transformed self: The psychology of religious conversion.* New York: Plenum Press.

Webster, D. M., & Kruglanski, A. W. (1994). Individual differences in need for cognitive closure. *Journal of Personality and Social Psychology, 67*(6), 1049–1062.

Westenberg, P. M., Treffers, P. D. A., & Drewes, M. J. (1998). A new version of the WUSCT: The sentence completion test for children and youths (SCT-Y). In J. Loevinger (Ed.), *Technical foundations for measuring ego development: The Washington University sentence completion test.* Mahwah, NJ: Erlbaum.

Wohlrab-Sahr, M. (1999). Conversion to Islam: Between syncretism and symbolic battle. *Social Compass, 46*(3), 351–362.

Zinnabauer, B. J., & Pargament, K. I. (1998). Spiritual converstion: A study of religious change among college students. *Journal for the Scientific Study of Religion, 37,* 161–180.

8

The Shared Pathways of Religious/Spiritual Engagement and Positive Youth Development

GABRIEL S. SPIEWAK AND LONNIE R. SHERROD

A POSITIVE APPROACH TO YOUTH DEVELOPMENT

Too often research on adolescence has centered on addressing the unique problems that arise during this period of development, viewing the period as a time of storm and stress. Historically, since Aristotle (1941; Muuss, 1988), this view has colored our research and policy on adolescence. However, in recent years, a new approach has arisen to guide scholarship on adolescent development. This approach challenges the idea that adolescence is necessarily a time of storm and stress (Lerner, 2004, 2007), and has come to be known as the positive youth development (PYD) approach to research (and policy) on adolescence.

PYD attends to the strengths of adolescents, rather than to their problems. It promotes the view that the best way to prevent or treat problems is to promote positive development. PYD recognizes that all youth have needs, so that youth vary according to whether their needs are met by the resources in their environments. This approach shifts the focus of both research and policy from fixing isolated issues of the individual to fixing environments such as families, schools, or neighborhoods. PYD has three important ideas: (1) Development is promoted by developmental assets, both internal and external; (2) communities vary in the qualities that promote the development of these assets; (3) societies vary in the qualities that promote these assets. In 1998, Benson and colleagues identified

40 developmental assets and showed that the more internal and external assets youth have, the healthier and more successful their development into adulthood is (Benson, 2007; Benson, Leffert, Scales, & Blyth, 1998; Benson, Scales, Hamilton, & Sesma, 2006). Overall, research indicates that young people have only 16.5 to 21.6 assets on average (Benson, 2007; Sherrod, 2007; Sherrod & Lauckhardt, 2008). Recent research has continued to examine and define the number and specific nature of developmental assets (Theokas, Almerigi, Lerner, Dowling, Benson, Scales, & Von Eye, 2005). Nonetheless, the PYD approach clearly highlights the need for youth policy to promote development based on the resources available to youth in their families, schools, and communities. Following decades of unsuccessful research and policy to eliminate risk and prevent negative outcomes, PYD advocates for examining the strengths youth have—rather than their risks—and for designing policies and programs oriented to promoting positive outcomes—rather than preventing negative ones (Sherrod, 2006).

The PYD approach does not promote the idea that adolescents do not have problems; some have problems that have quite serious negative implications for healthy development. Instead, it advocates the need, when addressing adolescent problem behaviors, to surround adolescents with healthy outlets that may neutralize or buffer them against the pervasive risk factors that can compromise development (Eccles, Barber, Stone, & Hunt, 2003). Hence, it is necessary to search for the most potent and generic protective resources when addressing adolescent problems. Religion and spirituality may offer one such protective resource (Abbott-Chapman & Denholm, 2001; Sinha, Cnaan, & Gelles, 2007).

The PYD model approaches developmental resources without the emphasis on amelioration, or even prevention, that characterizes approaches to psychopathology. Instead, the PYD approach seeks to identify an array of potential resources that may allow the adolescent to function as a resource to be developed (Roth & Brooks-Gunn, 2003). Previously, we have argued that PYD requires a starting point steeped in sensitivity toward individual differences and personal preferences (Sherrod & Spiewak, 2008). This view represents a substantially different orientation to adolescent research and policy than existed in prior eras of research (e.g., see Steinberg & Lerner, 2004). The aim in the PYD perspective is not to prevent a faltering developmental trajectory; rather, it is to promote whatever trajectory of strengths that may characterize a particular adolescent. Resources, in this context, are not directed toward diminishing a negative developmental path; rather, resources are used to promote optimal growth.

The Five Cs of positive youth development have been described: character, competence, confidence, connection, and caring (or compassion) (Bowers et al., 2010; Lerner et al., 2005; Phelps et al., 2009). Youth who exemplify these Five Cs are likely to be productive members of their community (Damon, Menon, & Bronk, 2003); that is, they are likely to be civically engaged. Contribution is often referred to as a sixth C (J. V. Lerner, Phelps, Forman, & Bowers, 2009). Connections between spirituality and each of these Cs can be articulated. Hence, it is important to examine the shared developmental pathways of spirituality and positive development. This chapter begins that task.

PYD AND RELIGIOSITY/SPIRITUALITY

Religiosity and spirituality are definite sources of PYD (Furrow, King, & White, 2004; King & Furrow, 2004; Lerner, Roeser, & Phelps, 2008; Youniss, McLellan, & Yates, 1999). Religiosity and spirituality uniquely expose young people to a wide variety of experiential interactions. The aim of this chapter is to explore and empirically examine the ways in which youth interact with spirituality/religiosity against the backdrop of the cognitive, affective, and behavioral tools that shape their development.

Head, Heart, and Hands: The 3H Model

In our previous research (Sherrod & Spiewak, 2008), we hypothesized three concentric domains of functioning common to both PYD and religion/spirituality: Head, Heart, and Hands. These domains capture the cognitive, affective, and behavioral dimensions of human experience. We argued that several developmental theories support such a holistic developmental approach under the rubric of the 3H model. The overlapping dimensions of Head, Heart, and Hands offer researchers a perspective that recognizes individual differences but acknowledges that people also have certain universal human tendencies. In this chapter, we review the essential tenets of the model and subject it to empirical analysis.

Head, Heart, and Hands, as a triangular perspective, are not without precedent. An implicit endorsement for this perspective is given by numerous articles concerned with cognitive, affective, and behavioral implications of various psychological constructs (e.g., Boyd & Yin, 1999; Hadjistravopoulos & Craig, 1994; Martin, Watson, & Wan, 2000); tripartite models are an aspect of several previous scholarly discussions of adolescent development. For example, one model of identity formation argues that there are three types of self-defining activities, ones that promote personal expressiveness, flow, and goal-directed behavior; together, these activities protect against problem behaviors in adolescence (Palen & Coatsworth, 2007).

The emphases of these three activities roughly shadow the broader Head, Heart, and Hands constructs. Personal expressiveness is manifest when an activity promotes subjective *emotional* satisfaction by projecting a sense of one's "true self." Flow also relies on matching subjective preferences with the activity, but in a manner that stimulates self-reflection and assists a *thought process* critical to constructing and affirming a burgeoning self-concept. Finally, goal-directed behaviors keep individuals *active* in a structured and meaningful manner.

Such work provides a rationale for why Head, Heart, and Hands should be the central dimensions on which to conceptualize adolescent development, especially in its positive orientation (i.e., the PYD model). This rationale can be summarized in three short arguments:

1. *The three Hs spur developmental growth.* While emotions inspire, thoughts compel, and effort engages, all three domains are equipped with the driving forces that transport youth along a healthy developmental track. Popular developmental initiatives, such as the national 4-H organization, where the three Hs of Head, Heart, and Hands are joined with Health to create the overarching mission of promoting positive youth development, provide testimony to the developmental efficacy of the 3H model.

2. *Seamlessly intertwined constructs reflect the complex systems of development.* It is easier to conceive of effective processes that merge these dimensions than it is to construct processes where only one dimension is in play. An adolescent's attitudes can be informed by any one of the three Hs, but, in turn, attitudes will seamlessly engage the other domains. Feelings can shape ideas and achievements can arouse feelings, and so on. There is no single direction or pathway from one domain to the next. For instance, one advocate for an integrated 3H model insisted that balancing the spiritual impulses of head, heart, and hands is paramount to achieving religious maturity (Hollinger, 2005).

3. *The 3H model fits adolescence.* Whereas earlier stages of development perceive individual differences largely through the lenses of genetic diversity or dramatic differences in the environment, adolescent differences have more diverse bases—especially when considering intentional, goal-directed behaviors. Fundamentally, PYD relies heavily on sparking adolescent initiative or motivating youth to engage in healthier activities or lifestyles (Eccles et al., 2003; Larson, 2000). For this reason, a focus on subjective fit between adolescents and self-defining activities is critical. The three Hs assist in sharpening this focus into a simple but comprehensive framework.

Spirituality/Religiosity

The 3H model necessarily shapes our perspective of what constitutes spirituality or religiosity. Some theorists exclusively approach the construct of spirituality as one of transcendence or as an experientially distinct form of consciousness (e.g., Elkins, 1998). Others approach religion in terms of social values or a core set of beliefs (e.g., Cornwall, 1989; Fuller, 2001). Still others, particularly sociologists, are most interested in measuring religious practice and ritual, leaving others to debate the differences between intrinsic and extrinsic religiosity (Smith & Denton, 2005). Of course, in the context of our model, these descriptions span the Head-Heart-Hands integration. The descriptions richly illustrate the full spectrum of human responses that the resources of spirituality and religion can provide.

Despite—or perhaps because of—the flexible range of spiritual leanings, the precise roles of religion or spirituality in positive development require more research. For instance, research about identity development has found that religion can be uniquely involved in reaching key developmental milestones (Erikson, 1968; Markstrom, 1999). In other words, religion promotes positive development. In one such formula, religion merges supportive environments with meaningful ideals and rituals to provide assets that underlie positive development (King, 2003). This role that we describe for religion is consistent with the most common approach in the PYD literature and is reflected in many of the chapters in this book.

However, spiritual development has also been treated in research as an independent path of development. In this case, both the processes and the outcomes of development acquire a distinctive character that differentiates them from the adolescent's general developmental trajectory. For instance, Fowler's stages of faith development, while inspired by mainstream developmental theorists such as Erikson and Kohlberg, is relatively independent of the stages of adolescent development. His theory of faith development concludes with a stage that reflects the highest faith achievement, but it does not necessarily represent the best psychological outcome (Fowler, 1981). Other examples of this approach that treats religion as a path independent of other developmental achievements include studies that seek to identify the determinants of religious or spiritual outcomes as intrinsically beneficial to the human condition (Cornwall, 1989; Waller et al., 1990; Neyrinck et al., 2006).

The 3H model is designed intentionally to reflect the shared paths of spiritual and positive adolescent development. Our model is predicated on a convergence between spiritual outcomes and PYD outcomes that evolve from the same essential human qualities, whether cognitive, affective, or behavioral. This model could be used for two distinct developmental purposes. One option would be to enroll spiritual or religious tools to assist in PYD growth. For example, transcendence can provide a foundation for improving generosity, another head-heart combination, as a developmental achievement. Alternatively, religious or spiritual development can benefit from PYD assets that are in accordance with the desired spiritual or religious outcomes. In many ways, spiritual and positive youth development are different sides of the same coin; they proceed fully interactively.

The Present Study

The present study is a first attempt at empirically confirming a model that we believe already has ample theoretical support. Utilizing constructs regarding both religiosity/spirituality and PYD, this study seeks to test a 3H model that links PYD outcomes with religious/spiritual outcomes. Specifically, we hypothesize that constructs of both religiosity/spirituality and PYD will fit into a measurement model that involves Head, Heart, and Hands as their underlying factors.

Method

The present study used data from the John Templeton Foundation (JTF)–sponsored study, "The Role of Spiritual Development in Growth of Purpose, Generosity, and Psychological Health in Adolescence," a cross-sectional and multimethod study conducted in the greater Boston area (Richard M. Lerner, Principal Investigator). Specifically, data from the *Positive Youth Development and Spirituality Questionnaire Sub-Study* were used. This substudy was designed to assess youth-centered perspectives on the relationship between PYD and spirituality during the second decade of life using questionnaires with samples of youth drawn from public schools, youth development programs, community colleges, and colleges and universities. The following research questions were explored: What are the relations among various indicators of PYD and spirituality in these samples? Do these relations vary by age, sex, and religious tradition?

Participants were recruited from the greater Boston, Massachusetts area. Four hundred eleven participants, ages 10 to 22 years, were recruited from middle schools, high schools, and after-school programs. An additional sample of 252 college participants, ages 18 to 23 years, was recruited. College participants were recruited using advertisements on Facebook and on college Web sites. Middle school and high school students were recruited using the personal connections of project staff (e.g., with local school administrators). The overall sample included 663 individuals ranging in age from 10 to 23 years. This sample included 31% middle school students, 31% high school students, and 38% college-age students. Participants were 49% female and 51% male; were ethnically diverse; and were mostly Jewish, Catholic, Protestant, Muslim, or had no religious affiliation.

Two versions of a questionnaire consisting of closed-ended items drawn from established measures of PYD and spirituality were constructed. The first version was delivered on a voice-enhanced personal digital assistant (PDA) for middle and high school students. The second version was a Web-based questionnaire for college-age participants using the same items.

Participants in middle school, high school, and after-school settings completed the questionnaire on the PDA after instructions were given on how to use the devices. Responses were downloaded from the PDAs to a computer. Participants who completed the questionnaire on the Web were assigned unique identification numbers.

For the present study, the biggest challenge was identifying survey responses that indexed the religious and PYD constructs as they relate to the 3H model. Because Head, Heart, and Hands are so pervasive, categorizing constructs is complicated. That is, some constructs might involve all three domains in some capacity, yet a scoring system that coded constructs as undifferentiated would defeat the purpose of these analyses. Accordingly, in cases where all three

Table 8.1 Expected Relationships Between Measured Constructs and Head, Heart, and Hands Factors

Variable	Head	Heart	Hands
Belief	X		
Religious practice	X		X
Transcendence	X	X	
Caring		X	
Generosity		X	X
Social conscience		X	X
Help			X

constructs were in evidence, coding was based on determining the most salient of the 3Hs. Moreover, as there was no existing scale for assessing Head, Heart, or Hands, we used correlational analyses to generate a measurement model using the constructs from the aforementioned questionnaires. Seven variables were chosen to assess Head, Heart, and Hands in a confirmatory factor analysis using LISREL 8.80 (Jöreskog & Sörbom, 1996; see Table 8.1).

The Head factor was indexed by the *belief* scale on the survey. This scale was composed originally of 21 items. An exploratory factor analysis revealed that about 14 of those items could be consolidated into a scale that represents fundamental questions of philosophy or theology. In this vein, items asking participants for their perspectives on the existence of God, life after death, and heaven and hell were included, whereas items asking whether people are generally good or sinful were omitted. We felt that this concentrated measure most directly tapped the cognitive faculty. As was the case with all variables, once the scale demonstrated sufficient reliability (Cronbach's alpha = .85), a scale was created by averaging the scores of individual items.

The Heart factor, in turn, was best reflected by the *caring* variable. This scale was composed of nine items (Cronbach's alpha = .84), for which participants indicated the extent to which they feel sorry or bothered by others' misfortune. This measure emphasizes the affective side of development without implying cognitive or behavioral corollaries. The Piedmont *Transcendence* scale (Piedmont, 1999) was composed of six items (Cronbach's alpha = .86), including formulations indicative of both cognitive and affective processes (e.g., "I believe that there is a larger plan to life"; "I generally feel an emotional bond with all of humanity").

The Hands factor was best reflected by eight *helping* items (Cronbach's alpha = .71). These items asked participants how often they help out in various contexts of daily living. We felt that this scale, bearing no connotative expression of affect or cognition, best reflected our conceptual notion of the Hands domain. The *generosity* scale has three items (Cronbach's alpha = .70), for which participants indicate whether they affectively enjoy engaging in benevolent action. This scale was linked to Heart and Hands in our model.

A *social conscience* scale composed of eight items (Cronbach's alpha = .90) was also used to assess both Heart and Hands factors in our model. Participants responded to items from this scale by indicating the degree to which it was important to them to act on behalf of social justice. We felt that the stem, "It is important to me . . ." captured a more subjective-affective inclination, whereas the content that completed the stem reflected the participant's drive to act. Finally, on the seven-item *religious practices* scale (Cronbach's alpha = .82), participants indicated the frequency with which they engage in various religious activities or initiatives, such as the study of scriptures, attending services, educational classes, or youth groups. We felt that this scale, while focusing primarily on the Hands factor, also assessed cognitive aspects of development because several of the items contain cognitive prerequisites (i.e., studying scriptures, talking with family about religion or God, attending educational classes).

It is important to note that the assessments available in the data set for the described model are not ideal. The Head factor is composed of solely religious or spiritual variables, for example. Nonetheless, we felt that in the absence of PYD variables that directly measured cognition, this choice of measures was based on fewer theoretical assumptions.

Results

Positive correlations among all seven variables were statistically significant at the .01 level (Table 8.2). Higher correlations of $r > .40$ were noted between *caring, generosity, social conscience,* and *transcendence;* between *belief, transcendence,* and *religious practices;* and between *help, religious practices, social conscience, transcendence,* and *generosity.* Except when theoretically implausible, these correlations informed the subsequent measurement model.

A confirmatory factor analysis of our model produced moderate fit indices: $\chi^2(7) = 38.94$, $p < .001$; RMSEA = .084. Significant correlations were also

Table 8.2 Correlations Between PYD and Religious/Spiritual Variables

	Generosity	Belief	Transcend	Religious Practices	Social Conscience	Help
Caring	.462(**)	.214(**)	.404(**)	.236(**)	.595(**)	.360(**)
Generosity		.172(**)	.486(**)	.227(**)	.596(**)	.448(**)
Belief			.493(**)	.553(**)	.201(**)	.240(**)
Transcendence				.392(**)	.564(**)	.418(**)
Religious Practices					.292(**)	.398(**)
Social Conscience						.477(**)

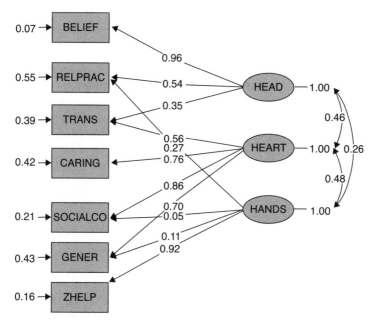

Figure 8.1   Standardized factor estimates and correlations from the CFA measuring the 3H model.

found between all three latent variables, though the correlation between Head and Hands was noticeably weaker than the other two correlations (see Figure 8.1). Moreover, with limited exceptions, most factor loadings between the latent variables of Head, Heart, and Hands and the PYD and spirituality scales contained significant *t*-values at the .05 level. The lone exceptions were factor loadings for *social conscience* and *generosity* from the Hands factor.

Discussion

Our results support the use of the 3H model as a means of exploring the relationship between religiosity/spirituality and positive youth development. While not a perfect fit, analyses indicate that the model is robust and that it is at least on the right track in terms of describing the shared nature of religiosity/spirituality and positive youth development.

We propose that the overlap of the three dimensions, Head, Heart, and Hands, captures the essence of PYD (Sherrod & Spiewak, 2008). The differentiation that we suggest among the three Hs should not obscure the fact that there is extensive overlap. In fact, we believe that their overlap allows their expression as positive development. For example, an adolescent who is developmentally engaged on both cognitive (Head) and conduct (Hands) dimensions will likely adopt the selfless act of giving charity as a profound sense of duty; in contrast, one who is motivated out of a humanistic selflessness—characteristic of the Heart dimension—will volunteer because it fulfills his or her sense of obligation to fellow citizens. Charity is a fitting combination of religiosity and civic engagement and volunteerism, and it nicely depicts the region shared by spirituality and civic engagement (Sherrod & Spiewak, 2008). We believe that our test of the model supports this position.

It is intriguing that the Head and Hands relationship is the weakest of the three. Interpretation of this finding can be approached on both technical and fundamental levels. On the technical side, the model had two features that predisposed an optimal balance between the three Hs: (1) the Head factor was exclusively restricted to religious/spiritual observed variables; and (2) the Hand factor was constrained by two nonsignificant pathways. Perhaps, the convergence of these two skewed elements in the model accounted for a weaker relationship.

Alternatively, a more fundamental explanation could be responsible for this finding. One question that occupies a great deal of thought in PYD research is how to motivate youth to engage in prosocial initiatives (Larson, 2000). In the context of this study, the question could be recast as to whether the Hands domain can be prompted more effectively by the Head or the Heart domains. Our finding that the Head–Hands relationship appears weaker than the other 3H relationships might signify empirical support that affective mechanisms are more effective motivators than their cognitive counterparts.

We previously used three major developmental theories—identity and life cycle, attachment, and social learning—to support our model. Through this sampling of developmental theories, we hoped not only to clarify this definitional model based on Head, Heart, and Hands but also to illustrate the conceptual strengths of the respective PYD dimensions (Sherrod & Spiewak, 2008). Head, Heart, and Hands can each be utilized for sharpening research questions and selecting meaningful measures and constructs.

Developmental research may pose hypotheses that seek to examine the trajectory of PYD constructs. The 3H model would be of significant assistance in this endeavor. A recognized PYD construct could be hypothesized to tap a certain dimension more in early adolescence and another more in late adolescence. New or undefined PYD constructs could use the 3H model to gain recognition in terms of their use of fundamental 3H resources.

Applied research stands to be informed by the theoretical implications of the 3H model. Programs can measure their effectiveness in terms of the relative gains in each of the three Hs. Programs seeking to have a positive impact on a diverse population of adolescents should look to integrate all three dimensions in order to ensure positive developmental outlets for everyone. Therefore, selecting measures that appeal to each of these three dimensions should be a standard practice in applied research.

Individual variability and development are critical considerations for using these research findings to address policy. By considering differentiated developmental trajectories, applied practitioners may prefer to accentuate areas in which an adolescent is naturally inclined to flourish, and then use these areas of strength to promote development in other weaker areas. This is the approach to policy inherent in PYD. An assessment tool is needed that identifies youth who are especially drawn toward one or two dimensions of the 3H model. Our measures did not allow this type of analysis.

The possibility that adolescents do not break down into categories of cognitive, affective, and behavioral preferences must also be considered. A latent class analysis would be useful here. Failure of a latent class analysis to converge would indicate that youth exhibit a normal range and distribution of all levels of competence among the three Hs. This possibility would also have meaningful assessment implications because means and standard deviations would acquire heightened significance in placing individual adolescents along the 3H spectrum of capabilities.

Limitations of the Study

The data used in this study were not collected to test the 3H model. As a result, the variables used in this study imperfectly represent the three dimensions of the model. The fact that the fit was as good as it was further verifies the robustness of the model. It would, for example, be interesting to examine the role that more traditional measures of cognition play in the Head dimension versus those of religious beliefs as used in this study. One such option would be to test how political beliefs, such as ideas about the rights and responsibilities of citizenship (Bogard & Sherrod, 2008; Sherrod, 2008), might serve as a traditional PYD construct in the Head dimension. Similarly, community service or political participation (Sherrod, 2003) could improve the Hands component in our model. Of the three components, Heart appeared to be most in sync with variables from the Templeton study. Better measures of the constructs would also contribute to the test of the overall model. The strength of the model is reflected by the significance of its test with post hoc measures that were not created with an eye for this study's specific aim. Refined measures will offer more sophisticated analytic possibilities in validating the 3H theory.

A latent class analysis will be instrumental in testing the usefulness of this theory in applied settings. One critical question is whether the three components of this model, Head, Heart, and Hands, differentiate today's population of youth. We would argue, given the significant positive correlations among all three latent variables in this study, that thriving youth would have a relatively balanced representation of the three Hs. If so, then one way to promote PYD is by promoting further development of that dimension in which the young person is weakest.

As soon as one considers developmental analysis, one must allow for differentiated pathways of development. Because of the cross-sectional nature of our sample, our analysis did not allow us to address development. Sample size, furthermore, prevented analysis of the role of age as a variable. Finally, we did not address any demographic variables of personal identity, such as gender, ethnicity, and immigrant status. Both longitudinal research and examination of diversity are clear directions for future research.

CONCLUSIONS

Our initial analysis of the 3H model can be labeled a modest success. Certainly, further analyses and research are needed to provide the empirical support that would justify full confidence in our theoretical proposition. At the same time, glimpses of empirical confirmation may be gleaned from the present study. These glimpses encourage a fresh perspective on the role of religiosity and spirituality in PYD. Our model suggests that religious and spiritual resources can be viewed as assets of PYD. In this way, they represent examples of PYD, and they promote continued healthy development and growth.

REFERENCES

Abbott-Chapman, J., & Denholm, C. (2001). Adolescents' risk activities, risk hierarchies and the influence of religiosity. *Journal of Youth Studies*, 4(3), 279–297.

Aristotle. (1941). Historia animalism. In R. McKeon (Ed.), *The basic works of Aristotle* (D. W. Thompson, trans). New York, NY: Random House.

Benson, P. L. (2007). Developmental assets and human development. In R. K. Silbereisen & R. M. Lerner (Eds.), *Approaches to positive youth development*. London, England: Sage.

Benson, P. L., Leffert, N., Scales, P. C., & Blyth, D. (1998). Beyond the village rhetoric: Creating healthy communities for children and adolescents. *Applied Developmental Science*, 2, 138–159.

Benson, P. L., Scales, P. C., Hamilton, S. F., & Sesma, A. (2006). Positive youth development: Theory, research and applications. In W. Damon & R. Lerner (Eds.), *Handbook of child psychology* (6th ed.): Vol. 1, R. M. Lerner (Ed.), *Theoretical models of human development* (pp. 894–941). Hoboken, NJ: Wiley.

Bogard, K., & Sherrod, L. (2008). Citizenship attitudes and allegiances in diverse youth. *Cultural Diversity and Ethnic Minority Psychology*, 14(4), 286–296.

Bowers, E. P., Li, Y., Kiely, M. K., Brittian, A., Lerner, J. V., & Lerner, R. M. (2010). The Five Cs Model of Positive Youth Development: A longitudinal analysis of confirmatory factor structure and measurement invariance. *Journal of Youth and Adolescnce*, 39(7), 720–735.

Boyd, M., & Yin, Z. (1999). Cognitive-affective and behavioral correlates of self-schemata in sport. *Journal of Sport Behavior*, 22(2), 288–301.

Cornwall, M. (1989). The determinants of religious behavior: A theoretical model and empirical test. *Social Forces*, 68(2), 572–592.

Damon, W., Menon, J., & Bronk, K. C. (2003). The development of purpose during adolescence. *Applied Developmental Science*, 7, 119–128.

Eccles, J. S., Barber, B. L., Stone, M., & Hunt, J. (2003). Extracurricular activities and adolescent development. *Journal of Social Issues, 59*(4), 865–889.

Elkins, D. N. (1998). *Beyond religion: Eight alternative paths to the sacred.* Wheaton, IL: QuestBooks.

Erikson, E. H. (1968). *Identity: Youth and crisis.* Oxford, England: Norton & Co.

Fowler, J. W. (1981). *Stages of faith: The psychology of human development and the quest for meaning.* New York, NY: Harper Collins.

Fuller, R. C. (2001). *Spiritual but not religious: Understanding unchurched America.* New York, NY: Oxford University Press.

Furrow, J. L., King, P. E., & White, K. (2004). Religion and positive youth development: Identity, meaning, and prosocial concerns. *Applied Developmental Science, 8*(1), 17–26.

Hadjistavropoulos, H. D., & Craig, K. D. (1994). Acute and chronic low back pain: Cognitive, affective, and behavioural dimensions. *Journal of Consulting and Clinical Psychology, 62,* 341–349.

Hollinger, D. P. (2005). *Head, heart & hands: Bringing together Christian thought, passion, and action.* Downers Grove, IL: InterVarsity Press.

Jöreskog, K. G., & Sörbom, D. (1996). *LISREL 8: User's reference guide.* Chicago, IL: Scientific Software International.

King, P. E. (2003). Religion and identity: The role of ideological, social, and spiritual contexts. *Applied Developmental Science, 7*(3), 197–204.

King, P. E., & Furrow, J. L. (2004). Religion as a resource for positive youth development: Religion, social capital, and moral outcomes. *Developmental Psychology, 40*(5), 703–713.

Larson, R. (2000). Toward a psychology of positive youth development. *American Psychologist, 55*(1), 170–183.

Lerner, J. V., Phelps, E., Forman, Y., & Bowers, E. P. (2009). Positive youth development. In R. M. Lerner & L. Steinberg (Eds.), *Handbook of adolescent psychology* (3rd ed., pp. 524–558). Hoboken, NJ: Wiley.

Lerner, R. M. (2004). *Liberty: Thriving and civic engagement among America's youth.* Thousand Oaks, CA: Sage.

Lerner, R. M. (2007). *The good teen.* New York, NY: Random House/Stonesong Press.

Lerner, R. M., Lerner, J. V., Almerigi, J., Theokas, C., Phelps, E., Gestsdottir, S., . . . & von Eye, A. (2005). Positive youth development, participation in community youth development programs, and community contributions of fifth grade adolescents: Findings from the first wave of the 4-H Study of Positive Youth Development. *Journal of Early Adolescence, 25,* 17–71.

Lerner, R. M., Roeser, R. W., & Phelps, E. (2008). Positive youth development, spirituality and generosity in youth. In R. M. Lerner, R. W. Roeser, & E. Phelps (Eds.), *Positive youth development and spirituality: From theory to research* (pp. 322–338). West Conshohocken, PA: Templeton Foundation Press.

Markstrom, C. A. (1999). Religious involvement and adolescent psychosocial development. *Journal of Adolescence, 22*(2), 205–221.

Martin, R., Watson, D., & Wan, C. K. (2000). A three-factor model of trait anger: Dimensions of affect, behavior, and cognition. *Journal of Personality, 68*(5), 869–897.

Muuss, R. E. (1988). *Theories of adolescence* (5th ed.). New York, NY: Random House.

Neyrinck, B., Vansteenkiste, M., Lens, W., Duriez, B., & Hutsebaut, D. (2006). Cognitive, affective and behavioral correlates of internalization of regulations for religious activities. *Motivation and Emotion, 30*(4), 323–334.

Palen, L., & Coatsworth, J. D. (2007). Activity-based identity experiences and their relations to problem behavior and psychological well-being in adolescence. *Journal of Adolescence, 30*(5), 721–737.

Phelps, E., Zimmerman, S., Warren, A. E. A., Jeličić, H., von Eye, A., & Lerner, R. M. (2009). The structure and developmental course of positive youth development (PYD) in early adolescence: Implications for theory and practice. *Journal of Applied Developmental Psychology, 30*(5), 571–584.

Piedmont, R. L. (1999). Does spirituality represent the sixth factor of personality? Spiritual transcendence and the Five-Factor Model. *Journal of Personality, 67*(6), 985–1013.

Roth, J. L., & Brooks-Gunn, J. (2003). What exactly is a youth development program? Answers from research and practice. *Applied Developmental Science, 7*, 94–111.

Sherrod, L. (2003). Promoting the development of citizenship in diverse youth. *PS: Political Science and Politics*, April, 287–292.

Sherrod, L. (2006). Promoting citizenship and activism in today's youth. In S. Ginwright & R. Watts (Eds.), *Beyond resistance! Youth activism and community change: New democratic possibilities for practice and policy for America's children*. New York, NY: Routledge.

Sherrod, L. (2007). Civic engagement as an expression of positive youth development. In R. Silbereisen & R. Lerner (Eds.), *Approaches to positive youth development*. Thousand Oaks, CA: Sage.

Sherrod, L. (2008). Adolescent's perceptions of rights as reflected in their views of citizenship. *Journal of Social Issues, 64*(4), 771–790.

Sherrod, L., & Lauckhardt, J. (2008). The development of citizenship. In R. M. Lerner & L. Steinberg (Eds.), *Handbook of adolescent psychology* (3rd ed., pp. 372–408). Hoboken, NJ: Wiley.

Sherrod, L., & Spiewak, G. (2008). Possible interrelationships between civic engagement, positive youth development, and spirituality/religiosity. In R. M. Lerner, R. W. Roeser, & E. Phelps (Eds.), *Positive youth development and spirituality: From theory to research* (pp. 322–338). West Conshohocken, PA: Templeton Foundation Press.

Sinha, J. W., Cnaan, R. A., & Gelles, R. J. (2007). Adolescent risk behaviors and religion: Findings from a national study. *Journal of Adolescence, 30*(2), 231–249.

Smith, C., & Denton, M. L. (2005). *Soul searching: The religious and spiritual lives of American teenagers*. New York, NY: Oxford University Press.

Steinberg, L., & Lerner, R. M. (2004). The scientific study of adolescence: A brief history. *Journal of Early Adolescence, 24*(1), 45–54.

Theokas, C., Almerigi, J., Lerner, R. M., Dowling, E. M., Benson, P. L., Scales, P. C., & von Eye, A. (2005). Conceptualizing and modeling individual and ecological asset components of thriving in early adolescence. *Journal of Early Adolescence, 25*(1), 113–143.

Waller, N. G., Kojetin, B. A., Bouchard, T. J., Jr., Lykken, D. T., & Tellegen, A. (1990). Genetic and environmental influences on religious interests, attitudes and values: A study of twins reared apart and together. *Psychological Science, 1*(2), 138–142.

Youniss, J., McLellan, J. A., & Yates, M. (1999). Religion, community service, and identity in American youth. *Journal of Adolescence, 22*(2), 243–253.

⟫━◆━⟪

Religious Adolescents' Views of Success and Spirituality

Jenni Menon Mariano, Robert W. Roeser, Paula Taylor
Greathouse, and Sonia S. Issac Koshy

Probably as long as spiritual traditions have existed, spiritual practice in its finest sense has been directed toward positive developmental outcomes. For instance, a goal of meditation is to gain insight and achieve personal enlightenment; the admonishments offered by the more enlightened philosophers and by religious scriptures inspire virtue and commitment to noble social purposes; and across the annals of human history many intellectual and technological advancements have coincided with the introduction and proliferation of new positive spiritual ideologies that offer novel solutions to the human problems of the day. All three of these examples describe an overlap between successful development and what it means to be spiritual that is at least theoretical.

As applied to the developing young person, however, the empirical evidence describing the potential shape and form of the convergence between development and spirituality has remained primarily anecdotal. It has been relegated to the domains of daily conversation, for example, but largely escaped systematic scientific inquiry (Benson & Roehlkepartain, 2008). This is likely because (among other reasons) the idea of spirituality can be difficult to grasp. As some writers have emphasized, spirituality may be experienced as a deeply personal quest for understanding answers to ultimate questions about life, meaning, and relationship to the sacred and transcendent, and it is conceptualized by some as a subjective, unifying realm that goes beyond the limits of materiality and the physical tendencies of humanity (Boyatzis, Dollahite, & Marks, 2005; Koenig, McCullough, & Larson, 2001). It is indeed difficult to grasp something that seems too ethereal and for which our everyday language eludes us.

We propose that the daily conversational language of young people—representing the insider's perspective if you will—is an important place to begin pinning down what is often a shifty concept in the youth development literature. This is because although theoretical conceptions of positive youth development (PYD) exist (and include the idea of spirituality) (Catalano, Berglund, Ryan, Lonczak, & Hawkins, 2004), measuring spirituality and other potentially subjective and dynamic developmental phenomena (i.e., purpose, ultimate concerns, Great Love-Compassion (GLC)—see Alberts Warren's chapter in this volume for a discussion of GLC) is still limited in prior research. The need for a consistent vernacular between practitioner and participants is imperative. We still need to develop a language of youth spirituality, based on the knowledge of the young people who experience it. Spiritual and religious practices are common experiences among people the world over (Gallup International Association, 1999; King & Furrow, 2004), so this goal is a compelling one.

In the attempt to put some empirical meat on this much-neglected subject and to potentially uncover what Hay, Nye, and Murphy (1996) refer to as "a rich spirituality of childhood" (p. 47) that has been overlooked by researchers, in this chapter we discuss results from a study of youth-centered responses to the notions of "being spiritual" and "being successful." Success (i.e., competence, achievement, etc.) and spirituality are both considered central facets of positive youth development (e.g., see Benson, Roehlkepartian, & Rude, 2003; Eccles & Gootman, 2002; Kerestes & Youniss, 2003; King, 2003; and Lerner, Dowling, & Anderson, 2003). A few studies have examined the language and terms used by adolescents to describe the experience of developing positively, or thriving (i.e., Alberts et al., 2006; King et al., 2005), and some work has even identified cross-generational similarities and divergences in descriptors of youth thriving and PYD (i.e., see Lerner et al.'s [2005] description of the Five Cs of PYD; and a comparison of parents', youth-serving practitioners', and adolescents' conceptions by King et al., 2005). But similar understandings have yet to be reached about adolescents' understandings of the meaning of spirituality and how such an understanding diverges or converges with notions of youths' vision of the successfully functioning young person.

BACKGROUND OF THE STUDY

As with other research presented in this book, the data from this study were drawn from the John Templeton Foundation (JTF)–sponsored investigation entitled, "The Role of Spiritual Development in Growth of Purpose, Generosity, and Psychological Health in Adolescence," designed in part by the second and fourth authors and their colleagues at Tufts University. Full details of the methodology of the JTF study have been presented in prior reports (e.g., Lerner, Roeser, & Phelps, 2008; Roeser et al., 2007). Accordingly, we present only those features of methodology pertinent to the focus of this investigation.

Survey Questions

The data analyzed were adolescents' responses to two open-ended survey questions tapping understandings about the meaning of positive development and spirituality. These questions were administered within a larger battery of measures. To study views of positive development, we noticed that other qualitative studies with the same aim have asked youth to identify characteristics of self and others by using terms like "doing really well" (Alberts et al., 2006; King et al., 2005) and "thriving" (King et al., 2005). In the present study we therefore sought to use different terms so that, at some future point, we might compare our findings with the results of these other studies. This might provide new insights not already offered by the empirical work on our subject to date and inform the design of future studies.

As a construct, we felt that the idea of success was broad enough to tap into the potential variation in young people's knowledge of higher-order concepts of "excelling," "thriving," "doing well," and "contributing to others." Success might simultaneously invoke the more practical and material concerns associated with achievement in common parlance (i.e., "making lots of money," "climbing the career ladder," or "having a fancy car"). It could also connect to aspects of youth development or PYD (i.e., "contributing to self," "being happy," and "being confident"; see Alberts et al., 2006). Depending on the individual, a young person might view success as occurring across overlapping life domains, such as school and work, relationships, and moral accomplishments. Depending on the respondent, therefore, we theorized that success might take on several connotations. The prompt for survey question one was, "Think about the people you know your age. What are two or three qualities or characteristics of someone that you would say is a successful young person?" Survey question two measured views of spirituality and asked, "What does it mean to be a spiritual person?"

Studying Youth in Faith-Based and Diverse Religious Contexts

In selecting the sample for this study, we were interested in capturing the potential diversity of experience of adolescents. A good deal of the research on spirituality, for example, is designed from Western and Christian perspectives, whereas inclusion of minority religious and cultural groups (i.e., in the United States, where the present study was conducted) may uncover alternate notions of spirituality that draw from other religious and cultural traditions (Rich & Cinamon, 2007). As with religious affiliation, other demographic variables may also describe differential experiences affecting views of spirituality and positive development. Therefore, we sought to sample from a group of adolescents who are diverse in religion, gender, age, and ethnicity.

To further address the role of context, we were particularly interested in understanding what success and spirituality mean to youth attending faith-based schools. Religious adolescents—or those immersed in religious schooling contexts on a daily basis—have rarely been studied to discover their views on spirituality. Furthermore, young people with frequent formal opportunities to reflect about spiritual matters in environments that integrate goals of spiritualization and education (i.e., religious schools and organizations) are potentially good candidates for uncovering new insights on adolescent spirituality. More than their less-religious peers, youth who attend religious schools and organizations may articulate profound and diverse views about adolescent spirituality. Spirituality has been conceived of as a universal process that transcends any one religious context because it speaks to human nature and to the wider human developmental experience. Therefore, it is seen as accessible to all people regardless of either type or absence of religious affiliation. Yet, it is likely that a high level of religious involvement will furnish religious youth with frequent opportunities to engage in public spiritual practices, study, and reflection that are less available to others their age.

On this note, in beginning this study we also wanted to develop a question that concerned us. We initially expected that religiously oriented youth would be likely to view positive development and spiritual development as similar, if not as the same, phenomena. In one study of 939 high school seniors, for example, one of the greatest spiritual doubts expressed by young people was based on feelings that one's religion failed to make people "better" (Hunsberger, Pratt, & Pancer, 2002), thus indicating the view in the minds of these adolescents that spirituality and positive development certainly *should* go together, even if this was not the case in reality. There is reason to believe that for religious adolescents this theoretical positive relationship will be even more pronounced, because religion is more frequently a part of their everyday lives. They would be less likely to subscribe to split, or dualistic, conceptions of positive development, because they move within a context that seeks integration of spirituality and successful functioning. The most recent report of the National Study of Youth and Religion (Denton, Pearce, & Smith, 2008), for instance, found that adolescents cited gaining positive benefits from their religion as a chief reason for their increase in spiritual commitment over a three-year period. For example, religion provided them with support in dealing with life's real problems or helped them to become better, happier people (Denton, Pearce, & Smith, 2008, p. 29).

However, we were aware that the assumption that religious youth would report a substantial overlap in conceptions of success and spirituality needed further investigation. After all, young people exist within diverse ecologies (Bronfenbrenner & Morris, 2006), and their beliefs are thus influenced by more than one social message. Although frequently exposed to spiritual worldviews through religious schools and organizations, therefore, this experience might affect some adolescents differently than others. School, family, peers, the media, and communities of faith within the broader culture simultaneously influence (*and are influenced by*) the developing adolescent. In actuality, therefore, there may in fact be a greater disconnect than we assume between how even religious young people define success when thinking about their daily lives and their spiritual lives. Success and spirituality could instead constitute separate, rather than overlapping, cognitive schemes, and this dissimilarity may be reflected in adolescents' reports.

A final qualification has to do with the methods used in this study. In keeping with the spirit of this volume, we grant that a more extensive understanding of the PYD ↔ spirituality relationship will eventually be best understood through triangulation of a range of methods and examination of the validity of various ways of studying these constructs. We agree with the editors of this volume that, at this stage, we do not know where the best methods to study youth spirituality will come from. Rich and Cinamon (2007) note, however, that to date a limitation of most research on spirituality is the virtually exclusive use of quantitative data alone. Much of this work has discovered correlations among aspects of spirituality and positive developmental variables, but getting at the deeper, more contextualized meanings of spirituality may be better served through qualitative approaches (Rich & Cinamon, 2007, p. 10).

Furthermore, mixed-method studies still represent a relatively new approach in the social science literature, which is perhaps reflective of the conventional qualitative/quantitative methods divide that still plagues some academic departments. Mixing qualitative and quantitative strategies, however, may offer valuable insights into the questions we pose. As in the study of other constructs that probe highly personal and internal phenomena (i.e., identity, self-understanding, youth purpose; see Damon & Hart, 1988; Moran, 2009), our initial probing for adolescents' personal understandings, which we describe in this chapter, seems appropriate. However, we then utilize quantitative analysis techniques to examine potential effects on views of success and spirituality of contexts indicated by demographic variables such as ethnicity, religious affiliation, school level, and gender. Also, by using a youth-centered response format, our contribution in this chapter is to present data that were generated in a way that contrasts with research paradigms that minimize the open and direct elicitation of responses from research subjects (Hart, Yates, Fegley, & Wilson, 1995).

Participants

Questionnaires for this study were originally administered to 269 youth. We discarded questionnaires in which participants failed to answer both survey questions, however. Respondents were, therefore, 244 adolescents from 20 religious youth organizations and schools in an urban area of the Northeastern United States. To recruit subjects, project staff tapped personal ties at these organizations. More than 87% of participants reported that they were being raised religious. Participants' ages ranged from 11 to 26 years ($M = 15.9$; $SD = 2.6$) and included students in middle school (36%), high school (51%), and college (13%). Fifty-five percent were female.

The ethnic composition of participants was diverse, including those identifying as Caucasian (27.9%), multiethnic (17%), African American or Black (7.8%), Arab American (7.4%), Latino/Hispanic (7%), Asian Indian (5.7%), Asian, Asian American, or Pacific Islander (5.3%), Native American (0.4%), and 11% identified with Other ethnicities, did not identify with any ethnic group, or were not sure of their identification. A remaining 10.2% of participants did not report ethnicity.

A little more than half (54.4%) of participants were affiliated with some branch of Christianity (34.1% were Protestant or "Other" Christian and 9.8% were Catholic). Only 10.2% identified with Judaism, 26.2% were Muslim, 8.2% were Unitarian/Universalist, and 1.6% were Buddhists. The remainder of the young people in the sample identified with no religion or were atheists (2.4%), or identified with multiple religions (0.4%) or some other religion (0.8%). A remaining 6.1% did not report or did not know their religious affiliation.

Qualitative Analysis

In applying a qualitative strategy of analysis, we went through various steps in interpreting the written responses in the data and developing reliability. First, for the data from question two, "What does it mean to be a spiritual person?" two coders together divided the participants' responses into sections and agreed that each section would be coded once. This step was not necessary for responses to question one, because that question provided three lines where participants were asked to merely list "two or three qualities or characteristics of someone that you would say is a successful young person" so that codable sections were automatically indicated by the respondent.

Second, a combination of methods was used by two coders to code the survey responses. Coder 1 first read a random sample of the responses for each question and developed a list of the characteristics (i.e., qualities or behaviors) mentioned. This process was repeated on a random sample of approximately one-third of the surveys until characteristics were repeated enough times to indicate that little new information was emerging from the data. The purpose of this strategy was to develop an initial coding scheme. Coder 1 and Coder 2 then examined the list and brainstormed potential labels that might emerge into broader category designations. The process described here mimics Strauss and Corbin's (1998) notion of "open coding" (p. 102) to the extent that we sought to examine the data in discrete parts, entertaining and exploring for differences and similarities in the mentioned characteristics, then creating our own abstract umbrella terms that could serve as organizers for the characteristics mentioned, which we called micro-categories (see Table 9.1).

Definitions for each micro-category were developed, then both coders applied these codes independently to a second randomly selected sample of more than one-third of the surveys (about 38%, or 92 surveys). We explored the inter-rater reliability of the new categories with the 92 surveys by calculating the degree of

Table 9.1 Macro- and Micro-Categories Describing Adolescents' Reports of Characteristics of a Successful Person

Macro-Category	Micro-Category	Examples
Knowledge	Wisdom	"Common sense"/ "Wise"/ "Thinks before acting"
	Independence/Openness	"Not afraid of what people think"/ "Open mind"
	Learning	"Good student"/ "Eager to learn"/ "Asks questions"
Moral Virtues	Moral Compass	"Integrity"/ "Honest"/ "Sense of right and wrong"
	Strengths of Humanity	"Nice"/ "Helps others"/ "Compassion"
Motivation	Purpose/Goals	"Purpose"/ "Dreams or aspirations"/ "Clear goals"
	Motivation/Energy	"Motivated"/ "Ambitious"/ "Determined"
Social Virtues	Positive Relationships	"Able to talk to people"
	Participation	"Involved in activities"/ "Extracurric. involvement"
Self-Oriented Virtues	Self-Esteem	"High self-esteem"/ "Self-respect"
	Self-Reliance	"Makes own decisions"/ "Independent"
Positive Emotions	Happiness	"Happy" / "Easygoing"
	Positive Outlook	"Optimistic"/ "(Good) attitude"
Social Status	Social Status	"Popular"/ "Good social life"
Spirituality	Spirituality	"Spiritual"
Temperance	Balance	"Balanced"/ "Manages time well"
Leadership	Leadership	"A good leader"/ "Takes charge and organizes"

agreement (Cohen's kappas) in application of each code between the two coders. With the exception of an "Other" category in the question about spirituality, the reliability of all micro-categories for both questions was satisfactory, ranging from 0.62 to 1, with most coefficients falling above 0.84. A third coder settled code discrepancies in cases of disagreement between the first two raters by choosing between one of two possible codes for each instance. In some cases, the third rater also suggested a third code. If both of the original two raters agreed, the third code was adopted. If they disagreed, the original code choice of the third rater was used in the analysis. The remainder of the transcripts were then coded by the first rater.

Next, the micro-categories were grouped under larger labels (or macro-categories) in order to reduce the number of units with which we were working to facilitate adequate frequency reports for quantitative analysis of between-groups differences. These macro-category labels also served as designators indicating the interpretation of the story about young people's views that we saw emerging from the data. We drew from previous theory and literature on positive youth development and positive psychology as starting points in developing both the micro- and macro-categories. For example, the concepts of strengths of humanity, temperance, leadership, and knowledge were derived in part from Peterson and Seligman's (2004) classification of character strengths and virtues. The idea of positive emotions came from the work of Fredrickson (2001), and motivation, purpose, and goals were drawn from the literature on motivation and youth development (i.e., see Damon, Menon, & Bronk, 2003). Tables 9.1 and 9.2 display the micro-categories, with examples developed for each question.

Quantitative Analysis

For the quantitative analysis, we examined frequencies and percentage of participants mentioning each of the micro- and macro-categories. Micro-category frequencies were summed in order to arrive at the macro-category results. We then conducted a set of chi-square analyses (binomial, i.e., 1 = code mentioned, 0 = code not mentioned) and a set of One Way Analyses of Variance (ANOVAs) on the macro-category sums in order to examine differences in youths' reports involving school level (age), gender, ethnicity, and religious affiliation. Given limited group sizes, ethnic groups were separated into Caucasian and Minorities, and religious group differences were examined according to Christian, Muslim, or Jewish affiliation.

Finally, to explore potential overlap in youth's conceptions of success and spirituality, we examined frequencies of responses on the three macro-categories that seemed to conceptually overlap most across the two questions. We simply calculated the percentage of participants who mentioned those macro-categories in their views about (a) *just* success; (b) *just* spirituality; and (c) *both* success and spirituality. Findings from the quantitative and qualitative analyses of responses to both questions are reported as follows. As the binomial analyses were supported by the ANOVA results, we report the ANOVA results.

RESULTS

Our analyses were conducted in order to test our hypotheses regarding adolescents' views about the convergence of positive development and spirituality. As stated previously, we believed that adolescents attending a religious school or youth group were given opportunities to explore notions of spirituality, as taught by their respective faith institutions, in order to speak about such concepts. As such, we carried out analyses to understand whether youth raised in faith traditions spontaneously generated ideas about being religious or spiritual as part of what it means to develop positively. The findings of our analyses follow.

Qualitative Coding Findings About Adolescents' Views of Success

The qualitative coding analysis of views of success resulted in 18 micro-categories. These in turn were grouped together into 10 macro-categories that were later used in the quantitative analysis. The *Knowledge* macro-category encompassed three micro-categories, including *Wisdom*, a commitment to learning and doing well in school (*Learning*), and independent thinking and openness to new knowledge (*Independence/Openness*). A *Moral Virtues* macro-category encompassed two codes, which were similar to classifications noted in Peterson and Seligman (2004): *Moral Compass* and *Strengths of Humanity*. *Moral Compass* referred to virtues akin to some of these authors' "strengths of courage," such as being honest and having integrity (p. 249). It also included virtues of reliability, fairness, and responsibility. *Strengths of Humanity* referred to any mention of caring-oriented attributes, such as generosity, kindness, and compassion (p. 325). A third macro-category, *Motivation*, included being focused on a purpose or goals (*purpose/goals*) and qualities related to investing one's energies in goal-directed behavior, such as perseverance, taking initiative, and willingness to take on challenges (*motivation/energy*). *Social Virtues* incorporated the ability to contribute to and engage in positive relationships (*positive relationships*) and notions of involvement in school and community activities (*participation*). *Self-Oriented Virtues* included *self-esteem* and *self-reliance*. A *Positive Emotions* macro-code included *happiness* and having a *positive outlook*. Remaining macro-codes were *Social Status*, *Spirituality*, *Temperance* (or having balance and organization in one's life), and *Leadership*. An *Other* code comprised remaining reports that were unable to be categorized elsewhere. Table 9.1 details examples of codes describing views of success.

Being wise, knowledgeable, and dedicated to learning, along with personal moral virtues, were the most frequently reported qualities attributed to successful young people by the adolescents in our sample. More than 50% (50.4%) of respondents said that being wise, independent and open thinkers, and dedicated to their education (Knowledge) were qualities of successful young people they knew, while 49.2% of all survey participants cited having moral integrity or caring and compassion for others (Moral Virtues) as central descriptors of successful peers. A sense of purpose and motivation (Motivation) was reported by 41.4% of respondents, followed by Social Virtues (30%), Positive Emotions (15.6%), Self-Oriented Virtues (14.8%), Spirituality (8.6%), Social Status (11.1%), Temperance (5.3%), and Leadership (3.7%). A host of "Other" qualities were reported by 21.7% of respondents, the most common being "athletic" (2.9%) and "talented/gifted" (2.9%). A few respondents (1.6%) said they did not know what a successful person was like. Table 9.2 shows these results.

Table 9.2 Characteristics of the Successful Person: Proportion of Adolescents Mentioning Codes, and Frequency of Times Each Code Was Mentioned

Categories	Frequency of Times Mentioned	Percentage of Sample Reporting
Knowledge	129	50.4
Wisdom	56	22.1
Independence/Openness	14	5.3
Learning	59	22.4
Moral Virtues	151	49.2
Moral Compass	82	25.8
Strengths of Humanity	69	23.4
Motivation	129	41.4
Purpose/Goals	30	11.5
Motivation/Energy	99	29.9
Social Virtues	91	30.0
Positive Relationships	69	23.4
Participation	22	6.6
Positive Emotions	39	15.6
Happiness	33	13.1
Positive Outlook	6	2.5
Self-Oriented Virtues	43	14.8
Self-Esteem	36	12.3
Self-Reliance	7	2.5
Social Status	32	11.1
Spirituality	25	8.6
Temperance	15	5.3
Leadership	10	3.7
I Don't Know	7	1.6

Group Differences in Adolescents' Views of Success

Our examination of between-groups differences in adolescents' views of success and corresponding post-hoc tests (specifically, Success × School Level, Success × Gender, Success × Religion, and Success × Ethnicity), revealed significant school-level (age) effects in reports of Motivation, Social Status, and Temperance as descriptors of the successful person. It seems that increasingly with age, having purpose and goals, and the determination to achieve them (i.e., Motivation:

$F = 10.527$; $df = 2$) is seen as a sign of success by the religious adolescents in this sample. This was evident in differences in mean frequencies of reports between middle schoolers and the two older age groups surveyed ($p < .01$). Social Status was a significantly stronger gauge of success for high schoolers than for college students ($F = 4.231$; $df = 2$; $p < .05$), and having balance in one's life (Temperance) was significantly more central to success to college students than it was to either high school or middle school students ($F = 3.482$; $df = 2$; $p < .05$).

Differences in views of success by religious group showed main effects for Motivation and Positive Emotions, where the Christian youth mentioned Motivation more frequently than the Muslim youth ($F = 3.913$; $df = 3$), and where the Jewish youth reported Positive Emotions more frequently than both the Christian and Muslim youth ($F = 3.026$; $df = 3$). We found no differences by gender or ethnic group.

Qualitative Coding Findings About Adolescents' Views of Spirituality

For question two, 16 micro-categories were organized under 8 macro-categories. In some cases, micro-categories were broken down into subgroups, and those subgroups were then allocated to different macro-categories. The Personal Connection macro-category included the micro-categories of *prayer and meditation*, *faith*, and feelings of connection to a power or force that transcends the self (*connection to a higher power*). A Beliefs macro-category included the micro-code *theism*, which had to do with beliefs in (a) an ultimate being, (b) an ultimate state of being, or (c) specific doctrines. Moral Virtues included two subgroups of a *good conduct* micro-category that had to do with (a) being virtuous and (b) bringing the teachings of one's religion into one's daily life. A Formal Worship macro-category referred to an *obedience* micro-category relating to obeying the laws and teachings of one's religion, including in some cases, "following" or "aligning oneself" with "God's will." Formal Worship also included mention of engagement in public worship activities, like attending church, temple, mosque, or religious school (*worship*), and *respect god*, which described mention of paying formal respect to a deity. Growth/Seeking included mention of study of religious texts (*study*) and a *spiritual learning* code that referred to an openness to spiritual growth and learning.

Spiritual Emotions included mention of feelings of *gratitude*, *serenity*, being *emotionally moved* by spiritual and religious phenomena in general, and feelings of deep connection to the world, including people, animals, and nature (*connection to world*). *Self-understanding* and a sense of connection to one's inner self (*connection to self*) constituted a Self-Orientation macro-code. *Undefined* was categorized under a macro-code of the same name and included any mention of spirituality not being connected to a specific definition or religion, or as being unique to each person. Codes that did not fit under any of the other macro-categories were grouped under "Other," examples of which were "happy," "spread/teach your religion," and "not closed about your religious beliefs." Definitions and examples of codes for question one appear in Table 9.3.

When describing what it means to be a spiritual person, adolescents overwhelmingly described a connection to one's inner life, engagement with internal experiences and practices such as prayer and meditation, having a sense of faith, and feeling connected to something greater than the self. This description was given by 61.9% of all participants surveyed. Beliefs were also considered central aspects of spirituality by 35.2% of respondents. These primarily included theistic beliefs in an ultimate being that transcends the self and doctrinal beliefs related to specific religious traditions. Moral Virtues were mentioned by 29.9% of respondents and implied personally embodying moral virtues, achieving congruence between one's beliefs and how one conducts oneself in life, and a sense of authenticity.

Formal Worship was the next most frequently mentioned cluster (26%), meaning to live that aspect of the spiritual life that has to do with obeying religious laws, attending formal public worship, and showing respect to the transcendent via specific public rituals and acts of worship. A Growth/Seeking orientation was evident in responses of 17.6% of adolescents. The Spiritual Emotions category codes (i.e., gratitude, serenity, feeling emotionally moved by spiritual matters, and feeling a deep connection to the world) were mentioned by 17.2% of respondents. Only 5.7% mentioned concepts having to do with a Self-Orientation, and 2% described spirituality as being unable to be defined. Notably, 9.8% of the sample mentioned terms that could not fit under any of the categories, and a remaining 5.7% of the sample ($n = 14$) left the question blank. Table 9.4 lists frequencies and percentages of micro- and macro-categories reported.

Group Differences in Adolescents' Views of Spirituality

As with their views of success, our between-groups analysis of adolescents' views of spirituality (specifically, Spirituality × School Level, Spirituality × Gender, Spirituality × Religion, and Spirituality × Ethnicity) suggested age and religious differences and no main effects by gender or ethnicity. College students emphasized Personal Connection significantly more frequently than middle schoolers ($F = 5.974$; $df = 2$). This trend was repeated for the Moral Virtues category ($F = 5.038$; $df = 2$). Personal Connection ($F = 9.070$; $df = 3$), Moral Virtues ($F = 3.232$; $df = 3$), and Self-Orientation ($F = 11.618$; $df = 3$) were all emphasized more by the Christian than by the Muslim youth, and the Jewish adolescents endorsed the Undefined category more frequently than the Christian adolescents.

Convergence of Adolescents' Views of Success and Spirituality

To explore potential convergence between conceptions of success and spirituality, we compared the percentage of adolescents who reported on the three most closely conceptually related macro-categories across the two survey questions.

Table 9.3 Macro- and Micro-Categories Describing Adolescents' Reports of Characteristics of a Spiritual Person

Macro-Category	Micro-Category	Examples
Personal Connection	Prayer and Meditation	"Pray"/ "Someone who meditates"
	Faith	"Faith in something higher"/ "Depend on God"
	Connection to a Higher Power	"Feeling some connection to a higher power"
Beliefs	Theism a) belief in ultimate being b) doctrinal acceptance c) ultimate state of being	"Believe in a higher being"/ "Believe in God" "To believe in your religion" "Feeling a connection to a higher power...within yourself"
Moral Virtues	Good Conduct a) embodying moral virtues b) congruence between one's beliefs and one's life	"To be compassionate"/ "To be virtuous" "To apply our beliefs in our everyday lives"
	Authenticity	"To be religious and not ashamed to show it outside church"
Formal Worship	Obedience	"Follow commandments"
	Worship	"Engage in symbolic events"/ "Attend church"
	Respect God	"To show respect to whomever you worship"
Growth/Seeking	Study	"Study"/ "Reading scripture"
	Spiritual Learning	"Trying to learn more and grow spiritually"
Spiritual Emotions	Gratitude	"To thank"/ "Be thankful to Allah"
	Serenity	"To be able to calm the mind"/ "inner peace"
	Emotionally Moved	"To be moved (i.e., by prayer, services)"
	Connection to World	"To feel like you're part of something bigger"/ "Deeply connected to people, nature, animals"/ "Close connection to the world around you"
Self-Orientation	Self-Understanding	"Fully aware of oneself"/ "Understand oneself"
	Connection to Self	"Deeply connected to oneself"
Undefined	Undefined	"There is no exact definition"

Table 9.4 Characteristics of the Spiritual Person: Proportion of Adolescents Mentioning Codes, and Frequency of Times Each Code Was Mentioned

Categories	Frequency of Times Mentioned	Percentage of Sample Reporting
Personal Connection	177	61.8
Prayer and Meditation	65	25.4
Faith	57	18.4
Connection to a Higher Power	55	18.0
Beliefs	86	35.2
Theism	86	35.2
a) belief in force greater than self	47	19.3
b) doctrinal acceptance	36	14.8
c) ultimate state of being	3	1.2
Moral Virtues	73	29.9
Good Conduct	66	27.0
a) embodying moral virtues	32	13.1
b) congruence between one's beliefs and one's life	34	13.9
Authenticity	7	2.9
Formal Worship	71	26.0
Obedience	30	12.3
Worship	34	13.9
Respect God	7	2.9
Growth/Seeking	43	17.6
Study	17	6.9
Spiritual Learning	26	10.7
Spiritual Emotions	42	17.2
Gratitude	8	3.3
Serenity	7	2.9
Emotionally Moved	12	4.9
Connection to World	15	6.1
Self-Orientation	14	5.7
Connection to Self	7	2.8
Self-Understanding	7	2.8
Undefined	5	2.0
Other	27	11.0

This examination was therefore limited to three macro-category pairs: Moral Virtues/Moral Virtues, Positive Emotions/Spiritual Emotions, and Self-Oriented Virtues/Self-Orientation. Though the within-pair terms were not completely congruent in their meanings, we felt that they were close enough to facilitate an exploratory examination that would offer hints into the degree to which success and spirituality constitute similar phenomena in the minds of the adolescents. For this analysis, we examined the percentage of the sample reporting *just one* of the macro-codes in each pair and *both* of the macro-codes in each pair. Fourteen subjects failed to report their views of spirituality, so our examination here was contained to a slightly smaller sample size than in the other analyses ($n = 230$). Overlap within each of the three pairs was relatively small when compared to the number of adolescents participating in the study, but notably, the most substantial overlap appeared within the Moral Virtues/Moral Virtues pair. Even though this occurred among a relatively small percentage of adolescents in this sample (9.1%), the moral domain seems to be the place where notions of being successful and being spiritual converge most in the minds of young people. Table 9.5 reports these percentages.

DISCUSSION

The results of this study highlight several important points. In regard to youths' views of success, we note that no single category commanded an overwhelming majority of responses. Overall, this suggests a theme of difference, rather than similarity, among adolescents in their conceptions of success. Yet, Knowledge, Moral Virtues, and Motivation may constitute a core cluster representing a good proportion of adolescents' views (mentioned by 41.4% to 50.4% of the sample). Social Virtues were also notable (mentioned by 30% of the sample). What is perhaps most striking here is the unremarkable presence of responses expressing

Table 9.5 Proportion of Sample Reporting Overlapping Views of Success and Spirituality ($n = 230$)

Overlapping Macro-Categories	Proportion of Sample Reporting Just Success Category	Proportion of Sample Reporting Just Spirituality Category	Proportion of Sample Reporting Both Categories
Moral Virtues/ Moral Virtues	29.6%	12.6%	9.1%
Positive Emotions/ Spiritual Emotions	11.3%	10.4%	3.0%
Self-Oriented Virtues/ Self-Orientation	13.0%	3.9%	1.7%

more conventional, materialistic views of success (i.e., being rich, having a big house, etc.). Even in the Knowledge category, for example, youth went beyond referencing academic achievement or being smart: They mentioned Wisdom, a form of knowing associated with an integration of insight and virtue (Staudinger, Maciel, Smith, & Baltes, 1998, p. 1) and a mature orientation to life (Wink & Helson, 1997). The fact that college students associate success more strongly with motivation and purpose than do the younger participants may be a defining characteristic of the emerging adulthood years (Arnett, 2000). Concerns about making something of oneself that were merely burgeoning in high school are brought more strongly to bear as youth work on fulfilling career, personal, and family goals during this period. Concerns of having balance in one's life (Temperance) also increase with age as youth of college age work to balance multiple responsibilities and commitments in ways they were not required to do when they were younger. Perhaps the more urgent focus on challenges of goal achievement and attaining a healthy balance in one's life in college also explains the decline in the primacy of social status (Social Status) as a gauge of success between high school and college.

It is not surprising that experiencing a personal connection was most frequently mentioned as a descriptor of the spiritual person (mentioned by 61.8% of participants). This finding corresponds with the thought of spirituality as relationship to the sacred and transcendent, which was discussed earlier. The mention of connection to a higher power, however, is a specifically religious notion that might be characteristic of religious youth, and especially those that subscribe to Christian, Muslim, and Jewish faiths (of which most of our sample was constituted). Reports of beliefs and acts of formal worship are, similarly, not surprising coming from this group.

As with adolescents' views of success, however, we were struck by the prominence of reports of moral virtues in adolescents' views of spirituality. Our results correspond with the National Study of Youth and Religion (Denton, Pearce, & Smith, 2008), which reports that youth feel that their faith should make them better people. We were also struck to find that personal connection and moral virtues were increasingly central to youth's views of spirituality with age, and specifically during the college years. As youth enter the period of emerging adulthood (Arnett, 2000), it may be that the standard for religious and spiritual practice and experience is raised. Spirituality must be felt as more authentic, more emotionally nourishing, more personally beneficial, and have a stronger impact on one's moral life than in the teenage years if it is to be real. This could correspond with the greater life demands of that period in contrast to the teenage years, and thus a more useful spirituality is seen as necessary for healthy adaptation.

At this point, we are more tentative about drawing conclusions about the religious group differences we observed. Religious group differences in reports could allude to use of different language to describe the same developmental and religious phenomena. It could refer to fundamental philosophical differences in conceptions as a result of different worldviews. Or, it could refer to different experiences of success and spirituality given the presence or absence of varied contextual variables and their interaction in the lives of the adolescents. It seems, for instance, that cultural variables might interact with religion, especially as they refer to the three long-established traditions to which the adolescents in our sample belong (Christian, Jewish, and Muslim). This interaction might in turn influence participants' views. Fundamentally, however, we underscore the similarities in religious youths' views across the religious groups studied.

This finding brings us to a question: Do religious youth's views reveal a convergence between what it means to be successful and what it means to be spiritual? In this study, we attempted to depict this overlap through comparison of percentage of adolescents reporting moral virtues on *each* and then *both* of the survey questions. At least using this method in this sample, the overlap does not seem great, but it is certainly present. The substantiality of this overlap will be more reliably ascertained when compared with views of less-religious youth in future studies. The most remarkable finding was that moral virtues constituted the greatest area of overlap in adolescents' views of success and spirituality: The moral domain was once again brought to the forefront.

METHODOLOGICAL ISSUES AND FUTURE POSSIBILITIES

Finally, because this volume is about "Research Perspectives and Future Possibilities," we believe it is important to discuss some methodological issues that are inevitably raised by the work we present here. Namely, we are aware that we employ some strategies that are not necessarily common practice among either qualitative *or* quantitative researchers. Specifically, Marques and McCall (2005) discuss how in the past several years inter-rater reliability has rarely been used in qualitative studies as a tool of verification. One reason for this is that many researchers feel that it is unrealistic to expect another qualitative researcher to derive similar insights from what are usually limited databases, and because the nature of qualitative accounts are to evoke understandings of the social world rather than to actually represent it.

On the other side of the argument, many quantitative researchers stress the importance of reclaiming reliability in qualitative studies (Marques & McCall, 2005, p. 443) and warn that post-hoc methods used by many qualitative researchers are inadequate. In reply to this argument, we appreciate the fact that our measure of reliability is certainly not sufficient—that further criteria should ideally be applied. We believe that multiple perspectives on the code definitions and arrangements that we devised—for instance, developed by groups of researchers from different cultural and theoretical bents—would ultimately make for a more reliable and varied study. Not only might reliability be increased in this manner, but new theoretical frameworks would be brought to bear upon data of this type, potentially offering a more broad-based understanding of young people's views on our subject. Each formulation in turn might be utilized alongside more quantitative-based measures for corroboration. A much richer story would result.

In addition, in this study we followed the suggestion to calculate inter-rater reliability "right *after* the initial attainment of themes by the researcher yet *before* formulating conclusions based on the themes registered" (Marques & McCall, 2005, p. 443). This method avoids finding that consistency in the study is unsatisfactory after the study has been completed, and allows the researcher to corroborate the study before it is too late (p. 443). Ideally, to substantiate the findings of our study, we need further data collection to confirm, explore, or potentially refute the early findings noted here. Open-ended survey questions might be complemented by in-depth interviews to grasp more fully the meaning of the written responses. In this study, for instance, several responses were classified as "Other" because it was impossible to ascertain their meaning within the context of our coding scheme. A more randomly selected sample, representing even greater diversity of religious affiliation, could be gathered.

Most important, however, we emphasize that from the outset our concerns about PYD and spirituality are firstly and fundamentally about *development*. As this is the case, we recommend a focus on theoretical frameworks that may best represent the reality of development. In recent years, cutting-edge theories in the natural sciences based on developmental and dynamic systems theories have inspired new understandings in the developmental sciences (Fischer & Bidell, 2006; Lewis, 2000; Thelen & Smith, 2006). These theories describe aspects of the child's world as a dynamic and integrated system that guides mastery of new skills. The story of development is one of *self-directedness* and *emergence* that is not adequately captured by more deterministic theories. We venture that this kind of theoretical framework may be most useful in capturing the potentially dynamic and emergent phenomena of spiritual development and its interaction with the growing adolescent.

However, in order to do this, longitudinal research is needed. In our study, developmental differences in views of success and spirituality were suggested, hinting, for instance, that critical changes in youths' conceptions may emerge across the course of adolescence. But even if we were to employ more extensive methods to cross-sectional designs of this type, our results would be limited. Ideally, a longitudinal follow-up, which tracks the same participants across time, is warranted. The ultimate purpose of such a design would be to paint a real picture of the diverse and multiple lines of change that characterize adolescent spiritual and positive development. This sort of study would constitute a unique and pioneering contribution to the field.

REFERENCES

Alberts, A. E., Christiansen, E. D., Chase, P., Naudeau, S., Phelps, E., & Lerner, R. M. (2006). Qualitative and quantitative assessments of thriving and contribution in early adolescence: Findings from the 4-H study of positive youth development. *Journal of Youth Development: Bridging Research and Practice*, *1*, http://www.nae4ha.org/directory/jyd/index.html.

Arnett, J. J. (2000). Emerging adulthood: A theory of development from the late teens through the early twenties. *American Psychologist*, *55*, 469–480.

Benson, P. L., & Roehlkepartain, E. C. (2008). Spiritual development: A missing priority in youth development. *New Directions for Youth Development*, *118*, 13–28.

Benson, P. L., Roehlkepartain, E. C., & Rude, S. P. (2003). Spiritual development in childhood and adolescence: Toward a field of inquiry. *Applied Developmental Science*, *7*(3), 204–212.

Boyatzis, C. J., Dollahite, D. C., & Marks, L. D. (2005). The family as a context for religious and spiritual development in children and youth. In E. C. Roehlkepartain, P. E. King, L. Wagener, & P. L. Benson (Eds.), *The handbook of spiritual development in childhood and adolescence* (pp. 297–309). Thousand Oaks, CA: Sage.

Bronfenbrenner, U., & Morris, P. A. (2006). The bioecological model of human development. In R. M. Lerner (Ed.), *Handbook of child psychology: Vol 1, Theoretical models of human development* (6th ed.). Hoboken, NJ: Wiley.

Catalano, R. F., Berglund, M. L., Ryan, J. A. M., Lonczak, H. S., & Hawkins, J. D. (2004). *Positive youth development in the United States: Research findings on evaluations of positive youth development programs*. Seattle, WA: U.S. Department of Health and Human Services.

Damon, W., & Hart, D. (1988). *Self-understanding in childhood and adolescence*. New York, NY: Cambridge University Press.

Damon, W., Menon, J., & Bronk, K. C. (2003). The development of purpose during adolescence. *Applied Developmental Science*, *7*(3), 119–128.

Denton, M. L., Pearce, L. D., & Smith, C. (2008). *Religion and spirituality on the path through adolescence: A research report of the National Study of Youth and Religion*, Number 8. Chapel Hill, NC: National Study of Youth and Religion.

Eccles, J., & Gootman, J. A. (Eds.). (2002). *Community programs to promote youth development*. Washington, DC: National Academies Press.

Fischer, W., & Bidell, T. R. (2006). Dynamic development of action and thought. In R. M. Lerner (Ed.), *Handbook of child psychology: Vol. 1, Theoretical models of human development* (6th ed., pp. 199–235). Hoboken, NJ: Wiley.

Fredrickson, B. L. (2001). The role of positive emotions in positive psychology: The broaden-and-build theory of positive emotions. *American Psychologist*, *56*(3), 218–226.

Gallup International Association. (1999). *Gallup international millennium survey*. Accessed on June 15, 2009, from www.gallup-international.com.

Hart, D., Yates, M., Fegley, S., & Wilson, G. (1995). Moral commitment in inner-city adolescents. In M. Killen & D. Hart (Eds.), *Morality in everyday lives: Developmental perspectives* (pp. 317–341). Cambridge, England: Cambridge University Press.

Hay, D., Nye, R., & Murphy, R. (1996). Thinking about childhood spirituality: Review of research and current directions. In L. Francis, W. Kay, & W. Campbell (Eds.), *Research in religious education* (pp. 47–71). Leominster, England: Gracewing.

Hunsberger, B., Pratt, M., & Pancer, S. M. (2002). Longitudinal study of religious doubts in high school and beyond: Relationships, stability, and searching for answers. *Journal for the Scientific Study of Religion, 41*, 255–266.

Kerestes, M., & Youniss, J. E. (2003). Rediscovering the importance of religion in adolescent development. In R. M. Lerner, F. Jacobs, & D. Wertlieb (Eds.), *Handbook of applied developmental science: Promoting positive child, adolescent, and family development through research, policies, and programs: Vol. 1, Applying developmental science for youth and families: Historical and theoretical foundations* (pp. 165–184). Thousand Oaks, CA: Sage.

King, P. E. (2003). Religion and identity: The role of ideological, social, and spiritual contexts. *Applied Developmental Science, 73*, 197–204.

King, P. E., Dowling, E. M., Mueller, R. A., White, K., Schultz, W., Osborn, P., . . . & Scales, P. C. (2005). Thriving in adolescence: The voices of youth-serving practitioners, parents, and early and late adolescents. *Journal of Early Adolescence, 25*(1), 94–112.

King, P. E., & Furrow, J. (2004). Religion as a resource for positive youth development: Religion, social capital, and moral outcomes. *Developmental Psychology, 40*, 703–713.

Koenig, H. G., McCullough, M. E., & Larson, D. B. (2001). *Handbook of religion and health.* New York, NY: Oxford University Press.

Lerner, R. M., Dowling, E. M., & Anderson, P. M. (2003). Positive youth development: Thriving as a basis of personhood and civil society. *Applied Developmental Science, 7*, 172–180.

Lerner, R. M., Lerner, J. V., Almerigi, J., Theokas, C., Phelps, E., Gestsdottir, S., . . . & von Eye, A. (2005). Positive youth development, participation in community youth development programs, and community contributions of fifth grade adolescents: Findings from the first wave of the 4-H Study of Positive Youth Development. *Journal of Early Adolescence, 25*(1), 17–71.

Lerner, R. M., Roeser, R. W., & Phelps, E. (2008). Positive development, spirituality, and generosity in youth: A view of the issues. In R. M. Lerner, R. W. Roeser, & E. Phelps (Eds.), *Positive youth development and spirituality: From theory to research* (pp. 3–22). West Conshohocken, PA: Templeton Foundation Press.

Lewis, M. D. (2000). The promise of dynamic systems approaches for an integrated account of human development. *Child Development, 71*(1), 36–43.

Marques, J. F., & McCall, C. (2005). The application of interrater reliability as a solidification instrument in a phenomenological study. *The Qualitative Report, 10*(3), 439–462.

Moran, S. (2009). Purpose: Giftedness in intrapersonal intelligence. *High Ability Studies, 20*(2), 143–159.

Peterson, C., & Seligman, M. E. P. (2004). *Character strengths and virtues: A handbook and classification.* Oxford, England: Oxford University Press.

Rich, Y., & Cinamon, R. G. (2007). Conceptions of spirituality among Israeli Arab and Jewish late adolescents. *Journal of Humanistic Psychology, 47*(1), 7–29.

Roeser, R. W., Lerner, R. M., Phelps, E., Urry, H. L., Lazar, S., Issac, S. S., . . . & Du, D. (2007, March). The role of spiritual development in growth of purpose, generosity, and psychological health in adolescence. Invited presentation to the Fourth Biennial SRCD Preconference on Religious and Spiritual Development, Society for Research in Child Development (SRCD), Boston, MA.

Staudinger, U. M., Maciel, A. G., Smith, J., & Baltes, P. B. (1998). What predicts wisdom-related performance? A first look at personality, intelligence, and facilitative experiential contexts. *European Journal of Personality, 12*, 1–17.

Strauss, A., & Corbin, J. (1998). *Basics of qualitative research: Techniques and procedures for developing grounded theory.* (2nd ed.). Thousand Oaks, CA: Sage.

Thelen, E., & Smith, L. B. (2006). Dynamic systems theories. In R. M. Lerner (Ed.), *Handbook of child psychology: Vol. 1, Theoretical models of human development* (6th ed., pp. 563–634). Hoboken, NJ: Wiley.

Wink, P., & Helson, R. (1997). Practical and transcendent wisdom: Their nature and some longitudinal findings. *Journal of Adult Development, 4*(1), 1–15.

10

————◆————

Assessing the Relationship Between Ethnic and Religious Identity Among and Between Diverse American Youth[1]

AERIKA S. BRITTIAN AND MARGARET BEALE SPENCER

Developmental systems thinking provides the significance for research that considers the influence and function of religion and spirituality, in multiple cultural contexts, for the promotion of positive youth development (Roeser, Isaac, Abo-Zena, Brittian, & Peck, 2008). The purpose of this chapter is to examine empirically the convergence of two prominent aspects of identity among a racially diverse group of adolescents (i.e., ethnic identity and religious identity). In addition, we will explore the moderating effect of ethnic and religious identity in promoting positive life outcomes.

To address these key research objectives, which are framed in a particular instance of developmental systems theory [i.e., the phenomenological variant of ecological systems theoretical (PVEST) model (Spencer, 2006)], we first present

---

[1] The writing of this chapter was supported by a grant from the John Templeton Foundation. The authors wish to acknowledge the support and contributions of Richard M. Lerner, Robert W. Roeser, Erin Phelps, Sonia Koshy, Mona Abo-Zena, Dan Du, Amy Eva Alberts Warren, and the Institute for Applied Research in Youth Development.

a theoretical discussion of identity as a key developmental construct of interest in adolescence. Second, we provide a brief dialogue regarding identity theory through the work of Erikson (1950) and Marcia (1980); this presentation is followed by a discussion of the contemporary approach to assessing multiple aspects of identity. Third, we will discuss previous research that has examined independently two prominent aspects of identity, ethnic and religious. Subsequently, we examine empirically the relationship between ethnic and religious identity and its influence on indicators of positive development. To conclude this chapter, we introduce directions for advancing this work in future studies, and we note implications for policy.

THE PHENOMENOLOGICAL VARIANT OF ECOLOGICAL SYSTEMS THEORY FRAMEWORK

The research we shall report is framed by the Phenomenological Variant of Ecological Systems Theory (PVEST; Spencer, 2006, 2008) framework. Spencer and colleagues have emphasized the importance of contextual and cultural experiences of all youth within this instance of a developmental systems perspective. PVEST accounts for the individual's interpretation of life experiences (i.e., phenomenology) throughout the life span. Whereas previous theories have acknowledged the importance of historical and political context on human development, the PVEST model stresses the significance of these factors in identity development for diverse youth, such as assessing the impact of affirmative action policies on African Americans' educational and occupational upward mobility (Spencer, 2006).

Spencer's (2006, 2008) perspective takes as foundational the view that *all humans are vulnerable*. This status is the result of humans' experience of unavoidable developmental tasks (see Havighurst, 1953) confronted across the life course that require coping responses. Spencer suggests that identity formation is attained through a series of cyclical processes experienced as individuals navigate social places and environmental places frequently characterized by both common and unique challenges; responding to them requires appropriate coping strategies. There are cyclical sets of processes that occur throughout the life span and across a variety of settings; these processes are accompanied and influenced by particular cultural practices and sociocultural traditions. Healthy human development is achieved through five components linked by bidirectional processes (see Figure 10.1).

The first component is an assessment of net *vulnerability level*, which is accomplished by examining the net balance between *risk conditions* and *protective factors*. The genetic and/or phenotypic makeup of minority youth, such as being born female or Latino, may expose young people to stereotypes or discrimination (e.g., increased level of vulnerability from the risks associated with discrimination and stereotyping). Conversely, and although less frequently acknowledged, Spencer

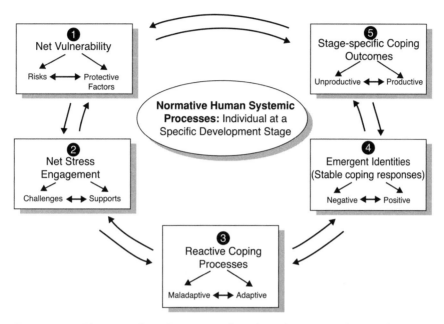

Figure 10.1   Phenomenological variant of ecological systems theory. (PVEST; Spencer, 2006)

Source: Spencer, M. B. (2006). Phenomenology and ecological systems theory: Development of diverse groups. In W. Damon and R. Lerner (Eds.), *Handbook of Child Psychology* (Theory Volume; 6th ed.). Hoboken, NJ: Wiley.

suggests that exposure to affluence may position youth for a particular level of risk as well (Luthar & Latendresse, 2002).

The second component, *net stress*, accounts for experiences that test one's psychosocial and physical well-being. These events, which are encountered in everyday life, may be buffered by social supports or exacerbated by challenges. For example, Spencer (2008) has used economic stress to explain the net stress level. The effects of an adolescent's parent's employment status or source of income may be both exacerbated by challenges and buffered by social support. The challenge is presented when limited access to resources is available, such as access to quality education or youth development programs. However, these challenges may be buffered by support from the adolescent's family, school, neighborhood, or religious community.

Reactive coping strategies, the third component, are expressed when an individual encounters stress-related events or dissonance associated with previous beliefs. The outcome of this stage depends on whether a person acts in adaptive or maladaptive ways. In some cases, a response that seems adaptive in one environment may be seen as maladaptive in another. For instance, consider a child who has suffered maltreatment or abuse in the home, who develops a sense of mistrust for caregivers, and who develops problematic coping behavior (e.g., aggression, delinquency, antisocial behavior, anxiety, and/or depression). These coping strategies may seem appropriate and adaptive given the circumstances, and perhaps even protective for the child in instances of neglect or abuse, but if the child was removed from the abusive environment and placed with nurturing caregivers, one would not expect the child to assume trusting behaviors immediately. On the contrary, children who have been abused react in a variety of ways once they are placed in a nurturing environment, including insecure and avoidant attachment to caregivers (Finzi, Ram, Har-Even, Shnit, & Weizman, 2001; McCarthy & Taylor, 1999; McWey, 2004), often to the disappointment of their eager foster families. Thus, coping strategies that were protective in one environment may function or be perceived as maladaptive in another.

As an individual consistently utilizes reactive coping strategies, the stability of the coping response emerges as a salient identity. Specifically, as the fourth component, *emergent identities—stable coping responses*, identity develops as a product of past experiences, interpretation of those experiences, and reaction to risk and stress. The development of stable coping strategies during the fourth stage leads to psychosocial stability over time and space. The product of the fifth stage, *life stage outcomes*, leads to productive or unproductive life choices.

PVEST differs from most theories that either ignore issues of human diversity or assume *a priori* pathology perspectives or assumptions that difference is equated with deviancy. Spencer (2008) asserts that PVEST is an *inclusive theory of human development applicable to all humans*. Its inclusive character involves considering the cultural traditions and contextual experiences of youth of color as well as youth living within many socioeconomic, religious, cultural, and historical systems. It is a theory that assesses not only the presence of risk but also the issue of privilege (e.g., race, skin color, or wealth) that is present in many societies. For instance, as the racial, cultural, and religious landscapes of the United States are rapidly changing, researchers using PVEST have called for a consideration of inclusive studies that examine how various psychological constructs influence human behavior. In particular, how do these psychological constructs contribute to developmental coping mechanisms, which, in turn, lead to positive developmental outcomes (Spencer, 2006)?

Before we begin to discuss theories of identity development, it is important to define *identity* as it has been typically treated in the literature. According to Erikson (1950), *identity* is continuity over time in awareness of one's values, attitudes, and ideology concerning the self and society. In adolescence, a young person first begins to think about his or her place in the world. Many young people begin to consider how their own family's values may be different or similar to those of other families. A young person may obtain his or her first part-time job while attending high school, or choose to become active in extracurricular activities (e.g., sports, drama, clubs) sponsored by the school. This time is also a developmental period when a young person may begin to think about his or future, in terms of attending college or choosing to work. According to Lerner (2002), identity development is an important aspect of an adolescent's life in the United States because of societal expectations, such that the beliefs that adolescents develop in this period of life will contribute to a positive and productive adulthood.

THEORETICAL CONCEPTIONS OF IDENTITY

Given the dynamic biological, psychological, and social changes that occur both within the individual and in his or her environment, adolescence is the quintessential developmental period most associated with identity exploration (Eccles, Brown, & Templeton, 2008). In fact, Erikson (1950) posited that identity bridges the gap between childhood—characterized by bodily self and parent's expectations—and adulthood, which is marked by an increase in social roles. It is in adolescence that a person may begin to ask him or herself, not only "Who am I?" but "Who am I in this particular context?" (Erikson, 1950; Schwartz, 2001). In conjunction with experiencing a myriad of biological changes, such as physical growth and sexual maturation, adolescents' expectations and social relationships are being redefined (Brown & Larson, 2009; Eccles, Brown, & Templeton, 2008; Laursen & Collins, 2009; Lerner, 2002).

The initial works of Erikson were based in a person-centered perspective. Within his eight-stage theory of human development, Erikson proposed that in each developmental stage an individual must adapt to challenges presented by the environment in order for healthy development to occur. Of particular importance for the study of adolescence, society places expectations on young people to develop a sense of identity or face the negative consequences of role confusion.

Furthering the work of Erikson, James Marcia (1966) proposed that more differentiated phases of development were involved in identity formation. According to Marcia, four identity statuses exist, differing in the degree to which individuals have explored aspects of their identity and how committed they were to their beliefs. The first status, *diffuse*, consists of individuals who have not explored various aspects of their identity. These individuals do not have a clear, coherent, and coalesced concept of their place in society. They are low on choice and low on commitment. Côté (2009) suggests that "diffusion is generally considered the least mature and least complex status, reflecting a lack of concern about directing one's present and future life" (p. 272).

The second status, *foreclosure*, occurs when young people accept the values and ideas to which they have been exposed by their parents or guardians. These individuals, who are low on choice but high on commitment, have been described as heavily influenced by obedience and authoritarianism, as well as by being overly identified with their parents (Adams, Dyk, & Bennion, 1987; Berman, Schwartz, Kurtines, & Berman, 2001; Côté & Levine, 1983). The third status, *moratorium*, includes individuals who are in the process of searching or exploring many statuses but are not committed to any of them. In contemporary U.S. society, adolescents are expected to explore many identities.

Conflicts between young people and their parents may occur as youth begin to challenge norms (e.g., gender, career, culture) within their family and as they attempt to establish an autonomous identity (Fuligini, 1998; Steinberg, 2001). In considering immigrant American adolescents, there is often conflict around cultural norms and family expectations between first-generation adolescents and their parents who were born in other countries (Gans, 1992; Portes, 1995). For example, children of immigrants evaluate themselves in comparison to the standards of the new country, whereas their immigrant parents attempt to retain the values of their cultural origin (Zhou, 1997). Côté (2009) posits that a moratorium status is associated with anxiety and uncertainty.

Achieved, the fourth status, occurs when individuals have explored options for their identity, found an identity, and resolved any pending questions about their values. This status is considered the most mature, as individuals have actively explored multiple aspects of the self and have made a commitment to a sound ideology. In addition, an achieved identity status has been found to be associated with several healthy life outcomes, such as high interpersonal skills and more developed cognitive processes (Kroger, 2003).

The contemporary study of identity as a psychological construct, which remains heavily influenced by the work of Erikson and Marcia, has expanded in various disciplines to include an examination of multiple, both independent and overlapping, instances of one's identity, including but not limited to ethnic/cultural identity (Ashmore, Deaux, & McLaughlin-Volpe, 2004; Phinney & Ong, 2007; Romero & Roberts, 2003), gender identity (Egan & Perry, 2001; Zucker, 2002), religious/spiritual identity (Furrow, King, & White, 2004; King, 2003), vocational identity (Gushue, Clarke, Pantzer, & Scanlan, 2006; Hargrove, Creagh, & Burgess, 2002; Robitschek & Cook, 1990), immigrant identity (Gibson, 2001; Lee & Bean, 2004), and national identity (Featherstone, 2003; Huntington, 2004; Orchard, 2002). For the purposes of this chapter, we will focus on what is known about two of the more prominent areas of current research: ethnic identity and religious identity.

THE DEVELOPMENT OF ETHNIC IDENTITY

Ethnic identity is an important construct to examine in ethnically diverse societies, such as those found in the United States (Worrell, Conyers, Mpofu, & Vandiver, 2006), because it is believed to influence several positive outcomes among adolescents, such as greater self-esteem, higher academic achievement, and effective coping against discrimination (Juang & Syed, 2008; Phinney, 2003; Quintana, 2007). This aspect of identity has been defined as "an individual's sense of belonging to a group of people [that] may be based upon shared physiology, as well as common values, beliefs and practices" (Smith, Walker, Fields, Brookins, & Seay, 1999). Ethnic identity also refers to "knowledge and understanding of one's ingroup affiliation . . . [that is] constructed over time" (Phinney & Ong, 2007). Although group affiliation has been associated with antisocial behavior from nongroup members, such as discrimination (Brown, 2000; Mummendey & Wenzel, 1999; Schlesinger, 1991), ethnic identity may nevertheless serve as a source of strength for individuals who experience discrimination and/or inequitable treatment in heterogeneous societies (Smith et al., 1999; Spencer & Markstrom-Adams, 1990).

The presence of positive ethnic identity has been linked to greater participation in political and civic activities, and volunteerism among ethnic minorities. It has been suggested that ethnic minorities who have internalized ethnicity as a part of their identity and are cognizant of social injustices committed against their ethnic group are more likely to engage in activities related to social change (Guitierrez, 1990; Juang & Syed, 2008; Zimmerman, 1995). Undoubtedly, from a PVEST perspective, positive ethnic identity functions as a protective factor and source of psychological support, especially when faced with human risks and challenges. However, less is known about other identifications (e.g., religious, philanthropic, or civic), which could function interactively with ethnic identity. These interactions might be particularly important for those individuals burdened with disproportionally high levels of risk and challenge.

At the same time, those who have significant and high levels of protective factors and support may also benefit by practicing coping strategies. Among such individuals, coping strategies may help address the challenges that may exist in society in regard to feeling that one is behaving morally. In addition, for those individuals with significant privilege or status, identifications associated with religiosity may provide sources of moral "salvation." Religiosity may be helpful in maintaining positive identity by offsetting the possible excesses of high privilege (Luthar & Latendresse, 2002).

INCREASING FOCUS ON RELIGIOUS IDENTITY

The study of religious identity has burgeoned over the past 30 years, with an increasing number of disciplines (e.g., psychology, sociology, anthropology and public health) beginning to focus on this aspect of the person. King (2003) stated that there has been a "revival of interest in religion and spirituality in the social sciences." Among adolescents, studies have reported that religion gives value to their life experiences and enhances their identity development (King, 2003; Youniss, McLellan, & Yates, 1999). Participation in religious communities may give adolescents the opportunities to consider their own beliefs, in conjunction with other worldviews and their own faith community. Furthermore, religious communities may provide youth with opportunities for building social support networks, as King (2003) indicated that "religions often provide opportunities for adolescents to interact with peers and build intergenerational relationships" (p. 199). Although research suggests that there are both psychological and social benefits for adolescents' participation in religious institutions, for the current study we will focus on the benefits gained through awareness of one's religious identity.

Previous studies have suggested that religiosity varies by racial group, such that European Americans reported higher instances of religious service attendance than African Americans, Asian Americans, and Latino Americans. In addition, African American youth reported that religion is more influential in their lives than did youth from other racial groups (Smith & Lundquist-Denton, 2002). We also know that Latino youth are more likely to engage in instances of prayer and religious commitment than are youth from other ethnic groups (Smith & Denton, 2005). Simply stated, religiosity has been narrowly explored as a protective factor and source of support. However, less is known about its downside, or about those conditions that lead to a negative identity or reactive coping responses.

Although many studies have focused on the positive effects of religious identity, the negative effects of religiosity on both individual and prosocial behavior have been acknowledged in the literature (Benson, 2006; Benson, Donahue, & Erickson, 1989). First, it has been suggested that religious communities may hinder identity exploration among adolescents, in favor of acceptance of group norms and identity foreclosure (Benson, 2006; Benson et al., 1989). In addition, it should be noted that religion may promote inclusive ideals and behavior among group members and prompt exclusivity toward nongroup members. Thus, the impact of religion, when combined with other indicators of group membership, is less well known. Accordingly, we know very little about the relationship between ethnic identity and religious identity and, in turn, how these identities relate to indicators of positive youth development. In the next section, we provide an overview of what previous research has suggested about how ethnic identity and religious identity may relate.

ETHNIC IDENTITY AND RELIGIOUS IDENTITY: OVERLAPPING FACETS OF IDENTITY

Contemporary research has begun to examine ethnic identity and religious identity as overlapping facets of identity. Facets of identity, such as one's ethnicity and religiosity, are social categorizations and are not always clearly defined in the literature. In addition, although empirical research often seeks to partition out the amount of variance accounted for by each individual construct, these social constructions may be connected within an individual. The potential overlap between these facets of identity has been referred to as *intersectionality* among Critical Race Theorists (Crenshaw, Gotanda, Peller, & Thomas, 1995; Hurtado, 1997; Juang & Syed, 2008).

Several methods have been proposed for examining how religious and ethnic identity may intersect for various racial and cultural groups. Qualitative research has contributed greatly to our understanding of how these aspects of identity may be related for some individuals. Juang and Syed (2008) stated that "for some individuals, their religious identities are less important, or even nonexistent, in relation to their ethnic identities" (p. 270). They go on to explain that aspects of identity may be: (a) fused, (b) distinct, with one taking precedence over the other, or (c) distinct, but in conflict. For individuals whose identities are fused, ethnic identity may be reinforced by participation in a same-ethnic group congregation (Mattis & Jagers, 2001; Taylor, Chatters, & Levin, 2004). For others, religious identity and ethnic identity may be distinct, with one facet taking precedence over another.

The relationship between these aspects of identity also may be nonexistent. For example, children growing up in a black Jewish community may or may not have socializing experiences that explicitly forge links between the formation of ethnic and religious identities. For some families or synagogue communities, the fact that the group is designated as members of a black Jewish community may be an imposed demarcation used for separating them from traditionally white American Jewish communities. For other families with the same synagogue membership, however, the designation may be viewed by parents as an opportunity for promoting ethnic socialization values and beliefs as well as for reinforcing the family's religious identity.

Within the study of adolescent identity development, three main branches of research have emerged as a product of healthy identity formation: prosocial behavior, psychological well-being, and academic achievement (see Figure 10.2).

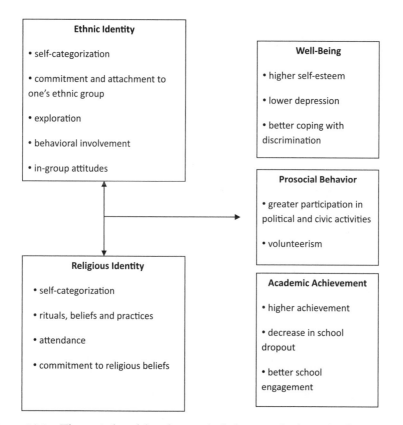

Figure 10.2   Theoretical model explaining the bidirectional relationship between ethnic identity and religious identity in promoting indicators of healthy development.

Why should the intersection of ethnic and religious identity be associated with these three outcomes? Prosocial behavior may be linked to one's degree of psychological well-being (e.g., see Spencer, Fegley, & Dupree 2006). That is, to the extent that one feels psychological comfort regarding the self, it may be more probable that prosocial behavioral orientations will occur. In turn, to the degree that one feels psychological well-being, it may also be that high risk-taking behavior is less likely (Cunningham, Swanson, & Spencer, 2003; Spencer, Fegley, Harpalani, & Seaton, 2004). Moreover, in regard to academic achievement, to the degree that youth feel comfortable in school and experience a positive school climate, positive academic outcomes may be achieved (e.g., see Youngblood & Spencer, 2002; Spencer 1999, 2001). In the current study, framed in the PVEST model, we will consider the outcomes of psychological well-being and reduction of risk in relation to the intersection of ethnic and religious identity.

CURRENT STUDY AND HYPOTHESES

Although the development of social identity (e.g., ethnicity) and personal identity (e.g., religiosity) have often been examined separately in previous literature, current scholarship has called for integrative research that examines both of these aspects of an individual's identity (Schwartz, Zamboanga, & Weisskirch, 2008). Many studies have examined the relationship between religion and positive outcomes in American adolescents (Wallace, Forman, Caldwell, & Willis, 2003), but to date few studies have explored the importance of religion in the lives of diverse youth. As such, this chapter will address three main research questions:

1. Is there convergence between ethnic identity and religious identity among youth from various racial backgrounds?
2. Does the relationship between ethnic identity and religious identity promote positive development (i.e., higher instances of well-being, decreased risk behaviors)?
3. Do ethnic identity and religious identity function in parallel fashion for adolescents from different racial groups (i.e., European American, African American, and multiracial youth)?

METHOD

Study Design and Participants

The John Templeton Foundation (JTF)–funded cross-sectional, mixed-methods study, "The Role of Spiritual Development in Growth of Purpose, Generosity, and Psychological Health in Adolescence," was designed to enhance our understanding of the relationship between spirituality and positive development during adolescence. The overall study consisted of multiple substudies designed to assess adolescents' biological, psychological, cognitive, and social understanding of religious/spiritual affiliation and, in turn, to explore implications of both individual and collective religious and spiritual experiences for positive youth development.

The data for the current study were selected from the *Positive Youth Development and Spirituality Questionnaire Sub-Study*. Participants were recruited from the greater Boston, Massachusetts area. Four hundred eleven participants aged 10 to 22 years were recruited from middle schools, high schools, and after-school programs. An additional sample of 252 college participants aged 18 to 23 years were recruited by word of mouth and advertisements on Facebook. The overall study sample, therefore, included 663 individuals ranging in age from 10 to 23 years. This group included 31% middle school students, 31% high school students, and 38% college-aged students. Participants were 49% female and 51% male, ethnically diverse, and mostly Jewish, Catholic, Protestant, Muslim, or of no religious affiliation.

For the purpose of conducting within-group analyses, we selected a subsample of African American ($n = 82$), European American ($n = 278$), and multiracial adolescents ($n = 111$) from the overall study sample. For this subsample, the age range was from 12 to 23 years ($M = 17.67$). The majority of participants reported religious affiliation as follows: 30.4%, Roman Catholic; 13.8%, Protestant; 10.3%, no religion; 10.6%, Jewish; 10.4%, other Christian group; and 3.0%, Eastern Orthodox.

Two versions of a questionnaire, consisting of closed-ended items drawn from established measures of PYD and spirituality, were constructed. Measures of reliability for the items used in the current study are reported in the measures section that follows. The survey was administered in one of two versions. The first version of the survey was delivered on a voice-enhanced personal digital assistant (PDA) for middle and high school students. Participants who completed the questionnaire on the PDA were given instructions on how to use the devices before completing the survey. Responses were downloaded from the PDAs to a computer. The second version was a Web-based questionnaire for college-aged participants that used the same items.

Measures

Ethnic Identity

Ten items were used from the Multigroup Ethnic Identity Measure (MEIM; Phinney, 1992) to construct a measure of ethnic identity. Sample items used in the present study included, "I have spent time trying to find out more about my culture, such as its history, traditions, and customs" and "I have a strong sense of belonging to my own culture." The response format ranged from 1 = *strongly disagree* to 4 = *strongly agree*. Higher scores on this measure indicated stronger cultural identity. The MEIM shows good reliability, with Cronbach's alphas above .80 across a wide range of ethnic groups and ages (Roberts et al., 1999). Cronbach's alphas for the overall MEIM for the current sample were

.85 for African Americans, .85 for European Americans, and .87 for multiracial adolescents.

Religious Identity

To assess religious identity, we used an eight-item composite comprising items related to (a) religious belief and (b) religious practices. One item was used to index religious belief: "I consider myself a religious person" (Fetzer Institute, 2003; Roeser, 2005; Smith & Denton, 2005). Seven items were used to assess level of religious practice. Sample items for religious practice included "How often do you seek help from God (i.e., Allah, G-d, Holy One, Buddha, Brahman, Great Spirit, etc.) through prayer or some other way when you experience problems or difficulties in your life?" and "How often do you go to a temple, synagogue, church, mosque, or some other religious/spiritual center to attend public services?" Cronbach's alphas for the religious identity measure by ethnic group were African Americans, $\alpha = .79$; European Americans, $\alpha = .83$; and multiracial, $\alpha = .86$.

Well-Being

This four-item measure assessed adolescents' self-reported overall well-being (Roeser, Galloway, et al., 2008). Participants responded to questions on a five-item response scale, ranging from $1 = $ *not at all* to $5 = $ *very true*. Sample questions included "How happy would you say you are with your life right now?" and "How satisfied are you with your life right now?" Previous research has reported Cronbach's alphas equaling .80. Cronbach's alphas for the current sample were .63 for African Americans, .63 for European Americans, and .70 for multiracial adolescents.

Risk Behaviors

Risk behaviors are measured through scales of substance use and delinquency derived from the Profile of Student Life—Attitudes and Behaviors Survey (PSL-AB; Leffert et al., 1998) and from the Monitoring the Future (2000) questionnaire. The five items we used to measure substance use asked participants to indicate during the past year whether they have done any of several risk behaviors. The questions used a forced-choice response format ranging from $1 = $ *never* to $5 = $ *often, 5 times or more*. Sample items included "Have you smoked pot?" and "Have you used illegal drugs other than marijuana?" The seven items we used to measure delinquency asked respondents how many times during the last 12 months they had engaged in delinquent behavior. These items used a forced-choice response format ranging from $1 = $ *never* to $5 = $ *often, 5 times or more*. Sample items included "Have you stolen something just for fun?" and "Have you cheated on school exams?" Cronbach's alphas for the current sample were .75 for African Americans, .78 for European Americans, and .85 for multiracial adolescents.

RESULTS

As we have noted, our research questions were: Is there convergence between ethnic identity and religious identity among youth from various ethnic backgrounds? Does the relationship between ethnic identity and religious identity promote positive development (i.e., higher instances of well-being, decreased risk behaviors)? Does the relationship function similarly for different racial groups (i.e., European American, African American, and multiracial youth)? In order to address these questions, we conducted a series of mean-level analyses, correlations, nested regression analyses, and within-group analyses.

Preliminary Analyses

Socioeconomic status (SES) is often confounded with race in the United States and, as such, its role in influencing developmental outcomes is often unclear. Therefore, we used mother's education to index SES and assessed variation among the different ethnic groups. The results of a one-way analysis of variance (ANOVA) indicated significant group differences, $F(2, 468) = 36.13, p < .001$. Post-hoc analyses revealed that European American adolescents' mothers reported higher levels of education ($M = 3.98, SD = 1.28$) than did multiracial adolescents' mothers ($M = 3.38, SD = 1.58$), and mothers of multiracial adolescents reported higher levels of education than did mothers of African American adolescents ($M = 2.45, SD = 1.77$). In turn, about one-fourth of the African American participants (26.8%) were born outside of the United States, compared to 6.8% of European American adolescents and 14.4% of multiracial adolescents. For this reason, to address the third question, we conducted within-group examinations of the role of religious and ethnic identity on well-being and risk behaviors. This approach provides a more accurate assessment of the influence of these potentially protective factors in the lives of the adolescents in this sample than would a between-group comparison. We conducted mean-level analyses for the key outcome variables by ethnic group for descriptive purposes only.

Although not included in our hypotheses, we compared the predictor variables by ethnic groups using analysis of variance (ANOVA). The first test indicated significant group differences for ethnic identity, $F(2, 468) = 21.86, p < .001$. A post-hoc analysis was used to determine where group differences existed. Results of Tukey's HSD suggested that African Americans ($M = 3.15, SD = .55$) and multiracial adolescents ($M = 2.97, SD = .53$) reported higher ethnic identity levels than did European Americans ($M = 2.73, SD = .54$). The second analysis, examining religious identity, indicated significant group differences by ethnic group, $F(2, 468) = 4.76, p < .01$. Therefore, we again followed up with a post-hoc analysis. Results of Tukey's HSD suggested that African Americans ($M = 3.84, SD = 1.74$) reported higher religious identity than did European Americans ($M = 3.19, SD = 1.61$).

Results of an ANOVA indicated significant group differences for well-being, $F(2, 468) = 10.34, p < .001$. Results of Tukey's HSD suggested that African

Americans (M = 3.77, SD = .67) and European Americans (M = 3.67, SD = .63) reported higher instances of well-being than did multiracial adolescents (M = 3.37, SD = .79). We found no significant mean differences on risk behaviors by ethnic group, F(2, 466) = 1.12, p > .05.

Because sex is associated with indicators of positive development, such as self-esteem and self-concept, we conducted a mean-level analysis examining the outcome variables by sex. Results of an independent samples t-test suggested significant sex differences for the outcome variables: well-being and risk behaviors. Well-being was lower among adolescent girls (M = 3.48, SD = .72) than adolescent boys (M = 3.76, SD = .64) in this sample, t(463) = −4.46, p < .05. Risk behaviors were higher among adolescent boys (M = 1.87, SD = .56) than adolescent girls (M = 1.75, SD = .56), t(432) = −2.02, p < .05. Given that significant differences were found for adolescent males and females, we included sex as a control variable in further analyses.

Ethnic Identity and Religious Identity: Is There Convergence?

To determine if ethnic identity and religious identity are related facets of identity among youth from three racial groups, within-group correlation analyses were examined. Results indicated a moderate positive relationship between ethnic identity and religious identity for all groups, such that higher ethnic identity was associated with higher religious identity: African Americans, r(82) = 0.23 p < .05; European Americans, r(278) = 0.29, p < .001; and multiracial adolescents, r(103) = 0.24, p < .05.

Is the Ethnic Identity–Religious Identity Relation Associated With Well-Being and Risk Behaviors?

To address the second research question, a series of nested regression analyses were computed in order to determine if religious identity and ethnic identity predicted well-being for the adolescents we studied. Using a hierarchical linear regression model, four explanatory variables were included in the first step, and ethnic identity and religious identity were added in the second step. This approach allows us to determine whether ethnic identity and religious identity explain a significant amount of the variance in the dependent variable above and beyond demographic variables that we expect to be related to adolescents' well-being. The demographic variables included adolescent's sex, self-reported age, mother's education, and immigration status. In the third step, an interaction term of religious identity by ethnic identity was included. The first step explained a small amount of variance in well-being, F(5, 464) = 7.42, p < .001, R² = .06. However, adding ethnic identity and religious identity in the second step only resulted in a small change in R squared. The third model, containing the main effects of religious and ethnic identity, demographic variables, and an interaction term, explained only 7% of the variance in well-being. Therefore, the second model was the most parsimonious one. There were main effects of sex and age on well-being. The strongest explanatory variable was sex ($\beta = .20, p < .001$), followed by age ($\beta = -.14, p < .01$). Adjusting for all other variables in the model, adolescent boys reported higher scores of well-being, such as satisfaction and happiness with life overall, than did adolescent girls. In addition, younger adolescents reported higher well-being than did older adolescents.

Second, we conducted a series of nested regression analyses to determine if there was a moderating relationship between religious identity and ethnic identity in predicting risk behaviors. Using a hierarchical model, the same demographic variables were included in the first step; we then added ethnic identity and religious identity in the second step. In the third step, an interaction term of religious identity by ethnic identity was included. The first step explained a significant amount of variance in risk behaviors, $F(4, 462) = 9.32, p < .001$, $R^2 = .08$. The second model, which added ethnic identity and religious identity, also accounted for a significant amount of variance in risk behaviors, $F(6, 460) = 7.16, p < .001, R^2 = .09$. However, the third model, containing the main effects of religious and ethnic identity, demographic variables, and an interaction term, explained 10% of the variance in risk factors, $F(7, 459) = 7.56, p < .001$. There was a main effect of sex ($\beta = .11, p < .05$), age ($\beta = .23, p < .001$), mother's education ($\beta = -.11, p < .05$), and an interaction between ethnic identity and religious identity on risk behaviors ($\beta = -3.04, p < .01$).

In sum, these findings show that boys reported more risk behaviors than did girls, older adolescents reported more risk behaviors than did younger adolescents, and higher mother's education was associated with lower risk behaviors. In addition, the significant interaction suggests that, in the high ethnic identity group, adolescents with low religious identity have significantly higher risk scores than do adolescents with high religious identity. However, in the low ethnic identity group, adolescents with low religious identity did not have higher risk scores than did adolescents with high religious identity.

Do Religious Identity and Ethnic Identity Function Differently Among Adolescents From Different Racial Backgrounds?

We expected that there would be a combined effect of ethnic and religious identity on adolescents' well-being and risk behaviors. However, previous research led us to believe that this relationship functions differently for youth from varying racial backgrounds. Thus, in the present study, we conducted within-group analyses to determine if and where these differences existed among African American, European American, and multiracial adolescents.

African American Adolescents

Similar to the steps we followed to address our second question, we first conducted a series of nested regression analyses to determine if religious identity and ethnic identity predicted well-being among African American adolescents. Using a hierarchical model, the aforementioned four control variables were again used in the first step in this analysis; also as before, ethnic identity and religious identity were added in the second step. In the third step, we included an interaction term between religious identity and ethnic identity. The first model explained a fairly large amount of variance in the well-being of African American adolescents, $F(4, 76) = 5.11, p \leq .001, R^2 = .21$. The second model also explained a fairly large amount of variance in the well-being of African American adolescents, $F(6, 74) = 3.91, p < .01, R^2 = .24$. We found a significant main effect of age and sex, such that boys were more likely than girls to report higher instances of well-being, and younger adolescents were more likely than older adolescents to report higher instances of well-being (see Table 10.1). The third model, containing the main effects of religious and ethnic identity, demographic variables, and an interaction term, explained 24% of the variance in well-being, $F(7, 73) = 3.32, p < .01, R^2 = .24$.

To assess the relationship between ethnic identity and religious identity, demographic variables, and risk, a series of linear regression models were examined. Using a hierarchical model, the same four demographic variables were included in the first step, and then ethnic identity and religious identity were added in the second step. In the third step, we included the interaction term between religious identity and ethnic identity. The first model explained 21% of the variance in African American adolescents' risk behaviors, $F(4, 74) = 4.93, p < .001$. The second model also explained a significant amount of variance in risk, $F(6, 72) = 5.01, p < .001, R^2 = .29$. We found a significant main effect of age and ethnic identity on risk behaviors among African American adolescents (see Table 10.2). Higher instances of ethnic identity were predictive of fewer risk behaviors among African Americans. The third model, containing the interaction between religious identity and ethnic identity, accounted for the same amount of variance as the second model, $F(7, 71) = 4.23, p < .001, R^2 = .29$.

European American Adolescents

Using the same within-group approach, we took similar data analytic steps with the European American sample. The first model explained a small amount of variance in the well-being of European Americans, $F(4, 272) = 2.57, p < .05, R^2 = .04$. The second model explained 5% of the variance in well-being, $F(6, 270) = 2.54, p < .05$. We found a significant main effect of age and sex, such that boys were again more likely to report higher instances of well-being than girls, and younger adolescents were more likely than older adolescents to report higher instances of well-being (see Table 10.1). The third model explained 6% of the variance in well-being, $F(7, 269) = 2.34, p < .05$.

To assess the relationship between ethnic identity, religious identity, demographic variables, and risk, we next conducted an analogous series of linear regression models. The first model explained 11% of the variance in European American

Table 10.1 Nested Regression Models Examining Ethnic Identity and Religious Identity With Well-Being as an Outcome

	African Americans (n = 82)			European Americans (n = 278)			Multi-racial (n = 111)		
	Step 1	Step 2	Step 3	Step 1	Step 2	Step 3	Step 1	Step 2	Step 3
Intercept	4.76***	4.91***	5.26***	4.13***	3.81***	4.21***	3.02***	2.56***	3.02***
Sex	.32**	.32**	.31**	.12	.12*	.12*	.30**	.31***	.30**
Age	−.34**	.38***	.38***	−.15*	−.13*	−.12	−.03	−.04	−.04
Caregiver's education	.02	.02	.03	.05	.03	.02	.06	.04	.05
Immigration status	−.02	−.04	−.04	−.02	−.02	−.01	.09	.09	.08
Ethnic identity	—	.07	−.01	—	.04	−.09	—	.14	.01
Religious identity	—	−.18	−.42	—	.12	−.23	—	.01	−.27
Ethnic identity*Religious identity	—	—	.27	—	—	.42	—	—	.34
R^2	0.21	0.24	0.24	0.04	0.05	0.06	0.1	0.12	0.12
df(Residual)	76	74	73	272	270	269	106	104	103
ΔR^2		0.03	0		0.01	0.01		0.02	0
df(ΔR^2)		1	1		1	1		1	1

$*p < .05; **p < .01; ***p < .001$

Table 10.2 Nested Regression Models Examining Ethnic Identity and Religious Identity With Risk as an Outcome

	African Americans (n = 82)			European Americans (n = 278)			Multi-racial (n = 111)		
	Step 1	Step 2	Step 3	Step 1	Step 2	Step 3	Step 1	Step 2	Step 3
Intercept	.59***	1.82***	1.89***	.63*	.58	.43***	1.40	1.84	.07
Sex	.20	.19	.19	.07	.07	.07	.13	.12	.14
Age	.30**	.26*	.26*	.33***	.33***	.33***	.06	.08	.07
Caregiver's education	−.16	−.15	−.15	−.05	−.03	−.03	−.09	−.07	−.10
Immigration status	.26*	.19	.18	−.04	−.05	−.05	.14	.14	.20*
Ethnic identity	—	−.23*	−.25	—	.09	.14	—	−.17	.32
Religious identity	—	−.15	−.21	—	−.18**	−.05	—	.05	1.15**
Ethnic identity*Religious identity	—	—	.06	—	—	−.16	—	—	−1.33**
R^2	0.21	0.29	0.29	0.11	0.14	0.14	0.04	0.07	0.15
df(Residual)	74	72	71	272	270	276	106	104	103
ΔR^2		0.08	0		0.03	0		0.03	0.08
df(ΔR^2)		1	1		1	1		1	1

*$p < .05$; **$p < .01$; ***$p < .001$

adolescents' risk behaviors, $F(4, 272) = 8.59, p < .001$. The second model also explained a significant amount of variance in risk, $F(6, 270) = 7.54, p < .001$, $R^2 = .14$. We found a significant main effect of age and religious identity on risk behaviors among European American adolescents (see Table 10.2). Higher instances of religious identity were predictive of less risk behaviors among European Americans. The third model accounted for the same amount of variance as the second model, $F(7, 269) = 6.47, p < .001, R^2 = .14$.

Multiracial Adolescents

Finally, we conducted the same within-group analyses among our multiracial participants. The first model explained a small amount of variance in well-being among multiracial adolescents, $F(4, 106) = 2.92, p < .05, R^2 = .09$. The second model explained a moderate amount of variance in well-being among multiracial adolescents, $F(6, 104) = 2.31, p < .05, R^2 = .12$. We found a significant main effect of sex, such that boys were more likely than girls to report higher instances of well-being (see Table 10.1). The third model was not significant, $F(7, 103) = 2.06, p > .05$.

To assess the relationship between ethnic identity, religious identity, demographic variables, and risk, we conducted again an analogous series of linear regression models. The first model explained 4% of the variance in multiracial adolescents' risk behaviors and was not significant, $F(4, 106) = 1.12, p > .05$. The second model was also not significant, $F(6, 104) = 1.21, p > .05, R^2 = .07$. However, the third model, containing the interaction between religious identity and ethnic identity, accounted for a significant amount of variance, $F(7, 103) = 2.54, p < .05, R^2 = .15$. We found a significant interaction between religious identity and ethnic identity among multiracial adolescents. In the high ethnic identity group, adolescents with low religious identity had significantly higher risk scores than did adolescents with high religious identity. However, in the low ethnic identity group, adolescents with low religious identity did not have higher risk scores than did adolescents with high religious identity.

DISCUSSION

Using the PVEST model (Spencer, 2006, 2008) as a frame, the purpose of this chapter was to examine empirically the convergence of ethnic identity and religious identity among a racially and socioeconomically diverse group of adolescents. In addition, we explored the effect of ethnic and religious identity in promoting various positive life outcomes (i.e., increased well-being and reduced risk).

Results of this study suggest some overlap between religious identity and ethnic identity. We found that a moderate relationship existed between these two facets of identity. Although only small percentages of variance were involved, individuals who reported a higher sense of belonging to their ethnic group and had spent more time learning about their ethnic group were more likely to consider themselves religious persons and, as such, engage in more instances of religious practice. It may be that both ethnic identity and religious identity are compo-nents of an overarching identity, and that adolescents may be on a journey of self-discovery investigating multiple aspects of their identity. If the cross-sectional data from the present research were extended longitudinally, this idea could be better tested, and adolescents' exploration of other aspects of identity, such as gender or national identity, could also be assessed.

The second hypothesis was that ethnic identity and religious identity would be predictive of indicators of positive development (i.e., higher instances of well-being, decreased risk behaviors). Contrary to expectations, results suggest that the strongest predictors of adolescent well-being in this sample were sex and age. Although it was expected that demographic characteristics would be associated with well-being, the finding that religious identity was not predictive of well-being was surprising. In turn, the strongest predictors of risk were sex, age, mother's education, and the interaction between religious identity and ethnic identity.

Our tests of our third research question assessed if the relationship between ethnic identity and religious identity functioned similarly for adolescents from dif-ferent racial groups (i.e., European American, African American, and multiracial youth). Juang and Syed (2008) posited that "ethnicity and religion/spirituality are overlapping [instances of] identity that cannot be separated" (p. 276). Although we agree with these authors, we would add that these instances of identity do seem to function differently for diverse American adolescents. Results of this study suggest that immigrant status was predictive of African American adolescents' risk behaviors, but this relationship was moderated by ethnic identity. U.S.-born adolescents in this sample were more likely to exhibit higher risk factors; how-ever, higher ethnic identity was associated with a lower level of risk behaviors. Religious identity was associated with lower levels of risk for European Amer-ican adolescents. For multiracial adolescents, we found an interaction between religious identity and ethnic identity. It may be that the collectivist sense of self, or being part of a larger identity (i.e., as part of a religious group or ethnic enclave), provides the sense of group membership that is less easily experienced for multiracial youth, and so any role of ethnic identity in risk behaviors may be attenuated. It may be that youth experience of multiracial socialization efforts by parents might account for this finding. Such a possibility may be a worthy target of future research.

Limitations and Directions for Future Research

Although this research begins to unpack the notion of overlapping instances of identity among diverse American youth, one limitation of this research is that the participants are all from a Northeastern geographic region. We know that the cultural climate of New England may vary from many other regional contexts (e.g., Midwestern, Southern). For example, a large percentage of the Black/African American population in New England comprises Afro-Caribbean individuals, such as Haitians, Dominicans, and Jamaicans. This background adds not only a racial and cultural component to the layers of complexity in assessing the effects of identity, but one must also take into account the influence of language. Therefore, we caution readers not to generalize the results of this work to all people of African descent in the United States. Rather, future research would benefit from replicating this work in different regions and among diverse racial and ethnic groups in the United States in order to determine if similar associations between ethnic identity and religious identity exist among diverse youth.

A second limitation is that results of this study are cross-sectional. Identity formation is marked by continuity over time in awareness of one's values, attitudes, and ideology concerning the self and society (Erikson, 1950). Therefore, while the results of this study are informative in elucidating the relations between two prominent aspects of identity and, in turn, in furthering our understanding of the associations between identity and positive youth outcomes, this study is not able to describe the process of development that occurs in diverse adolescents' identities. Directions for future research should include a developmental (longitudinal) examination of how ethnic identity and religious identity may co-develop across adolescence.

REFERENCES

Adams, G. R., Dyk, P. A. H., & Bennion, L. D. (1987). Parent–adolescent relationships and identity formation. *Family Perspective, 21*, 249–260.

Ashmore, R. D., Deaux, K., & McLaughlin-Volpe, T. (2004). An organizing framework for collective identity: Articulation and significance of multidimensionality. *Psychological Bulletin, 130*, 80–114.

Benson, P. L. (2006). *All kids are our kids: What communities must do to raise caring and responsible children and adolescents* (2nd ed.). San Francisco, CA: Jossey-Bass.

Benson, P. L., Donahue, M. J., & Erickson, J. A. (1989). Adolescence and religion: A review of the literature from 1970 to 1986. In M. L. Lynn & D. O. Moberg (Eds.), *Research in the social scientific study of religion* (Vol. 1, pp. 153–181). Greenwich, CT: JAI Press.

Berman, A. M., Schwartz, S. J., Kurtines, W. M., & Berman, S. L. (2001). The process of exploration in identity formation: The role of style and competence. *Journal of Adolescence, 24*, 513–528.

Brown, R. (2000). Social identity theory: Past achievements, current problems and future challenges. *European Journal of Social Psychology, 30*(6), 745–778.

Brown, B. B., & Larson, J. (2009). Peers relationships in adolescence. In R. M. Lerner & L. Steinberg (Eds.), *Handbook of adolescent psychology: Vol. 2, Contextual influences on adolescent development* (3rd ed., pp. 74–103). Hoboken, NJ: Wiley.

Côté, J. E. (2009). Identity formation and self-development in adolescence. In R. M. Lerner & L. Steinberg (Eds.), *Handbook of Adolescent Psychology*, (3rd ed., Vol. 1, pp. 266–304). Hoboken, NJ: Wiley.

Côté, J. E., & Levine, C. (1983). Marcia and Erikson: The relationships between ego identity status, neuroticism, dogmatism, and purpose of life. *Journal of Youth and Adolescence, 12*, 43–53.

Crenshaw, K., Gotanda, N., Peller, G., & Thomas, K. (1995). *Critical race theory: The key writings that formed the movement*. New York, NY: The Free Press.

Cunningham, M., Swanson, D. P., & Spencer, M. B. (2003). Black males' structural conditions, achievement patterns, normative needs and opportunities. *Urban Education, 38*, 608–603.

Eccles, J., Brown, B., & Templeton, J. (2008). A developmental framework for selecting indicators of well-being during the adolescent and young adult years. In B. V. Brown (Ed.), *Key indicators of child and youth well-being: Completing the picture*. Mahwah, NJ: Erlbaum.

Egan, S., & Perry, D. (2001). Gender identity: A multidimensional analysis with implications for psychosocial adjustment. *Developmental Psychology, 37*(4), 451–463.

Erikson, E. H. (1950). *Childhood and society*. New York, NY: Norton.

Featherstone, M. (2003). Localism, globalism and cultural identity. In L. M. Alcoff & E. Mendieta (Eds.), *Identities: Race, class, gender, and nationality* (pp. 342–359). Oxford, UK: Blackwell Publishing Ltd.

Fetzer Institute & National Institute on Aging Working Group. (2003). *Measurement of religiousness/spirituality for use in health research: A report of the Fetzer Institute/National Institute on Aging Working Group*. Kalamazoo, MI: Fetzer Institute.

Finzi, R., Ram, A., Har-Even, D., Shnit, D., & Weizman, A. (2001). Attachment styles and aggression in physically abused and neglected children. *Journal of Youth and Adolescence, 30*, 769–786.

Fuligini, A. (1998). The adjustment of children from immigrant families. *Current Directions in Psychological Science, 7*(4), 99–103.

Furrow, J. L., King, P. E., & White, K. (2004). Religion and positive youth development: Identity, meaning, and prosocial concerns. *Applied Development Science, 8*(1), 17–26.

Gans, H. (1992). Second generation decline: Scenarios for the economic and ethnic futures of the post-1965 American immigrants. *Ethnic and Racial Studies, 15*, 173–191.

Gibson, M. A. (2001). Immigrant adaptation and patterns of acculturation. *Human Development, 44*, 19–23.

Guitierrez, L. (1990). Working with women of color: An empowerment perspective. *Social Work, 35*, 149–153.

Gushue, G. V., Clarke, C. P., Pantzer, K. M., & Scanlan, K. R. (2006). Self-efficacy, perceptions or barriers, vocational identity and career exploration behavior of Latino/a high school students. *Career Development Quarterly, 54*(4), 307–317.

Hargrove, B. K., Creagh, M. G., & Burgess, B. L. (2002). Family interaction patterns as predictors of vocational identity and self-efficacy. *Journal of Vocational Behavior, 61*(2), 185–201.

Havighurst, R. (1953). *Human development and education.* New York: McKay.

Huntington, S. P. (2004). The Hispanic challenge. *Foreign Policy, 141,* 30–45.

Hurtado, A. (1997). Understanding multiple group identities: Inserting women into cultural transformation. *Journal of Social Issues, 52*(2), 299–328.

Juang, L., & Syed, M. (2008). Ethnic identity and spirituality. In R. Roeser, R. M. Lerner, & E. Phelps (Eds.), *Positive youth development and spirituality: From theory to research.* West Conshohocken, PA: John Templeton Press.

King, P. E. (2003). Religion and identity: The role of ideological, social, and spiritual contexts. *Applied Developmental Science, 7*(3), 197–204.

Kroger, J. K. (2003). Long-term memories, features, and novelty. *Behavior and Brain Sciences, 26*(6), 744–745.

Laursen, B., & Collins, W. A. (2009). Parent-child relationships during adolescence. In R. M. Lerner & L. Steinberg (Eds.), *Handbook of adolescent psychology: Vol. 2, Contextual influences on adolescent development* (3rd ed., pp. 3–42). Hoboken, NJ: Wiley.

Lee, J., & Bean, F. D. (2004). America's changing color lines: Immigration, race/ethnicity, and multiracial identification. *Annual Review of Sociology, 30,* 221–242.

Leffert, N., Benson, P. L., Scales, P. C., Sharma, A. R., Drake, D. R., &, Blyth, D. A. (1998). Developmental assets: Measurement and prediction of risk behaviors among adolescents. *Applied Developmental Science, 2*(4), 209–230.

Lerner, R. M. (2002). *Concepts and theories of human development* (3rd ed.). Mahwah, NJ: Erlbaum.

Luthar, S. S., & Latendresse, S. J. (2002). Adolescent risk: The cost of affluence. In R. M. Lerner, C. S. Taylor, & A. Von Eye (Eds.), *Pathways to positive development among diverse youth: New directions for youth development* (pp. 101–121). San Francisco, CA: Jossey-Bass.

Marcia, J. E. (1966). Development and validation of ego identity status. *Journal of Youth and Adolescence, 13,* 419–438.

Marcia, J. E. (1980). Identity in adolescence. In J. Andelson (Ed.), *Handbook of adolescent psychology.* New York, NY: Wiley.

Mattis, J. S., & Jagers, R. J. (2001). A relational framework for the study of religiosity and spirituality in the lives of African Americans. *Journal of Community Psychology, 29*(5), 519–539.

McCarthy, G., & Taylor, A. (1999). Avoidant/ambivalent attachment style as a mediator between abusive childhood experiences and adult relationship difficulties. *Journal of Child Psychology and Psychiatry, 40,* 465–478.

McWey, L. M. (2004). Predictors of attachment styles of children in foster care: An attachment theory model. *Journal of Marital and Family Therapy, 30*(4), 439–452.

Monitoring the Future. (2000). *National survey on drug use, 1975-2000*. Bethesda, MD: National Institute on Drug Abuse.

Mummendey, A., & Wenzel, M. (1999). Social discrimination and tolerance in intergroup relations: Reactions to intergroup difference. *Personality and Social Psychology Review*, 3(2), 158–174.

Orchard, V. (2002). Culture as opposed to what? *European Journal of Social Theory*, 5(4), 419–433.

Phinney, J. S. (1992). The Multi-Group Ethnic Identity Measure: A new scale for use with adolescents and young adults from diverse groups. *Journal of Adolescent Research*, 7, 156–176.

Phinney, J. S. (2003). Ethnic identity and acculturation. In K. M. Chun, P. B. Organista, & G. Marin (Eds.), *Acculturation: Advances in theory, measurement, and applied research* (pp. 63–81). Washington, DC: American Psychological Association.

Phinney, J. S., & Ong, A. D. (2007). Conceptualization and measurement of ethnic identity: Current status and future directions. *Journal of Counseling Psychology*, 54(3), 271–281.

Portes, A. (1995). *The economic sociology of immigration*. New York, NY: Russell Sage.

Quintana, S. M. (2007). Racial and ethnic identity: Developmental perspectives and research. *Journal of Counseling Psychology*, 54(3), 259–270.

Roberts, R., Phinney, J. S., Masse, L., Chen, Y., Roberts, C., & Romero, A. (1999). The structure of ethnic identity in young adolescents from diverse ethnocultural groups. *Journal of Early Adolescence*, 19, 301–322.

Robitschek, C., & Cook, C. (1990). The influence of personal growth initiative and coping styles on career exploration and vocational identity. *Journal of Vocational Behavior*, 54(1), 127–141.

Roeser, R. W. (2005). *Fulbright survey of identity, schooling, and spirituality in adolescence*. Unpublished manuscript.

Roeser, R. W., Galloway, M., Casey-Cannon, S., Watson, C., Keller, L., & Tan, E. (2008). Identity representations in patterns of school achievement and well-being among early adolescent girls. *Journal of Early Adolescence*, 28(1), 115–152.

Roeser, R. W., Isaac, S. I., Abo-Zena, M., Brittian, A. S., & Peck, S. C. (2008). Self and identity processes in spirituality and positive youth development. In R. M. Lerner, R. W. Roeser, & E. Phelps (Eds.), *Positive youth development and spirituality: From theory to research*. West Conshohocken, PA: John Templeton Press.

Romero, A., & Roberts, R. (1998). Perception of discrimination and ethnocultural variables in a diverse group of adolescents. *Journal of Adolescence*, 21, 641–656.

Romero, A., & Roberts, R. (2003). The impact of multiple dimensions of ethnic identity on discrimination and adolescents' self-esteem. *Journal of Applied Social Psychology*, 33, 2288–2305.

Schlesinger, P. (1991). *Media, state and nation: Political violence and collective identities*. London, England: Sage.

Schwartz, S. J. (2001). The evolution of Eriksonian and neo-Eriksonian identity theory and research: A review and integration. *Identity: An International Journal of Theory and Research, 1*(1), 7–58.

Schwartz, S. J., Zamboanga, B. L., & Weisskirch, R. S. (2008). Broadening the study of the self: Integrating the study of personal identity and cultural identity. *Social and Personality Psychology Compass, 2*(2), 635–651.

Smith, C., & Denton, M. L. (2005). *Soul searching: The religious and spiritual lives of American teenagers.* New York, NY: Oxford University Press.

Smith, C., & Lundquist-Denton, M. (2002). Mapping American adolescent religious participation. *Journal for the Scientific Study of Religion, 41*, 597–612.

Smith, E. P., Walker, K., Fields, L., Brookins, C. G., & Seay, R. C. (1999). Ethnic identity and its relationship to self-esteem, perceived efficacy and prosocial attitudes in early adolescence. *Journal of Adolescence, 22*(6), 867–880.

Spencer, M. B. (1999). Social and cultural influences on school adjustment: The application of an identity-focused cultural ecological perspective. *Educational Psychologist, 34*(1), 43–57.

Spencer, M. B. (2001). Identity, achievement orientation and race: "Lessons learned" about the normative developmental experiences of African American males. In W. Watkins, et al. (Eds.), *Race and education* (pp. 100–127). Needham Heights, MA: Allyn & Bacon.

Spencer, M. B. (2006). Phenomenology and ecological systems theory: Development of diverse groups. In W. Damon & R. Lerner (Eds.), *Handbook of child psychology* (6th ed.). Hoboken, NJ: Wiley.

Spencer, M. B. (2008). Phenomenology and ecological systems theory: Development of diverse groups. In W. Damon & R. Lerner (Eds.), *Child and adolescent development: An advanced course* (pp. 696–740). Hoboken, NJ: Wiley.

Spencer, M. B., Fegley, S., & Dupree, D. (2006). Investigating and linking social conditions of African-American children and adolescents with emotional well-being. *Ethnicity & Disease, 16*(2), 63–67.

Spencer, M. B., Fegley, S., Harpalani, V., & Seaton, G. (2004). Understanding hyper-masculinity in context: A theory-driven analysis of urban adolescent males' coping responses. *Research in Human Development, 1*(4), 229–257.

Spencer, M. B., & Markstrom-Adams, C. (1990). Identity processes among racial and ethnic minority children in America. *Child Development, 61*(2), 290–310.

Steinberg, L. (2001). We know some things: Parent-adolescent relationships in retrospect and prospect. *Journal of Research on Adolescence, 11*(1), 1–19.

Taylor, R. J., Chatters, L. M., & Levin, J. (2004). *Religion in the lives of African Americans: Social, psychological, and health perspectives.* Thousand Oaks, CA: Sage.

Wallace, J. M., Forman, T. A., Caldwell, C. H., & Willis, D. S. (2003). Religion and U.S. secondary school students: Current patterns, recent trends, and sociodemographic correlates. *Youth & Society, 35*(1), 98–125.

Worrell, F. C., Conyers, L. M., Mpofu, E., & Vandiver, B. J. (2006). Multigroup ethnic identity measure scores in a sample of adolescents of Zimbabwe. *Identity: An International Journal of Theory and Research, 6*(1), 35–59.

Youniss, J., McLellan, J. A., & Yates, M. (1999). Religion, community service, and identity in American youth. *Journal of Adolescence, 22*, 243–253.

Youngblood, J., & Spencer, M. B. (2002). Integrating normative identity processes and academic support requirements for special needs adolescents: The application of an identity-focused cultural ecological (ICE) perspective. *Journal of Applied Developmental Science, 6*(2), 95–108.

Zhou, M. (1997). Growing up American: The challenge confronting immigrant children and the children of immigrants. *Annual Review of Sociology, 23*, 63–95.

Zimmerman, M. A. (1995). Psychological empowerment: Issues and illustrations. *American Journal of Community Psychology, 23*, 581–599.

Zucker, K. J. (2002). Intersexuality and gender differentiation. *Journal of Pediatric and Adolescent Gynecology, 15*, 3–13.

Social and Cultural Contexts of Positive Youth Development and Spirituality

CHAPTER

11

━━━➤⊶⊰━━━

Contributions Despite Challenges

Exploring Positive Youth Development
Among Muslim American Youth

Selcuk R. Sirin, Mona M. Abo-Zena, and Hala Shehadeh

Young people's positive development and their contributions to the social and
cultural milieu has seen more attention recently, both in terms of research and
theory (Jensen & Flanagan, 2008; Lerner, 2008, 2009). Positive youth outcomes
refer to both personal assets as well as taking an active role in the social and
cultural life of one's own community (Damon, 2004; Larson, 2000; Lerner, 2007;
Search Institute, 2004). In this study we will examine how young Muslims in the
United States develop positive outcomes despite significant challenges resulting
from their religious background in the post-9/11 United States. Before we provide
specific findings, a brief demographic introduction of this unique population is
presented next.

The history of Muslims in the United States is also a history of immigration that
took place in two waves, one that spread from the late 19th century to the early
20th century and one that began around the mid-1960s and continued through
the 1990s. We must also add to these waves of immigrants those people, mostly
African American, along with some European-American and most recently Latin
American Muslims, who have converted to Islam. At this point we do not have
a very good estimate of how many Muslims live in the United States, partly
because the U.S. Census Bureau, by law, does not gather any information about
religious affiliation, and unlike churches, mosques do not have membership rolls

that can be used as a proxy. Different estimates based on nationwide surveys put the number of Muslims in the United States anywhere between 2 and 8 million. However, we have better estimates about the growth rate of this population using data gathered from surveys conducted at multiple time points. For example, the American Religious Identification Survey (ARIS), conducted twice in 1990 and 2001, shows an increase of more than 108% during this decade (Kosmin, Mayer, & Keysar, 2001). An evaluation of Census ancestry data for those with birthplaces in Islamic countries also confirms the same trend during the same period.

The Muslim population in the United States reflects a very diverse group (Zogby, 2004). South Asians, those who come from Pakistan, Bangladesh, and India, represent about 30% of the population. African American Muslims represent the largest indigenous Muslim group in the United States, representing around 25% of the Muslim American population. The third major group is Arab Americans, who represent an additional 25% of the U.S. Muslim population. Despite some misconceptions, the majority of Arab Americans are Christian; in addition to these three major groups, there is also a very large Iranian population and much smaller immigrant groups from Malaysia, Indonesia, Turkey, Afghanistan, sub-Saharan Africa, and central and eastern Europe, as well as Caucasian and Latin American converts.

Given this diversity, it is important to note that, particularly since the 9/11 attacks, a growing number of Americans have chosen to use the label of Muslim American both at the national and local levels (Leonard, 2003). At this point, it became imperative for Muslim Americans to voice their concerns and gain representation at the American table. This movement was marked by articulating aggregate Muslim foundations and sources of power at the social, economic, and political levels (Gallup, 2009). As a result, multiple organizations and groups were formulated, such as the Muslim student organizations on most college campuses, instead of ethnic (e.g., Arab Student Clubs) or home country–based organizations (e.g., Pakistani Student Organizations).

POSITIVE YOUTH DEVELOPMENT AMONG IMMIGRANT YOUTH

Studies examining immigrants' community contributions suggest that immigrant-origin youth in the United States tend to be more heavily involved in religious activities than their native-born peers and, thus, more heavily involved in their respective communities (Stepick & Stepick, 2002; see also Haitians in Miami, Stepick, 1998; Vietnamese in New Orleans, Zhou & Bankston, 1998; and Korean Presbyterians nationwide, Hurh & Kim, 1990 and Kim & Kim, 2001). The link between religious commitment and positive youth development (PYD) has also received some attention in the literature. Several studies have shown that deeper religious commitment brings about higher levels of involvement of religious youth in the social and cultural affairs of their community compared to their nonreligious peers (Crystal & DeBell, 2002; Youniss, McLellan, & Yates, 1999; Youniss & Yates, 1997, 1999). The researchers attributed religious saliency and religious commitment as affecting community engagement for the following reasons: (a) being a part of a social network fosters a sense of caring for the community; (b) religious spaces are venues for public issues to be discussed; and (c) religion often fosters values that are consistent with being a "good citizen" and being socially responsible (Crystal & DeBell, 2002, p. 117).

Furrow, King, and White (2004) created a model for understanding the dynamics of this relationship after surveying 801 adolescents. Those with a religious identity tended to have a personal meaning system in place that gave the adolescents a sense of direction and fulfilment in life. Having this meaning system in place, religious youth are associated with positive developmental resources such as higher levels of personal restraint, parental and adult support, positive values, prosocial behavior, school bonding, civic engagement, and social competence (King & Furrow, 2004; Miller & Thoresen, 2003; Wagener, Furrow, King, Leffert, & Benson, 2003). Another study implicated that spirituality and religion were associated with thriving, which implies the absence of problem behaviors and the presence of healthy behaviors (Dowling et al., 2004).

In this chapter we examined positive youth outcomes among Muslim American youth using two complementary methods in two independent studies. In Study 1, using survey methodology, we examined the degree to which religiosity, perceived discrimination, and collective Muslim and American identities influence Muslim youths' positive outcomes. In Study 2, we examined similar issues using qualitative research methodology. The first study, conducted in the New York metropolitan area, was sampled as part of a larger project on Muslim American youth (Selcuk R. Sirin, PI). The second study, conducted in the Boston metropolitan area, was a part of the John Templeton Foundation (JTF)–supported study of the role of spiritual development in growth of purpose, generosity, and psychological health in adolescence (Richard M. Lerner, PI).

STUDY 1

One of the most disturbing findings from our studies with Muslim youth over the past five years was the degree to which discriminatory acts have been woven intimately into the lives of Muslim American youth (Sirin & Fine, 2007, 2008). Further, converging lines of evidence also implicate that post-9/11 Muslim American youth have been enduring different levels of "minority stress" in the form of prejudice and discrimination. Multiple recent studies and surveys with Muslim American youth, ages varying from 12 to 25, indicated that discriminatory experiences were reported in different settings, such as school, college campus, on the street, on the playground, and even while shopping (Sirin et al., 2008; Sirin & Fine, 2007). The majority of participants in these studies reported that they experienced this discrimination only *because they are Muslims*.

In the current study we explored the factors that influence positive youth outcomes among Muslim American youth. Specifically, this study examined the roles of discrimination, religiosity, identification with Muslim communities, and identification with American society in the positive youth outcomes of immigrant Muslim youth in the United States. We also explored whether the experiences of Muslim young men and women differ.

Method

Data were gathered from 134 college students, all of whom self-identified as Muslim American. The participants ranged in age from 18 to 28 years ($M = 21.78$, $SD = 2.38$). The sample was 56% female and 44% male. Participants were either first generation (53%; i.e., born abroad) or second generation (47%; i.e., born in the United States to Muslim immigrant parents). In terms of parental education, 63% of fathers and 38% of mothers had college or advanced degrees. In terms of ethnicity, 35% of the participants were of Pakistani origins, 27% came from Arab backgrounds (Egypt, Palestine, Jordan, Lebanon, Saudi Arabia, Syria, Kuwait, and Yemen), and the remaining participants came from a diverse group of countries from which Muslims originate, including Iran, Turkey, West Indian nations (Trinidad and Guyana), Venezuela, Guatemala, and Puerto Rico. These demographic characteristics reflect the general population parameters for Muslim immigrants in the United States. An analysis of variance revealed no statistically significant ethnic group differences for the key study variables after correction for Type I error.

Measures

We used a demographic questionnaire to gather all of the relevant background information, including age, gender, racial and ethnic background, generational status in the United States (first- vs. second-generation immigrant status), and parental education.

Positive Youth Outcomes

We measured positive youth outcomes using the internal assets subscales of the *Developmental Assets Profile* (DAP; Search Institute, 2004). Specifically, we focused on two indicators of positive youth development: *Positive Values* and *Positive Identity*. Positive Values refers to young people's guiding principles that help them make healthy life choices. Positive Identity, on the other hand, refers to young people's belief in their own self-worth and feelings of control over the things that happen to them. A total of 17 items were designed to measure positive youth outcomes, using a four-point Likert scale ranging from *not at all or rarely* to *extremely or almost always*. In order to confirm these two components, we employed principal component analysis of 17 DAP items using a Varimax rotation with

Kaiser normalization. Two distinct components did emerge from the analysis of DAP items, accounting for 52% of the variance across all 17 items. The first component, Positive Values, accounted for 38% of the variance, while the second component, Positive Identity, accounted for an additional 14% of the variance.

The Positive Values scale assesses the values of caring (placing high value on helping other people), equality and social justice, integrity, honesty, responsibility, and restraint from using drugs and alcohol. Sample survey items include "I stand up for what I believe in," "I am trying to help solve social problems," "I tell the truth even when it is not easy," and "I am helping to make my community a better place." Cronbach's alpha for the 11-item scale for the current sample was .82.

The Positive Identity scale has six items that capture the positive feelings of young people in terms of personal power, self-esteem, sense of purpose, and positive view of the future. Sample survey items include, "I am developing a sense of purpose in my life," "I feel in control of my life and future," and "I feel good about myself." Cronbach's alpha for the six-item scale for the current sample was .87.

Religiosity

Because of a lack of standard measures designed for this population, we developed a six-item index that measures religious engagement in terms of the degree of participation in religious activities, such as praying, fasting, attending mosque, and the degree to which one relies on religion in daily life (e.g., "I put my trust in Allah," "I seek Allah's help," and "I try to find comfort in Islam"). Because the response sets for the questions ranged from a dichotomy (e.g., whether or not one fasts) to a four-point Likert scale for the last three items, we first standardized all of the items before calculating the composite score. Higher scores indicated a greater degree of religiosity. Cronbach's alpha for the items was .84.

Muslim Collective Identity and American Collective Identity

We measured the two variables independently using two "race-specific" versions of the *Collective Self-Esteem* measure (CSE; Luhtanen & Crocker, 1992). This scale is designed to assess perception of one's group membership. In this study, both the domains of Muslim and American identity were measured in terms of three CSE components: (a) *group membership*, which measures one's judgment of self-worth as a member of one's cultural group; (b) *private regard*, which measures one's personal evaluation of one's cultural group; and (c) *identity importance*, which captures how the significance of one's social group membership(s) influences one's own self-concept. An example item from the *Muslim version* for the first component is: "I am a worthy member of the Muslim community." An illustrative item from the second component for the *American version* is: "In general, I am glad to be a member of American society." Examples of the third component for both versions are: "Overall, my Muslim identity has very little to do with how I feel about myself," and "In general, belonging to American society is an important part of my self-image." The seven-point scale ranges from 1 (*strongly disagree*) to 7 (*strongly agree*). For the present sample, Cronbach's alpha for the full, 12-item Muslim identity was .87 and for the full, 12-item American collective identity was .90.

Discrimination

Muslim American discrimination-related stress was measured by a modified version of the *Societal, Attitudinal, Familial, and Environmental—Revised—Short Form* (SAFE-Short; Mena, Padilla, & Maldonado, 1987). The full SAFE form is designed to assess negative stressors experienced by minority immigrants. In this study we used a modified version based on Amer and Hovey's (2005) study with Arab Americans, which provided evidence for construct validity and better than acceptable reliability for the items. The 13-item version tapped experiences of and stress related to discrimination from the mainstream society (e.g., "It bothers me when the media portrays a negative image of Muslims or Muslim Americans," "I am upset that most people consider the Muslim American community to be more dangerous than other groups," or "I feel uncomfortable when others make jokes about or put down Muslims"). A four-point Likert scale ranged from 0 (*not at all stressful*) to 4 (*very stressful*). For the current sample, Cronbach's alpha was .83.

Procedure

Participants for the study were recruited using the snowballing method with attention to gender, country of origin, and generation level. The participants were recruited through fliers posted in coffee shops, campus buildings, community centers, and mosques throughout the New York/New Jersey metropolitan area. Surveys were administered individually during 2006–2007. All participants were compensated for their time with a $20 gift certificate.

Results

Descriptive statistics and intercorrelations among study variables are presented in Table 11.1. There was a significant correlation between religiosity and Muslim collective identity ($r = .64$ and $p < .005$) and between religiosity and positive values (PV) ($r = .36$, $p < .001$). In order to address the main research question—Do religiosity, discrimination, identification with the Muslim community, and identification with the mainstream U.S. society influence positive youth outcomes?—we ran two separate regression models. The results for the Positive Values and Positive Identity models are presented in Table 11.2.

Table 11.1 Means, Standard Deviations, and Correlations (N = 136)

	M	SD	1	2	3	4	5
Positive Values	2.20	.49					
Positive Identity	1.99	.62	.54**				
Religiosity	−.01	.74	.36**	.11			
Discrimination	1.23	.53	.15	−.15	.29**		
American CSE	5.03	1.14	.16	.12	−.10	−.24**	
Muslim CSE	5.76	.96	.42**	.24**	.64**	.28**	.16

Notes: CSE = Collective Self Esteem
*$p < .05$. **$p < .01$. ***$p < .001$.

Overall, the results showed that, for Positive Values, religiosity and Muslim identification were significant predictors. Higher degrees of religious practice contributed to more positive values, and deeper identification with the Muslim communities also influenced young people's positive values in this study. On the other hand, for the Positive Identity model, while Muslim identification again contributed significantly, the degree to which young people experience acculturative stress seems to negatively affect their positive identities. In other words, while religiosity seems to play a role in values, it did not seem to affect how young people feel about their identities. At the same time, the degree to which young immigrants in this study identify with the mainstream U.S. society—an indicator of their integration—did not seem to play a significant role in forming their positive values or identities.

There was no statistically significant difference in positive youth outcomes between Muslim women and men. There was, however, a significant difference

Table 11.2 Multiple Regression Models Predicting Positive Values and Positive Identity

	Positive Values			Positive Identity		
Variable	B	SE B	β	B	SE B	β
Religiosity	.14	.70	.21*	−.02	.09	−.03
Acculturative Stress	.06	.08	.07	−.26	.11	−.22*
American Identification	.69	.36	.16	.01	.05	.02
Muslim Identification	.35	.64	.22*	.20	.07	.31**
R^2	.20			.11		
F	8.21***			3.89**		

*$p < .05$. **$p < .01$. ***$p < .001$.

between Muslim men and women on Muslim identification ($t = 2.92$, $p < .005$) and on acculturative stress ($t = 2.53$, $p < .05$). Women reported deeper identification with the Muslim community ($M = 5.52$, $SD = 1.08$) than did men ($M = 5.52$, $SD = .82$), and they also reported more acculturative stress ($M = 1.34$, $SD = .54$) than did their male counterparts ($M = 1.08$, $SD = .48$). There was no statistically significant difference in their identification with the mainstream U.S. society or religiosity.

Discussion

The field of positive youth development has witnessed an increased interest of scholars and practitioners, where multiple developmental factors have been examined (Furrow, King, & White, 2004). Recently, religiosity and spirituality have been associated with the promotion of personal meaning and positive attitudes among youth (Dowling et al., 2004; Lerner, 2008). In our study with Muslim youth in the New York/New Jersey metropolitan area, we sought to shed light on the relationship between religiosity and youth positive values and identity. We also explored the roles of acculturative stress and youth identifications with their own community and the mainstream U.S. society. An important finding in this study is the unique relationship between religiosity and positive values. Muslim American youth who are more religious and who are more strongly identified with the Muslim society tend to develop stronger positive values. Acculturative stress, however, seems to diminish young people's positive feelings about themselves and their community. In their study with Roman Catholic and Protestant youth, Hart and Fegley (1995) observed a similar trend, noting the positive role of religiosity and spirituality in the lives of youth who were recognized for their civic engagement and contributions to others in their community. Hence, religiosity and engagement in one's own local ethnic or religious community seem to be significant indicators for promoting positive values.

STUDY 2

This study also focused on religiosity, perceived discrimination, and positive youth development, but used qualitative research methodology. Data came from the John Templeton Foundation–supported study of *The Role of Spiritual Development in Growth of Purpose, Generosity, and Psychological Health in Adolescence* (Richard M. Lerner, PI). The current inquiry is part of a larger study of the role of religion in the lives of youth during the second decade of life. This study used mixed methods to explore how the religious beliefs and participation of youth relate to contribution and positive youth development. Comprehensive explanations of the purpose and the methodology of the study have been presented previously (see Lerner, Roeser, & Phelps, 2008). This report will summarize only the features of the methodology relevant to the current study.

Method

Participants in this study were recruited because they attended a religious school or youth group. Although the full study included participants with a range of religious affiliations, the present analysis focuses on participants who self-identified as Muslim. Participants completed a written survey and participated in focus groups. The focus groups ranged from 3 to 15 participants in each group; a total of 11 focus groups were conducted, and the groups were drawn from 6 research sites. The size and the gender composition of the focus groups depended on the nature of the site (e.g., depending on the number of participants, some sites preferred sex-segregated focus groups, and other sites preferred grouping participants by age).

This analysis was part of a cross-sectional study of 74 youth and young adults who self-identified as Muslim (49% female). Participants were recruited from private religious schools and religious youth groups in the greater Boston area. In the present study, 45.9% of the participants were in middle school, 36.5% in high school, and 17.6% in college or of traditional college age. The sample was racially diverse. The sample was 29.2% Arab American, 26.2% other, 16.9% black or African American, 15.4% multiethnic, 10.7% Asian American or South Asian, and 1.5% not sure.

Borrowing from the established field of marketing research (see Greenbaum, 1993), these group interviews sought to provide a more efficient way rather than individual interviews of collecting in-depth, qualitative data (Morgan, 1997). Focus group interviews were selected as the method in order to try to demonstrate the range of perspectives participants may have had. Given that psychology of religion literature has been dominated by a largely Protestant Christian orientation (see Hill & Pargament, 2003), a goal of this study was to gather data on previously underrepresented youth perspectives. Although focus groups do not provide the detailed responses of individual interviews, they give voice to youth and provide important insights, different from the ones afforded by quantitative data. Because focus groups are inherently social (Stewart, Shamdasani, & Rook, 2007), they lend themselves to the study of religion, which usually involves a collective experience. Focus groups may help to shed light on quantitative data already collected (Krueger & Casey, 2000), and they may be particularly useful in identifying core themes, especially in understudied topics, when there is sufficient heterogeneity of participants to achieve conceptual saturation of the topic (Morgan, 1997).

Analysis

Although survey data were collected for this study, this analysis employed only focus group data. While approaches to analyze focus groups may include various considerations, such as the amount of time spent on an issue or the intensity of expression of various individuals or the group as a whole (Stewart et al.,

2007), this analysis will be a thematic focus on the central constructs outlined in the research questions: youth perspectives on positive youth development, a description of youth volunteering or civic engagement, motivation or reason for engaging, and challenges to their religious affiliation that may affect how and whether youth choose to volunteer or be civically engaged.

Focus group responses to particular questions in the focus group protocol were listed, noting the demographic descriptors related to the participant (e.g., research site marking the urban or suburban location and proxy for socioeconomic status, sex of participant, and in some cases the ethnicity of the participant). These social address variables marked the "positionality" of the participant, suggesting that one's social position may affect how one engages and is perceived to engage with others (Hurtado, 1997). The participant data were then open-coded based on emergent descriptive themes from the data (Corbin & Strauss, 2008), and there was an attempt to explore thematic similarity and variation within and across groups.

Results

Qualitative findings revealed themes in youth perspectives about what constitutes positive youth development, volunteering or civic engagement, reasons for volunteering, and challenges or reasons that may guide or limit such engagement.

We found several themes associated with the perspective of youth about positive development. These themes concerned skills and achievement, purpose, and personal qualities.

Skills and Achievement

Across all focus groups, youth reported that positive development required a set of skills and school-related achievement, but they varied in the particular characteristics they noted and the degree to which they were highlighted. Youth reported needing to be educated, responsible, a good leader, and organized. One female student from an Islamic high school discussed the importance of balance and the need to "get good grades without killing yourself." Male middle school students from the same Islamic high school discussed doing well academically but avoiding overachieving, "[b]ecause then they'd be like a geek, and they wouldn't be fun to be with." Another peer added that, "[h]e'd be too serious. He won't be fun at all. He'd just look at everything as a fact and say, 'That's not right.' Say if you're kidding around, he wouldn't laugh at it."

Sense of Purpose

A male participant from a Somalian after-school program reported that a positively developing person "knows what he's doing. He knows his goals in his life." Similarly, other participants noted the importance of being determined and not

giving up. One high school religious youth group attendee indicated the importance of being able to solve problems and keep things in perspective when things
do not go smoothly.

Admirable Personal Qualities

Across all focus groups, participants provided personal qualities that they felt
were admirable, positive, and worthy of emulation. Themes of being respectful to
adults, particularly parents and teachers, were common across age groups, gender,
ethnicities, and sites. In addition, participants highlighted characteristics such as
being truthful, trustworthy, loyal, kind, helpful, well behaved and mannered, religious, social, outgoing, and confident. A female middle school student discussed
the need to be confident enough to "lead your own self instead of following
somebody else." In a discussion about how to advocate for one's own opinion,
the female middle school student discussed "being able to interact" without being
bossy and disagreeing in a manner that does not seem anti-social. Rather, the girls
discussed "being able to state your opinion and . . . being sure of your opinion,"
while also balancing the need to, "think about accepting other people's opinions
even though you don't agree with them."

Male high school Muslim students in a religious youth group noted that what
may be considered to be an admirable quality is based on the perspective of the
social group. As one of the participants noted, "I think it's like if you're talking
about school or society or if you're talking about, like, the Muslim community, like
there's two different things. . . ." While the participants discussed whether what
is considered popular in broader U.S. society may be considered inappropriate in
Islamic settings, one participant summarized the relative standards of determining
what qualities are admirable:

> I think the biggest characteristics of someone that is, what's the word,
> you can admire him or her, I think like, well, your intentions can be
> different. I mean, if you admire him for being religious or being very,
> like, nice, if you admire him for his, like status in the community. But I
> think like—I think for different people it's what they admire him for so
> that they like, mostly a successful person is someone that you would like
> to be like and you admire very much, or the person he is.

Description of Volunteering

We found several themes related to volunteering behavior that seemed to range
from proximal to distal. The range from proximal to distal volunteering included
helping family, friends, and neighbors to helping the Muslim community and the
broader U.S. society.

Helping Family

Across all focus groups and research sites, the most common type of volunteering involved helping at home or with the family. Several participants indicated that they do not volunteer regularly. One female high school student at an Islamic school did not respond initially to the question about volunteering until being prompted by the interviewer, who had observed the student helping with activities in the community (e.g., volunteering with a children's program, preparing mailings). The participant discussed her difficulty in assessing her own volunteering:

> . . . I don't know. There's kind of an idea of what it means to volunteer, like helping at a shelter or things like that that are typical of what volunteering means. And I feel like I don't do that, or I don't do that with that kind of intention. It's usually just [to] help friends or to make things run smoothly . . .

When prompted to discuss their helping behavior at home, including help with translation, no participants indicated that they did not volunteer. Males and females reported helping with housework and dishes, but only males discussed doing yardwork; these helping activities were generally considered to be helping parents. Males and females discussed helping with babysitting and providing homework assistance for younger siblings. Outside of the context of home, but still a form of family support, one female middle school student discussed helping her mother "in the lab by doing stuff the undergrads won't do." Several male students in the Islamic high school discussed helping their parents in a family bakery or family business. Participants discussed whether this type of activity is truly volunteer if there is some pay, or if it is somehow forced or there is limited option not to participate (e.g., expected by parents).

Helping Friends and Neighbors

Many participants reported helping friends and neighbors with tasks similar to the help they provide at home. Helping friends and neighbors included babysitting for neighborhood children and doing yardwork for neighbors. Helping nonrelated but familiar others seemed particularly the case for participants who do not have younger siblings.

Helping the Muslim Community and the Broader Community

The most common type of volunteering beyond friends and family was helping at the mosque or at other events organized by the Muslim community. Service to the Muslim community included cleaning the mosque, providing humanitarian relief (e.g., sorting food at a food bank), volunteering at events including babysitting, and teaching Arabic or serving as a teacher assistant for elementary-age children. A male high school student noted that participating in the focus group is a type of volunteering, and another participant in the group described fielding questions on a public bus about Islam. Beyond the Muslim community, participants from a nonimmigrant, mostly African American mosque discussed participating in student council, going on the radio and performing, and selling goods at the store down the street in order to stay off the streets. College students discussed tutoring and working in student groups, particularly Muslim student organizations. One participant in the Somalian after-school program indicated that she does not do anything consistently, "But I take the opportunity when it arises, like I ushered at a graduation recently."

Reasons for Volunteering

Participants reported various reasons for their volunteering behavior. We found that different motivations for volunteering were grouped into four categories. These categories included that volunteering in part served the needs or goals of the participant, provided needed services, contributed to a greater good of self or beyond, or fulfilled a religious obligation (greatest good).

Helping Others Also Helps Myself

Several participants indicated that they completed volunteer activities in part to promote their own development. These participant goals included building their resume, strengthening their college or scholarship applications, developing their own skill set, and completing community service requirements at school. Generally, participants who indicated such reasons for volunteering were critiqued by their peers for having self-serving objectives in their service of others. Furthermore, in several focus groups, participants engaged in lengthy discussions about whether required service (e.g., service required by parents or school, but notably not by religion) would qualify as volunteering. Although some participants indicated that that is forced and you have to comply, others, such as a male participant in a Somalian after-school setting, stated that "Your family brings you up like that."

In other discussions about what constitutes volunteering, participants questioned whether service that benefits the service provider should count as volunteering. For example, in a discussion in the Somalian after-school group, the participants discussed the example of cleaning the house. Both male and female participants indicated that they would want their house to be clean. In addition to wanting a clean space, one female participant added that, "You want to do it because you want to make your parents happy." Another female participant illustrated how the context determines whether an action is volunteering:

The difference between doing it in your house is because you're doing it for yourself. So you're not volunteering yourself, your time. You know? If you clean up somebody else's house, like an elderly person, that would be volunteering. But when you're doing it for your own benefit, then it's not volunteering.

Participants expanded the example to include cleaning the yard, which may help provide a clean view for others. One male participant maintained that in cleaning the lawn, "You still do it for yourself. But you do it for others, too. . . ." Unconvinced, a female participant challenged the self-service implicit in the behavior by questioning, "By cleaning up your yard? You get the *your* part?"

Provide Needed Services

Whether they provided services to a particular person (e.g., parent) or an organization, participants discussed how volunteering helped provide needed services. One male Somalian after-school participant said that he volunteered in order "to make it easier for someone." Another male Somalian participant said that, "If I just see something wrong, I just like to fix it. If the kids are like misbehaving and I know them and the teachers need help, I help the students, make them listen. Help them out." One female Islamic school student indicated that most of her volunteer work is facilitated by friends:

. . . A lot of times I end up volunteering for an event or something because a friend asked me to or I can see that they need help, like they're really drowning. So a lot of times it's to help out friends and things like that.

In several instances, participants indicated that they were bored and then found themselves in situations where work needed to be done, so they, often through parental influence, started to volunteer. In helping her younger sibling, one middle school female participant provided an example that was relatively common:

It might be first kind of hard, but when you kind of get used to it you kind of start liking it and helping other people. Until now, I don't really like helping my brother out, but still I have to.

Contribute to a Greater Good (of Self and Beyond)

Participants frequently discussed how volunteering positively contributes to their own sense of self, to the well-being of others, or to a broader level of well-being. Participants across focus groups discussed how volunteering made them feel good, either immediately or over time. One male middle school student summarized,

"It's just the right thing to do." Another participant in the same group continued, ". . . sometimes you just want to do something that's going to make people happy, and at the same time, you're going to feel happy about yourself . . . like you've accomplished something." A female middle school student discussed her desire "to reach out because we think about giving someone something. You always have to think about fulfilling their needs—not like every need, but fulfilling whatever you can give." In reflecting on her service in daycare, babysitting, mentoring, and tutoring, one participant in the Somalian after-school program indicated that, "My motive for that is not only to put it on my college resume, but just to make a difference. To help somebody. So you can say you helped someone or you made a difference. You were a change in somebody's life."

Religious Obligation

Some participants indicated that they volunteer because of their religious commitment. When specifically prompted as to whether volunteering is a part of Islam, almost all respondents indicated that it was and either detailed the various forms of volunteering (e.g., time, money generally, and through the specific alms) or provided accounts from Islamic history of well-known examples of volunteering or contribution. A few participants indicated that they were not sure whether volunteering is a part of Islam. Several participants discussed that they are motivated to receive religious rewards or blessings for their service; one male middle school student at an Islamic school reflected on the rewards for good deeds, "and, in turn, you could go to heaven for that. Even though you think it's small, it counts a lot in your book of good deeds."

Across focus groups, participants discussed the necessity of being obedient and respectful to one's parents. One Muslim middle school student discussed the connection between parental obedience and volunteering: ". . . Helping your parents is essential for being a good Muslim—to help your parents to be nice to them and do whatever they want." Reflecting on Islamic beliefs, one female high school student discussed recycling and taking care of the earth as a form of volunteering because, ". . . I've always felt that that's something that you have to do because, I mean, there are prophets who explicitly said, 'Don't waste,' and things like that. . . . " One middle school female discussed the religious obligation to project a positive image and that when you volunteer, "people see you as a better person, and Islam as a better religion."

Challenges

Participants discussed the challenges associated with the sociocultural context that provides the context for their development, their volunteering, and how it is received. Participants also highlighted issues of post-9/11 backlash, negative images of Muslims, and local and global issues as challenges to their positive development.

Post-9/11 Backlash

Across all focus groups, participants discussed the overt and covert challenges they have faced given the post-9/11 environment. One male high school participant framed the issue:

> . . . after 9/11 happened we experienced the taking away of our pride, basically because we were blamed for something that allegedly even if a Muslim did it and he's not just claiming he did it, even if he did it, just one person, maybe one extremist if you want to say, it doesn't reflect a whole community. Like if you look at an extremist and what community he belongs to, you're not supposed to relate that person to the community itself. You can't take one person and take the whole community based on that person. . . .

Many participants provided personal accounts or related anecdotes, such as the middle school male who shared the example of "my friend's dad, he went to BJs. He had to pray. They called the SWAT team." Males and females discussed how they felt they were being looked at like terrorists. One male high school student discussed his fear of being deported after the attacks.

Negative Social Portrayals

Participants provided numerous examples of how they experienced negative social portrayals related to their religious affiliation. In reflecting on his previous experience in public school, one middle school student discussed his teachers not liking him because he is Muslim. Other middle school students discussed peers (e.g., on a soccer team and in other contexts) not liking them because they are Muslim. A female middle school student discussed being told to go back to her country; many of the girls noted that if they wore the head covering they were more identifiable as Muslim. Some participants noted the negative portrayals of Islam by the U.S. media. Further, one middle school Muslim student indicated that the U.S. media does not give credit to the contributions of Muslims, but that Arabic media does note the service.

Local and Global Issues

Although less prevalent than the other themes, many participants referenced local and global issues about being Muslim that were challenging. A female high school student recalled being in middle school and the only one who wore hijab. Another female high school student discussed the difficult transition from attendance at an Islamic school to taking classes at a community college and interacting with a broader range of people. Another female Muslim discussed the challenge of being a spokesperson for Islam with her new neighbors. In reflecting on her role as a spokesperson, she responded, "Well, things like hajj and Ramadan stuff it's easy, but if they ask things that are more personal and stuff, it's harder. Things that are straightforward, it's just straightforward." Several participants reflected on historical or global challenges, including the split between Sunni and Shi'ite. In addition, a high school male discussed the difficulty of "seeing Muslims killed around the world" and specifically mentioned Chechnya and Bosnia, Iraq, Afghanistan, and Palestine.

Discussion

There was significant discussion about what counts as volunteering, particularly around the themes of forced/encouraged volunteering and the beneficiaries of such volunteering. The preponderance of youth contribution reports had to do with serving within their respective communities (serving their Muslim community and family); there were fewer examples of serving the broader society, particularly in the more formal sense of civic engagement and politics. Immigrant-origin youth may have less access to parental and adult models who are civically involved, in part because of the stress of the acculturation process and also in part because of many cultural and linguistic barriers. An additional limitation to civic engagement of Muslim youth in particular may be the negative social environment, particularly post-9/11. Obstacles to civic involvement or particular types of volunteering may be related to the acculturation process or to negative aspects of the social environment. Irrespective of what may limit volunteering, contribution and civic engagement are important both to the individual from the perspective of youth development and to the society so that it may maintain itself (Lerner, 2000).

Overall, then, it may be that volunteering contributes to a sense of self for the Muslim youth, but additional research is needed to determine what factors may be related to higher levels of political participation. For example, there may be a difference between immigrant-origin and non-immigrant-origin participants, as well as between first- and second-generation participants, where higher levels of participation are generally associated with longer periods of time in the United States (i.e., the individual and/or group are more acculturated, including aware of systems for civic engagement). Political scientists have tracked the civic participation and political attitudes of immigrant religious groups and have found that participation levels may vary based on the religious group and the area of political advocacy (Soysal, 1997).

There was evidence to suggest gendered themes in youth perceptions of PYD. For example, in discussing what constitutes admirable personal qualities, male participants seemed to highlight a balance between achievement and fun, whereas female participants referenced the balance between achievement and maintaining positive relations with others. In addition, the types of contribution behavior in which youth reported participating seemed to vary by gender, where males seemed to engage in more activities that were outside the home and formal (e.g., working in a family business) and females seemed to engage in less formal activities inside the home (e.g., providing care for younger siblings). Such evidence that suggests gendered differences indicates the need for further research.

CONCLUSIONS

Many psychology of religion scholars have acknowledged that, to date, the field has been dominated by a largely Protestant Christian orientation (see Hill & Pargament, 2003). Consequently, the perspectives of religious minority youth (e.g., Muslim, Jewish, Buddhist, and Sikh) are largely underrepresented. Because Christianity serves as a prominent factor in the ideology of U.S. culture (Schlosser, 2003), religious minority youth may encounter religious discrimination and exclusion (Sirin & Balsano, 2007; Sirin & Fine, 2007). Given the post-9/11 sociocultural context, Muslim youth in the West face particular challenges in reconciling their religious affiliation with the often negative portrayals of Islam and Muslims (Sirin et al., 2008).

There exist significant differences among Muslim youth in terms of the salience of religious beliefs and practices. Furthermore, the indigenous, immigrant, and refugee origins of Muslim youth give rise to a range and diversity of cultural, ethnic, socioeconomic, race, and gender differences. In this chapter, we explored how Muslim youth develop positive outcomes despite many challenges. The two studies provided an overview of a range of Muslim youth, in terms of age, immigrant-origin status, gender, and socioeconomic status. Study 1 revealed that identifying with one's own religious group, along with religiosity, serves as a critical factor in the formation of positive values and positive identities for Muslim youth in the United States. Study 2 provided a detailed account of the nature of civic engagement and volunteer behavior, as well as the motivation for participating in these behaviors. Combined, these studies highlight key factors and processes related to the positive development of Muslim American youth, a group of young people whose identity has been under scrutiny because of historical forces outside of their control.

While these two studies provided initial evidence of PYD within an understudied population, several limitations need to be taken seriously when interpreting the findings of these studies. First, we used a cross-sectional method to understand a developmental phenomenon, the formation of positive youth outcomes. Some of the themes and constructs that emerged in these studies may point to developmental processes, but the cross-sectional nature of the study does not allow for developmental change to be noted. A longitudinal study built on these findings is needed to adequately understand young people's PYD.

Second, while we used survey and focus group methods, we could not fully benefit from the mixed-methods approach, because we employed two independently planned projects with two different samples. A project that combines multiple qualitative and quantitative methods would have highlighted key factors and processes in PYD.

Finally, although both studies focused on Muslim youth, we worked with two different groups of youth who live in two different settings. Because of the design of these studies, we were unable to examine the contextual-level factors that may help or hinder young people's positive outcomes. Thus, in order to address these major limitations, future research on PYD should utilize a longitudinal design with mixed research methods and recruit youth across multiple settings in a planned fashion.

REFERENCES

Amer, M., & Hovey, J. (2005). Examination of the impact of accultration, stress, and religiosity on mental health variables for second-generation Arab Americans. *Ethnicity and Disease, 15*, 111–112.

Corbin, J., & Stauss, A. (2008). *Basics of qualitative research: Techniques and procedures for developing grounded theory* (3rd ed.). Thousand Oaks, CA: Sage.

Crystal, D. S., & DeBell, M. (2002). Sources of civic orientation among American youth: Trust, religious valuation, and attributions of responsibility. *Political Psychology, 23*(1), 113–132.

Damon, W. (2004). What is positive youth development? *The Annals of the American Academy of Political and Social Science, 591*(1), 13–24.

Dowling, E. M., Gestsdottir, S., Anderson, P. M., von Eye, A., Almerigi, J., & Lerner, R. M. (2004). Structural relations among spirituality, religiosity, and thriving in adolescence. *Applied Developmental Science, 8*, 7–16.

Furrow, J. L, King, P. E., & White K. (2004). Religion and positive youth development: Identity, meaning, and prosocial concerns. *Applied Development Science, 8*(1), 17–26.

Gallup and the Coexist Foundation. (2009). Muslim Americans: A national portrait: An in-depth analysis of America's most diverse religious community. Retrieved from   http://www.muslimwestfacts.com/mwf/116074/Muslim-Americans-National-Portrait.aspx

Greenbaum, T. L. (1993). *The handbook for focus group research*. New York, NY: Macmillan.

Hart, D., & Fegley, S. (1995). Prosocial behaviour and caring in adolescence: Relations to self-understanding and social judgement. *Child Development, 66*, 1346–1359.

Hill, P. C., & Pargament K. (2003). Advances in the conceptualization and measurement of religion and spirituality. *American Psychologist, 58*, 64–74.

Hurh, W. M., & Kim, K. C. (1990). Religious participation of Korean immigrants in the United States. *Journal of the Scientific Study of Religion, 29*, 19–34.

Hurtado, A. (1997). Understanding multiple group identities: Inserting women into cultural transformations. *Journal of Social Issues, 53*(2), 299–328.

Jensen, L., & Flanagan, C. (2008). Immigrant civic engagement: New translations. *Applied Development Science, 12*(2), 55–56.

Kim, C., & Kim, S. (2001). Ethnic roles of Korean immigrant churches in the United States. In K. Ho-Youn, K. K. Chung, & R. S. Warner (Eds.), *Korean Americans and their religion* (pp. 71–94). University Park: Pennsylvania State University Press.

King, P. E., & Furrow, J. L. (2004). Religion as a resource for positive youth development: Religion, social capital, and moral outcomes. *Developmental Psychology, 40*(5), 703–713.

Kosmin, B. A., Mayer, E., & Keysar, A. (2001). *American religious identification survey*. New York: City University of New York.

Krueger, R. A., & Casey, M. A. (2000). *Focus groups: A practical guide for applied research* (3rd ed.). Thousand Oaks, CA: Sage.

Larson, R. (2000). Towards a psychology of positive youth development. *American Psychologist, 55*, 170–183.

Leonard, K. I. (2003). *Muslims in the United States: The state of the research*. New York, NY: Russell Sage.

Lerner, R. M. (2000). Developing civil society through the promotion of positive youth development. *Journal of Developmental and Behavioral Pediatrics, 21*, 48–49.

Lerner, R. M. (2007). *The good teen: Rescuing adolescents from the myths of the storm and stress years*. New York, NY: Crown.

Lerner, R. M. (2008). Spirituality, positive purpose, wisdom, and positive development in adolescence: Comments on Oman, Flinders and Thoresen's Ideas about "integrating spiritual modeling into education." *International Journal for the Psychology of Religion, 18*(2), 108–118.

Lerner, R. M. (2009). The positive youth development perspective: Theoretical and empirical bases of a strength-based approach to adolescent development. In C. R. Snyder & S. J. Lopez (Eds.), *Oxford handbook of positive psychology* (2nd ed., pp. 149–163). Oxford, England: Oxford University Press.

Lerner, R. M., Roeser, W., & Phelps, E. (2008). *Positive youth development and spirituality: From theory to research*. West Conshohocken, PA: Templeton Foundation Press.

Luhtanen, R., & Crocker, J. (1992). A collective self-esteem scale: Self-evaluation of one's social identity. *Personality and Social Psychology Bulletin, 18*, 302–318.

Mena, F. J., Padilla, A. M., & Maldonado, M. (1987). Acculturative stress and specific coping strategies among immigrant and later generation college students. *Hispanic Journal of Behavioral Sciences, 9*(2), 207–225.

Miller, W. R., & Thoresen, C. E. (2003), Spirituality, religion, and health: An emerging research field. *American Psychologist, 58*(1), 24–35.

Morgan, D. L. (1997). *Focus groups as qualitative research* (2nd ed.). Qualitative research methods series (Vol. 16). Thousand Oaks, CA: Sage.

Schlosser, L. (2003). Christian privilege: Breaking a sacred taboo. *Journal of Multicultural Counseling and Development, 31*, 44–51.

Search Institute. (2004). *Developmental assets profile*. Minneapolis, MN: Author.

Sirin, S. R., & Balsano, A. (2007). Pathways to identity and positive development among Muslim youth in the West. *Applied Developmental Science, 11*(3), 109–111.

Sirin, S. R., Bikmen, N., Mir, M., Zaal, M., Fine, M., & Katciaficas, D. (2008). Exploring dual identification among Muslim-American emerging adults: A mixed methods study. *Journal of Adolescence, 31*, 2.

Sirin, S. R., & Fine, M. (2007). Hyphenated selves: Muslim American youth negotiating their identities across the fault lines of global conflict. *Applied Developmental Science, 11*(3), 151–163.

Sirin, S. R., & Fine, M. (2008). *Muslim American youth: Understanding hyphenated identities through multiple methods.* New York: New York University Press.

Soysal, Y. (1997). Changing parameters of citizenship and claims-making: Organized Islam in European public spheres. *Theory and Society, 26,* 509–527.

Stepick, A. (1998). *Pride against prejudice: Haitians in the United States.* Boston, MA: Allyn & Bacon.

Stepick, A., & Stepick, C. D. (2002). Becoming American, constructing ethnicity: Immigrant youth and civic engagement. *Applied Developmental Science, 6*(4), 246–257.

Stewart, D. W., Shamdasani, P. N., & Rook, D. W. (2007). *Focus groups: Theory and practice.* Applied Social Research Method Series (Vol. 20). Thousand Oaks, CA: Sage.

Wagener, L. M., Furrow, J. L., King, P. E., Leffert, N., & Benson, P. L. (2003). Religion and developmental resources. *Review of Religious Research, 44,* 271–284.

Youniss, J., McLellan, J. A., & Yates, M. (1999). Religion, community service, and identity in American youth. *Journal of Adolescence, 22,* 243–253.

Youniss, J., & Yates, M. (1997). *Community service and social responsibility in youth.* Chicago, IL: University of Chicago Press.

Youniss, J., & Yates, M. (1999). Youth service and moral-civic identity: A case for everyday morality. *Educational Psychology Review, 11*(4), 361–376.

Zhou, M., & Bankston, C. L. (1998). *Growing up American: How Vietnamese children adapt to life in the United States.* New York: Russell Sage Foundation.

Zogby, J. (2004). Muslims in the American public square: Shifting political winds and fallout from 9/11, Afghanistan, and Iraq. Online press release and report: http://www.projectmaps.com/AMP2004report.pdf

CHAPTER

12

⊰⊷◈⊷⊱

The Role of Religion
and Worship Communities
in the Positive Development
of Immigrant Youth

Carola Suárez-Orozco,[1] Sukhmani Singh,[1]
Mona M. Abo-Zena,[2] Dan Du,[2] and Robert W. Roeser

The children of immigrants are the fastest growing sector of the child population in the United States today. Nearly one quarter of the U.S. population is
either immigrant or the children of immigrants (Alba & Nee, 2003), and 12.6%
of the U.S. population is born abroad (Terrazas & Batalva, 2008). This rapidly
growing population is highly diverse—in terms of national origin, race, ethnicity, socioeconomic background, language (Hernandez, Denton, & McCartney,

[1]The Longitudinal Immigration Student Adaptation (LISA) study was funded by the
National Science Foundation, the W. T. Grant Foundation, and the Spencer Foundation.
We thank Nora Thompson for developing the religion questions for the LISA study.

[2]The Role of Spiritual Development in Growth of Purpose, Generosity, and Psychological
Health in Adolescence was supported in part by a grant to Richard M. Lerner from the
John Templeton Foundation. We thank Drs. Richard M. Lerner (PI), Erin Phelps and
Heather Urry (Co-Investigators), Sonia Issac and Alan Poey (graduate student research
assistants), Mari Rutkin and Emma Blumstein (project assistants), and Pamela Anderson
(consultant) for their assistance with this project. Earlier versions of the Tufts contributions
to this paper were presented at the 2009 Biennial Meeting of the Society for Research in
Child Development, in Denver, Colorado.

255

2007), and religion (Eck, 2002). While much has been written about the first five dimensions of diversity and their implications for the study of immigrant youth adaptation, the role of religion has been neglected in the developmental literature (Holden & Vittrup, 2009).

Newcomer immigrant youth face a variety of challenges as they settle in their new homeland. Immigration is a stressful event (Falicov, 1998; Suárez-Orozco & Suárez-Orozco, 2001) that removes youth from predictable contexts while stripping them of significant social ties (Suárez-Orozco, Suárez-Orozco, & Todorova, 2008), and it presents them with the particular acculturative challenge of navigating two worlds simultaneously (Berry, Phinney, Sam, & Vedder, 2006). Within a Western context, youth are often asked to take on responsibilities beyond their years, including sibling care, translation, and advocacy (Faulstich-Orellana, 2009), which at times undermine traditional patterns of parental authority. These responsibilities often involve tasks that represent highly gendered roles, which may have both positive and negative consequences for development (Suárez-Orozco & Qin-Hillard, 2004).

Just as native-born youth, children of immigrants face the challenge of forging an integrated identity. In addition, however, their experiences also include the task of developing a sense of belonging to their new homeland while still honoring their parental origins (Suárez-Orozco, 2004). For immigrant-origin youth and particularly for newcomer youth, acculturative stress has been linked to both psychological distress (García-Coll & Magnuson, 1997; Noh, Beiser, Kaspar, Hou, & Rummens, 1999) and academic problems (Suárez-Orozco et al., 2008). Thus, for many immigrant youth, religion and the framework it provides can play an important role in the negotiations of immigration in a new land, in understanding and making meaning of new life circumstances, in developing a network of social support that fosters a sense of belonging, and in constructing an identity that is purposeful and hopeful with respect to the future.

Religion is a fundamental part of life for most people throughout the world (Holden & Vittrup, 2009; Spiro, 1987; Weber, 1905/2008). As a result, it has been a topic of consideration in the social sciences from the very beginning of the disciplines. Religion has been related to the search for meaning and transcendence (Berger, 1974), existential questions and the human psyche (Freud, 1913/2009), the problem of false consciousness (Marx & Engels, 2002), and the need to make meaning of suffering and the biological finality of life (Spiro, 1987). Durkheim (1912/2008) has written about the function of religion in solidifying social belonging, and William James (1902/2009) has eloquently discussed its role in a search for personal belonging. Sociologists have pointed to humans' particular turn to religion in times of rapid social change (Wallace, 1956; Weber, 1950/2008). Despite these important theoretical contributions, the developmental implications of religion for youth from diverse backgrounds remain fundamentally understudied (Holden & Vittrup, 2009).

Psychologists have argued that religion can provide a variety of protective functions during various phases of the life cycle. For example, research among nonimmigrant adolescents suggests various ways that religion can shape the adolescent experience (Furrow, King, & White, 2004; Regenerus, Smith, & Smith, 2004; Roehlkepartain, King, Wagener, & Benson, 2006). Religious involvement, the combination of religious attendance and private devotion, has been reported to positively influence a sense of purpose (King & Furrow, 2004) and subjective well-being (Ellison, 1991). Religious involvement may also help individuals and groups of individuals adjust positively to life circumstances, as suggested by studies of adolescents who report positive correlations between religious involvement and adolescent school engagement (Dowling et al., 2004; Dowling, Gestsdottir, Anderson, von Eye, & Lerner, 2003; Regenerus, 2003).

Furthermore, religious participation is widely considered to be a protective factor in decreasing the likelihood of adolescent engagement in risk behavior (Bridges & Moore, 2002; Jessor, 1991; Michalak, Trocki, & Bond, 2007; Rostosky, Wilcox, Wright, & Randall, 2004). There is also compelling evidence that religion may particularly serve a protective function for urban youth. A study of African-American female, urban adolescents found that greater religiosity was significantly associated with higher self-esteem and greater psychological functioning (Ball, Armistead, & Austin, 2003). Another study on urban African-American adolescents reported that youth who were more "religiously active" (Steinman & Zimmerman, 2004, p. 158) tended to engage less in a variety of risk behaviors, including alcohol, cigarette, and marijuana use as well as sexual involvement (Steinman & Zimmerman, 2004). Further, Latino youth who attend church on a weekly basis are significantly less likely to be involved in violent encounters then their peers who attend church less frequently (Pew Hispanic Center, 2009).

For new arrivals who are often disoriented and striving to establish themselves in a new land, religion and religious participation may be particularly helpful in serving to bolster well-being. Religiosity and participation in worship communities are likely to serve similar functions as those established in nonimmigrant populations, such as providing hope, a moral compass that promotes charity, compassion, and justice (Furrow et al., 2004), being associated with better mental health outcomes (Wong, Rew, & Slaikeu, 2006), fostering academic achievement, and reducing participation in risk behaviors (Nooney, 2005; Regenerus, 2000, 2003). These functions are important for individuals all over the world, but they may be particularly compelling for immigrants who are uprooted and feel disconnected from their familiar roles and social ties. It has been shown that belonging to a worship community provides a sense of fellowship (Durkheim, 1912/2008), social support, and tangible support to its members (King & Roeser, 2009; Portes & Rumbaut, 2006).

For many immigrants, participation in worship communities provides the opportunity for ethnic continuity and preservation of ties to their ethnic community (Bankston & Zhou, 1995; Min, 2005). Participation in religious communities can also serve as a pathway to acculturation; a substantial body of research has claimed that for the children of immigrants—particularly the second generation and beyond—religion has served the function of "turn[ing] immigrants into Americans and giv[ing] them a sense of belonging and membership" (Foner & Alba, 2008, p. 365). Worship communities can also serve as safe places and "surrogate families" (Cao, 2005, p. 183) for immigrant youth, whose parents may not be able to readily guide them with an accurate map of their new land (Suárez-Orozco et al., 2008).

Sociologists have made substantive theoretical, empirical, and methodological contributions to the intersectionality of the study of religion and immigration. From their contributions we know that new arrivals tend to be more religious than they were before they migrated (Foley & Hoge, 2007); immigrants are substantially more "actively religious than other Americans" (Foley & Hoge, 2007, p. 15). The elegant work of Levitt (2007) demonstrates the ways in which immigrants engage in transnational religious practices to maintain a sense of connectedness with their homeland. For immigrants who may feel disoriented and displaced in their new land, religion and religious places of worship serve the role of "transcending boundaries" of space and time, allowing "followers to feel a part of a chain of memory, connected to a past, a present, and a future" (Levitt, 2007, p. 13). For new immigrants, worship communities may be safe havens in what they perceive to be unwelcoming new homelands (Foley & Hoge, 2007); sources of bridging capital for information about jobs, housing, and other resources; as well as providers of tangible resources such as food, clothing, child care, and money in an emergency (Stepick, 2005). Religious organizations also have a long tradition, dating back to settlement houses, of activism for immigrant rights; in more recent years, religious organizations and communities have been at the forefront of providing assistance to refugees and advocating for immigrant rights (Hondagneu-Sotelo, 2007).

This body of sociological research provides substantial insights into the importance of religion in the lives of immigrants and, indeed, substantiates that, as Stepick (2005) wryly points out, if Nietzsche "were still alive and visited various immigrant communities, he would observe, that among immigrants, at least, God is very much alive" (p. 13). But the sociological corpus, to date, does little to shed light on the religious experiences or perspectives of immigrant adolescents or young adults. This body of work is nearly entirely focused on the adult perspective and on the particular role of religious social organizations rather than on the individual experience. While developmental perspectives have provided insights into the substantial potential positive role that religion and religious organizations play in positive youth development (Holden & Vittrup, 2009; Lerner, Lerner, Almerigi, & Theokas, 2005), there is very limited developmental research with immigrant populations. Thus, the role of religion in the lives of immigrant youth is also understudied and little understood, which, given the dynamic growth in this population, is a significant gap in knowledge.

In this chapter, we sought to focus the spotlight on the intersection of immigration, religion, and positive youth development (PYD) using data from two separate studies. The *Longitudinal Immigrant Student Adaptation Study* was developed to examine the adaptation of immigrant newcomer youth from several sending countries with a focus on educational outcomes. As a part of the study, we collected data from the parents about their religious practices and asked students to reflect on the role of God and religion in their lives. The data presented in this chapter provide evidence of the importance of religion in their lives—the youths' words provide insights into how they express their connection with God and religion.

In the second study, using data from the cross-sectional study, the "Role of Spiritual Development in Growth of Purpose, Generosity, and Psychological Health in Adolescence" (see Lerner, Roeser, & Phelps, 2008), we compared young adults of diverse origins (222 immigrant-origin youth) to explore the mediating roles of positive peer affiliations and social support in predicting the positive outcomes of well-being, sense of purpose, and reduced risk behavior. Data and analyses from this data set provide insight into possible mediating mechanisms that explain relations between religious involvements on the one hand and indices of PYD on the other. Overall, this chapter presents early evidence of the need to study the role of religion and spirituality in the lives of immigrant youth and the children of immigrants, a topic that is understudied but important for our understanding of adolescent development writ large (King & Roeser, 2009).

STUDY 1: THE LONGITUDINAL IMMIGRANT STUDENT ADAPTATION STUDY

The data presented here came from the *Longitudinal Immigration Student Adaptation* (LISA) study (Carola Suárez-Orozco and Marcelo Suárez-Orozco, PIs), a five-year longitudinal study that used interdisciplinary and comparative approaches, mixed methods, and triangulated data in order to document patterns of adaptation among recently arrived immigrant youth from Central America, China, the Dominican Republic, Haiti, and Mexico (Suárez-Orozco et al., 2008). The original study was not designed primarily to examine questions of religion—rather, it was focused on academic adaptations of newcomer adolescents over time. As part of the larger study, however, we collected parent and student data on religious participation and asked youth to tell us about the role of God and religion in their lives as migrants in a new country. Here we provided quantitative descriptions of the parents' reports of their religious participation (and corroborated the information by including their children's reports) and then, using qualitative data, explored in the youths' own words the significance of religion in their lives.

Participants

A diverse sample ($N = 407$; 53% female) of newcomer immigrant students was recruited from the Boston and San Francisco metropolitan areas in 1997. This research was designed to be a study of newcomers arriving just at the cusp of adolescence. The recruited participants were between the ages of 9 and 14 years ($M = 11.7$); by year five, when the student data reported here were collected, participants were ages 14 to 19 years ($M = 16.7$). Participants were restricted to youth who had been in the United States no more than one third of their life ($M = 1.93$ years in the United States at the beginning of the study). By year five, the final sample included 309 students (Chinese = 72; Dominican = 60; Central American = 57; Haitian = 50; Mexican = 70); note that the selected countries are among the largest sending countries of immigrants in the areas we recruited. The attrition rate was 5% annually; students of Chinese origin had significantly higher completion rates (90%) than Dominicans, Mexicans, or Central Americans (approximately 75%) or Haitians (69%), and significantly more girls than boys completed the five interviews (81% vs. 70%). Relative to completers, noncompleters reported witnessing more school violence (37% vs. 23%), but they were otherwise nearly identical to those who completed the study (see Suárez-Orozco et al., 2008).

On average, students' mothers (or maternal figures) received 9.2 years of schooling, with a range from no formal schooling to 21 years of formal education. One third of the mothers had completed high school. On average, Dominican mothers reported the most years of schooling ($M = 11$ years), whereas Central American mothers reported the fewest ($M = 7.3$ years). These ranges in years of education are consistent with national norms for immigrants (U.S. Census Bureau, 2006). During the first year of the study (in 2002), 96% of the total sample of immigrant fathers was working. By the fifth year of this study, only 64% of the fathers were employed, reflecting the economic downturn following the attacks of September 11th. Central American fathers were the most likely to be unemployed in the first year of the study (11%), whereas by the fifth year Dominican fathers were the most likely to be unemployed (58%). Mothers were less likely to be employed outside the home than fathers. Twenty percent of the total population of mothers reported staying at home, with significant differences among the groups. Central American mothers were most likely to work outside the home (91% the first year and 86.8% the last year).

Students lived in a wide variety of family constellations, ranging from single-parent households to crowded, shared spaces with several families and boarders. Participants lived in households ranging in size from 2 to 17 people. Central American and Mexican participants lived in the largest households ($M = 6.40$ and 6.38, respectively), whereas the Chinese lived in the smallest ($M = 4.38$). Consistent with most immigrant youth, only 37% of the sample lived in a traditional two-parent, no-extended-family household arrangement. Twenty-six percent lived in households headed by two adults, which included extended family members such as grandparents, aunts, uncles, and cousins. The remaining 42% of the sample lived in an arrangement that was headed by a mother only, a father only, a combined arrangement including a stepparent, or a family headed by a nonparent relative such as grandparents, uncles, aunts, or older siblings.

Procedure

Students in our study were recruited from more than 50 schools in 7 districts representing typical contexts of reception for newcomer students from each of the groups of origin (U.S. Census Bureau, 2000). District, principal, parent, and student permissions were obtained before students were signed on to participate in the study. Each year, students completed interviews either during or after school, depending on the participant's availability and the activities occurring at school on the day of the interview. Trained research assistants conducted all interviews on an individual basis in the participant's preferred language. The student interviews took from 1.5 to 2 hours to administer and involved a variety of question formats (e.g., open-ended, fill-in-the-blank, Likert scales). The scales were administered in the native language, if the participant so preferred, on an oral basis so as not to jeopardize the validity of responses given by students with limited literacy skills. Parent interviews were conducted in the native language the first and last year of the study in the participants' homes.

In this chapter we report on parent interview data collected during the first year of the study, at which point we asked the following questions: What religion were you born into? What religion are you part of now? Do you attend church or temple? Do you teach your children about religion? and Some immigrants receive help from religious organizations when they arrive. Is that true for you? If so, what kind of help have you received? Students were also asked questions about whether they attended church or temple (as well as the frequency) in the last year of the study. In addition, they were asked to respond to: Is religion or a belief in God important to you? And, if so, in what ways is religion or God a part of your life?

Data Analysis

Data for parents and adolescents were analyzed separately. Because there were no qualitative data available for parents, we ran means and frequencies for the parent religious participation questions using SPSS. Chi-square analyses were also calculated to determine whether these variables differed significantly across the different country of origin groups, between parents and their children's responses, and between genders.

An open-coding process using phrases as the units of analysis was employed to analyze the qualitative data (Strauss & Corbin, 1990). During the first stage of the coding, emergent descriptive themes from all of the transcripts were identified. The initial set of independently identified themes was compared and integrated into a single comprehensive list of coding categories (Miles & Huberman, 1994.) The coders (who were not involved in the data collection process to guard against bias during the analytic and interpretative processes) refined the coding scheme "by discussing the meanings of, and relationships between, each coding category, and identified rules for determining when a particular coding category should be assigned to a response" (Mattis et al., 2008, pp. 420–421). The two coders assessed the reliability of the coding scheme using randomly selected narrative samples from 34 of the 397 interviews. The formula for inter-rater reliability was: inter-rater reliability = agreement/(agreement + disagreement) with a target rate of 85% reliability as the lowest acceptable level for each category (Miles & Huberman, 1994). The level of reliability for the coding derived for this study reached an average rate of 89.7%.

Findings on Religious Participation

The majority of the parents in the sample reported being born into a Catholic tradition (74.1%). This finding is consistent with the fact that four of the groups of origin of this sample originated from predominantly Catholic countries in Latin America or the Caribbean (i.e., Mexico, Dominican Republic, Central America, and Haiti; Pew Forum on Religion and Public Life, 2008). The majority of the Chinese reported either not being affiliated to a religion (47.1%) or coming from a tradition of practicing ancestor worship (30.9%) or Buddhism (19.1%) (see Table 12.1). The religious affiliations of the Chinese parents are in keeping with the official Chinese governmental policy of atheism.

Table 12.1 Parental Reports of Religious Affiliation Born Into by Nation of Origin

	Parental Nation of Origin				
	Dominican Republic	Central America	Mexico	Haiti	China
Ancestor worship					30.9%
Baptist				15.4%	
Buddhist					19.1%
Catholic	97%	94.1%	94.2%	78.8%	2.9%
Evangelical		2.9%			
Jehovah's Witness			3.5%		
Pentecostal	1.5%			5.8%	
Protestant		1.5%			
No religious affiliation	1.5%	1.5%	2.3%		47.1%

Table 12.2 Parental Report of Religious Conversions

Country of Origin	Conversion
Dominican	18.2%
Central American	37.3%
Mexican	13.1%
Haitian	25%
Chinese	23.8%
Total	25.4%

Religious Conversions

Within Haiti and Central America, evangelical churches have demonstrated rapid growth in their membership in the last several decades of political and social unrest in these regions (Vasquez, 2005). Consequently, we expected that there would be a substantial percentage of families who might have converted from their family of origin religion. Thus, we asked parents if they currently considered themselves a part of the religion into which they had been born. Notably, 25.4% of our sample had converted. The Central Americans were most likely to have converted, and the Mexicans were least likely to do so. Central Americans and Haitians were most likely to become members of Evangelical, Pentecostal, or Jehovah's Witness religious communities, whereas Chinese parents largely reported becoming agnostic (a small number had converted to Catholic or Protestant churches) (see Table 12.2). The percentages of Evangelical participants from Mexico and the Dominican Republic in our study were in keeping with those reported by a recent Pew Hispanic Foundation summary, but the percentage of Evangelicals in our study, however, was approximately one-third higher (Pew Hispanic Center, 2007).

Church Attendance

Parents were asked to report on whether they attend church or temple on a regular basis. The majority of the Dominican (77.9%), Central American (87%), Mexican (86.2%), and Haitian (89.6%) immigrant parents reported that they attend church regularly. Not surprisingly, the only group that reported a different kind of pattern of attendance was the Chinese, because they have a very low religious affiliation; they reported low attendance at church or temple (32.9%). In the fifth year of the study, students reported in the affirmative about regular attendance as follows: Dominican (65%), Central American (87.7%), Mexican (90%), Haitian (89.6%), and Chinese (35.2%). It is notable that parent and student reports on church or temple attendance were quite consistent, given

Table 12.3 Frequency of Church/Temple Attendance Reported by Students

	Dominican	Central Am.	Mexican	Haitian	Chinese
Never	35	12.3	10	10.4	64.8
Few times a year	26.7	24.6	20	16.7	16.9
Few times a month	13.3	24.6	24.3	6.3	7
Weekly	21.7	15.8	32.9	43.8	8.5
Few times a week	3.3	22.8	12.9	22.9	2.8

that different sources were asked five years apart, $\chi^2(4, N = 280) = 44.09, p < .0005$. This finding speaks to the notion of parental influences and socialization practices.

Apart from the Chinese group, the youth reported that church attendance was a regular event in their lives (see Table 12.3). The Central American, Haitian, and Mexican participants were particularly engaged in their worship communities as measured by attendance. The attendance rates for the Hispanic groups in this sample were consistent with patterns reported by the Pew Hispanic Center (2007). Notably, there was no difference in attendance rates between girls and boys, when it came to church attendance, $\chi^2(4, N = 306) = 6.42, p = .169$.

Teaching About Religion

We also asked parents to tell us whether they taught their children about religion. With the exception of the Chinese group, approximately 92% of parents of all other groups reported teaching their children about religion.

Getting Tangible Help

It is well documented that religious organizations and the faith community are active in promoting and fighting for social justice for immigrants (Hondagneu-Sotelo, 2007). Churches and faith-based organizations also provide a variety of supports to new immigrants and refugees, from food, housing, information, shelter, water, and "know-your-rights" booklets to undocumented immigrants, to political advocacy promoting citizenship and human rights for migrants (Hondagneu-Sotelo, 2007). Only 11% of our participants, however, reported that they had received tangible help from religious organizations. Our qualitative analysis of open-ended responses indicated that when parents reported getting help, it tended to be in the form of being provided with clothing, help in finding work, receiving small sums of money in a crisis, and very rarely, securing their child's immigration into the United States. Thus, in this sample, the help they seemed to derive from their participation in church had more to do with continuation of cultural practices (Eck, 2002) and a sense of belonging (Portes & Rumbaut, 2006) to the faith community rather than tangible supports.

Findings: Youth Perspectives on the Role of Religion and God

In the last year of the study, the first-generation adolescent immigrants were asked to reflect on the role of religion and God in their lives. Their responses were quite revealing of the different ways in which religion and God are a part of their lives.

Guidance About How to Behave

Emerging directly from the data were many examples from our participants of how religion and God provide them with a system of guidance or a charter for belief about how to behave. A 19-year-old Chinese girl said: "It provides me with guidelines." An 18-year-old Dominican girl told us, "It helps me to think better, to make better decisions," and a 19-year-old Haitian girl noted, "The Bible has a good way of telling you how to live your life." These statements were consistent with theories of religion providing a moral compass and a charter for belief (Dowling et al., 2004; Malinowski, 1948; Mariano & Damon, 2008). Participants who gave these kinds of responses indicated that the guidance they received was a clear, positive roadmap of behavior.

Guidance About How NOT to Behave

An extension of the moral compass and charter for belief theme, which also frequently emerged, were statements in which our informants indicated that religion and God provided guidance about how *not* to behave. For example, a 17-year-old Dominican girl said that religion "tells me about what I am not supposed to do like with somebody if you are not married to him." A 16-year-old Chinese boy told us that religion had taught him to "stay away from bad stuff—drugs, sex, smoking." Thus, for these youth, religion functioned as a kind of super-ego guiding the adolescents away from risk behaviors they might otherwise have been lured into. Often these statements implied a fear of punishment. As a 17-year-old Dominican girl noted, "I have faith and I believe that when you do something bad, God will punish you."

Religion and God as Sources of Ever-Present Help

For many of the youth in our study, participants reported that God and religion provide an umbrella of safety and protection, an ever-present and ever-felt source of help, and a source of comfort in an unsafe world. A 17-year-old Chinese girl said: "It's been with me all my life. I worship God and I go to church. I follow the 10 commandments. It's a big part of my life. It keeps me safe." A 14-year-old

Haitian boy noted, "God helps me and protects me," and a 17-year-old Mexican girl confided that she feels "I am protected and kept away from evil."

Turning to God in Moments of Need

In contrast to the participants who indicated that God was ever-present, many others noted that God was someone to turn to explicitly in a moment of need or crisis. So, for example, an 18-year-old Chinese girl said, "When I am in trouble, I pray." A 19-year-old Dominican girl told us, "I pray—when I need something I ask God." A 14-year-old Haitian girl confided, "He helps me through troubles," and a 19-year-old Dominican boy told us, "God helps you with any problem. You ask him and he helps you." While the earlier responses were proactive, the nature of this second category was more reactive.

Religious Practices

Other participants did not specifically speak about the ways in which religion and God provide them with a moral compass or a sense of protection in a new and often unsafe land, but rather they spoke directly to practicing *acts* that demonstrate their religious participation. In response to the open-ended question about the role of God or religion in their life, participants talked about such acts of religious participation as attending church, praying, participating in Catechism, and making an offering to deities. Thus, for example, a 16-year-old Dominican girl said, "I go to church and pray" and an 18-year-old Dominican boy said, "I participate in religious services every week." A 16-year-old Mexican girl volunteered, "You have to be baptized, do communion, and all that." A 17-year-old Chinese boy told us, "I make offerings to the folk deities so I can have a peace of mind." For these youth, simple participation in religious acts and rituals (Turner, 1969) signified a fellowship and an affiliation with a cause greater than themselves.

God Without Religious Practice

A few participants indicated that they believe in God, but that they neither attend church nor engage in religious practices. A 16-year-old Dominican boy mentioned, "I don't go to church but I believe in God." A 17-year-old Central American boy noted, "I believe in God even though I don't go to church. I believe that you have to believe in something or someone." These responses occurred fairly infrequently in this sample; nevertheless, they are important because they suggest the importance of future research on religiosity, even in the absence of religious practice or attendance at places of worship.

Nonbelieving [3]

Some participants indicated that they were not religious, did not identify as a part of any religion, or did not participate in religious practices. Examples of such responses were, "I don't have any religion or any belief" from a 19-year-old Chinese female, and "Religion does not impact me. It does not play a role in my life" from an 18-year-old Chinese male respondent. Notably, nearly all of the students who provided such responses were of Chinese origin; this finding is consistent with the nonbelieving patterns reported by their parents and reflects the strength of parents as important socialization influences.

Familial Values

Listening carefully to the participants' responses, it was clear that, for many immigrant youth, religion was a cultural *value* that was being transmitted across generations. An 18-year-old Haitian girl explained, "God is a part of my life because first of all I was born and raised in a Christian family. Therefore, I feel like it's a part of my life and what I do." A 15-year-old Central American girl told us, "I have been raised in the Evangelical religion. It is something I practice. It is something I am into." An 18-year-old Mexican girl said, "I have to do what my mom tells me because parents are to be respected and they show us the right way." A 16-year-old Mexican boy explained the importance of family in transmitting religion: "I grew up believing in God. Same as my family. And with the idea that one has to go to Church and be good. I grew up believing in religion, it is something my family has taught me." These responses are consistent with the developmental theories that articulate how adults and, more specifically, families actively socialize youth and channel them toward religious learning and experiences (Martin, White, & Perlman, 2003; Smith & Denton, 2005). Interestingly, at the point when we collected the data, participants were largely in late adolescence, yet they were still quite affiliated with their parents' religion.

---

[3]Nonbelieving could fall into three distinct categories. Many of the youth could be labeled *areligious*, which we would juxtapose against *agnosticism* and *atheism*. These three terms are overlapping but distinct. According to Webster's Dictionary, *agnostics* are individuals "who hold the view that any ultimate reality (such as God) is unknown and probably unknowable." *Atheists* are defined as individuals "who believe that there is no deity." While atheists take a stance of active disbelief, agnostics take a stance that one simply cannot know. The areligious, on the other hand, often do not take an active stance; rather, as a result of their life circumstances, they may have simply not given religion much thought. They may not have actively received a religious education, or they may have parents with two religious backgrounds or with varying degrees of commitment to religious practice.

"It Just Is"

A last significant theme that surfaced in many responses was the inability of participants to articulate the specific function of religion or God in their lives; nonetheless, they clearly affirmed their *belief* in God. This belief tended to be unarticulated and unquestioned, and was not linked in their responses to family, practices, values, personal well-being, or a guide to behavior. A 16-year-old Central American girl, for example, said, "I just believe in God." Examples of these responses included an 18-year-old Central American boy's response: "Because . . . I don't know . . . because it is a good thing to believe in God. He gave his life for us." A 15-year-old Dominican girl stated, "I love God. I will always love God. I can't explain it." Another 13-year-old Central American boy summed up this way of thinking, "It just is." For these participants, religion may not be fully examined or considered—analogous to other identities Marcia (1966) described during the stage of foreclosure. Perhaps these young people have yet to reach a stage in development where they closely examine and understand their beliefs. Nonetheless, participation in religious practices and incorporation of religious beliefs clearly plays a central role in their lives.

STUDY 2: THE ROLE OF SPIRITUAL DEVELOPMENT IN GROWTH OF PURPOSE, GENEROSITY, AND PSYCHOLOGICAL HEALTH IN ADOLESCENCE

The role of religion and spirituality in the lives of immigrant adolescents was also examined in a recent study of positive youth development in the Northeastern United States (see Lerner et al., 2008). Although a nationally representative study of youth in America has shown that adolescents in the Northeast are generally the least religious of all youth in the country (Smith & Denton, 2005), this is clearly not the case for immigrant youth and children of immigrants. For example, despite declines in church membership among U.S.-born Catholics, the membership of the Catholic church has remained stable (24%) in the United States over the last few decades primarily because of immigrants, mostly from Latin America, the Philippines, and, to some extent, Vietnam, who identify as Catholic (Pew Forum on Religion and Public Life, 2008; Portes & Rumbaut, 2006). In addition, since the 1960s, a small but increasingly significant number of immigrant Americans and their offspring identify religiously as Muslim, Hindu, Buddhist, or Orthodox Christian (e.g., Eck, 2002). Thus, in this study, we were interested in examining the role of religion and spirituality to indicators of PYD among the growing segment of the U.S. population who are immigrants, as well as the mediating processes by which religious involvement might affect positive development.

Perhaps the most studied variables indexing religiosity beyond religious self-identification is individuals' self-rated importance of religion to themselves (or in their lives) and their frequency of involvement in various religious activities (e.g., formal religious services). These measures are often combined and called religiosity or religiousness—an unfortunate mixing of what can be considered psychological identity beliefs and religious behavior. Nonetheless, these two variables have been linked to positive outcomes among youth (King & Roeser, 2009), including a sense of life purpose (Mariano & Damon, 2008), well-being (Benson, Scales, Sesma, & Roehlkepartain, 2005; George, Ellison, & Larson, 2002), and decreased engagement in risky behaviors (Bridges & Moore, 2002). In this study, we were particularly interested in how religious involvement, defined as self-reported frequency of *behavioral engagement* in religious activities and practices, was associated with indicators of positive development (e.g., purpose, well-being, risk behavior), as well as the potential mediating mechanisms behind such associations. We sought to address the question: By what processes does engagement in religious practices and organized activities affect youth development?

Based on the extant research, in this study, we focused on a small subset of the processes theorized to mediate between involvement in religious practices and institutions and positive, constructive aspects of youth development (see Smith, 2003). First, we considered the role of identity, in this case religious identity, in mediating the previously documented relations between behavioral involvement in religious practices and activities and the development of a sense of purpose (Mariano & Damon, 2008). Various studies have identified different links in the hypothesized chain of effect from religious involvement to religious identity to meaning and purpose. For instance, the positive association between religious involvement and adolescents' development of a sense of personal meaning, purpose, and hope for the future has been established (Francis, 2000; Markstrom, 1999; Smith & Denton, 2005). In addition, Furrow and colleagues (2004) showed that adolescents who reported a strong religious identity were also more likely to report more purpose and meaning in their lives compared to their nonreligious peers. However, we know of no study that has examined the hypothesis articulated by Smith (2003) that religious involvement affects positive development by fostering religious identity that affords a sense of purpose and meaning in life.

In addition, we examined whether religious identity, cultivated through religious involvement, also cultivates a sense of well-being as established in previous research (Donahue & Benson, 1995). Further, other work has shown that adolescents' religious identities provide a mediating mechanism that can explain how their participation in religious activities is associated with a greater sense of well-being (Greenfield & Marks, 2007); in this study, we examined if immigrant adolescents' religious identity mediates the relation of their religious involvement and their sense of well-being. Our hypothesis is that religious identity is important in mediating many of the effects of religiosity on developmental outcomes (Roeser, Issac, Abo-Zena, Brittain, & Peck, 2008b) and that the process by which religious institutions socialize the young is rather universal (e.g., involvement affects identity and related senses of purpose), whereas the particular content of this socialization process is culturally and temporally situated. Thus, we expected religious identities to be stronger among immigrant youth who show more frequent behavioral engagement in religious activities, and that their religious identity in turn would be associated with a sense of purpose and well-being.

A second mediating mechanism we investigated concerns the role of social support. As Smith (2003) theorized, the social resources available to individuals who participate in religious organizations are considerable. Furthermore, some evidence shows that social support mediates the link between religious affiliation and well-being in adults (George et al., 2002). We expected that perceived social support from adults would be higher for immigrant youth who participated more in religious institutions and activities, and that such support would be linked to youths' well-being, especially given youths' needs for belonging and support in their new homeland (Roeser et al., 2008b).

A third mediating mechanism between religious involvement and PYD we explored concerned adolescents' self-reported peers and their values. The fostering of active religious institutional involvement among youth is often a conscious parenting process on the part of adults to steer their children toward positive peers and away from those who encourage involvement in risk behavior (Smith, 2003). Indeed, peer relationships formed in the context of religious congregations have been shown to predict both reduced contact with negative peers (Schreck, Burek, & Clark-Miller, 2007) and decreased risk behaviors (King, Furrow, & Roth, 2002). Thus, we expect affiliations with peers with prosocial values will be stronger among immigrant youth who show more frequent behavioral engagement in religious activities, and that such peer associations, in turn, will be associated with less involvement in risk behavior.

In sum, we sought to explore the link between religious involvement and indicators of PYD (i.e., purpose, well-being, and low levels of risk behaviors) among a sample of immigrant-origin youth, as well as three potential processes that might mediate such relations, including religious identity, social support, and positive peer affiliations. We hypothesized that (1) involvement in religious practices would be associated with a religious identity that is linked with a sense of meaning and purpose in life and a sense of well-being; (2) religious involvement would be correlated with social support, which in turn would mediate relations between their religious involvement and well-being; and (3) religious involvement would be coupled with lower levels of engagement in risk behaviors and associated with higher levels of positive peer affiliations.

Participants

A diverse sample ($N = 222$; 47.5% female) of middle school (27.9%), high school (36.3%), and college-aged (35.8%) immigrant participants (11 to 24 years old), completed surveys assessing aspects of religion/spirituality and PYD. The sample was racially and religiously diverse. Participants' self-identified religious affiliations were Christian (60%), other religions (9%), nonreligious (8%), Muslim (7%), multiple religions (7%), atheist (6%), and Jewish (3%). Data about the number of participants in each Christian denomination were not used in the present research. The sample was 29% multiethnic, 27% Asian American, 20% Hispanic, 16% white, 3% African American, 4% other, and 1% none reported. In addition, based on participant self-report, 29.6% belonged to 1.5-generation families and 69.4% belonged to second-generation immigrant families. We defined 1.5-generation individuals as children or adolescents who emigrate with their parents and second-generation as those who were born to immigrants in a host country (Portes & Rumbaut, 2001).

Procedures

Data came from the John Templeton Foundation (JTF)–supported study of "The Role of Spiritual Development in Growth of Purpose, Generosity, and Psychological Health in Adolescence" (Richard M. Lerner, PI). Participants included convenience samples of middle and high school as well as college students who were recruited from the greater Boston area. Middle and high school students completed study questionnaires in school and after-school settings. For these age groups, surveys were administered on handheld personal digital assistant (PDA) devices with voice enhancement. Participants were given a PDA, a pair of headphones, a stylus, and instructions about how to complete the survey at their own pace. Once the research team demonstrated how to use the PDA, participants independently completed the survey. For college students, recruitment was done via Web-based advertising and word of mouth. College students who agreed to be in the study were provided with a unique identification number and completed the survey through a Web-based survey platform.

Survey Measures

The survey consisted of established self-report measures drawn from the field (e.g., Fetzer Institute, 2003). The measures were all statistically reliable.

Religious Involvement

Religious involvement was indicated by self-reported frequency of engagement in various religious practices, such as praying or meditating by oneself or with a group, as well as attending religious services, schools, retreats, and youth groups. The validity and reliability of this measure has been demonstrated in previous research (Fetzer Institute, 2003; Smith & Denton, 2005). The scale items range from 1 = *never* to 11 = *several times a day*.

Positive Youth Development Indicators

Following in the tradition of research that emphasizes positive developmental outcomes in adolescents (e.g., Lerner et al., 2005; Lerner et al., 2008), we investigated the following indicators:

1. *Purpose.* Single item asking youth if they believe that their life has a purpose was asked (1 = *not at all true*, 5 = *very true*; purpose, adapted from Leffert et al., 1998).
2. *Well-being.* A three-item scale of subjective happiness and life satisfaction was used (Lerner et. al, 2005; Roeser et al., 2008a). Items ranged from 1 = *not at all happy*, 5 = *very happy/satisfied*).
3. *Risk Behaviors.* We asked youth about the frequency of their involvement in risk behaviors (e.g. drinking, smoking, drug use). These items ranged from 1 = *never* to 5 = *often* (five times or more in the past year), and items were modified from the PSL-AB Scale (Leffert et al., 1998) and the Monitoring the Future (2000) questionnaire.

Mediating Processes

We examined the following three factors as possible mediators of the relations between religious involvement and PYD:

1. *Religious Identity.* Participants were asked their identification with a religion, participants' identification of oneself as a religious person; and their religious worldview beliefs (Fetzer Institute, 2003; Koltko-Rivera, 2004; Roeser et al., 2008a).
2. *Social Support.* To measure social support, we created a sum of the number of 22 different people from which youth say they could seek assistance in the face of difficulties (Roeser et al., 2008b).
3. *Positive Peer Affiliations.* To measure positive peer affiliations, we asked youth how many of their friends demonstrated positive behaviors, such as good grades in school, volunteering, and caring about the environment (Roeser & Peck, 2003). These items ranged from 1 = *none* to 3 = *most of my friends*.

Demographic Characteristics

In order to account for the demographic backgrounds of the adolescents in our study, we included their sex, their age, and their self-reported proficiency in English in all analyses. Age was computed by subtracting the date of birth from the date of survey administration. For the purpose of analysis, participants were grouped based on self-reported grade levels into three age-related groups based on school context of middle school age (grades 6–8), high-school-age (grades 9–12), and college age (beyond grade 12 to age 23). Gender was determined by participants' self-reported response, with dichotomous choices of male or female provided. Participants' self-reported English proficiency was determined based on a four-item scale of how well participants reported understanding, speaking, reading, and writing English (Padilla & Gonzalez, 2001; Roeser & Peck, 2003). We were interested if religious involvement had incremental predictive validity for the mediators and outcomes after accounting for these demographic variables.

Data Analysis

Descriptive statistics and bivariate correlations among the religious involvement, PYD, and hypothesized mediating variables are summarized in Table 12.4. Consistent with the prerequisites for ascertaining mediating effects (e.g., Baron & Kenny, 1986), Table 12.4 presents significant correlations between the independent variable (religious involvement), the dependent variables (purpose, well-being, and risk behavior), and the mediators. These correlations are modest to small in size and range from −.16 to .28. Tests of mediation, therefore, involved seeing if such significant relations are reduced or eliminated in the presence of the hypothesized mediators.

Based on this pattern of bivariate relations, we next conducted a series of path analyses. First, we regressed the mediators on religious involvement controlling for participants' demographic characteristics. These results are presented in Table 12.5 and show that, as hypothesized, the more frequent immigrant youths' religious involvement, the stronger their religious identities, the greater their reported levels of social support, and the more likely youth were to say that their friends were characterized by prosocial values and behavior. The relations between religious involvement and these outcomes were significant after accounting for participants' demographic characteristics (see Table 12.5).

Having established a bivariate relation between the independent variable religious involvement and the PYD outcomes (Table 12.4) and a multivariate relation of the independent variable with each of the three mediators (Table 12.5), we moved on to test if the relation between the independent variable and the PYD outcomes was reduced in the regression equations that included the mediators (Baron & Kenny, 1986). For each of these final regression models, the three PYD outcomes (purpose, well-being, and lower levels of risk behaviors) were each regressed on the mediating variables, religious involvement, and demographic factors. Evidence for the hypothesized mediated effects was found and is presented in Table 12.6. The full results of the path analyses are presented in Figures 12.1 to 12.3.

In the first path analysis, we examined if immigrant adolescents' religious identity mediated the relation of their religious involvement and their sense of purpose. As shown in Figure 12.1 and Table 12.6, we found evidence that the relation of religious involvement and life purpose was mediated through religious identity as predicted. As shown in Table 12.6, the direct relation of religious

Table 12.4 Descriptive Statistics and Bivariate Correlations Among Religious Involvement, Hypothesized Mediating Processes, PYD Outcomes, and Demographic Characteristics

	1	2	3	4	5	6	7	8	9	10
1. Religious Involvement	—									
Hypothesized Mediators										
2. Religious Identity	.58**	—								
3. Social Support	.42**	.35**	—							
4. Positive Peer Affiliation	.25**	.13	.34**	—						
Positive Youth Development Outcomes										
5. Purpose	.28**	.46**	.23**	.18*	—					
6. Well Being	.22**	.13	.34**	.27**	.26**	—				
7. Risk Behaviors	−.16*	−.18**	−.18*	−.29**	−.19**	−.20**	—			
Participant Demographic Characteristics										
8. Sex (0 = male, 1 = female)	−.03	.04	−.10	.15*	.06	−.14**	−.17*	—		
9. Age	.00	−.08	.07	.23**	.08	.10	−.10	.10	—	
10. English Proficiency	−.21**	−.37**	−.13	.23**	−.23**	−.09	.19**	.05	.16*	—
Mean	3.15	−.17	8.75	2.23	4.03	3.63	1.85	.48	2.01	3.75
S.D.	2.01	.73	3.34	.39	1.20	.88	.67	.50	.80	.52
Range	1–10	−1.67 to 1.10	0–15	1–3	1–5	1–5	1–4	0–1	1–3	1–4

*p < .05; **p < .01.

Table 12.5 Standardized Beta Coefficients: Regression Analyses Predicting of Mediators with Frequency of Religious Involvement and Participant Demographic Characteristics

Predictors	Religious Identity	Social Support	Positive Peers
Involvement and Demography			
Religious Involvement	.55**	.40**	.43**
Sex (0 = male, 1 = female)	.08	−.09	.15*
Middle school-aged (1 = yes)	.19**	.05	−.31**
High-school-aged (1 = yes)	.23**	.15	−.21*
English proficiency	−.04	.03	.13
Adjusted R-Squared	.38	.16	.25

$^*p < .05; ^{**}p < .01.$

involvement and purpose is zero in the final equations. In addition, we found that positive peer affiliations also mediated this relation. To the extent that immigrant youth participated more in religious activities, they reported more prosocial friends, and such peer affiliation in turn positively predicted their sense of life purpose. No effect from social support to purpose was hypothesized or found. In the second path analysis, we examined if immigrant adolescents' self-reported

Table 12.6 Standardized Beta Coefficients: Regression Analyses Predicting of PYD Outcomes With Frequency of Religious Involvement, Participant Demographic Characteristics, and Mediating Processes as Predictors

Predictors	Sense of Purpose	Well-Being	Risk Behaviors
Involvement and Demography			
Frequency religious practices	.00	.00	−.11
Sex (0 = male, 1 = female)	.06	−.17*	−.08
Middle school-aged (1 = yes)	.20*	.25**	−.28**
High-school-aged (1 = yes)	.23**	.06	−.19*
English Proficiency	.17*	.15*	.14
Mediating Processes			
Religious Identity	.40**	−.03	−.01
Social Support	−.03	.18*	−.05
Positive Peer Affiliation	.19*	.24**	−.25**
Adjusted R-squares	.29	.28	.17

$^*p < .05; ^{**}p < .01.$

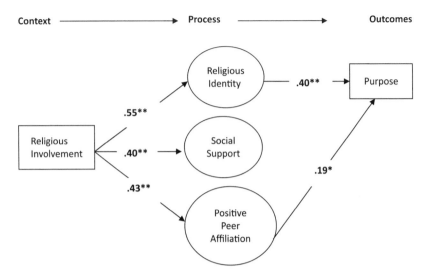

Only statistically significant effects are represented. Demographic effects are omitted from the figure for the sake of clarity. *$p < .05$, **$p < .01$.

Figure 12.1 Path analyses predicting purpose: Summary of standardized betas and adjusted R-squares, controlling for demographic factors.

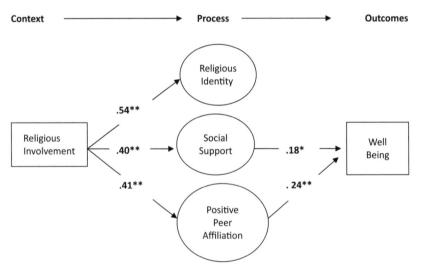

Only statistically significant effects are represented. Demographic effects are omitted from the figure for the sake of clarity. *$p < .05$, **$p < .01$.

Figure 12.2 Path analyses predicting well being: Summary of standardized betas and adjusted R-squares, controlling for demographic factors.

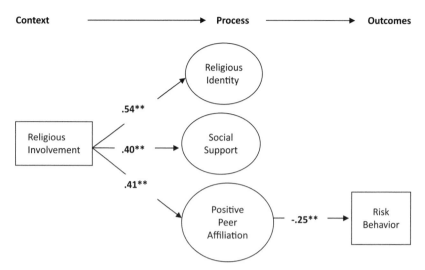

Only statistically significant effects are represented. Demographic effects are omitted from the figure for the sake of clarity. *p < .05, **p < .01.

Figure 12.3   Path analyses predicting engagement in risk behavior: Summary of standardized betas and adjusted R-squares, controlling for demographic factors.

levels of social support mediated the relation of their religious involvement and their sense of well-being.

As shown in Figure 12.2 and Table 12.6, we found evidence, as predicted, that the relation of religious involvement and well-being was mediated through social support. As one can see in Table 12.6, the direct relation of religious involvement and well-being is zero in the final equations. In addition, this relation was also mediated through positive peer affiliations. To the extent youth participated more, they felt more social support and reported a greater number of prosocial peers. These factors, in turn, predicted greater happiness and life satisfaction. No association between religious identity and well-being was found.

In the final path analysis, we examined if immigrant adolescents' self-reported peer affiliations mediated the relation of their religious involvement and the frequency of their engagement in various risk behaviors. As shown in Figure 12.3 and Table 12.6, we found evidence for this mediated relationship. As one can see in Table 12.6, the direct relation of religious involvement and well-being is reduced to nonsignificant in the final equations, whereas positive peer affiliations emerged as a significant negative predictor of youths' involvement in risk behavior. To the extent youth participated more in religious activities, they reported a greater number of prosocial peers and less involvement in risky behavior.

Discussion

As Holden and Vittrup (2009) state, "religion is a fundamental force of human development for most of the world's population" (p. 281). Further, immigrants are particularly likely to be religious; they are apt to be more religious than the average native-born resident of the ever more secular, postmodern nation-states, to which they migrate. Moreover, the experience of immigration is likely to redouble their faiths (Foley & Hoge, 2007). As the data in the first study presented here indicate, immigrant-origin children are likely to come of age in religious homes, and many will internalize religious beliefs and values held by their parents, and perhaps carry these practices into their late adolescence and adult lives. The second study demonstrated the important health-promotion and protective functions of religious involvement and its effects on identity formation and the social networks that 1.5- and second-generation young adults are exposed to and develop during adolescence.

From Study 1, we learned that, for first-generation adolescents from Mexico, the Dominican Republic, Central America, and Haiti, religion plays a promi-nent role in their lives. Their parents taught them about religion and indicated that they regularly attended church; the adolescents confirmed this information. This finding is consistent with previous research demonstrating how adolescents tend to carry forward their parents' religious convictions and practices (Holden & Vittrup, 2009). Given the countries of origin from which they arrived, not surpris-ingly, the majority of participants practiced Catholicism (Pew Hispanic Center, 2007). Our data, however, showed a high proportion of conversions to Evangel-ical or Pentecostal faiths, which is consistent with the trends reported in other research (Pew Hispanic Center, 2007; Vasquez, 2005).

Immigrant youth spoke eloquently about the role of God and religion in their lives. Some noted that religion served as a moral compass for how to (or how not to) behave (Malinowski, 1948; Smith & Denton, 2005; Weber, 1905/2008). For some it was a north star guiding them in the right direction, whereas for others it provided warnings of danger ahead. In both cases, the participants' responses gave indication of how religion could function as a way to deter risk behaviors. Other youth spoke of the warm, encompassing protective function of religion. For some, simply knowing God provided ever-present comfort, whereas for others, God was someone to turn to in moments of crisis and need.

Participant responses also distinguished between (a) *religious actions*, (b) *reli-gious values*, and (c) the *belief* in God and religion. Some adolescents spoke about their active participation in religion, such as going to church or praying, whereas others made the distinction between believing in God and formal religion, and still others (mostly the Chinese youth) casually noted that they were not in-volved in religious practices. Many participants talked about how their affiliation to a church was a continuation of a family value that they had been taught and that they honored (Holden & Vittrup, 2009). For a last group of youth, the role of God was central and obvious in their lives, yet they could not articulate any specific function of religion; they seemed almost mystified by the question, as they affirmed the importance of religion in their lives. "I was raised to believe in God," a Mexican teenager told us. This unwavering faith at the end of adolescence was a value, a belief, and a practice expressed by a majority of the youth in this study.

In Study 2, we considered the role of religion and participation in religious community for various positive development outcomes (i.e., sense of purpose, reported well-being, and lower risk behaviors) for a diverse sample of 1.5- and second-generation immigrant-origin youth. We learned that religious involvement was positively related to the belief that life has a purpose and that the relation was mediated through both religious identity and positive peer affiliation. Religious involvement was also positively related to well-being, and social support and positive peer affiliation mediated this relationship. Finally, the more youth were involved in religious activities, the less they were likely to report engaging in risk behaviors; again, this relationship was mediated by positive peer affiliation. These findings are consistent with the theorizing of Smith (2003) and provided evidence of the hypothesized mediating relationships that may explain in part why religious involvement affects positive youth development.

Overall, the findings in this chapter support the general hypothesis about the important role of religion in the lives of immigrant-origin youth and thus represent findings among this understudied group. Worship communities play a vital role in supporting immigrant-origin youth in numerous ways. These communities can provide immigrants with some semblance of the cultural community they left behind and, thus, with a ripe context for identity development, social support, and positive peer affiliation. These communities can serve as "a familiar anchor in the midst of novel and challenging experiences associated with adaptation to a new country" (Juang & Syed, 2008, p. 268). They provide refuge and serve as a source of psychological (Hirschman, 2004), social (Min, 2000), and instrumental (Hirschman, 2004) support. Such a social network has several protective functions that may mediate the relationship between religious involvement and positive outcomes.

Limitations

The first study was designed not with the intention of studying religious practices and their connection to a variety of outcomes, such as well-being and academic performance. Further, although LISA is a longitudinal study, religious values, beliefs, and practices were not captured longitudinally. Lastly, the sample was one of convenience. Random sampling was not possible given the specific inclusion criteria of the study, the need for signed permission forms from school personnel and parents, and the required commitment of five years of participation. These criteria limit our ability to generalize from this sample to the larger immigrant youth population. However, comparisons between our descriptive statistics (parental education, parental employment, etc.) and census data descriptions of each target population's recent immigrants revealed similar profiles (Suárez-Orozco et al.,

2008). Our sample was also largely Latin American and Caribbean (and thus heavily Catholic); while such a sample represents more than half of the immigrants currently entering the United States (Pew Hispanic Center, 2007), it does not capture the rich religious diversity of immigrant experience (Eck, 2002).

Although Study 2 expands beyond past empirical work on adolescent religiosity by including a large sample of previously underrepresented groups of religious minorities (e.g., Muslims), the sample sizes for most of the subgroups are small. In the context of this limitation, our contributions to the extant literature are modest. Ideally, in future research, there would be a larger sample of each religious and nonreligious cohort in order to ensure diversity within each religious group in terms of age and gender, as well as other sources of diversity such as ethnic affiliation and frequency of religious practice by the participant and their family. Study 2 was designed to explore the role of religious involvement in certain positive outcomes for a diverse sample of youth, but it was not designed to explore the particular context of immigrant-origin youth.

Even though significant findings from this cross-sectional study may point to some developmental processes, Study 2 does not provide the longitudinal data required to indicate developmental change or, specifically, to highlight the intersection between religion, positive development, and the acculturative process. Although the finding that positive peer affiliation mediates the relationship between religious involvement and each of the three positive outcomes indicates that peer relationships may do more than simply buffer risk behaviors, a longitudinal exploration into the role of peer relationships, as well as other explanatory pathways, is needed. Qualitative research examining the processes at play would also provide critical insights.

Nonetheless, taken together, these two unique data sets afforded a glimpse into the important role of religion in the lives of immigrant-origin youth. These data provided evidence that religion is indeed important for immigrant youth and that religious involvement and participation in religious communities are associated with positive outcomes.

FUTURE RESEARCH

Future research will need to address many topics in what should become a burgeoning field at the intersection of immigration, religion, and developmental studies. It is vital that more diverse samples be included, representing a range of religious orientations and practices. Research that considers how transnational beliefs, values, and practices influence child development would be particularly valuable (Levitt, 2007). Interdisciplinary efforts that concurrently take into consideration developmental, intrapsychic and behavioral (psychological), social (sociological), and cultural (anthropological) perspectives would shed the greatest light on this complex domain.

Gendered patterns of socialization and participation would be important to consider. Qualitatively, we noted that girls were often more articulate in their responses. Further, though we did not present these data here, we noticed a trend in which grandmothers, aunts, and mothers took a more active role in the religious socialization of youth in the predominantly Catholic sample of Study 1. Future studies should actively examine gender.

It is important to conduct studies that examine developmental trajectories from mid-to-late adolescence through adulthood. As such, longitudinal research is vital. Clearly, during early childhood, parental socializing influences are very strong. In our sample, these influences carried into late adolescence. Do these influences continue across ontogeny? Even well-designed cross-sectional studies cannot shed light on these changing patterns; again, longitudinal studies are essential.

It also would be important to develop studies examining first-, second-, and third-generation immigrants, as research suggests that these patterns work differently across generations (Foner & Alba, 2008; Hirschman, 2007). Whereas in the first generation the role of the church may principally serve to maintain ethnic identity, in subsequent generations its function may be more to Americanize. But the intersection between an individual immigrant's development and religion is likely to vary across receiving contexts; in Europe, which is more secular and has less of a history of religious pluralism and tolerance, immigrant religious communities may work in the opposite direction, serving to solidify and even rigidify ethnic identity through religious and cultural practices (Foner & Alba, 2008).

Tied to the generational issue is the use of language in ceremonies and other kinds of accommodations that churches, temples, and mosques are willing to make for the second generation and beyond, in order to make them feel welcome members of the faith community. Because language attrition is a prevalent problem across generations, how connected can immigrants feel if they do not understand what is being said?

Conversion is another interesting phenomenon. Our data show that parents are converting. Do children maintain the original religious affiliation of their parents, or do children also convert? If children do convert, do they eventually lose their attachment to Pentecostal and Evangelical faiths, which require a large time commitment?

Using qualitative, quantitative, as well as mixed-method approaches, we need to examine the ways in which religious beliefs, practices, and ties to faith-based communities are linked to various indicators of PYD for immigrant-origin youth, such as optimism, future outlook, peer relations, relative abstention from risk behaviors, academic engagement, and family relations, among others. What processes make a difference in these various outcomes?

We should also consider the potential negative effects of involvement in religious communities. These negative effects may arise when there are tensions between family beliefs and practices and the receiving communities in which they arrive; when parents have different beliefs, such as when one parent converts and another does not; when an adolescent begins to resist regular church attendance—these scenarios are important areas of study.

Intervention studies examining ways in which links with religious communities can facilitate integration for immigrant families is another important area of research. Immigrants trust their religious communities in ways they often do not trust outsiders. Thus, worship communities and religious organizations are potential spaces with which schools, after-school programs, and intervention programs could and should make liaisons if they want to successfully reach immigrant families. Research assessing intervention partnerships could be an excellent contribution to the field.

IMPLICATIONS

Taken together, these two exploratory studies have implications for our understanding of immigrant youth, human development, and religion. These unique data sets provide a window into the importance of religion in the lives of a portion of "the neglected 95%" (Arnett, 2008). The immigrant youth spoke quite clearly—for most, God and religion are important. Religion was probably important for their families before they arrived, but the transition of immigration may have further brought religion to the forefront of their lives. Malinowski (1948) argued that religion provides a charter for belief in uncertain times. As immigrant youth move from one culture to another, they are in a state of "betwixt and between" (Turner, 1969), often living in conditions of liminality (van Gennep, 1960), uncertainty, and transition. Disorientation is a part of the immigrant experience: "I had to learn all over again how to talk, how to dress, how to eat," a young Mexican informant once summarized (Suárez-Orozco & Suárez-Orozco, 2001). Immigrant parents, whose compass in an unknown territory may also be a bit off-kilter, are often not able to guide their children in the rules of the new land. Thus, predictable rituals (Turner, 1969) that religion offers, as well as its protective umbrella, serve an even greater human need than they might have prior to migration.

The qualitative themes articulated by the youth were quite clear. Religion provides guidance on how to behave or not to behave—all the more necessary when the rules in the new land may not be so evident. Religion provides a sense of ever-present protection in an uncertain, unsafe, and sometimes hostile new environment, and God is someone to ask for explicit help when one needs it. Further, the quantitative data demonstrated that religious involvement is associated with three separate positive youth outcomes—sense of purpose, reported well-being, and abstention from risk behaviors—demonstrating the protective function of religion in immigrant youth's lives.

Worship communities provide a system of belonging, social supports, and social networks. For immigrants, these communities provide a social center of co-ethnics, providing religious and cultural continuity across the span of borders (Levitt, 2007). Worship communities provide spaces where religious rituals that are encoded in the culture can be practiced collectively, serving to stabilize cultural traditions (Turner, 1969). For immigrant adolescent newcomers, who often report feelings of deep loneliness (Suárez-Orozco, Pimentel, & Martin, 2009), worship communities may become sources of important friendships and "surrogate families" (Cao, 2005, p. 183). These important supportive relationships (Suárez-Orozco et al., 2009), networks of information and tangible help (Portes & Rumbaut, 2006), as well as advocacy (Hondagneu-Sotelo, 2007) provided by the worship communities, are likely critical factors that contribute to mediating positive youth outcomes.

REFERENCES

Alba, R., & Nee, V. (2003). *Remaking the American mainstream: Assimilation and contemporary immigration.* Cambridge, MA: Harvard University Press.

Arnett, J. J. (2008). The neglected 95%: Why American psychology needs to become less American. *American Psychologist, 63*(7), 602–614.

Ball, J., Armistead, L., & Austin, B.-J. (2003). The relationship between religiosity and adjustment among African-American, female, urban adolescents. *Journal of Adolescence, 26,* 431–446.

Bankston, C. L., & Zhou, M. (1995). Religious participation, ethnic identification and adaptation of Vietnamese adolescents in and immigrant community. *Sociological Quarterly, 36,* 523–534.

Baron, R. M., & Kenny, D. A. (1986). The moderator-mediator variable distinction in social psychological research: Conceptual, strategic, and statistical considerations. *Journal of Personality and Social Psychology, 51,* 1173–1182.

Benson, P. L., Scales, P. C., Sesma, A., Jr., & Roehlkepartain, E. C. (2005). Adolescent spirituality. In K. A. Moore & L. H. Lippman (Eds.), *What do children need to flourish? Conceptualizing and measuring indicators of positive development* (pp. 25–40). New York, NY: Springer.

Berger, P. L. (1974). Some second thoughts on substantive versus functional definitions of religion. *Journal for the Scientific Study of Religion, 13*(2), 125–133.

Berry, J. W., Phinney, J. S., Sam, D. L., & Vedder, P. (Eds.). (2006). *Immigrant youth in cultural transition: Acculturation, identity, and adaptation across national contexts.* Mahwah, NJ: Erlbaum.

Bridges, L. J., & Moore, K. A. (2002). *Religion and spirituality in childhood and adolescence.* Washington, DC: Child Trends.

Cao, N. (2005). The church as a surrogate family for working class immigrant Chinese youth: An ethnography of segmented assimilation. *Sociology of Religion, 66*(2), 183–200.

Donahue, M. J., & Benson, P. L. (1995). Religion and the well being of adolescents. *Journal of Social Issues, 51,* 145–160.

Dowling, E. M., Gestsdottir, S., Anderson, P., von Eye, A., & Lerner, R. M. (2003). Spirituality, religiosity, and thriving among adolescents: Identification and confirmation of factor structures. *Applied Developmental Science, 7*(4), 253–260.

Dowling, E. M., Gestsdottir, S., Anderson, P., von Eye, A., Almerigi, J., & Lerner, R. M. (2004). Structural relations among spirituality, religiosity, and thriving in adolescence. *Applied Developmental Science*, 9(1), 7–16.

Durkheim, E. (1912/2008). *The elementary forms of the religious life*. New York, NY: Oxford University Press.

Eck, D. L. (2002). *A new religious America: How a "Christian Country" has become the world's most religiously diverse nation*. New York, NY: HarperCollins.

Ellison, C. G. (1991). Religious involvement and subjective well-being. *Journal of Health and Social Behavior*, 32(1), 80–99.

Falicov, C. J. (1998). *Latino families in therapy: A guide to multicultural practice*. New York, NY: Guilford Press.

Faulstich-Orellana, M. (2009). *Translating childhoods: Immigrant youth, language, and culture*. Piscataway, NJ: Rutgers Press.

Foley, M. W., & Hoge, D. R. (2007). *Religion and the new immigrants: How faith communities form our newest citizens*. Oxford, England: Oxford University Press.

Foner, N., & Alba, R. (2008). Immigrant religion in the U.S. and Western Europe: Bridge or barrier to inclusion? *International Migration Research*, 42(2), 360–392.

Fetzer Institute, & National Institute on Aging Working Group. (2003). *Measurement of religiousness/spirituality for use in health research: A report of the Fetzer Institute/National Institute on Aging Working Group*. Kalamazoo, MI: Fetzer Institute.

Francis, L. J. (2000). The relationship between Bible reading and purpose in life among 13–15 year olds. *Mental Health, Religion & Culture*, 3, 27–36.

Freud, S. (1913/2009). *Totem and taboo: Resemblances between the psychic lives of savages and neurotics*. Elbridge, NY: BiblioBazzar.

Furrow, J. L., King, P. E., & White, K. (2004). Religion and positive youth development: Identity, meaning, and pro-social concerns. *Applied Developmental Science*, 8(1), 17–26.

García-Coll, C., & Magnuson, K. (1997). The psychological experience of immigration: A developmental perspective. In A. Booth, A. C. Crouter, & N. Landale (Eds.), *Immigration and the family* (pp. 91–132). Mahwah, NJ: Erlbaum.

George, L. K., Ellison, C. G., & Larson, D. B. (2002). Explaining the relationships between religious involvement and health. *Psychological Inquiry*, 13, 190–200.

Greenfield, E., & Marks, N. F. (2007). Religious social identity as an exploratory factor for associations between more frequent formal religious participation and psychological well-being. *International Journal for the Psychology of Religion*, 17(3), 245–259.

Hernandez, D., Denton, N., & McCartney, S. (2007). *Family circumstances of children in immigrant families: Looking to the future of America*. New York. NY: Guilford Press.

Hirschman, C. (2004). The role of religion in the origins and adaptation of immigrant groups in the United States. *International Migration Review*, 38, 1206–1233.

Hirschman, C. (2007). The role of religion in the origins and adaptation of immigrant groups in the United States. In A. Portes & J. DeWind (Eds.), *Rethinking migration: New theoretical and empirical perspectives*. New York, NY: Berghahn Books.

Holden, G. W., & Vittrup B. (2009). Religion. In M. H. Bornstein (Ed.), *Handbook of cultural developmental science* (pp. 279–295). New York, NY: Routledge.

Hondagneu-Sotelo, P. (Ed.). (2007). *Religion and social justice for immigrants*. New Brunswick, NJ: Rutgers University Press.

James, W. (1902/2009). *The varieties of religious experience: A study in human nature*. Charlotte, NC: Information Age Publishing.

Jessor, R. (1991). Risk behavior in adolescence: A psychosocial framework for understanding and action. *Journal of Adolescent Health, 12*(8), 597–605.

Juang, L., & Syed, L. M. (2008). Ethnic identity and spirituality. In R. M. Lerner, R. W. Roeser, & E. Phelps (Eds.), *Positive youth development and spirituality: From theory to research* (pp. 262–284). West Conshohocken, PA: Templeton Foundation Press.

King, P. E., & Furrow, J. L. (2004). Religion as a resource for positive youth development: Religion, social capital, and moral outcomes. *Developmental Psychology, 40*(5), 703–713.

King, P. E., Furrow, J. L., & Roth, N. (2002). The influence of families and peers on adolescent religiousness. *Journal of Psychology and Christianity, 21*(2), 109–120.

King, P. D., & Roeser, R. W. (2009). Religion and spirituality in adolescent development. In R. M. Lerner & L. Steinberg (Eds.), *Handbook of adolescent psychology* (3rd ed., pp. 435–478). Hoboken, NJ: Wiley.

Koltko-Rivera, M. E. (2004). The psychology of worldviews. *Review of General Psychology, 8*, 3–58.

Leffert, N., Benson, P. L., Scales, P. C., Sharma, A. R., Drake, D. R., & Blyth, D. A. (1998). Developmental assets: Measurement and prediction of risk behaviors among adolescents. *Applied Developmental Science, 2*(4), 209–230.

Lerner, R. M., Lerner, J. V., Almerigi, J., & Theokas, C. (2005). Positive youth development: Current research perspectives. *Journal of Early Adolescence, 25*(1), 10–16.

Lerner, R. M., Roeser, R. W., & Phelps, E. (Eds.). (2008). *Positive youth development and spirituality: From theory to research*. West Conshohocken, PA: Templeton Foundation Press.

Levitt, P. (2007). *God needs no passports: Immigrants and the changing American religious landscape*. New York, NY: New Press.

Malinowski, B. (1948). *Magic, science, religion, and other essays*. Glencoe, IL: Free Press.

Marcia, J. (1966). Development and validation of ego-identity status. *Journal of Personality and Social Psychology, 3*, 551–558.

Mariano, J. M., & Damon, W. (2008). The role of spirituality and religious faith in supporting purpose in adolescence. In R. M. Lerner, R. W. Roeser, & E. Phelps (Eds.), *Positive youth development and spirituality: From theory to research* (pp. 210–230). West Conshohocken, PA: Templeton Foundation Press.

Markstrom, C. A. (1999). Religious involvement and adolescent psychosocial development. *Journal of Adolescence, 22*, 205–221.

Martin, T. F., White, J. M., & Perlman, D. (2003). Religious socialization: A test of the channeling hypothesis of parental influence on adolescent faith maturity. *Journal of Adolescent Research*, 18(2), 169–187.

Marx, K., & Engels, F. (2002). *Marx and Engels on religion*. Fredonia, NY: Fredonia Press.

Mattis, J. S., Grayman, N. A., Cowle, S., Winston, C., Watson, C., & Jackson, D. (2008). Intersectional identities and the politics of altruistic care in a low-income, urban community. *Sex Roles*, 59, 418–428.

Michalak, L., Trocki, K., & Bond, J. (2007). Religion and alcohol in the U.S. National Alcohol Survey: How important is religion for abstention and drinking? *Drug and Alcohol Dependence*, 87(2-3), 268–280.

Miles, M., & Huberman, A. (1994). *Qualitative data analysis: A sourcebook* (2nd ed.). Thousand Oaks, CA: Sage.

Min, P. G. (2000). The structure and social functions of Korean immigrant churches in the United States. In M. Zhou & J. V. Gatewood (Eds.), *Contemporary Asian America: A multidisciplinary reader* (pp. 372–390). New York: New York University Press.

Min, P. G. (2005). Religion and the maintenance of ethnicity among immigrants: A comparison of Hindus and Korean Protestants. In K. Leonard, A. Stepick, M. A. Vasquez, & J. Holdaway (Eds.), *Immigrant faiths: Transforming religious life in America* (pp. 11–38). Lanham, MD: Alta Mira Press.

Monitoring the Future. (2000). *National survey on drug use, 1975–2000*. Bethesda, MD: National Institute on Drug Abuse.

Noh, S., Beiser, M., Kaspar, V., Hou, F., & Rummens, J. (1999). Perceived racial discrimination, depression, and coping: A study of Southeast Asian refugees in Canada. *The Journal of Health and Social Behavior*, 40, 193–207.

Nooney, J. G. (2005). Religion, stress, and mental health in adolescence: Findings from Add Health. *Review of Religious Research*, 46(4), 341–354.

Padilla, A. M., & Gonzalez, R. (2001). Academic performance of immigrant and U.S.-born Mexican heritage students: Effects of schooling in Mexico and bilingual/English language instruction. *American Educational Research Journal*, 38(3), 727–742.

Pew Forum on Religion and Public Life. (2008). *U.S. religious landscape survey*. Washington, DC: Pew Research Center.

Pew Hispanic Center. (2007). *Changing faiths: Latinos and the transformation of American religion*. Washington, DC: Pew Hispanic Center.

Pew Hispanic Center. (2009). *Between two worlds: How young Latinos come of age in America*. Washington, DC: Pew Hispanic Center.

Portes, A., & Rumbaut, R. G. (2001). *Legacies: The story of the immigrant second generation*. Berkeley: University of California Press.

Portes, A., & Rumbaut, R. G. (2006). *Immigrant America: A portrait*. Berkeley: University of California Press.

Regenerus, M. D. (2000). Shaping schooling success: Religious socialization and educational outcomes in metropolitan public schools. *Journal of the Scientific Study of Religion*, 39(3), 363–370.

Regenerus, M. D. (2003). Religion and positive adolescent outcomes: A review of research and theory. *Review of Religious Research, 44*(4), 394–413.

Regenerus, M. D., Smith, C., & Smith, B. (2004). Social context in the development of adolescent religiosity. *Applied Developmental Science, 8*(1), 27–38.

Roehlkepartain, E. C., King, P. E., Wagener, L. M., & Benson, P. L. (2005). *The handbook of spiritual development in childhood and adolescence* (The SAGE Program on Applied Developmental Science). New York, NY: Sage.

Roeser, R. W., Galloway, M., Casey-Cannon, S., Watson, C., Keller, L., & Tan, E. (2008a). Identity representations in patterns of school achievement and well-being among early adolescent girls: Variable- and person-centered approaches. *Journal of Early Adolescence, 28*, 115–152.

Roeser, R. W., Issac, S. S., Abo-Zena, M., Brittian, A., & Peck, S. J. (2008b). Self and identity processes in spirituality and positive youth development. In R. M. Lerner, R. W. Roeser, & E. Phelps (Eds.), *Positive youth development and spirituality: From theory to research* (pp. 74–105). West Conshohocken, PA: Templeton Foundation Press.

Roeser, R. W., & Peck, S. C. (2003). Patterns and pathways of educational achievement across adolescence: A holistic-developmental perspective. In W. Damon (Series Ed.) & S. C. Peck & R. W. Roeser (Vol. Eds.), *New directions for child and adolescent development: Vol. 101, Person-centered approaches to studying development in context* (pp. 39–62). San Francisco, CA: Jossey-Bass.

Rostosky, S. S., Wilcox, B. L., Wright, M. L. C., & Randall, B. A. (2004). The impact of religiosity on adolescent sexual behavior: A review of the evidence. *Journal of Adolescent Research, 19*, 677–697.

Schreck, C. J., Burek, M. W., & Clark-Miller, J. (2007). He sends rain upon the wicked: A panel study of the influence of religiosity on violent victimization. *Journal of Interpersonal Violence, 22*, 872–893.

Smith, C. (2003). Theorizing religious effects among American adolescents. *Journal for the Scientific Study of Religion, 42*, 17–30.

Smith, C., & Denton, M. L. (2005). *Soul searching: The religious and spiritual lives of American teenagers.* New York, NY: Oxford University Press.

Spiro, M. E. (1987). *Culture and human nature.* Chicago, IL: University of Chicago Press.

Steinman, K. J., & Zimmerman, M. A. (2004). Religious activity and risk behavior among African American adolescents: Concurrent and developmental effects. *American Journal of Community Psychology, 33*(3/4), 151–161.

Stepick, A. (2005). God is apparently not dead: The obvious, the emergent, and the still unknown in immigration and religion. In K. Leonard, A. Stepick, M. A. Vasquez, & J. Holdaway (Eds.), *Immigrant faiths: Transforming religious life in America* (pp. 11–38). Lanham, MD: Alta Mira Press.

Strauss, A., & Corbin, J. (1990). *Basics of qualitative research: Grounded theory procedures and techniques.* Newbury Park, CA: Sage.

Suárez-Orozco, C. (2004). Formulating identity in a globalized world. In M. Suárez-Orozco & D. B. Qin-Hilliard (Eds.), *Globalization: Culture and education in the new millennium* (pp. 173–202). Berkeley: University of California Press.

Suárez-Orozco, C., Pimentel, A., & Martin, M. (2009). The significance of relationships: Academic engagement and achievement among newcomer immigrant youth. *Teacher's College Review, 111*(3), 712–749.

Suárez-Orozco, C., & Qin-Hillard, D. B. (2004). The cultural psychology of academic engagement: Immigrant boys' experiences in U.S. schools. In N. Way & J. Chu (Eds.), *Adolescent boys: Exploring diverse cultures of boyhood*. New York: New York University Press.

Suárez-Orozco, C., & Suárez-Orozco, M. M. (2001). *Children of immigration*. Cambridge, MA: Harvard University Press.

Suárez-Orozco, C., Suárez-Orozco, M. M., & Todorova, I. (2008). *Learning a new land*. Cambridge, MA: Harvard University Press.

Terrazas, A., & Batalva, J. (2008). U.S. in focus: The most up-to-date frequently requested statistics on immigrants in the United States. Washington, DC: Migration Policy Institute. http://www.migrationinformation.org/USfocus/display.cfm?ID=714 (Accessed May 30, 2009).

Turner, V. W. (1969). *The ritual process: Structure and anti-structure*. Chicago, IL: Aldine.

U.S. Census Bureau. (2000). Selected characteristics of the native and foreign-born populations. American community survey. http://factfinder.census.gov/servlet/STTable?_bm=y&-geo_id=01000US&-qr_name=ACS_2007_1YR_G00_S0501&-ds_name=ACS_2007_1YR_G00_&-_lang=en&-redoLog=false (Accessed June 28, 2009).

U.S. Census Bureau. (2006). American community survey. Table B15002i: Sex by Educational Attainment for the Population 25 Years and over. http://factfinder.census.gov/servlet/DTTable?_bm=y&-state=dt&-ds_name=ACS_2006_EST_G00_&-CONTEXT=dt&-mt_name=ACS_2006_EST_G2000_B15002I&-redoLog=true&-_caller=geoselect&-geo_id=01000US&-geo_id=NBSP&-format=&-_lang=en (Accessed June 28, 2009)

van Gennep, A. (1960). *The rites of passage*. Chicago, IL: University of Chicago Press.

Vasquez, M. A. (2005). Historicizing and materializing the study of religion: The contribution of migration studies. In K. Leonard, A. Stepick, M. A. Vasquez, & J. Holdaway (Eds.), *Immigrant faiths: Transforming religious life in America* (pp. 11–38). Lanham, MD: Alta Mira Press.

Wallace, A. F. (1956). Revitalization movements. *American Anthropologist, 58*(2), 264–281.

Weber, M. (1905/2008). *The Protestant ethic and the spirit of capitalism*. Charlotte, NC: Information Age Publishing.

Wong, Y. J., Rew, L., & Slaikeu, K. D. (2006). A systematic review of recent research on adolescent religiosity/spirituality and mental health. *Issues in Mental Health Nursing, 27*(2), 161–183.

13

The Interplay of Self-Transcendence and Psychological Maturity Among Israeli College Students

OFRA MAYSELESS AND PNINIT RUSSO-NETZER

INTRODUCTION

Spirituality is considered a core, universal facet of human development (for a review, see Oser, Scarlett, & Bucher, 2006; Wulff, 1997). Yet, for several decades it has been relegated to a peripheral place within the developmental science literature (Roehlkepartain, Benson, King, & Wagener, 2005). Pertinent to such neglect is a conceptual and empirical lacuna in investigating the place of spiritual development vis-à-vis other domains of development, such as emotional development (but see discussions of these issues in Lerner, Roeser, & Phelps, 2008).

This chapter presents the results of a study conducted with Israeli youth that examined the interplay of spiritual development and the development of psychological and emotional maturity. The transition from adolescence to adulthood has been recognized as an important and crucial developmental phase, in which youth develop their identity to become emotionally mature adults in their society (Arnett, 2000; Donnellan, Conger, & Burzette, 2007). Consequently, it is an especially significant period to examine the interplay between these two realms.

We first discuss several conceptualizations that suggest how these two domains may be related and then present the study, which examined concurrent associations between these two realms of development and psychosocial characteristics in four areas: self-perceptions, orientation to others, values, and the relational context. We conclude with a discussion of the findings, which accord with some of the conceptualizations and highlight the urgent need to undertake longitudinal research to examine how these two lines of development are interrelated.

SPIRITUALITY AND SPIRITUAL DEVELOPMENT

Despite the existence of a large number of current approaches to and definitions of spiritual development, most incorporate several common themes. These themes include an aspect of transcendence that reflects a realization that "there exists a broader paradigm for understanding existence that transcends the immediacy of our own individual consciousness and that binds all things into a more unitive harmony" (Piedmont, 1999, p. 988). In line with this viewpoint, the development of spirituality is thought to involve the development of the capacity of individuals to consider and experience this transcendence and this unity and to act accordingly (Lerner et al., 2008). A related theme focuses on meaning and suggests that spirituality involves addressing ultimate questions about the nature, purpose, and meaning of life, thus constructing a relationship to the sacred (e.g., Kiesling, Sorell, Montgomery, & Colwell, 2006). In line with Benson, Roehlkepartain, and Rude (2003, pp. 205–206), we refer to both themes and define *spiritual development* as the "process of growing the intrinsic human capacity for self-transcendence, in which the self is embedded in something greater than the self, including the sacred. It is the developmental engine that propels the search for connectedness, meaning, purpose, and contribution."

Following Lerner et al. (2008), we assessed spiritual development in this study by reference mostly to its transcendent aspect. In line with many other scholars and extant research findings (e.g., Benson, Roehlkepartain, & Rude, 2003; Lerner et al., 2008), we contend that spiritual development and self-transcendence are cultivated both within and outside religious traditions. Hence, belonging to a religious community does not have to be a necessary precursor of such development. This is especially pertinent to the Israeli context, which unlike the United States, includes a majority of individuals who perceive themselves as secular and even have negative views regarding traditional religiosity (Ezrachi, 2004). In terms of antecedents of spiritual development and based on studies assessing religious involvement of youth (Furrow, King, & White, 2004; Hunsberger, Pratt, & Pancer, 2001; Markstrom, 1999), it seems plausible that a warm and accepting relational context will be fertile ground for the promotion of such development. Yet, difficult relational background and interpersonal challenges may also promote seeking of spiritual meaning and the development of spirituality and transcendence (Kirkpatrick, 1999). Thus, the developmental path from relational context to spiritual development may be complex.

In terms of psychosocial outcomes of spiritual development, self-transcendence, which involves the capacity to extend beyond the self, is expected to be associated with corresponding values, such as having a strong social conscience and low endorsement of material and self-aggrandizement values. Furthermore, self-transcendence should also be revealed in positive orientation toward others, such as in empathy, benevolence, and generosity (Lerner et al., 2008).

PSYCHOLOGICAL AND EMOTIONAL MATURITY

Psychological maturity relates to the attainment of certain qualities and capacities that are expected of a mature person in a given society (Arnett, 2000; Badger, Nelson, & Barry, 2006; Donnellan, Conger, & Burzette, 2007). Interestingly, there is a high level of agreement regarding the expectations of a mature adult among members within cultures and also across cultures, at least in the Western world (Arnett & Galambos, 2003).

In a series of studies, Arnett (1998, 2000) identified several major domains of markers of adulthood. These included biological or age-related attributes such as reaching a certain age and the biological capacity to bear children, and role transitions and family capacities such as marriage, independent residence, being employed full time, and parenting. However, when appraising maturity, psychological aspects were perceived as most central. These psychological aspects included issues of *separation and individuation*, such as the negotiation of a mature and equal stance vis-à-vis parents and the capacity to make independent decisions and to care for oneself, and *emotional maturity*, namely the capacity to control impulses, the adoption of a broad unselfish perspective, and acceptance of responsibility for the consequences of one's action. In a study conducted with Israeli youth, emotional maturity and, in particular, accepting responsibility for your own actions emerged as the most central and important marker of mature adulthood as perceived by adolescents, college students, and parents of adolescents (Mayseless & Scharf, 2003).

Emotional and psychological maturity involves a sense of resilience and meaning, and connectedness with others and with the community (Donnellan, Conger, & Burzette, 2007; Greenberger & Bond, 1984). Hence, in terms of psychosocial characteristics, it should be associated with a strong and coherent self-image and high resiliency. In addition, it is expected to be associated with general positive orientation toward close others as well as toward the community and society at large. These latter characteristics are expected to be observed in empathy toward others, tendency to contribute to others, and values that go along with such tendencies. With regard to antecedents of emotional and psychological maturity, it has been shown to be cultivated mostly in a warm, accepting, and autonomy-promoting relational context (Scharf, Mayseless, & Kivenson Bar-On, 2004).

HOW MIGHT SPIRITUAL DEVELOPMENT BE RELATED TO PSYCHOLOGICAL AND EMOTIONAL MATURITY?

As becomes apparent from this analysis, the two domains of spiritual development and the development of emotional and psychological maturity may be highly related and similar. It seems that both could emerge from the same antecedents (e.g., warm and thriving relational context) and that both have similar outcomes or psychosocial characteristics, such as consideration of others, empathy, and social conscience. If this is indeed the case—namely that a high correlation exist between emotional maturity and self-transcendence—it could be argued that the two domains actually reflect the same analogous developmental processes but that for various reasons they have been titled differently by scholars from different disciplines. For example, it might be argued that what some scholars from the traditional developmental psychology described as positive emotional development or emotional maturity is in fact what other scholars (e.g., within the psychology of religion) would term spiritual development.

Several conceptualizations regarding the possible interplay between these two domains of development have been discussed. One of the most illuminating conceptualizations emerged within transpersonal psychology, a distinct school of psychology that is interested in studying human experiences that transcend the traditional boundaries of the ego (Hartelius, Caplan, & Rardin, 2007).

TRANSPERSONAL PSYCHOLOGY

Abraham Maslow, the founder of transpersonal psychology in the late 1960s (Maslow, 1971), asserted an interesting and challenging view in relation to the place of spirituality in human development. Maslow is most known for his theory of a hierarchy of needs. At the bottom of this hierarchy are *Deficiency-needs*, such as physiological needs, the need for safety, the need for love and belongingness, and the need for esteem, and at the top are *Being-needs*, or growth needs, in particular self-actualization. Maslow postulated a hierarchical organization in which all needs are seen as central and primary, yet those lower in the hierarchy (e.g., physiological needs) have to be at least partly satisfied before needs at the higher level in the hierarchy (e.g., need for self-actualization) become dominant.

Satisfaction of these needs promotes the development of a healthy actualized self and reflects a *personal* developmental sphere. However, in exploring the farthest reaches of human nature, Maslow (1971) suggested that there were possibilities beyond self-actualization. Maslow postulated another developmental level—*transpersonal*—in which the actualized person transcends his or her own self to find spiritual fulfillment and self-transcendence. Maslow's self-transcendence level recognizes the human needs for creativity, compassion, and spirituality. It involves states of consciousness in which the sense of self is expanded beyond the ordinary definitions and self-images of the individual personality. Self-transcendence refers to the direct experience of a fundamental connection, harmony, or unity with others and the world through "peak experiences" and "plateau experiences." In such situations the sense of self dissolves into awareness of a greater unity, and individuals have a deep sense of peacefulness or tranquility; feel in tune, in harmony, or at one with the universe; and experience a deep or profound understanding along with strong or deep positive emotions (Walsh & Vaughan, 1993).

The self which is transcended is the personality or ego-self, the collection of self-concepts, self-images, and roles that develops through one's interactions with others and with the environment. Transpersonal approaches hold that this ego-self is not the same as one's true nature or essence and that self-transcendence opens one to the experience of this deeper nature. Maslow described those who had achieved self-actualization as having "strong identities, people who know who they are, where they are going, what they want, what they are good for, in a word, as, strong Selves, using themselves well and authentically and in accordance with their own true nature" (Maslow, 1971, p. 280). Yet he viewed the next level in the hierarchy—the transpersonal level—as going beyond this strong and positive self-identity to involve relation to the sacred and the transcendence of the self. In line with his hierarchical view, individuals were expected to first reach a certain level of fulfillment of needs for safety, self-esteem, love, and belongingness, as well as reach a certain level of self-identity and self-actualization (i.e., emotional maturity) before they transcend this self and develop their spirituality to its fullest potential.

Yet Maslow acknowledged that individuals could experience what he termed "peak experiences" and have a sense of self-transcendence even when they have not yet satisfied deficiency needs. He stated (Maslow, 1971, p. 281):

> I have recently found it more and more useful to differentiate between two kinds (or better, degrees) of self-actualizing people, those who were clearly healthy, but with little or no experiences of transcendence, and those in whom transcendent experiencing was important and even central.

And then he continues:

> It is unfortunate that I can no longer be theoretically neat at this level. I find not only self-actualizing persons who transcend, but also non-healthy people, non-self-actualizers who have important transcendent experiences. It seems to me that I have found some degree of transcendence in many people other than self-actualizing ones as I have defined this term. Perhaps it will be found even more widely as we develop better techniques and better conceptualizations. After all, I am reporting here my impressions from the most preliminary of explorations.

This statement may be viewed as a forerunner of one of the most important issues regarding spiritual development, namely the ways in which spiritual development is related to psychological and emotional development and maturity. Is a certain level of psychological and emotional maturity required before spiritual development and self-transcendence come to the forefront? How is spirituality and self-transcendence experienced by an individual who is not psychologically and emotionally mature or healthy? Are spiritual development and psychological and emotional maturity two separate domains of development? Are they totally independent domains, or does each contribute to and advance the other?

Interestingly, Maslow's expectation that true or positive transcendence necessitates a certain level of self-actualization and a certain level of emotional maturity accords with similar conceptions within Judaism, wherein individuals are expected to turn to the mystical realm (i.e., the study of Kabbalah) only after a certain age and after a certain maturity has been achieved. Similar notions are discussed also within Hinduism thought.

Other scholars, such as Ken Wilber, who started his intellectual journey within transpersonal psychology, discussed somewhat different possibilities. Wilber (1996, 2000) distinguished between *Pre-personal* stages of development, prior to the development of a stable sense of self; *Personal* stages, wherein the development of a coherent self-identity is achieved; and *Transpersonal* stages, in which a stable holistic awareness of a whole that is larger than the individual ego is developed. Wilber viewed higher stages of development as incorporating the lower stages, rather than dissolving them. He postulated the existence of several somewhat independent lines of development, such as emotional, cognitive, moral, and spiritual, which influence each other but only partly. Hence, he argued that a person can be developed in one line (e.g., cognitive) but less developed in another (e.g., emotional or spiritual).

Furthermore, like Maslow, he argued that experiences of transcendence could occur at any stage of development, but he added that how these experiences are interpreted depends on the stage of development of the individual (i.e., pre-personal, personal, or transpersonal). He further suggested that transcendental experiences at lower stages can propel the developmental process toward higher levels of consciousness. Though a certain level of emotional maturity and self-identity must be reached before a person moves to the transpersonal stage, according to Wilber, spiritual development has its own independent line of development, which starts before a transpersonal stage is reached. Further, according to Wilber, there might be certain cross-influences between the different developmental lines. However, he did not specify how these lines of development are expected to be associated and to what extent.

MODELS OF INTERRELATIONS BETWEEN THE TWO DOMAINS

Assuming that the two domains or lines of development (spiritual and psychological/emotional) are somewhat independent, what might be their interrelations? In general, there might be several ways by which these two domains of development could be related: The two domains may share similar antecedents, and they may be associated with similar outcomes and each may or may not affect development in the other domain. Four models reflecting these possibilities are suggested:

1. *Independent—shared outcomes*. According to this model, the two domains may be mostly unrelated and develop quite independent of each other. In such case, the antecedents that contribute to or impede development in each of these domains may be distinct. Yet, development in each domain (spiritual and emotional) may independently contribute to or be associated with similar psychosocial outcomes. For example, development in each domain may be independently associated with the capacity for empathy and for consideration of others' points of views.

2. *Independent—shared antecedents*. Alternatively, the two domains may be independent (i.e., they do not affect each other) yet may be related, namely similar antecedents (e.g., a supportive and cohesive relational context) may promote development in each domain. In such case, development in one domain is expected to be related to development in the other domain through a common causal factor.

3. *Unidirectional dependence—emotional maturity as prerequisite to spiritual development*. As suggested by Maslow, one possibility of dependence is that a certain level of emotional maturity and psychological development is required before spiritual development and, in particular, true self transcendence can be cultivated; namely, a certain level of emotional maturity is a prerequisite for true transcendence. In such case, spiritual experiences without the emotional maturity will be colored by this immaturity and may lead to problematic outcomes, such as self-aggrandizement or low resilience.

4. *Bidirectional contribution*. A fourth model involves a situation in which each domain contributes to the other. In such case, spiritual experiences can trigger processes that lead to better emotional integration and foster higher levels of psychological maturity. Such developmental processes are expected when spiritual experiences are perceived as positive and benign but may also occur when spiritual or transcendental experiences trigger anxiety, distress, and sometimes acute crisis. In such case, the crisis may trigger new psychological organization and personal growth. Similarly, emotional and psychological maturity may contribute to the emergence of a quest for ultimate meaning and transcendence and promote the spiritual development of the individual.

The study presented in this chapter provided a first step in examining these four models in a sample of Israeli college students. In the study we examined concurrently self-transcendence and psychological/emotional maturity. We assessed the correlation between these two lines of development and looked at their association with possible antecedents, in particular with indicators of a positive and supportive relational context. In addition, we investigated their association with various outcomes, in particular, with orientation to others, values, and the self system. The patterns of associations that would emerge could throw light on the various models and suggest future avenues for longitudinal research.

ISRAELI CULTURE

The study was conducted in a unique cultural milieu—the Israeli cultural context. In line with a developmental systems approach, it is clear the development of the individuals examined in the study is highly interconnected, influenced by, and influencing the cultural context. Hence a brief portrayal of some of the relevant characteristics of Israeli culture is undertaken. Israel is a young country, founded in May 1948. It is also quite small geographically and in terms of population (about 7 million citizens). Throughout the years, Israel has engaged in several wars with its Arab neighboring countries, including frequent armed clashes with the Palestinian Arabs in the West Bank and Gaza Strip. These constant hostilities have led most Israelis to experience anxiety, loss, and trauma (Milgram, 1993), and may have propelled many Israelis to seek spiritual meaning.

Like many other countries, Israel is composed of various subcultures with distinct ethnic origins and socioeconomic levels. Most Israeli citizens are Jewish (80%), with about half regarding themselves as secular. For this secular population, the Jewish origin reflects a national identity rather than a religious one. Along with an ambivalent stance toward institutionalized religion, during the past decade Israel has seen a large surge of interest in spirituality broadly defined. This includes interest in Eastern spiritual traditions such as Buddhism and Hinduism (Valley, 2006), New Religious Movements, New Age groups (Ezrachi, 2004), as well as a return to Judaism with a stronger accent on its spiritual or mystical facets such as Kabbalah (Huss, 2007). Hence, notions of spirituality and self-transcendence are moderately common among college students.

Israel also has a large minority (20%) of Arabs who are further divided into various religions, mostly Muslim, Christian, and Druze. In general, Israel is a developed, industrialized, Western culture, and the Israeli Jewish secular middle class is very similar to the North American one in its focus on individualistic values (Schwartz, 1994). In contrast, many individuals from the Arab minority and orthodox Jews are more communal and traditional in their values.

Two unique features of Israeli society are relevant with respect to the transition from adolescence to adulthood. In Israel, the great majority of the 18-year-old cohort of Jewish youngsters (92% men and 65% women) leave their parents' home for a period of two to three years' mandatory service in the Israel Defense Forces (Mayseless, 1993). The timing of the military service is determined by one's age and is not affected by maturity. Furthermore, many Israeli youth, who plan to go to college, take a year or two after their military service to travel abroad, work, or study to improve their grades before they enter college. Hence, many Israeli college students are in their mid-twenties and have had more life experience and perhaps are more emotionally mature than the typical college student in North America or Europe (Salomon & Mayseless, 2003). This moratorium and, in particular, the journeys of youth in Israel to the Far East or to South America have been discussed as both reflecting and enhancing the spiritual quests of these youth (Maoz, 2007; Noy, 2004).

Another important characteristic of Israeli society has to do with its emphasis on communal values and practices (Elon, 1971). Israeli society is conspicuous in placing high value on the family and on belonging to a social group (Peres & Katz, 1981). Hence, though Israel is a Western industrialized society with mostly individualistic values, it is more communal and more collectivist than the United States (Salomon & Mayseless, 2003). Many college students live at home and, if they don't, their contact with their family of origin is quite frequent (e.g., visiting the family almost every week, having phone calls every other day). These characteristics should be considered when examining the findings regarding spiritual development and emotional and psychological maturity.

METHOD

Participants and Procedure

Participants of this study were 215 college students (154 female and 61 male) from a medium-sized university in Israel. Ages ranged from 19 to 30 years ($M = 24.5$; $SD = 2.89$). The sample included 111 (51.6%) freshman, 51 (23.7%) sophomore, and 40 (18.6%) senior undergraduate students (13 did not identify their year of study). Of the participants, 72% reported an average of B and above in their grades. The majority of the students (187; 87%) were single, whereas 22 (10%) indicated they were married and 6 (2%) were divorced or separated.

The sample included 152 (70.5%) Jews, 27 (12.5%) Muslims, 19 (9%) Druze, and 17 (8%) Christians. Seventy students (32.5%) indicated they were raised as religious. Students' parents were mostly middle-class, with 52% having an academic degree. Number of siblings ranged from 0 (only child) to 6 ($M = 1.92$; $SD = 1.13$).

Students completed the questionnaires after they were informed of the purpose of the study and signed an informed consent form.

Measures

The packet of questionnaires included various measures, translated from English into Hebrew and back-translated into English. For the purpose of this study, we report on part of the measures included in this packet: a demographic questionnaire, measures assessing the two domains of development (emotional maturity and spiritual development), and measures pertaining to four areas: self-perceptions, orientation to others, values, and relational context.

Demographic Questionnaire

A short demographic questionnaire was administered to participants requesting information such as their age, religion, gender, grades, and year of study.

Domains of Development

Emotional maturity was assessed by means of five items reflecting the indicators identified by Arnett and Galambos (2003) and others (Mayseless & Scharf, 2003) as representing emotional maturity (e.g., "taking responsibility for my actions," "controlling my temper"; participants used a Likert scale ranging from 1 = *not true at all* to 5 = *very true*; α = .70). High scores denote high levels of emotional and psychological maturity.

Spiritual development was assessed using items from the *Piedmont Transcendence Scale* (Piedmont, 1999; e.g., "I feel that on a higher level all of us share a common bond"). The measure contained seven items, and participants were asked to respond using a five-point Likert scale (1 = *strongly disagree* to 5 = *strongly agree*; Cronbach α = .88)

Self-Perceptions

Scholastic Competence (Harter, 1988) was assessed by four items from the Harter scale (1988) using the response scale devised by Harter (1988) with higher scores denoting higher self-esteem (Cronbach α = .64).

Resilience was assessed using items adapted from the Symptom Checklist-90-R inventory (Derogatis, 1994). The measure contained five items, and participants were asked to respond using a five-point Likert scale (1 = *strongly disagree* to 5 = *strongly agree*; e.g., "I am good at resolving conflicts I have with other people," "I am good at bouncing back when bad things happen to me"; Cronbach α = .65).

Orientation to Others

Empathy was assessed by a measure created and developed by Lerner et al. (2005), based on the Eisenberg Sympathy Scale (ESS; Eisenberg et al., 1996) and the Empathic Concern Subscale of the Interpersonal Reactivity Index (IRI; Davis, 1983). The measure contained nine items and participants were asked to respond using a five-point Likert scale (1 = *strongly disagree* to 5 = *strongly agree*; e.g., "It bothers me when bad things happen to good people"; Cronbach α = .79).

Contribution Behavior was assessed using items adapted from the 4-H Study of PYD (Lerner et al., 2005). The measure contained four items, and participants were asked to respond using a five-point Likert scale (1 = *never* to 5 = *every day*; e.g., "tutoring others"; Cronbach α = .62).

Efficacy Regarding Contribution to Community was assessed using three items (e.g., "I believe that I can make a change in my community;" Likert scale ranging from 1 = *strongly disagree* to 5 = *strongly agree*; Cronbach α = .78).

Generosity (Kasser, 2002) was assessed using a six-item scale, and participants were asked to respond using a five-point Likert scale (1 = *strongly disagree* to 5 = *strongly agree*; e.g., "I am a pretty generous person when it comes to my money and sharing my things"; Cronbach α = .72).

Values

Religious Pluralism (Roeser, 2005) was assessed using a three-item scale, and participants were asked to respond using a five-point Likert scale (1 = *strongly disagree* to 5 = *strongly agree*; e.g., "I believe all students should have to take a world religions class"; Cronbach α = .74).

Social Conscience was assessed using items adapted from various sources (Benson, Leffert, Scales, & Blyth, 1998; Leffert et al., 1998; Greenberger & Bond, 1984; Kasser & Ryan, 1996). The measure contained five items, and participants were asked to respond using a five-point Likert scale (1 = *not important to me at all* to 5 = *very important to me*; e.g., "It is important for me to reduce hunger and poverty in the world"; Cronbach α = .83).

Relational Context

Social Support was assessed using a measure containing 16 items (Roeser et al., 2008). Participants were requested to report if they could rely on support from various persons (e.g., parents, friends) using a *yes, no*, or *unsure* response scale; Cronbach α = .78).

Positive Ethnic Identity scale contained 13 items (e.g., "I feel good about my cultural/ethnic background"; Phinney, 1992). Participants were asked to respond using a five-point Likert scale (1 = *strongly disagree* to 5 = *strongly agree*; Cronbach α = .90).

Positive Peer Characteristics (Roeser & Peck, 2003) comprised five items, and participants were asked to respond using a three-point Likert scale (1 = *none of them* to 3 = *most of them*; e.g., "My friends get good grades in school"; Cronbach α = .60).

Frequency of Religious Practices was assessed by five items (Smith, 2005), and participants were asked to respond using an 11-point Likert scale (1 = *never* to 11 = *several times a day*; e.g., "How often do you go to religious services?" "How often do you study religious scriptures?"; Cronbach α = .84).

Frequency of Spiritual Practices, which are not directly associated with an established religion, was assessed by four items (Smith, 2005), and participants were asked to respond using an 11-point Likert scale (1 = *never* to 11 = *several times a day*; e.g., "How often do you meditate by yourself?" "How often do you participate in retreats whose purpose is spiritual?"; Cronbach α = .74). Frequency of religious practices was moderately correlated with frequency of spiritual practices attesting to their associated yet distinct nature (r = .42, p < .01)

Table 13.1 The Associations Between Spiritual Development and Emotional
Maturity and Psychosocial Characteristics

Psychosocial Characteristics	Domains of Development	
	Emotional Maturity	Spiritual Development
Self-Perceptions		
Scholastic competence	0.21**	0.05
Resilience	0.39**	0.38**
Orientation to Others		
Empathy	0.34**	0.27**
Contribution behavior	0.28**	0.26**
Efficacy: contribution to community	0.29**	0.34**
Generosity	0.34**	0.44**
Values		
Religious pluralism	0.23**	0.33**
Social conscience	0.53**	0.37**
Relational Context		
Social support	0.23**	0.44**
Ethnic identity	0.14*	0.26**
Positive peer characteristics	0.30**	0.35**
Frequency of religious practices	0.29**	0.55**
Frequency of spiritual practices	0.15*	0.41**

Note: $N = 209$–215. *$p < 0.05$ (2-tailed); **$p < 0.01$ (2-tailed).

RESULTS

Emotional maturity and spiritual development were moderately correlated ($r = .35$, $p < .01$), indicating that the two domains of development are associated but are also quite distinct. We further examined the zero-order Pearson correlations between the indicators of development in the two domains and the psychosocial characteristics assessed in this study: self-perceptions, orientation to others, values, and relational context. As can be seen in Table 13.1, both emotional maturity and spiritual development were significantly correlated with most psychosocial characteristics: scholastic competence (only emotional development), resilience, empathy, contribution behavior, efficacy to contribute to community, generosity, religious pluralism, social conscience, social support, positive ethnic identity, positive peer characteristics, and frequency of religious and spiritual practices.

This pattern of correlations may indicate a positive common core for both domains, which is the one driving the positive and significant correlations with better self-perceptions, more positive orientation to others, moral values, and helpful and reliable social context. To examine the joint and unique effects of each of these two domains and, in particular, to examine the possibility of an interaction whereby high levels of spiritual development coupled with low levels of emotional maturity would be associated with problematic psychosocial characteristics, we conducted the following analysis. For each domain of development, we created two groups, (1) low—below the median, and (2) high—above the median (i.e., one group low in emotional maturity and another high in emotional maturity). We performed a two-by-two MANOVA, with both groups of emotional maturity (low and high) and both groups of spiritual development (low and high) serving as independent variables and the psychosocial characteristics serving as dependent variables. The general effect of emotional maturity was significant (Wilks $= .615$; $F(13, 174) = 8.40, p < .001$; partial Eta Squared $= .385$), as was the general effect of spiritual development (Wilks $= .77$; $F (13, 174) = 4.01, p < .001$; partial Eta Squared $= .23$). The interaction was not significant.

As can be seen in Table 13.2 with the spiritual development groups, there was a significant effect for all of the variables except scholastic competence. Inspection of the means showed that in all of them the high spirituality group demonstrated superior functioning, which was evident in resiliency, positive orientation to others (empathy, contribution behavior, efficacy to contribute, generosity), moral values (religious pluralism, social conscience), and positive relational context (social support, strong ethnic identity, positive peer characteristics, high frequency of religious and spiritual practices). The emotional maturity groups showed a similar pattern, yet effects were not significant for some of the variables: efficacy to contribute, generosity, religious pluralism, social support, ethnic identity, and frequency of spiritual practices.

To further examine the joint contribution of the two developmental domains, while controlling for demographic variables and taking advantage of the whole variance of the indicators of development, we conducted 11 hierarchical regressions with each of the dependent variables. In the first step we entered age and gender (dummy-coded), and in the second step we entered emotional maturity and spiritual development. For all variables, except four, both emotional maturity and spiritual development were significant predictors. For scholastic competence, only emotional maturity was a significant predictor, and for social support, ethnic identity, and frequency of spiritual practices, only spiritual development was a significant predictor.

DISCUSSION

Our data provided cross-national and cross-cultural validity to the assessment of spirituality and positive youth development, as well as suggested important variability in the developmental trajectories of spirituality and positive youth development among youth. The results of this study presented a clear and coherent picture. The two domains of development were found to be associated to a moderate degree. Hence, they cannot be described as totally independent of each other, nor as mostly parallel or similar to each other. Such a moderate correlation can ensue from a common antecedent, which similarly contributed to the development of each domain. For example, we postulated that warm

Table 13.2 Results of MANOVA With Emotional Maturity and Spiritual Development

Domains of Development	Emotional Maturity		Spiritual Development		Emotional F Value (1, 186)	Spiritual F Value (1, 186)
Psychosocial Characteristics	Low (n=99)	High (n=91)	Low (n=99)	High (n=91)		
	Mean (SD)	Mean (SD)	Mean (SD)	Mean (SD)		
Self-Perceptions						
Scholastic	3.43	3.63	3.52	3.53	6.10**	0.39
competence	(.61)	(.55)	(.63)	(.55)		
Resilience	−0.19	0.26	−0.17	0.23	17.42***	11.78***
	(.60)	(.59)	(.58)	(.62)		
Orientation to Others						
Empathy	3.84	4.17	3.86	4.15	7.96**	5.14*
	(.62)	(.61)	(.66)	(.57)		
Contribution behavior	−0.17	0.20	−0.14	0.17	9.04**	4.78*
	(.59)	(.77)	(.65)	(.73)		
Efficacy: contribution	3.32	3.57	3.17	3.72	0.52	18.25***
to community	(.88)	(.78)	(.86)	(.72)		
Generosity	3.37	3.68	3.27	3.78	3.04	21.76***
	(.63)	(.72)	(.68)	(.61)		
Values						
Religious pluralism	2.73	3.06	2.60	3.22	0.86	12.18***
	(1.1)	(1.13)	(1.13)	(1.03)		
Social conscience	3.10	3.74	3.14	3.70	18.29***	11.35***
	(.86)	(.75)	(.82)	(.82)		
Relational Context						
Social support	1.91	2.06	1.81	2.16	0.82	36.70***
	(.41)	(.39)	(.36)	(.37)		
Ethnic identity	2.72	2.89	2.64	2.98	0.95	12.98***
	(.55)	(.62)	(.50)	(.64)		
Positive peer	2.08	2.28	2.05	2.32	6.55*	20.63***
characteristics	(.35)	(.36)	(.32)	(.36)		
Frequency of	3.56	5.37	3.16	5.80	13.07***	56.55***
religious practices	(2.03)	(2.54)	(1.79)	(2.34)		
Frequency of	2.06	2.75	1.62	3.22	0.82	40.80***
spiritual practices	(1.45)	(1.99)	(1.17)	(1.91)		

Note: $*p < .05$; $**p < .01$; $***p < .001$.

and nurturing relational environments may similarly promote development in each of these domains. The results of this study do not tend to support such an interpretation. The indicators of positive relational context were associated with both domains, when examining the zero-order correlations. However, in the MANOVA and in the hierarchical regressions, general social support and strong ethnic identity were associated more consistently with spiritual development than with emotional maturity.

This profile of results may reflect the importance of the community, perhaps a religious community, in supporting and promoting spiritual development. The findings in the MANOVA, where sense of efficacy in contributing to the community was only significant with spiritual development, accord with this interpretation. Further, in line with this interpretation, spiritual development was moderate to highly associated with frequency of religious practice. This interesting finding attests to the possible importance of the religious community in promoting spiritual development in youth even in a country, such as Israel, which is highly secular. Still, spiritual development was similarly associated with frequency of spiritual practices not directly related to an established religion, which was only moderately associated with the religious practice items. It seems that there may be several routes to the development of spiritual transcendence, both inside and outside traditional religious groups. Yet in both cases a supportive relational context seems to be highly important.

Why was such a context not as important for emotional maturity? One possibility is that emotional maturity is more strongly related to intimate and trustworthy close relationships with a few significant others and not to a sense of general support and embeddedness in a community. The measures that we employed in this study did not allow the assessment of this quality in the relationship and instead assessed a sense of support in the general network. If these interpretations are correct, future research may need to disentangle the different kinds of relational closeness and support and examine the possibility that they are distinctly associated with development in each domain.

One of the most illuminating findings of this study is that both domains were significantly and independently associated with the same positive outcomes, such as with moral values (i.e., social conscience), and with an empathic and benevolent stance toward others. In other words, the two domains of development seem to act independently in contributing to the individual's prosocial and benevolent perspective and behavior. Together these findings suggest that spiritual development as assessed in this study and emotional maturity are not associated with each other, because they are affected by the same common antecedent and are not redundant in predicting various positive outcomes. In short, the results of this study do not support the first two models that were described in the introduction: the one assuming that the two domains are *Independent with shared outcomes* and the other assuming that they are *Independent with shared antecedents*. In fact, the two domains seem to be interrelated, but is there *unidirectional dependence* as Maslow (1971) suggested or a *bidirectional contribution?*

The results of the study are also quite clear with regard to the issue addressed by Maslow regarding his hierarchy of needs. The analyses of our data do not support the notion that a certain level of maturity is required before spiritual development can be achieved. Further, our analyses do not support the contention that transcendental experiences in less-mature individuals lead to negative phenomena. At least in our sample of highly functioning emerging adults, this was not the case. The cross-sectional nature of our study did not allow us to directly examine the possibility of bidirectional contributions. The current profile of results neither supports nor contradicts this possibility, and so this model remains highly plausible.

Several considerations should be noted. Our study relied on self-report measures and assessed some of the constructs (e.g., emotional maturity) using a rather short questionnaire. Future research needs to examine the questions addressed in this study with a multimethod, multisource design to enrich and strengthen its findings. Furthermore, our results reflect the specific cultural milieu and age group that we studied. The participants of our study were well-functioning, highly articulate young Israeli men and women. Other samples of non-college-bound youth or youth who are younger and less experienced and youth in other cultures may reveal yet other profiles of results. Similarly, our sample was moderately secular, reflecting the normative population of college students in Israel. Future research may also examine populations that are more religious in their orientation. Finally, the research questions addressed in this study were examined in a cross-sectional research design. Though these questions lend themselves to such inquiry, to fully understand the developmental processes of spiritual development and emotional maturity and in particular to assess the possibility that each developmental domain contributes to the other necessitates a longitudinal design.

During the period of the transition from adolescence to adulthood, youth develop in different domains, including two highly related ones: emotional development and spiritual development. For the past several decades, large research efforts have been invested to conceptualize and understand processes that lead to maturity and to positive emotional development. Consequently, we now have a sound body of knowledge regarding the core characteristics of positive emotional development and the processes that enable such development in adolescence (e.g., Steinberg, 2001). However, the study of spiritual development has only more recently become a focus of research attention. Hence, we know much less about spiritual development (but see Benson et al., 1998; Lerner et al., 2008) and, in particular, we know even less about how these two lines of development are related. To fully address these important questions and to assess the complex interrelations between these two developmental domains, a longitudinal research design is required in which the voices of the youth themselves will also be heard.

REFERENCES

Arnett, J. J. (1998). Learning to stand alone: The contemporary American transition to adulthood in cultural and historical context. *Human Development, 41*, 295–315.

Arnett, J. J. (2000). Emerging adulthood: A theory of development from the late teens through the twenties. *American Psychologist, 55,* 469–480.

Arnett, J. J., & Galambos, N. L. (Eds.) (2003). *New directions for child and adolescent development: Exploring cultural conceptions of the transition to adulthood.* San Francisco, CA: Jossey-Bass.

Badger, S., Nelson, L. J., & Barry, C. M. N. (2006). Perceptions of the transition to adulthood among Chinese and American emerging adults. *International Journal of Behavioral Development, 30,* 84–93.

Benson, P. L., Leffert, N., Scales, P. C., & Blyth, D. A. (1998). Beyond the "village" rhetoric: Creating healthy communities for children and adolescents. *Applied Developmental Science, 2,* 138–159.

Benson, P. L., Roehlkepartain, E. C., & Rude, S. P. (2003). Spiritual development in childhood and adolescence. *Applied Developmental Science, 7,* 205–213.

Davis, M. (1983). Measuring individual differences in empathy: Evidence for a multidimensional approach. *Journal of Personality and Social Psychology, 44,* 113–126.

Derogatis, L. R. (1994). *Symptoms checklist 90 revised (SCL-90-R): Administration, scoring, and procedure manual* (3rd ed.). Minneapolis, MN: National Computer Systems.

Donnellan, M. B., Conger, R. D., & Burzette, R. G. (2007). Personality development from late adolescence to young adulthood: Differential stability, normative maturity, and evidence for the maturity-stability hypothesis. *Journal of Personality, 75,* 237–264.

Eisenberg, N., Fabes, R. A., Murphy, B. C., Karbon, M., Smith, M., & Maszk, P. (1996). The relations of children's dispositional empathy-related responding to their emotionality, regulation, and social functioning. *Developmental Psychology, 32,* 195–209.

Elon, A. (1971). *The Israelis: Founders and sons.* New York, NY: Holt, Rinehart & Winston.

Ezrachi, E. (2004). The quest for spirituality among secular Israelis. In U. Rebhun & C. I. Waxman (Eds.), *Jews in Israel: Contemporary social and cultural patterns* (pp. 315–330). Boston, MA: Brandeis University Press.

Furrow, J. L., King, P. E., & White, K. (2004). Religion and positive youth development: Identity, meaning, and prosocial concerns. *Applied Developmental Science, 8,* 17–26.

Greenberger, E., & Bond, L. (1984). *Psychosocial maturity inventory.* Irvine: University of California, Irvine, Department of Social Ecology.

Hartelius, G., Caplan, M., & Rardin, M. A. (2007). Transpersonal psychology: Defining the past, divining the future. *The Humanistic Psychologist, 35,* 135–160.

Harter, S. (1988). *Manual for the self-perception profile for adolescents.* Denver, CO: University of Denver.

Hunsberger, B., Pratt, M., & Pancer, S. M. (2001). Adolescent identity formation: Religious exploration and commitment. *Identity: An International Journal of Theory and Research, 1,* 365–386.

Huss, B. (2007). The new age of Kabbalah: Contemporary Kabbalah, the new age and postmodern spirituality. *Journal of Modern Jewish Studies, 6,* 107–125.

Kasser, T. (2002). *The high price of materialism.* Cambridge, MA: MIT Press.

Kasser, T., & Ryan, R. M. (1996). Further examining the American dream: Differential correlates of intrinsic and extrinsic goals. *Personality and Social Psychology Bulletin, 22*, 280–287.

Kiesling, C., Sorell, G. T., Montgomery, M. J., & Colwell, R. J. (2006). Identity and spirituality: A psychosocial exploration of the sense of spiritual self. *Developmental Psychology, 42*, 1269–1277.

Kirkpatrick, L. A. (1999). Attachment and religious representations and behavior. In J. Cassidy & P. R. Shaver (Eds.), *Handbook of attachment theory and research* (pp. 803–822). New York, NY: Guilford Press.

Leffert, N., Benson, P. L., Scales, P. C., Sharma, A. R., Drake, D. R., & Blyth, D. A. (1998). Developmental assets: Measurement and prediction of risk behaviors among adolescents. *Applied Developmental Science, 2*, 209–230.

Lerner, R. M., Lerner, J. V., Almerigi, J., Theokas, C., Phelps, E., Gestsdottir, S., ... & von Eye, A. (2005). Positive youth development, participation in community youth development programs, and community contributions of fifth grade adolescents: Findings from the first wave of the 4-H Study of Positive Youth Development. *Journal of Early Adolescence, 25*, 17–71.

Lerner, R. M., Roeser, R. W., & Phelps, E. (2008). *Positive youth development and spirituality: From theory to research.* West Conshohocken, PA: Templeton Foundation Press.

Maoz, D. (2007), Backpackers' motivations: The role of culture and nationality. *Annals of Tourism Research, 34*, 122–140.

Markstrom, C. A. (1999). Religious involvement and adolescent psychosocial development. *Journal of Adolescence, 22*, 205–221.

Maslow, A. (1971). *The farther reaches of human nature.* New York, NY: Viking.

Mayseless, O. (1993). Attitudes toward military service among Israeli youth. In D. Ashkenazy (Ed.), *The military in the service of society and democracy* (pp. 32–35). Westport, CT: Greenwood Press.

Mayseless, O., & Scharf, M. (2003). What does it mean to be an adult? The Israeli experience. In J. J. Arnett & N. L. Galambos (Eds.), *New directions for child and adolescent development: Exploring cultural conceptions of the transition to adulthood* (pp. 5–20). San Francisco, CA: Jossey-Bass.

Milgram, N. A. (1993). War-related trauma and victimization: Principles of traumatic stress prevention in Israel. In J. P. Wilson & B. Raphael (Eds.), *International handbook of traumatic stress syndromes* (pp. 811–820). New York, NY: Plenum Press.

Noy, C. (2004). This trip really changed me: Backpackers' narratives of self-change. *Annals of Tourism Research, 31*, 78–102.

Oser, F. K., Scarlett, W. G., & Bucher, A. (2006). Religious and spiritual development throughout the life span. In W. Damon & R. M. Lerner (Eds.), *Handbook of child psychology: Vol. 1, Theoretical models of human development* (6th ed., pp. 942–998). Hoboken, NJ: Wiley.

Peres, Y., & Katz, R. (1981). Stability and centrality: The nuclear family in modern Israel. *Social Forces, 59*, 687–704.

Phinney, J. S. (1992). The multi-group ethnic identity measure: A new scale for use with adolescents and young adults from diverse groups. *Journal of Adolescent Research, 7,* 156–176.

Piedmont, R. L. (1999). Does spirituality represent the sixth factor of personality? Spiritual transcendence and the five-factor model. *Journal of Personality, 67,* 985–1013.

Roehlkepartain, E. C., Benson, P. L., King, P. E., & Wagener, L. M. (Eds.). (2005). *The handbook of spiritual development in childhood and adolescence.* Thousand Oaks, CA: Sage.

Roeser, R. W. (2005). *Fulbright survey of identity, schooling, and spirituality in adolescence.* Unpublished manuscript.

Roeser, R. W., & Peck, S. C. (2003). Patterns and pathways of educational achievement across adolescence: A holistic-developmental perspective. In W. Damon (Series Ed.), S. C. Peck & R. W. Roeser (Vol. Eds.), *New directions for child and adolescent development: Vol. 101, Person-centered approaches to studying development in context* (pp. 39–62). San Francisco, CA: Jossey-Bass.

Roeser, R. W., Galloway, M., Casey-Cannon, S., Watson, C., Keller, L., & Tan, E. (2008). Identity representations in patterns of school achievement and well-being among early adolescent girls: Variable- and person-centered approaches. *Journal of Early Adolescence, 28,* 115–152.

Salomon, G., & Mayseless, O. (2003). Dialectic contradictions in the experiences of Israeli Jewish adolescents: Efficacy and stress, closeness and friction, and conformity and non-compliance. In F. Pajares & T. Urdan (Eds.), *Adolescence and education: Vol. 3, International perspectives on adolescence* (pp. 149–171). Greenwich, CT: Information Age Publishing.

Scharf, M., Mayseless, O., & Kivenson Bar-on, I. (2004). Adolescents' attachment representations and developmental tasks in emerging adulthood. *Developmental Psychology, 40,* 430–444.

Schwartz, S. H. (1994). Are there universal aspects in the content and structure of values? *Journal of Social Issues, 50,* 19–46.

Smith, C. (2005). *Soul searching: The religious and spiritual lives of American teenagers.* New York, NY: Oxford University Press.

Steinberg, L. (2001). We know some things: Parent–adolescent relationships in retrospect and prospect. *Journal of Research on Adolescence, 11,* 1–19.

Valley, A. (2006). Jewish redemption by way of the Buddha: A post-modern tale of exile and return. *Jewish Culture and History, 8,* 22–39.

Walsh, R., & Vaughan, F. (1993). On transpersonal definitions. *Journal of Transpersonal Psychology, 25,* 125–182.

Wilber, K. A. (1996). *A brief history of everything.* Boston, MA: Shambhala.

Wilber, K. A. (2000). *Integral psychology: Consciousness, spirit, psychology, therapy.* Boston, MA: Shambhala.

Wulff, D. M. (1997). *Psychology of religion: Classic and contemporary.* New York, NY: John Wiley & Sons.

14

Belief Systems and Positive Youth Development Among Chinese and American Youth[1]

WEI ZHANG, DAN DU, AND SHUANGJU ZHEN

The biggest difference between human beings and other animals is that every human being has certain beliefs and a spiritual world of his or her own. Many studies have shown that the United States stands out as one of the most religious nations in the developed world (Roehlkepartain, King, Wagener, & Benson, 2006; Smith & Denton, 2005). Although current data suggest that the number of religious Americans is gradually decreasing (Meacham, 2009; Pew Forum, 2008), religion still remains an important element of most Americans' daily activities and spiritual life. Currently, only 14% to 16% of American adults affiliate with no religious tradition (Meacham, 2009; Portes & Rumbaut, 2006).

Similar to the high levels of religiosity among American adults, the vast majority of youth in the United States also tend to affiliate with a particular religious group, with a rate of 84% to 87% (Smith & Denton, 2005; Wallace, Forman, Caldwell, & Willis, 2003). Religion and religious activities take up a very important place in American adolescents' daily lives and spiritual world.

[1]The preparation of this chapter was supported by a grant from the Innovative Team Project of Guangdong Humanities and Social Sciences Research to Wei Zhang and by a grant from the John Templeton Foundation to Richard M. Lerner.

Although religious and spiritual activities are an important facet of adolescents' lives in the United States and in many Western countries and regions, from a historical perspective this topic has been neglected for much of the latter part of the 20th century. Although significant attention was devoted to the religious development of adolescents in the early part of the 20th century (Hall, 1904), and again in the 1960s and 1970s (Spilka, Hood, Hunsberger, & Gorsuch, 2003), only in the last 10 to 20 years has the topic of religious and spiritual development (RSD) during adolescence begun to draw attention from fields related to the developmental sciences. Today, RSD has become a new frontier in developmental research (King & Roeser, 2009).

The emergence and development of human beings' spirituality and their engagement with the spiritual world have had a long period of biological and historical evolution. At the same time, the formation of an individual's spirituality and his or her spiritual world is influenced by the sociocultural context in which he or she lives and develops. According to developmental systems theories (DSTs; e.g., Bronfenbrenner, 1979; Lerner, 2006), individual development is the result of bidirectional, person ↔ context interactions. Therefore, the formation and development of one's spirituality and spiritual world is a product of the interaction between the vertical power of his or her group's biological and historical evolution and the horizontal power of the actual environment.

There are many differences between the United States and China; they differ in their historical origin, social structure, and ideology. The United States is a young country where many residents are immigrants (Alba & Nee, 2003), most of whom are religious (Cadge & Ecklund, 2006; Hirschman, 2007; Levitt, 2007). It is also a revolutionary country founded on modern democratic principles, such as freedom and equality. It is a country where individualism as a core concept is strongly advocated. Within a few hundred years, the United States has grown into a modernized country in possession of the most comprehensive social systems and mechanisms in the world, one with the most powerful economy and military forces, and the most benefits for its people.

In contrast, China is an old country with a recorded history of 5,000 years, and with a tradition of feudalism that has existed for ages. Agnation (e.g., patrilineal descent) and kin relation have been the basic units of the country's social structure, social ranking and political centralization have been highly stressed, and collectivism has been a leading value in China for centuries. The five prominent religions in China nowadays—Buddhism, Taoism, Christianity, Catholicism, and Islam—are mostly foreign. Modern democratic principles such as freedom and equality did not permeate this country until the last 100 years or so, while the promotion of individualism and the pursuit of personal liberty did not emerge until the last 30 years.

The differences between America and China in history, religion, culture, and society have led to large differences in the two countries' group and individual spiritual belief systems and structures. For various reasons, extant psychological research in China on spiritual beliefs was mostly conducted by researchers with specific religious backgrounds, and participants in these studies were usually from these same religious groups. However, more recently, there have been a few psychological studies on the Chinese spiritual belief system, work conducted either by Chinese or by Western researchers (see Shek, 2010, for a review). Even fewer studies have explored, from a developmental perspective, the formation of Chinese adolescent spiritual beliefs and the influences spiritual beliefs have on adolescent development.

This chapter explores, from a cross-cultural perspective, the characteristics of contemporary American and Chinese adolescents' spiritual beliefs, the differences between these groups, and the influences and effects that spiritual beliefs have on adolescent development in these different cultural settings. Specifically, we discuss three studies. Study 1 examined the influence of American youth's spirituality on their development, and Study 2 probed the structure and content of contemporary Chinese adolescents' belief systems. Finally, Study 3 explored the influence of Chinese adolescents' belief systems on their development.

STUDY 1: SPIRITUALITY AND PYD AMONG AMERICAN YOUTH

In the past decade, there has been increased research about the relationships between adolescent spirituality and/or religiosity and developmental outcomes. Despite variability in the quality of this research, studies from Western countries have suggested a link between adolescent religiosity and/or spirituality and positive development, as indicated by scores on various indices of well-being and risk behaviors (e.g., Cotton, Zebracki, Rosenthal, Tsevat, & Drotar, 2006; Dew et al., 2008; Josephson & Dell, 2004; King & Roeser, 2009; Lerner, Roeser, & Phelps, 2008; Weaver, Pargament, & Oppenheimer, 2006).

According to the developmental systems view of human development (Lerner, 2006), as a consequence of the presence of plasticity and the ubiquity of developmental regulations (i.e., mutually influential individual $\leftrightarrow$ context relations), there exists the potential in every young person for healthy and successful development. In adolescence, spirituality may be important for the healthy, positive development of a person's sense of self—his or her identity—and for enabling identity to frame the individual's pursuit of a life path eventuating in ideal adulthood, that is, an adulthood involving mutually beneficial relations (*adaptive* developmental regulations) between the individual and his or her social world. The research project, "The Role of Spiritual Development in Growth of Purpose, Generosity, and Psychological Health in Adolescence," a study supported by the John Templeton Foundation, was aimed to elucidate the role of spirituality in creating such self-defining characteristics among adolescents.

Method

Participants

Participants were 751 American high school and college students between the ages of 13 and 24 years (mean age = 18.1 years, 52% female) who completed surveys assessing aspects of religion/spirituality and positive youth development (PYD). Participants were recruited from 15 different religious schools and religious youth programs in the greater Boston area. The sample was racially and religiously diverse.

Survey Measures

Religiosity. The definition of youth religion in this study consisted of two subconcepts: religious identity and religious practices. Religious identity refers to participants' beliefs about being religious or spiritual (Fetzer Institute, 2003). Religious practices includes youths' self-reported frequency of engagement in various religious practices, such as praying or meditating by oneself or with a group, as well as attending religious services, schools, retreats, and youth groups. The validity and reliability of these measures have been demonstrated in previous research (Fetzer Institute, 2003).

Spiritual transcendence. Spiritual transcendence, which may be distinguished from youth religion, was used as a main indicator of youth spirituality. Spiritual transcendence is a shared sense of humanity and the belief that one is not alone in confronting the trials and tribulations of life. The six-item scale we used was adapted from the Spiritual Transcendence Scale (Piedmont, 1999).

Resilience. Resilience was defined as a capacity to bounce back and learn from life's changes and challenges. In this study, it was measured by items from the Symptom Checklist-90-Revised (Derogatis, 1994).

Risk behaviors. We used youth self-reported frequency of involvement in risk behaviors (e.g., drinking, smoking, drug use) as an indicator of risk behaviors. Items were modified from the PSL-AB Scale (Leffert et al., 1998) and the Monitoring the Future (2000) questionnaire.

Well-being. In this study, this construct was defined as subjective happiness and life satisfaction (Roeser et al., 2008).

Competence. Adapted from Harter's scale (1988), 12 items were used to measure the self-perceived competence of participants. Two domains of competence were assessed in this study—six items pertained to social competence and six items pertained to scholastic competence.

All scales used in the study had Cronbach's alpha levels of at least .65.

Procedure

Data come from the John Templeton Foundation (JTF)–supported study of "The Role of Spiritual Development in Growth of Purpose, Generosity, and

Table 14.1 Percent of Variance Accounted for PYD Indicators in Regression Analyses of Religiosity and Spirituality (Study 1)

	Scholastic Competence (n = 483)	Social Competence (n = 484)	Well-Being (n = 484)	Resilience (n = 222)	Reduced Risk (n = 484)
Religiosity	7%*	ns	ns	ns	3%*
Spirituality	ns	4%*	2%*	6%*	ns

*$p < .01$.

Psychological Health in Adolescence." Surveys were administered to high school students on handheld devices with voice enhancement; a Web-based survey was used for college students.

Results

Regression analyses were used to test the associations between religion and spirituality and various indicators of PYD. As shown in Table 14.1, among U.S. high school and college students, religiosity was positively related to scholastic competence, $R^2 = .07$, $F(2, 480) = 14.13$, $p < .01$, and reduced risk behaviors, $R^2 = .03$, $F(2, 481) = 14.13$, $p < .01$. These results correspond with previous findings suggesting that adolescents' religiosity may diminish risk behaviors (Furrow & Wagener, 2000; Smith & Denton, 2005; Wallace et al., 2003). Moreover, past research has also indicated that students with a high level of religiosity were more likely to have a higher GPA than were nonreligious students (Oh, 1999). Both past findings and the present results are consistent with earlier work showing that religious students are willing to devote more time and concentration to academic studies than are nonreligious students (Poulson, Eppler, Satterwhite, Wuensch, & Bass, 1998).

In turn, spiritual transcendence predicted such positive outcomes as social competence $R^2 = .04$, $F(2, 481) = 8.40$, $p < .01$, well-being $R^2 = .02$, $F(1, 482) = 10.10$, $p < .01$, and resilience $R^2 = .06$, $F(1, 220) = 14.37$, $p < .01$. Spiritual transcendence, as a deeply felt connection with universal facets of life, could afford individuals with social-control competency as well as a positive orientation to life. A greater sense of well-being is possible, because the roots of depressive rumination—a sense of isolation, self-pity, hopelessness, and disconnection—would be diminished.

Summary and Conclusions

Results from this study show that, to a large extent, religiosity and spirituality are positively related to different aspects of positive development among American youth (such as resilience, competence, well-being, and low incidences of risk behaviors). Such results support the idea of the developmental systems view and emphasize the usefulness of studying the connections between individuals and their social contexts. Indeed, as noted by Roehlkepartain et al. (2006), the field of adolescent religious and spiritual development is emerging as a multidimensional area of research, with a focus on dynamic developmental processes, ecological perspectives, and a strength-based approach to youth. The present findings, if they were to be extended longitudinally, could add substantive significance to this domain of scholarship. As well, future research should address what remains as critical research challenges, including definitional clarity, measurement, the study of the nonreligious context of spiritual development, a greater focus on religious diversity, and taking a global perspective toward the study of religious and spiritual development. As a means to advance this last challenge, the study of religion and spirituality among youth in China may be timely and valuable.

STUDY 2: THE BELIEF SYSTEMS OF CONTEMPORARY CHINESE YOUTH

Currently, Chinese spiritual beliefs are becoming increasingly liberalized and diversified. These shifts have resulted in a change over the last 30 years in the way researchers view these beliefs: Researchers have begun to frame the study of Chinese and Chinese adolescents' belief systems and structure from a developmental systems viewpoint instead of from a political perspective.

Using the sentence-completion method, Song and Yue (2005) asked 200 Chinese university students to finish sentences such as "Spiritual belief is . . ." or "My spiritual belief is . . ." Cognitions about the attributes and contents of spiritual beliefs were determined first by coding the completed sentences. Next, a free-association test was used to identify the vocabulary used to depict spiritual beliefs. Finally, the structure of spiritual beliefs was determined through using the ratings of 25 undergraduate students and 10 individuals with doctorates in psychology. Results indicated that university students' beliefs were diversified in content and roughly divided into three dimensions: supernatural beliefs, social beliefs, and practical beliefs. Supernatural beliefs included religious beliefs and divinity worship; social beliefs were composed of political beliefs, nationalism, and statism. Practical beliefs consisted of worship of life, money, and familism.

However, this prior study of Chinese adolescents' spiritual beliefs was not sufficiently clear about the definitions and structure of spiritual belief. Moreover, the definitions seemed to have incomplete coverage of the possible content of the beliefs. Thus, in the present study we tried to assess further the content and structure of Chinese adolescents' belief systems. We used a bottom-up strategy based on Chinese adolescents' own explanations about their belief systems.

Method

Participants and Procedure

First, using the technique of free association, 15 psychology graduate students were asked to answer the question "What is spiritual belief?" Using these answers, combined with the definitions of spiritual belief gained from previous studies at home and abroad, this group discussed what 20 items best describe spiritual belief. A questionnaire was created after three psychology professors carefully examined and approved all of the items. Next, first-year college students answered the same question based on this 20-item questionnaire. There were 310 students (63.2% female), aged 16 to 22 years (mean = 19.1 years, $SD = 0.86$ years) from three local universities in the Guangzhou area of southern China. The students were asked to choose those items they agreed with most and to answer two other questions: "Do you have any spiritual belief?" "What are your spiritual beliefs?" All answers were coded and analyzed in order to identify the structure and description of Chinese youth's spiritual beliefs.

Results

In this survey, 83.2% of the 310 adolescents indicated that they had some kind of spiritual beliefs. Answers to the question "What is spiritual belief?" could be divided into the following six types of beliefs (Table 14.2):

1. Spiritual beliefs are equivalent to religious beliefs (11.57%), i.e., embracing a religion and the rituals as well as the canons and tenets of a religion.
2. Spiritual beliefs mean beliefs about the soul (14.15%), i.e., believing in the existence of soul and supernatural beings, such as Jinn.
3. Spiritual beliefs are spiritual transcendence beliefs (31.45%), i.e., these beliefs pertain to the spiritual world of people and not necessarily to religion. These beliefs include embracing destiny, worshiping mystical power, and believing in a spiritual world beyond the material one.

Table 14.2 Percentage (Rounded) of Respondents Who Indicated That "Spiritual Beliefs Are About:" (n = 258) (Study 2)

Religiosity	12%
The soul	14%
Spiritual transcendence	31%
Inner power	63%
Social beliefs	20%
Practical beliefs	23%
No response	17%

4. Spiritual beliefs are the individual's spiritual power for survival and living (63.43%). Here beliefs refer to inner power beliefs, consisting of spirituality as a pillar and a resource for survival, psychological needs, the ideals an individual pursues in life, individuals' beliefs about life, and guides for a healthy and positive life.

5. Spiritual beliefs mean social beliefs (20.15%), i.e., the belief and experience of the individual that nations, countries, politics, and public benefits are the most important things in life.

6. Spiritual beliefs as practical beliefs (22.57%), i.e., the living conditions and life values related closely to individual survival, in particular including gaining tools that improve living conditions, pursuing specific goals of life, and practical values.

Summary

It may be seen that most of the Chinese youth in this sample were explicitly aware of their spiritual beliefs; moreover, the content of their beliefs seems to be diverse. Six types of spiritual beliefs were identified within this sample of contemporary Chinese youth. They are religious beliefs, soul beliefs, spiritual transcendence beliefs, inner power beliefs, social beliefs, and practical beliefs. Adolescents who see spiritual beliefs as involving inner power for survival and living constitute the largest group in the data set. That is, this type of belief is found among 63.43% of the participants: In short, then, inner power beliefs are the dominant component in the spiritual belief systems of the Chinese youth assessed in the present research.

In turn, some 31.45% of adolescents emphasized spiritual transcendence, believing that there is a spiritual world beyond religion. This finding indicates that, similar to American adolescents, spiritual transcendence beliefs are also an important component of the belief systems of contemporary Chinese youth. Fewer adolescents regarded spiritual beliefs as religious beliefs or beliefs about the soul, accounting for 11.57% and 14.15% of the sample, respectively. These two types of spiritual beliefs appear to be less important to this sample of contemporary Chinese youth.

STUDY 3: RELATIONS BETWEEN THE BELIEF SYSTEMS AND THE DEVELOPMENT OF CHINESE YOUTH

China may differ in many significant ways from Western countries (e.g., from the United States), in its ideology, cultural traditions, and belief structure. Nevertheless, Chinese researchers study many of the same issues that Western developmental scientists study in regard to the role of religion and spirituality in the lives of Chinese youth. For instance, they assess aspects of spiritual or religious life, such as the possible effect of spiritual beliefs on individuals' worldviews and values, whether such beliefs have a behavior-directing effect, and the comfort and support provided by spiritual life.

Song, Jin, and Li (2004) examined the relationship between spiritual beliefs and mental health in Chinese university students. Results showed that supernatural beliefs positively predicted interpersonal sensitivity, compulsion, depression, and anxiety; in turn, social beliefs negatively predicted all of these variables. Practical beliefs positively predicted interpersonal sensitivity and compulsion. Tian and Jin (2005) examined the relationship between spiritual beliefs and satisfaction with life among middle school students in a Guangzhou city. Findings indicated that spiritual beliefs significantly predicted satisfaction with life, in both general and specific domains, and that spiritual beliefs were important in predicting subjective life quality. By examining 1,745 Chinese postgraduates between the ages of 22 and 25 years, Ye (2006) found that spiritual beliefs significantly predicted the self-reported health of youth and had an important effect on youth satisfaction with life and on their emotions.

In general, it is still the case that links between spiritual beliefs and Chinese adolescent developmental outcomes have not been sufficiently and systematically studied. Thus, drawing on the results of Studies 1 and 2, we examined the association between the spiritual beliefs of Chinese adolescents and positive and negative developmental outcomes.

Method

Participants

Participants were 926 adolescents between the ages of 14 and 23 years (average age = 17.98 years, SD = 1.83). Participants were recruited from five middle schools (n = 448, 47.3% female) and five universities (n = 456, 52.6% female) in Guangdong province, southern China.

Survey Measures

Six scales were used to measure six types of beliefs among these adolescents:

1. *Religious beliefs*. Seven items were selected by drawing on the JTF project discussed in Study 1. Examples of these items are "How often do you study religious scriptures?" and "How often do you attend religious group?" The items were scored on a six-point Likert scale ranging from 1 = *never* to 6 = *always*. The Cronbach's alpha coefficient was 0.78 in the present study.
2. *Soul beliefs*. Four items were selected from the JTF study, such as "I believe I have a spirit or soul that can survive my death." The items were scored on a six-point Likert scale ranging from 1 = *totally disagree* to 6 = *totally agree*. The Cronbach's alpha coefficient was 0.84 in the present study.

3. *Spiritual transcendence beliefs.* Four items were selected from the JTF study (e.g., "I consider myself spiritual, but not necessarily religious."). The items were scored on a six-point Likert scale ranging from 1 = *totally disagree* to 6 = *totally agree*. The Cronbach's alpha coefficient in the present study was 0.85.

4. *Inner power beliefs.* An inner power belief questionnaire containing 21 items was developed by Zhang, Zhen, and Yu (2009). Representative items are "Life is always hopeful" and "Efforts always produce good outcomes." All of the items were scored on a six-point Likert scale ranging from 1 = *totally disagree* to 6 = *totally agree*. The Cronbach's alpha coefficient in the present study was 0.87.

5. *Social beliefs.* A nine-item social belief subscale from the Spiritual Belief Questionnaire for Middle School Students (Tian & Jin, 2005) was employed. All of the items were scored on a six-point Likert scale ranging from 1 = *totally disagree* to 6 = *totally agree*. The Cronbach's alpha coefficient in the present study was 0.83.

6. *Practical beliefs.* An 11-item practical belief subscale from the Spiritual Belief Questionnaire for Middle School Students (Tian & Jin, 2005) was used to measure adolescents' levels of practical belief. The items were scored on a six-point Likert scale ranging from 1 = *totally disagree* to 6 = *totally agree*. The Cronbach's alpha coefficient in the present study was 0.75.

In addition, eight scales were used to examine eight developmental outcomes:

1. *Academic competence.* A five-item subscale for academic competence from the Self-Perception Profile for Adolescents (SPPA; Harter, 1988) was used. The SPPA involves a structured-alternative response format. An example is "Some kids feel like they are just as smart as other kids their age, but other kids aren't so sure and wonder if they are as smart." The Cronbach's alpha coefficient for this scale was 0.59 in the present study.

2. *Social competence.* A five-item subscale of social competence was derived from the Self-Perception Profile for Adolescents (SPPA; Harter, 1988). A representative item is "Some kids have a lot of friends, but other kids don't have many friends." The Cronbach's alpha coefficient was 0.57 in the present study.

3. *General self-worth.* A five-item general self-worth subscale was derived from the Self-Perception Profile for Adolescents (SPPA; Harter, 1988). An example of an item from this scale is "Some teenagers don't like the way they are leading their life, but other teenagers like the way they are leading their life." The Cronbach's alpha coefficient was 0.50 in the present study.

4. *School engagement.* The 15-item School Engagement Scale (Li, Phelps, Lerner, & Lerner, 2009) was used. Five of these items have a

forced-choice response format. An example is "At school I try as hard as I can to do my best work." The other 10 items used a four-point Likert scale. An example is "I am happy at school." The Cronbach's alpha coefficient was 0.82 in the present study.

5. *Well-being.* The five-item Satisfaction with Life Scale (SWLS; Diener, Emmons, Larsen, & Griffin, 1985) was used. A representative item is "In most ways my life is close to my ideal." The items were scored on a seven-point Likert scale ranging from 1 = *strongly disagree* to 7 = *strongly agree.* The Cronbach's alpha coefficient was 0.77 in the present study.

6. *Resilience.* Eight items were selected from the Symptom Checklist-90-R Inventory (Derogatis, 1994). A representative item is "I am good at figuring out how to solve problems in my life." The Cronbach's alpha coefficient was 0.80 in the present study.

7. *Depression.* Depression was measured by the 20-item Center for Epidemiological Studies Depression Scale (CES-D; Radloff, 1977). Using a forced-choice response format, participants reported how often they felt a particular way during the past week. A representative item is "I was bothered by things that usually don't bother me." The Cronbach's alpha coefficient was 0.88 in the current study.

8. *Risk behaviors.* A 16-item scale was adapted for the present study by drawing on scales of substance use and delinquency derived from the PSL-AB Scale (Leffert et al., 1998), from the Monitoring the Future (2000) questionnaire, and from knowledge about common externalizing behavioral problems among Chinese youth. Representative items are "Do you smoke?" and "Do you drink alcohol?" The participants were asked to report the frequency of certain behaviors during the past year through use of a five-point Likert scale. The Cronbach's alpha coefficient for this scale was 0.81 in the current study.

Procedure

The study was conducted in a classroom setting, after informed consents were obtained from schools and the participants. The researchers were trained postgraduates. Using standard instructions, they explained to all participants the requirements of the questionnaires and emphasized the need for honest and independent answers. They also promised confidentiality about all information collected. If participants had any questions within the course of the testing session, they were asked to raise their hands and ask the researchers. The testing session lasted approximately 40 minutes.

Results

With the six types of beliefs as independent variables and academic competence, social competence, self-worth, school engagement, well-being, resilience, depression, and risk behaviors as dependent variables, we examined the predictive effects of all six beliefs on both positive and negative outcomes of youth development, using regression analysis (Table 14.3).

Results showed that only inner power beliefs and religious beliefs significantly predicted academic competence, combining to explain 9.3% of all variance. Inner power beliefs uniquely explained 8.6% of the variance in academic competence. Youth with higher inner power beliefs and lower religious beliefs had stronger academic competence.

Inner power beliefs and social beliefs significantly predicted social competence, together explaining 7.0% of the total variance. Inner power beliefs had a stronger effect, with a unique explained variance of 5.7%. Adolescents with inner power beliefs and social beliefs were found to have stronger social competence. In addition, only inner power beliefs predicted self-worth, uniquely explaining 8.2% of the total variance in self-worth.

Among the six predictor variables, five of them (i.e., inner power beliefs, social beliefs, practical beliefs, spiritual transcendence beliefs, and soul beliefs) significantly predicted individual school engagement. Together, these variables explained 30.1% of the total variance. Explaining uniquely 25.6% of the variance in school engagement, inner power belief had the strongest predictive effect among the five variables. Youth with more inner power beliefs, social beliefs, and spiritual transcendence beliefs had higher levels of school engagement, whereas practical beliefs and soul beliefs were associated with lower levels of school engagement.

Two variables (i.e., inner power beliefs and religious beliefs) significantly predicted individual subjective well-being. They combined to explain 7.9% of the total variance. Adolescents with inner power beliefs and religious beliefs had higher levels of subjective well-being. Resilience was also predicted by these same two variables. Together they explained 21.9% of the variance in resilience. Inner power beliefs had the stronger predictive effect, explaining 21% of the variance uniquely. Adolescents who had inner power beliefs seemed to be more resilient, whereas religious beliefs slightly hindered the resilience of youth.

In addition, four variables (i.e., inner power beliefs, soul beliefs, social beliefs, and practical beliefs) significantly predicted depression, combining to explain 21.5% of the variance. Uniquely explaining 17.4% of the variance, inner power beliefs had the strongest effect on depression compared to the other three variables. Adolescents having soul beliefs and practical beliefs were found to have higher levels of depression, whereas higher levels of inner power beliefs and social beliefs seemed to decrease the depression levels of adolescents.

Among all of the predictor variables, three (i.e., religious beliefs, social beliefs, and practical beliefs) significantly predicted individual risk behaviors, combining to explain 7.7% of the variance. Youth with higher religious beliefs and practical beliefs had more risk behaviors, whereas higher levels of social beliefs seemed to reduce adolescent risk behaviors.

Table 14.3 Percent of Variance Accounted and Direction of Effects for PYD Indicators in Regression Analyses of Chinese Religiosity and Spirituality (n = 926) (Study 3)

	Academic Competence	Social Competence	Self Worth	School Engagement	Well-Being	Resilience	Depression	Decreased Risk
Inner Power	8.60%	5.70%	8.20%	25.60%	+	21.00%	17.4% (−)	
Religiosity	−				+	−		−
Social Beliefs		+		+				+
Practical Beliefs				−			+	−
Spiritual Transcendence				+			+	
Soul				−			−	
% variance accounted for	9.30%	7.00%	8.20%	30.10%	7.90%	21.90%	21.50%	7.70%

Note: For variables that were predicted more strongly by one variable, the % accounted for is shown in the body of the table, with the direction of other effects indicated. For Well-Being and Risk, the predictor variables contributed approximately equally to the overall effects, so only the direction of effects is indicated.

Summary

It can be seen from the results of the aforementioned regression analyses that spiritual beliefs have important associations with indicators of the development of youth, with especially strong predictive effects on school engagement, resilience, depression, and scholastic competence. Spiritual beliefs explain 30.1%, 21.9%, 21.5%, and 9.3% of the variance in these indicators of development, respectively. Among the six types of beliefs, inner power beliefs have the greatest effect, significantly predicting all the indices of adolescent development except for risk behaviors; inner power beliefs had the greatest effect on school engagement, resilience, and depression, by uniquely explaining 25.6%, 21%, and 17.4% of the variance, respectively.

In turn, spiritual transcendence beliefs were linked to the school engagement of Chinese adolescents, explaining 0.3% of the variance. However, religious beliefs had both positive and negative associations with youth development. Specifically, religious beliefs were linked to the well-being of adolescents (explaining 0.8% of the variance); at the same time, they were associated with slightly lower scores for adolescent resilience and academic competence (explaining 0.9% and 0.7% of the variance, respectively) as well as with higher scores for risk behaviors (explaining 4.8% of the variance).

DISCUSSION

Carl Jung (1933) said,

> the larger part of mankind does not know why the body needs salt,
> everyone demands it none the less because of an instinctive need. . . .
> A large majority of people have from time immemorial felt the need of
> believing in a continuance of life. (p. 115)

Belief is a part of the fundamental nature of human beings. Beliefs involve the awareness and pursuit of what humans do to create the conditions of their lives and, as well, to provide meaning for their existence. In this way, beliefs are a basic necessity for our survival; however, while every person has his or her own personal set of beliefs, some people possess systematic or definite beliefs that can be expressed clearly, whereas others have vague or unsystematic beliefs that are not easily expressed or understood.

Personal beliefs exist along with beliefs that are part of one's cultural context. Each nation has its own cultures, religions, and beliefs, which together form a distinct national ethos. Similarly, due to demographic, cultural, historical, and ideological differences, there may be a disparity between different countries and regions of the world in terms of beliefs and spiritual life. This diversity is important to recognize because we are now in an era of globalization. Our world is becoming an interdependent global village, with the gradual formation of world economic integration and the conveniences of efficient communication afforded by technological innovations. Given the need to respond effectively to global issues, now, more than ever, people of different cultures, races, and belief systems need to communicate with and learn from each other. From the perspective of cross-cultural communication, knowledge of diverse religions and belief systems in various countries and nations would help people gain understanding of diverse cultures and customs, to predict and explain the behaviors of people with different beliefs, and eliminate misunderstandings caused by misinterpretation of others' behaviors based on one's own culture and beliefs. In this way, a respectful attitude toward all kinds of cultures and beliefs can be shaped so as to avoid unnecessary conflicts and confrontations between different ethnic groups, belief systems, and even countries.

From the perspective of China, the United States is a new country that has been built in part by the pursuit of new religions. Its immigrants are mostly from countries and regions with strong religious backgrounds. Therefore, it goes without saying that religion plays an essential role in the daily lives of Americans as well as in their social and cultural activities; their belief systems are greatly influenced by religion. "In God we trust" is a belief emblazoned on the currency of America.

By looking at our study and at past research on American youth, RSD, and its impact on development, we can draw two basic conclusions: First, most American youth identify themselves with a certain religion and often take part in religious activities or rituals. Religion and spirituality are core and dominant components of the belief systems of American youth. Second, in most cases, religion, spirituality, and religious institutional affiliation and related activities (e.g., church attendance) are conducive to youth academic achievement, mental health, and adjustment. Such links also are associated with lower levels of depression and many risk behaviors.

In China, because the lack of empirical research on youth belief systems is obvious, we needed to be creative about using different methods to discern what might have been expected to be low-frequency behaviors. Accordingly, we adopted methods such as free association and questionnaire development to study the belief systems of contemporary Chinese youth. We found six components of the belief systems of Chinese youth, namely religious beliefs, soul beliefs, spiritual transcendence beliefs, inner power beliefs, social beliefs, and practical beliefs. For the samples we tested, inner power beliefs were most salient. A higher proportion of youth also had spiritual transcendence beliefs, which suggests that it is also an important part of Chinese youth belief systems. Comparatively speaking, lower proportions of youth reported religious beliefs, indicating that it takes a relatively secondary role in their belief systems.

Our research on the association between spiritual beliefs and youth developmental outcomes indicates that inner power beliefs have the greatest influence. Inner power beliefs are significantly associated with youth school engagement, resilience, scholastic competence, general self-worth, and well-being, while being linked as well with low depression. Comparatively, religious beliefs and spiritual transcendence beliefs may play a smaller role in the lives of youth in China. Spiritual transcendence beliefs are linked only to school engagement. Although religious beliefs are positively linked to youth well-being, these beliefs are also associated with lower levels of youth resilience and academic competence, as well as with increases in risk behaviors.

Therefore, we can see that there are differences in how belief systems function among Chinese and American youth. For the latter group, religious and spiritual beliefs appear to be dominant components of their belief system, which plays a more positive role in youth mental health and behaviors and is a more crucial factor for positive youth development than is the case among Chinese youth. For Chinese youth, inner power beliefs primarily serve as an important predictor of positive youth development. Although spiritual transcendence beliefs are also a prominent part of the Chinese youth belief system, and are somewhat linked to positive youth development, their effect is small on the whole. Religious beliefs, however, take only a secondary place in the Chinese youth belief system. They have some positive influence on youth development, but they have more to do with negative outcomes, such as risk behaviors.

Confronted with these structural and functional disparities, we believe the best interpretation of the American and Chinese data we have presented can be obtained by drawing on developmental systems theories (DSTs). Bronfenbrenner's ecological model (1979), one instance of DSTs, proposes that individuals are significantly affected by interactions among several overlapping ecosystems: for example, microsystems (i.e., family, peer groups, classrooms, and neighborhoods), mesosystems (i.e., the connections among microsystems), exosystems (i.e., the educational system), and macrosystems (i.e., cultural values, political philosophies). Moreover, Lerner's DST further emphasizes the roles of plasticity, contextual variation, and developmental regulation (J. V. Lerner, Phelps, Forman, & Bowers, 2009; R. M. Lerner, 2004, 2006) in the links individuals have with their complex and changing ecologies.

We can see from the findings of the three studies reported that the difference in the structure and system of the youth belief systems in the two countries is mainly accounted for by their respective exosystems (i.e., the educational system) and macrosystems (i.e., cultural values, political philosophies). It is fair to say that developmental psychologists have mostly focused on individual youth or their interactions with such microsystems as family and peer groups. Perhaps because of the difficulty of research assessing the influence of exosystems and macrosystems on youth development, such studies are few in number.

However, the development of a single individual is the reflection, in miniature, of his or her social culture and history as a whole and is a result of person ↔ context transactions within his or her ecology. If, as we have suggested, the United States is a country that was established in part by pursuit of new religions and where religion plays a crucial role in Americans' education, culture, politics, family, and community, then transactions with a context during one's development will create a belief system that has religion at its core. Furthermore, given the salience of religious beliefs for American youth and mainstream American society as a whole, we would expect those teenagers who are more pious to develop positive outcomes conforming to the mainstream beliefs and to refrain from negative and undesirable behaviors. Simply put, religious beliefs and activities may help improve individual developmental regulations or resilience (Urry & Poey, 2008).

Comparatively speaking, throughout China's history, religion and its related beliefs have had a limited scope of influence on the daily life and social management of Chinese people. Chinese people's belief system was Jinn-oriented (i.e., soul oriented) in the early part of its long history, but in the first 80 years of the last century, political beliefs that were connected with social revolutions became the dominant belief orientation in China. In the last 30 years, with the great transformation in China's economy, society, politics, education, and culture, people's spiritual belief systems have also undergone a change. People became less devoted to religious beliefs or to soul beliefs, and instead beliefs related to one's positive development and to the prosperity of the society and country began to be dominant. Such beliefs served as a reflection of changes in China's current social environment.

After periods of war and political conflicts, lasting for more than 100 years, China today focuses on the economy in its development and adopts a set of policies, like opening up, that boost the standards of many Chinese people's living conditions, education, and health. In such social transformation, the Chinese people have developed their own social beliefs about the future of their society and country—beliefs that are quite distinct from the political culture of the past. This new belief system involves the expectation of positive social development as well as a set of understandings and experiences of the relationship between individuals and the society.

At the same time, during these changes, many Chinese have witnessed what each of them is capable of doing. Each individual and the society have embraced success again and again, which leads people to develop inner power beliefs that worship individual power and expect positive development. Finally, these inner power beliefs have become the dominant belief among contemporary Chinese people. This development is an interesting change, and one that is noteworthy, because in their history the Chinese people have always believed in Jinn, the government, and authority; in contrast, seldom have they dared to believe in themselves. This change shows that the Chinese people seem to be switching from their values and beliefs of collectivism to that of individualism, and that the pursuit of humanism and individualism is becoming a mainstream trend for contemporary Chinese people.

From another point of view, although the Chinese government has attached more importance to freedom of religious belief in the last three decades, and the number of religious believers has increased given that their rights are guaranteed, with the swift development of its economy, there seems not to be much of a difference in the salience of inner power beliefs between believers and nonbelievers or among believers of various religions in this sea change. One reason for the low influence of religious beliefs may be that, from time immemorial, religion has always been haunted by some negative images, because some impious believers often led others to connect religion with ghosts or evil tricks. In short, then, religion is currently not very important for most Chinese in their belief system, nor is there a social environment for promoting and advocating religious beliefs in China.

Growing up and receiving education in this sort of social environment, Chinese youth are likely to develop a belief system with inner power beliefs at its core. Religion and its related beliefs would be only of secondary importance. Furthermore, those youth with higher levels of inner power beliefs tend to develop positive outcomes or behaviors that conform to the mainstream, including higher levels of school engagement, scholastic competence, general self-worth, and well-being, and to lower levels of negative outcomes such as depression. Although youth religious beliefs and attendance can improve well-being, our data indicate that risk behaviors will also be increased. Alternatively, however, inner power beliefs can significantly enhance Chinese youth resilience, whereas religious beliefs may only slightly decrease their resilience. Such results could be explained by the nondominating role of religions in China: Adolescents and young adults who are religious may face the risk of deviating from the mainstream society, which might result in the development of negative behaviors.

Therefore, while discussing the influence of religion and its related beliefs on youth (be it negative or positive), and how these influences might occur, we cannot confine our analysis to features of the individual or to an individual's interaction with microsystems such as the family and peer group. Research must also take exosystems and macrosystems into consideration. In those societies and cultures that place religious beliefs at the center of all social beliefs and activities, religion and its related beliefs may be a positive force in youth development. On the contrary, in those societies and cultures that lack religious belief systems or in which religious beliefs are not the most valued instance of beliefs, other types of beliefs may play larger roles in youth development. Religious beliefs might not be of much use or may even be a negative force. This caution is exactly what DSTs ask us to consider: Broad contextual levels of organization, such as society and culture, may play a more crucial role in youth development than proximal levels of the context.

CONCLUSIONS AND FUTURE DIRECTIONS

The United States and China differ greatly in many dimensions, such as historical origin, cultural tradition, social structure, and ideology. This chapter compared youth spiritual beliefs and their associations with key developmental outcomes in China and America. It can be seen that religiosity and spirituality—the core and dominant components in the spiritual belief systems of American youth—are associated with their positive development and with lower levels of depression and many risk behaviors. Comparatively speaking, however, although religiosity and spirituality also predict the positive development of Chinese youth to some extent (e.g., spirituality is linked to youth school engagement and religiosity is associated with youth well-being), inner power beliefs are the core and dominant component in the belief systems of Chinese youth, and these beliefs are associated most significantly with the positive development of youth. Confronted with such structural and functional differences, we believe the best interpretation of these differences can be obtained by drawing on developmental systems theories.

Until now, there have been remarkably few large-scale comparative studies across different cultures and countries on such an important topic as spiritual belief and its development. In this chapter, for the first time, an empirical study was conducted on adolescent spiritual beliefs and their influences on adolescent development both in China and the United States, two of the most typical countries representing the Eastern and Western traditions. They also have greatly different historical origins, ideologies, and social development contexts. Inevitably, however, there are still some problems and limitations in the research we have presented. These limitations should be addressed in future research that is aimed at bringing data to bear on the following questions.

First, there exists a problem with the consistency in defining religiosity and spirituality and with the relation between the two terms in different cultural contexts. In this study, although we have tried to borrow American researchers' definitions about religiosity and spirituality, the components of the belief systems of Chinese youth were still mainly defined by coding qualitative data from Chinese adolescents. Religious beliefs were defined as faith in religious canon and doctrine and by participation in religious activities and ceremonies; spirituality was defined as faith in the existence of a super-material spiritual world, but not by religion. In addition, components of spiritual beliefs were arbitrarily distinguished as different from and independent of each other for the convenience of research.

In fact, however, there are many definitions of religiosity and spirituality and many different opinions about their relationship. For example, some researchers view religiosity as a subset of spirituality, but others view religiosity as more inclusive than spirituality; some researchers view religiosity and spirituality as two overlapping constructs (Hill & Pargament, 2003; Ho & Ho, 2007; Richards & Bergin, 1997). In addition, many researchers view religiosity and spirituality as distinguishable and parallel structures (Dowling, Gestsdóttir, Anderson, von Eye, & Lerner, 2003; Good & Willoughby, 2006; Harris et al., 2008; King et al., 2006). In the future, how should we solve the problem? Shall we use a kind of uniform definition and conceptualization of the RSD structural relationship, or shall we choose different concepts and structural relationships suitable for different cultural backgrounds? This question presents a challenge that must be considered and solved for future cross-cultural studies.

A second problem concerns the cultural equivalence of questionnaires designed for use in different countries. This issue is the most common problem that cross-cultural studies might encounter (Nicolas & DeSilva, 2008), and it might be especially evident in this study because we focused on youth spiritual beliefs, which have a close relationship with cultural and social differences. Most measures and items in the research we reported were selected from Western researchers' measures, and only a few changes were made to these measures or items. Although we reported adequate Cronbach's alpha coefficients for each questionnaire in this study, can these questionnaires and their items be just as effective, fair, and comprehensive when applied to Chinese adolescents as when they are used with American adolescents, especially when many of these questionnaires have been applied to Chinese adolescents for the first time? This question is worth repeated exploration in future studies.

Third, it is necessary to conduct longitudinal follow-up studies involving a cross-cultural comparison of the United States and China. The cross-cultural research reported in this chapter is a valuable first step, intended to inform future comparative research on this topic. The present research also provides an important reference and framework for multicultural comparative studies on similar topics. On the basis of this work, if longitudinal research on this topic, targeting adolescents of the United States and China, can be carried out in the future, we may be able to reveal in a more scientifically thorough way the mechanisms and processes through which cultural and social environment variables such as ideology and educational systems influence the formation of adolescent spiritual beliefs. Such work will provide a scientific basis for the positive cultivation of adolescent spiritual beliefs and healthy development.

REFERENCES

Alba, R., & Nee, V. (2003). *Remaking the American mainstream: Assimilation and contemporary immigration.* Cambridge, MA: Harvard University Press.

Bronfenbrenner, U. (1979). *The ecology of human development.* Cambridge, MA: Harvard University Press.

Cadge, W., & Ecklund, E. H. (2006). Religious service attendance among immigrants: Evidence from the new immigrant survey-pilot. *American Behavioral Scientist, 49*(11), 1574–1595.

Cotton, S., Zebracki, K., Rosenthal, S. L., Tsevat, J., & Drotar, D. (2006). Religion/spirituality and adolescent health outcomes: A review. *Journal of Adolescent Health, 38,* 472–480.

Dew, R. E., Daniel, S. S., Armstrong, T. D., Goldson, D. B., Triplett, M. F., & Koening, H. G. (2008). Religion/spirituality and adolescent psychiatric symptoms: A review. *Child Psychiatry and Human Development, 39,* 381–398.

Derogatis, L. R. (1994). *Symptoms checklist-90-revised (SCL-90-R): Administration, scoring, and procedure manual* (3rd ed.). Minneapolis, MN: National Computer Systems.

Diener, E., Emmons, R. A., Larsen, R. J., & Griffin, S. (1985). The satisfaction with life scale. *Journal of Personality Assessment, 49,* 71–75.

Dowling, E. M., Gestsdóttir, S., Anderson, P. M., von Eye, A., & Lerner, R. M. (2003). Spirituality, religiosity, and thriving among adolescents: Identification and confirmation of factor structures. *Applied Developmental Science, 7*(4), 253–260.

Fetzer Institute & National Institute on Aging Working Group. (2003). *Measurement of religiousness/spirituality for use in health research: A report of the Fetzer Institute/National Institute on Aging Working Group.* Kalamazoo, MI: Fetzer Institute.

Furrow, J. L., & Wagener, L. M. (2000). Lessons learned: The role of religion in the development of wisdom in adolescence. In W. S. Brown (Ed.), *Understanding wisdom: Sources, science, & society* (pp. 361–391). Philadelphia, PA: Templeton Foundation.

Good, M., & Willoughby, T. (2006). The role of spirituality versus religiosity in adolescent psychosocial adjustment. *Journal of Youth and Adolescence, 35,* 41–55.

Hall, G. S. (1904). *Adolescence: Its psychology and its relations to physiology, anthropology, sociology, sex, crime, religion, and education.* New York, NY: Appleton.

Harris, S. K., Sherritt, L. R., Holder, D. W., Kulig, J., Shrier, L. A., & Knight, J. R. (2008). Reliability and validity of the brief multidimensional measure of religiousness/spirituality among adolescents. *Journal of Religion and Health, 47,* 438–457.

Harter, S. (1988). *Manual for the self-perception profile for adolescents.* Denver, CO: University of Denver.

Hill, P. C., & Pargament, K. I. (2003). Advances in the conceptualization and measurement of religion and spirituality: Implications for physical and mental health research. *American Psychologist, 58,* 64–74.

Hirschman, C. (2007). The role of religion in the origins and adaptation of immigrant groups in the United States. In A. Portes & J. DeWind (Eds.), *Rethinking migration: New theoretical and empirical perspectives* (pp. 391–418). New York, NY: Berghahn Books.

Ho, D. Y. F., & Ho, R. T. H. (2007). Measuring spirituality and spiritual emptiness: Toward ecumenicity and transcultural applicability. *Review of General Psychology, 11,* 62–74.

Josephson, A. M., & Dell, M. L. (2004). Religion and spirituality in child and adolescent psychiatry: A new frontier. *Child and Adolescent Psychiatric Clinics of North America, 13,* 1–15.

Jung, C. G. (1933). *Modern man in search of a soul.* New York, NY: Harcourt, Brace & World.

King, M., Jones, L., Barnes, K., Low, J., Walker, C., Wilkinson, S., . . . & Tookman, A. (2006). Measuring spiritual belief: Development and standardization of a beliefs and values scale. *Psychological Medicine, 36,* 417–425.

King, P. E., & Roeser, R. W. (2009). Religion and spirituality in adolescent development. In R. M. Lerner & L. Sternberg (Eds.), *Handbook of adolescent psychology: Vol. 1, Individual bases of adolescent development* (3rd ed., pp. 435–478). Hoboken, NJ: Wiley.

Leffert, N., Benson, P. L., Scales, P. C., Sharma, A. R., Drake, D. R., & Blyth, D. A. (1998). Developmental assets: Measurement and prediction of risk behaviors among adolescents. *Applied Developmental Science, 2*(4), 209–230.

Lerner, J. V., Phelps, E., Forman, Y., & Bowers, E. P. (2009). Positive youth development. In R. M. Lerner & L. Sternberg (Eds.), *Handbook of adolescent psychology: Vol. 1, Individual bases of adolescent development* (3rd ed., pp. 524–558). Hoboken, NJ: Wiley.

Lerner, R. M. (2004). Innovative methods for studying lives in context: A view of the issues. *Research in Human Development, 1*(1&2), 5–7.

Lerner, R. M. (2006). Developmental science, developmental systems, and contemporary theories of human development. In R. M. Lerner (Ed.), *Handbook of child psychology: Vol. 1, Theoretical models of human development* (6th ed., pp. 1–17). (Editors-in-chief: W. Damon & R. M. Lerner.). Hoboken, NJ: Wiley.

Lerner, R. M., Roeser, R. W., & Phelps, E. (Eds.). (2008). *Positive youth development & spirituality: From theory to research*. West Conshohocken, PA: Templeton Foundation Press.

Levitt, P. (2007). *God needs no passport: Immigrants and the changing American religious landscape*. New York, NY: New Press.

Li, Y., Phelps, E., Lerner, R. M., & Lerner, J. V. (2009). Educational expectations and academic achievement in adolescence: The mediating role of school engagement and intentional self-regulation. Presentation at the Society for Research in Child Development (SRCD) Biennial Meeting, Denver, CO.

Meacham, J. (2009). The end of Christian America. *Newsweek, 153*(15), 34–38.

Monitoring the Future. (2000). *National survey on drug use, 1975–2000*. Bethesda, MD: National Institute on Drug Abuse.

Nicolas, G., & DeSilva, A. M. (2008). Application of the ecological model. In R. M. Lerner, R. W. Roeser, & E. Phelps (Eds.), *Positive youth development & spirituality: From theory to research* (pp. 305–321). West Conshohocken, PA: Templeton Foundation Press.

Oh, D. M. (1999). Evidence on the correlation between religiosity and social/psychological behavior and the resulting impact on student performance. *Dissertation Abstracts International Section A: Humanities & Social Sciences, 59*(11-A), 4102.

Pew Forum on Religion and Public Life. (2008). *U.S. religious landscape survey*. Washington, DC: Pew Research Center.

Piedmont, R. L. (1999). Does spirituality represent the sixth factor of personality? Spiritual transcendence and the five-factor model. *Journal of Personality, 67*(6), 985–1013.

Portes, A., & Rumbaut, R. G. (2006). *Immigrant American*. Berkeley: University of California Press.

Poulson, R. L., Eppler, M. A., Satterwhite, T. N., Wuensch, K. L., & Bass, L. A. (1998). Alcohol consumption, strength of religious beliefs, and risky sexual behavior in college students. *Journal of American College Health, 46*, 227–232.

Radloff, L. S. (1977). The CES-D Scale: A self-report depression scale for research in the general population. *Applied Psychological Measurement, 1*, 385–401.

Richards, P. S., & Bergin, A. E. (1997). *A spiritual strategy for counseling and psychotherapy*. Washington, DC: American Psychological Association.

Roehlkepartain, E. C., King, P. C., Wagener, L. M., & Benson, P. L. (2006). *The handbook of spiritual development in childhood and adolescence.* Thousand Oaks, CA: Sage.

Roeser, R. W., Galloway, M., Casey-Cannon, S., Watson, C., Keller, L., & Tan, E. (2008). Identity representations in patterns of school achievement and well-being among early adolescent girls: Variable- and person-centered approaches. *Journal of Early Adolescence, 28,* 115–152.

Shek, D. T. (2010). The spirituality of the Chinese people: A critical review. In M. H. Bond (Ed.), *The Oxford handbook of Chinese psychology* (pp. 343–366). New York, NY: Oxford University Press.

Song, X., Jin, S., & Li, B. (2004). Correlations of beliefs and mental health. *Chinese Mental Health, 18,* 554–556.

Song, X., & Yue, G. (2005). Spiritual belief structure in university students. *Chinese Journal of Clinical Rehabilitation, 16,* 46–47.

Smith, C., & Denton, M. (2005). *Soul searching: The religious and spiritual lives of American teenagers.* New York: Oxford University Press.

Spilka, B., Hood, R. W., Hunsberger, B., & Gorsuch, R. (2003). *Psychology of religion: An empirical approach* (3rd ed.). New York, NY: Guilford Press.

Tian, L., & Jin, S. (2005). Research on the characteristics of junior high school students' spiritual beliefs. *Psychological Development and Education, 2,* 87–91.

Urry, H. L., & Poey, A. P. (2008). How religious/spiritual practices contribute to well-being: The role of emotion regulation. In R. M. Lerner, R. W. Roeser, & E. Phelps (Eds.), *Positive youth development & spirituality: From theory to research* (pp. 145–163). West Conshohocken, PA: Templeton Foundation Press.

Wallace, J. M., Forman, T. A., Caldwell, C. H., & Willis, D. S. (2003). Religion and American youth: Recent pattern, historical trends and sociodemographic correlates. *Youth and Society, 35,* 98–125.

Weaver, A. J., Pargament, K. J., & Oppenheimer, J. E. (2006). Trends in the scientific study of religion, spirituality, and health: 1965–2000. *Journal of Religion and Health, 45,* 208–214.

Ye, Y. (2006). Research on spiritual belief and its relationship with the self-rated health and subjective well-being of postgraduates. Thesis for Master's Degree, South China Normal University, Guangzhou, China.

Zhang, W., Zhen, S., & Yu, C. (2009). Development of inner power belief scale for adolescent. Unpublished manuscript.

Afterword

This volume is a signpost, signifying that the field of spirituality and positive youth development has arrived. It was almost exactly 10 years before the completion of this volume that I was swinging on a hammock in Maine having a phone conversation with Peter Benson, then President of the Search Institute. The conversation is a vivid memory, not just because of the beautiful setting, but because Peter and I spoke of our shared desire to "be a voice of spirituality in the field of psychology." We acknowledged the hesitation that existed among scholars within the field of developmental psychology to address, or perhaps even regard with suspicion, transcendent domains of development such as spirituality and religiousness. In our conversation, we discussed the potential relevance of spirituality to adolescent development—particularly the role of spiritual development and thriving. We spoke of the need to engage in solid theoretical work and rigorous empirical research in order to have the role of spirituality in the lives of young people be taken seriously by developmental scholars. We wondered together how to build a field of adolescent spiritual development. At the time of our conversation, this concept of building a field of spiritual development was more a part of our imaginations than it was reality. However, this volume is evidence that at the time this volume was placed into production, in the fall of 2010, the field not only exists but is flourishing.

Although traces of the study of spirituality have existed within the field of psychology for the last century, the field of adolescent spiritual development has exploded in the last decade. Founding fathers of the field of psychology, such as William James, G. Stanley Hall, J. H. Leuba, and Edwin Starbuck, considered religiousness and spirituality to be integral to an understanding of human psychology; however, the study of such topics was marginalized throughout much of the 20th century. Nevertheless, scholars within the subfield of Psychology of Religion continued to examine issues of religiousness, but the study of spirituality, as a domain of human functioning existing apart from religious traditions, has only relatively recently begun to be explored (Paloutzian & Park, 2005). In addition, the study of religiousness has mainly focused on adult populations, with children and adolescents only seldom considered.

However, since the turn of the 20th century, research activity within psychology, and within developmental psychology, or developmental science, more specifically, has involved significant increases in the study of adolescent populations. Although a focus on adolescent religiousness and spirituality remain relatively rare topics of inquiry in the field of developmental science, interest has increased (see King & Roeser, 2009, for historical review). Indeed, special issues in peer-reviewed journals, the publication of the *Handbook of Spiritual Development in Childhood and Adolescence* (Roehlkepartain, Benson, King, & Wagener, 2006), and the inclusion of a chapter on "Religion and Spirituality in Adolescent Development" in the *Handbook of Adolescent Psychology* (Lerner & Steinberg, 2009) indicate that a field of scientific inquiry has been established. This volume builds on this foundation and propels the field to a new level.

The groundbreaking work of this volume is multifaceted. First, this book emphasizes adolescent spirituality and its relationship to positive youth development and generosity. Before this volume, most existing empirical work examined issues of religiousness, rather than expressions of spirituality outside of religious traditions. Although the word *spirituality* has been used, it is often used more for the sake of semantics, rather than actual operationalization. As one of the editors of the *Handbook of Spiritual Development in Childhood and Adolescence* (Roehlkepartain et al., 2006), I can attest to the fact that in most chapters our contributing authors had to stretch to include research on child and adolescent spirituality as opposed to religiousness. On the other hand, the research represented in this volume explicitly focuses on deepening an understanding of adolescent spirituality, both inside and outside religious traditions, as it relates to positive youth development and generosity.

One of the foremost contributions of the work found in this volume is the theoretical foundation that is offered for understanding adolescent spirituality. Although much ink has been spilt on different definitions and understandings of spirituality or spiritual development, there is little conceptual coherence in the existing body of literature (Roehlkepartain et al., 2006). Given the emergent nature of the field, providing a strong theoretical footing is timely and, furthermore, necessary for the field to move forward. Predicated on the developmental systems concepts of plasticity, diversity, and developmental regulation (Lerner, 2006), the editors of this volume offer a theoretical lens through which to understand and further investigate the links between spirituality, positive youth development, and generosity. They explain that as adolescents embark on both the search for identity and belonging, healthy development can be observed within mutually beneficial relationships between a young person and the many contexts in which his or her life is embedded. Recognizing that making a contribution to the greater good is a hallmark of positive youth development, Warren, Lerner, and Phelps make the case that spirituality is perhaps the orientation to transcend one's own focus on oneself, and to live in such a way that benefits others and society. As such, spirituality may provide the emotional and cognitive motivation to transcend the self and to sustain commitments to contributing to others.

Basing an understanding of spirituality on concepts found within developmental systems theories provides for an exploration of the potential and complexity of spiritual development. Developmental systems theory perspectives recognize plasticity and the capacity for change and growth in development generally, and in spirituality specifically. In addition, a developmental systems emphasis on diversity and the interactions between individual and context acknowledges the complexity of spiritual development. From this perspective, young people are viewed in all of their diversity and potential as they interact with their various settings. Furthermore, developmental systems theory provides an integrative approach to human development and acknowledges that spirituality impacts all of the developmental system, allowing for the consideration of biological, psychological, social, and cultural variables. In addition, although this volume presents cross-sectional research, this theoretical perspective provides a framework for the study of the change component that is necessary for understanding development in the associations among spirituality, positive youth development, and generosity.

The empirical findings presented in this volume, based in large part on the research conducted through the John Templeton Foundation (JTF)–supported study, "The Role of Spiritual Development in the Growth of Purpose, Generosity, and Psychological Health in Adolescence" are truly groundbreaking. The volume consists of leading scientists drawing from multiple disciplines to yield an interdisciplinary masterpiece. Drawing on cutting-edge theory, methodology, and technology, this volume offers insight into adolescent spirituality and its relationship to positive youth development and generosity.

To date, the biological context of spirituality and positive youth development has remained almost completely unexplored. This book forges new ground by considering the relations between biological-level variables and psychological-level constructs and behavior. Although the findings from the four studies presented in this volume that address biological variables are certainly not definitive, the results point to the pertinence of understanding the neuronal and physiological dimensions of spirituality and positive youth development. Addressing one of the key issues of positive youth development and spirituality—social connections—Grigorenko examined the potential link between affiliative behaviors and the presence of neuropeptides oxytocin (OXT) and arginine vasopressin (AVP). Her review of the literature presents a convincing case for how these biological agents are not only important for demonstrating affiliative behavior and forming affiliation and contributing to the development of the higher-order personality trait of affiliation, but may also be involved with experiencing affiliation or connection with a transcendent other that is central to spirituality and religiousness.

Although not examining spirituality directly, the chapter by Paus and colleagues examined the connections between positive youth development and brain development. Their investigation of the relationship between indicators of positive youth development based on the Five Cs of positive youth development (see Lerner, 2006) and the variation in the thickness of the cortex and the frontal, parietal, temporal, and occipital lobes of the brain is consistent with other studies on physiological effects of negative social support (Eisenberger, Lieberman, & Williams, 2003) and suggests that compromised social contexts may impact the maturation of the temporal cortex during adolescence. As such, the study serves a precursor to the study of spirituality and brain development by pointing to the potential physiological significance of social connections.

In the following chapter, Lazar and her colleagues also found preliminary findings that warrant the continued exploration of the relationship between brain structure, spirituality, and positive youth development. Using fMRI measurements and questionnaires, data suggest that being engaged in prayer and meditation may correlate with the thickness of the right anterior insula and that a specific subregion of the prefrontal cortex is related to self-regulation. These findings affirm the importance of biological-level variables in the study of spirituality and positive youth development.

Building on the existing literature that documents that religious and spiritual beliefs and practices are associated with higher levels of psychological well-being, brain imaging data analyzed by Urry and her colleagues found that meditation practice is associated with prefrontal cortex activation during cognitive reappraisal and that prefrontal cortex activation is related to positive emotion in daily life. These preliminary results provide support for the idea that emotional regulation may be an important factor that moderates the positive association between religious and spiritual beliefs and practices and well-being.

Although not conclusive, the findings from these studies suggest that there may be neural markers to spirituality and positive youth development. By examining defining aspects of spirituality and positive youth development, such as social connection, spiritual beliefs and practices, and emotional regulations, the chapters included in this section bring insight into what parts of the brain might be activated, the biological agents that may be present, and what physiological factors might be involved with spirituality and positive youth development. Although not definitive, the scholarship in these chapters points to the importance of understanding the biological context of spirituality and positive youth development and underscores the idea that it is not a coincidence that, during adolescence, the brain matures to a substantial degree, while adolescence is also a time of major behavior, cognitive, and social change.

In addition to the groundbreaking efforts of elucidating the potential role of biological-level processes, the volume builds on the existing small foundation of literature on the psychological processes involved in the relations between spirituality, positive youth development, and generosity. In particular, the contributors to this volume take the field's understanding to a new level by exploring specific psychological issues related to spirituality and positive youth development. For example, Warren's chapter enhances the clarity of the concept of transcendence that dominates much of the conceptual literature on spiritual development (Benson, Scales, Sesma, & Roehlkepartain, 2005; King & Roeser, 2009; Lerner, Dowling, & Anderson, 2003; Pargament & Mahoney, 2005). Recognizing that all developing entities are open systems and integrally connected, Warren explores a structural model that suggests that an important aspect of transcendence is a personal and ideational commitment to the whole of humanity, which she calls Great Love-Compassion. Specifically, she showed that one key outcome of elaborative development is having a commitment to all of humanity.

Also emphasizing a holistic view of human development, Feldman and colleagues demonstrate how religious and spiritual conversion is likely to affect and be affected by other aspects of development (Overton, 2009). Specifically, their chapter describes three case studies of individuals who converted to Islam, and suggests that religious conversion may coincide with aspects of positive youth development, such as a desire to better and grow the self as well as to contribute to something greater than the self. These findings warrant the further exploration of the role of religious conversion and positive youth development, especially as spiritual identities, commitments, and practices may relate to processes and indicators of positive youth development.

Spiewak and Sherrod shed light on the potentially shared developmental pathways between religiousness and spirituality and positive youth development. Their description and initial empirical testing of the 3H model, involving Head, Heart, and Hands, suggest that religious and spiritual development may overlap with positive youth development in cognitive, affective, and behavioral domains. Their chapter highlights both the complexity of religiousness and spirituality. They emphasize that both domains include beliefs, feelings, and behaviors and are also part of positive development in young people.

In an effort to understand young people's perspectives regarding the nature of being spiritual, and to elucidate the relationship between spirituality and positive development, Mariano and colleagues' qualitative and quantitative exploration of youth responses to notions of "being spiritual" and "being successful" reveals further potential connections between spirituality and youth thriving. Although the results suggest that diverse religious young people conceive of successful development and spirituality quite differently, with the exception of moral virtue, their findings reveal that young people define success with indicators that are relevant to spirituality. Youth descriptions of success were less aligned with materialism and included descriptions of knowledge and wisdom, moral virtues, purpose and motivation, and social connection. From the perspective of youth, spirituality most frequently involved personal awareness and transcendence, beliefs, moral virtue, and spiritual practices. This study points to not only the potential conceptual connections between adolescent thriving and spirituality, but also highlights some important distinctions between the two. Furthermore, the findings challenge our understanding of the role of moral development in both of these domains.

This section on individual- and psychological-level variables related to adolescent spirituality and positive development emphasizes the integrative nature of human development. All four of these chapters affirm a holistic perspective and maintain that adolescent spirituality is no exception to the integrative character of human development. The research presented in these chapters suggests significant conceptual overlap between spirituality and positive youth development by highlighting the commonality of a commitment to a whole or to the greater good; the chapters demonstrate that religious conversion often entails an intentional bettering of self and society; the chapters indicate also that spirituality and positive youth development both involve cognitive, affective, and behavioral functions; the chapters also point to the role of moral virtue in the spirituality–positive youth development relation. Taken together, these chapters highlight the commonality of both individual development (i.e., identity, purpose) and a connection to something beyond the self (i.e., helping others, belonging to community).

Again confirming the importance of this volume, the scope of material covered in the book is not limited to the study of spirituality and positive youth development among individual-level variables. The last section of the book explores the often neglected social and cultural context of spiritual development by considering potential resources of religious traditions and congregations, and the roles of immigration, race, and international settings among understudied populations. Through two studies on Muslim American youth, the first chapter in this section considers the roles of context and demographics and its relation to religious discrimination, identity, and practice. The findings reveal that religiosity and engagement in one's own ethnic or religious community may be significant indicators for promoting positive values. The second study points to the importance of understanding the cultural meanings of positive youth development–related behaviors, such as volunteerism, and demonstrates that cultural, ethnic, socioeconomic, race, and gender differences impact the meaning of youth outcomes.

In another study highlighting the role of context and culture, Suárez-Orozco and colleagues took on the important task of exploring the association between religion and social support among adolescent immigrants. Their study not only highlights some of the unique attributes of immigrant populations, but their findings also shed light on the importance and complexity of the mediating roles of peer affiliations and social support in predicting positive outcomes, such as well-being, sense of purpose, and lower levels of risk behaviors. Such work emphasizes the potential importance of the social context of religion.

Examining the impact of religious and racial identities on positive youth development from the perspective of the PVEST model (Spencer, 2006), Brittian and Spencer's work reveals that although age and sex were the most salient predictors of well-being and risk behaviors, ethnic identity and religious identity were important factors in understanding youth outcomes. The PVEST model stresses the significance of culture and context in identity development for diverse youth, allowing for the investigation of the interplay of ethnic and religious identities and facilitating the study of potential opportunities and constraints on the process of spiritual development and positive youth development.

Providing an international perspective about the relationship between spirituality and positive youth development, two chapters explore the uniqueness of different national contexts as a means of furthering an understanding of spirituality and positive youth development. In one of these chapters, involving the analysis of a sample of Israeli college youth, Mayseless and Russo-Netzer examined the link between spirituality and emotional maturity. Providing cross-national and cross-cultural perspectives, they argue for the importance of religious community in nurturing spiritual development in Israel. In addition to religious practices, they found that supportive, relational contexts seem to be important for the development of spiritual transcendence. They also found that emotional maturity and spirituality development were independently associated with prosocial actions and a benevolent stance toward others.

Also providing a national framework for understanding the ecological embeddedness of the development of spirituality and positive youth development, Zhang and colleagues compare Chinese and American samples in regards to their spiritual beliefs and their associations with adolescent developmental outcomes. Qualitative data reveal that Chinese youth have substantially different religious beliefs from American youth. Furthermore, their quantitative findings revealed that, whereas for American youth, religiousness and spirituality were central to spiritual belief systems and were associated with positive development and with lower reported levels of depression and other risk factors, for Chinese youth, beliefs that guide life meaning and survival, or inner power beliefs, were the core component of youth belief systems; these beliefs were associated with positive development. These findings illustrate the complexity of spirituality, highlighting that the content of spiritual ideology is culturally influenced and is related to youth outcomes differently across cultures.

These chapters not only give specific insight into several understudied populations, but they also demonstrate the necessity of a developmental systems approach, which allows for the study of contextual and cultural influences on the processes of spiritual development and positive youth development. These chapters point out that ideologically and socially rich contexts may be fertile ground for positive youth development. They also reveal that spirituality and positive youth development must be contextualized in order to be studied effectively in different cultural contexts. For example, these studies illustrate that beliefs, social support, and behaviors have the potential to mean different things in each context.

In sum, taken together this volume sheds great light on the processes and relationship between spiritual development and positive youth development. At the conclusion of reading these exciting chapters, a myriad of questions came to mind. Which regions of the brain are engaged in spirituality and positive youth development? What is the role of moral development in spirituality and its relationship to positive youth development? How is contribution culturally informed, and how do we effectively study these concepts across religious and cultural contexts? How can we further use mixed methods and available technology to answer these questions? How, in this economy, can we fund such endeavors!? However, the questions that stood out were "What is the difference between adolescent spirituality and positive youth development? Are they synonymous? Or are they distinct concepts?"

From a developmental systems perspective, spiritual development occurs in the ongoing transactions between people and their multiple embedded contexts.

It is through these interactions that young people experience something of significance beyond themselves and gain a growing sense of transcendence. As the content of this volume illustrates, this connection can be to a transcendent other, it can involve a sense of all of humanity, or it may pertain to a specific religious community, to peers, or perhaps even to nature. Such experiences of transcendence provide meaning for and motivate young people to contribute to the well-being of the world beyond themselves. From this perspective, the heart of spiritual development lies in the interaction between the self and some form of other that informs one's beliefs and commitments, and propels the young person to live in a manner that is mindful of others. As such, spirituality development involves transcendence (awareness of self and connection to other), fidelity (clarity and conviction of beliefs and ideology), and behavior (prosocial action benefiting others).

Given that defining features of positive youth development include social connections, positive values, and giving back to society (Benson, Scales, Hamilton, & Sesma, 2006; Bundick, Yeager, King, & Damon, 2010; Damon, 2004; Lerner et al., 2003), what is the difference between spirituality and positive youth development? Clearly, as this volume portrays, there is significant overlap; however, I would argue that perhaps the processes that involve transcending the self and fidelity are unique to spiritual development. A young person's experience of transcendence may lead to self-awareness, as experienced as identity, purpose, inner power, and a commitment to an ideology. The transcending of self and connection to something beyond the self provides meaning and clarity and conviction of beliefs, or fidelity. In turn, this devotion to, in most cases, a prosocial ideology motivates a manner of living that is respectful of and beneficial to others. Consequently, youth contribution may be both an indicator of spiritual development and of positive youth development, but transcendence and fidelity are specific to spiritual development. Further research will begin to address such possibilities.

The editors of and the contributors to this volume are to be congratulated for the groundbreaking contribution of this book. Richard Lerner as the principal investigator and convener of this study, "The Role of Spiritual Development in the Growth of Purpose, Generosity, and Psychological Health in Adolescence," and his colleagues Erin Phelps and Amy Alberts Warren are deeply appreciated for their visionary, creative, and tireless efforts to bring together an interdisciplinary group of scholars in order to further the theoretical and empirical knowledge of the relationship between spirituality and positive youth development. Truthfully, the field has not been the same since Richard Lerner entered it.

In all, this volume provides an ecological exploration of the developmental system of spirituality and positive youth development. Although it is broad in its scope in regard to examining biological, psychological, social, and cultural-level variables and their relationship to the processes of spiritual development and positive youth development, the contributors of the volume raise many important questions. In many ways, this watershed volume is not only hypothesis testing but also hypothesis generating. The editors and contributors have given a gift to the literature by providing the developmental science of adolescent spirituality with strong theoretical foundations and empirical girding that will allow scholars and practitioners alike to continue to build this new and important field of study. Only as we continue to fortify our understanding of spirituality and positive youth development will we be able to most effectively promote policy, programs, and most importantly, researchers and practitioners who will enable young people to thrive and flourish.

PAMELA EBSTYNE KING, PHD, MDIV
Fuller Theological Seminary

REFERENCES

Benson, P. L., Scales, P. C., Hamilton, S. F., & Sesma, A. (2006). Positive youth development: Theory, research, and applications. In W. Damon & R. M. Lerner (Eds.), *Handbook of child psychology, Volume 1: Theoretical models of human development* (6th ed., pp. 894–941). Hoboken, NJ: Wiley.

Benson, P. L., Scales, P. C., Sesma, A., Jr., & Roehlkepartain, E. C. (2005). Adolescent spirituality. In K. A. Moore & L. H. Lippman (Eds.), *What do children need to flourish? Conceptualizing and measuring indicators of positive development* (pp. 25–40). New York, NY: Springer Science + Business Media.

Bundick, M. J., Yeager, D. S., King, P. E., & Damon, W. (2010). Thriving across the life span. In W. F. Overton (Ed.), *Handbook of life span development: Methods, biology, neuroscience, & cognitive development* (3rd ed., Vol. 1). Hoboken, NJ: Wiley.

Damon, W. (2004). What is positive youth development? *Annals of the American Academy of Political and Social Science, 591,* 13–24.

Eisenberger, N. I., Lieberman, M. D., & Williams, K. D. (2003). Does rejection hurt? An fMRI study of social exclusion. *Science, 302*(5643), 290–292.

King, P. E., Ramos, J. S., & Clardy, C. E. (2010). Religion & spirituality in diverse adolescents. In D. P. Swanson & M. B. Spenncer (Eds.), *Adolescence: Development during a global era.* Amsterdam, The Netherlands: Elsevier Press.

King, P. E., & Roeser, R. W. (2009). Religion and spirituality in adolescent development. In R. M. Lerner & L. Steinberg (Eds.), *Handbook of adolescent psychology: Volume 1, Individual bases of adolescent development* (pp. 435–478). Hoboken, NJ: Wiley.

Lerner, R. M. (2006). Developmental science, developmental systems, and contemporary theories of human development. In R. M. Lerner & W. Damon (Eds.), *Handbook of child psychology: Vol. 1, Theoretical models of human development* (6th ed., pp. 1–17). Hoboken, NJ: Wiley.

Lerner, R. M., Dowling, E. M., & Anderson, P. M. (2003). Positive youth development: Thriving as the basis of personhood and civil society. *Applied Developmental Sciences, 7,* 172–180.

Lerner, R. M., & Steinberg, L. (Eds.) (2009). *Handbook of adolescent psychology: Volume 1, Individual bases of adolescent development.* Hoboken, NJ: Wiley.

Overton, W. S. (2009). Developmental psychology: Philosophy, concepts, methodology. In R. M. Lerner & W. Damon (Ed.), *Handbook of child psychology: Theoretical models of human development* (Vol. 1, pp. 18–88). Hoboken, NJ: Wiley.

Paloutzian, R. F., & Park, C. L. (2005). *Handbook of the psychology of religion and spirituality.* New York, NY: Guilford Press.

Pargament, K. I., & Mahoney, A. (2005). Sacred matters: Sanctification as a vital topic for the psychology of religion. *International Journal for the Psychology of Religion, 15,* 179–198.

Roehlkepartain, E. C., Benson, P. L., King, P. E., & Wagener, L. M. (Eds.). (2006). Spiritual development in childhood and adolescence: Moving to the scientific mainstream. In *The handbook of spiritual development in childhood and adolescence* (pp. 1–15). Thousand Oaks, CA: Sage.

Spencer, M. B. (2006). Phenomenology and ecological systems theory: Development of diverse groups. In R. M. Lerner & W. Damon (Eds.), *Handbook of child psychology: Vol. 1, Theoretical models of human development* (6th ed., pp. 829–893). Hoboken, NJ: Wiley.

Author Index

Subject Index